P9-CJM-782

PEARSON

PEARSON CUSTOM LIBRARY

IBM 307
Promotional Strategies
Cal Poly Pomona

PEARSON

5 16

ISBN 10: 1-323-33877-2
ISBN 13: 978-1-323-33877-3

Table of Contents

Integrated Marketing Communications

From Chapter 1 of *Integrated Advertising, Promotion, and Marketing Communications,* Seventh Edition. Kenneth E. Clow, Donald Baack.

Integrated Marketing Communications

Chapter Objectives

After reading this chapter, you should be able to answer the following questions:

1 How does communication take place?

2 What is an integrated marketing communications program?

3 What trends are affecting marketing communications?

4 What are the components of an integrated marketing communications program?

5 What does the term *GIMC* mean?

MyMarketingLab™

⭐ **Improve Your Grade!**

Over 10 million students improved their results using the Pearson MyLabs. Visit **mymktlab.com** for simulations, tutorials, and end-of-chapter problems.

Overview

Advertising and promotion face a rapidly shifting landscape. A decline in traditional media viewing combined with the rise in internet usage and the use of social media have created a new order. The wide variety of available media means that an effective advertising and marketing campaign now requires more than just one well-made commercial. Current advertising and marketing methods range from simple stand-alone billboard advertisements to complex, multilingual global websites. As a result, the number of ways to reach potential customers continually increases while alternative methods expand and become increasingly popular.

In the face of these sophisticated and cluttered market conditions, firms seek to be heard. Marketing experts know that a company's communications should speak with a clear voice. Customers must understand the essence of a business along with the benefits of its goods and services. The new variety of advertising and promotional venues combined with a multitude of companies bombarding potential customers with messages makes the task challenging. In response, some advertisers and companies have moved to innovative new approaches that utilize the concepts presented in this chapter.

Recent advertising promoted Miracle Whip in a surprising new way. Consumers were asked if they "loved" or "hated" the product. The advertising agency mcgarrybowen directed the entire advertising and social media campaign featuring the concept, "We're not for everyone." The campaign acknowledged the inherent polarization of the product by inviting consumers to say whether they love or hate Miracle Whip.

Advertisements premiered as major primetime placements on *Glee* and *American Idol*. The work included a cast of celebrities and everyday people. Pundit James Carville proclaimed "Miracle Whip is America" alongside an unknown actor stating it "tastes like spreadable disappointment." Jersey Shore's Pauly D reported, "I'd never eat it. I'd never put it in my hair. It's just wrong." Comic actor Amy Sedaris offered, "It's always great in the bedroom." Soon, full-page ads were used in major newspapers to support the launch with the tagline "Are You Miracle Whip?"

Next, the marketing team established social media channels for people who both love and hate Miracle Whip. The campaign urged the public to "Take a Side." A YouTube consumer contest asked consumers to declare their feelings in an effort to win a prize of $25,000. The site tallied the numbers of "lovers" and "haters," creating a huge buzz. In an attempt to reach a target market of nonusers and lapsed users, the site included a form for ordering a free sample, suggesting that, "It's okay if you don't like us, but give us a try." In all, 500,000 sample packets were sent out, quickly exhausting the supply.

The company's marketers took to the streets asking people to talk about their relationships, even reaching out to some just married in Las Vegas. Buzz grew quickly, as did a wave of

Jason Stitt/Fotolia

▲ The "Are You Miracle Whip" campaign featured an innovative approach to presenting a marketing communications message.

disapproval. Critics suggested the approach trivialized both marriage and divorce; however, none of these efforts impeded the campaign. Instead, Miracle Whip continued the conversation, tying the themes of either loving or hating the condiment. The campaign's buzz lasted for more than six months.[1]

The Miracle Whip program highlights many of the themes present in this chapter, including how to use the communications process to reach consumers and break through advertising clutter. It illustrates the importance of integrating all communications and how company leaders must understand the current trends sweeping the advertising and marketing world in order to succeed.

The Nature of Communication

Communication involves transmitting, receiving, and processing information. As a person, group, or organization attempts to transfer an idea or message, communication occurs when the receiver (another person or group) comprehends the information. The model of communication shown in Figure 1 displays the pathway a message takes from one person to another or others.[2]

Communication plays a key role in any advertising or marketing program. Consider a person planning to dine at a quick-serve chicken restaurant. In the communications model (Figure 1), the **senders** include the chains KFC, Chick-fil-A, Popeye's, Church's

objective 1
How does communication take place?

▶ **FIGURE 1**
The Communication Process

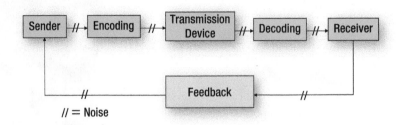

Sender //→ Encoding //→ Transmission Device //→ Decoding //→ Receiver

Feedback

// = Noise

Chicken, Bojangles, and Raising Cain's Chicken Fingers. Each one tries to capture the customer's attention. Most of these firms hire advertising agencies, although some utilize in-house teams.

Encoding is forming verbal and nonverbal cues. In marketing, the person in charge of designing an advertisement takes an idea and transforms it into an attention-getting message. The commercial consists of cues being placed in various media, such as television, magazines, and billboards. The message may also be encoded on the firm's website, a social media page, or on a Twitter account.

Messages travel to audiences through various **transmission devices**. Marketing communications move through various channels or media. The channel may be a television station carrying an advertisement, a Sunday paper with a coupon placed in it, the internet, or a billboard placed along the interstate.

▼ Decoding occurs when a consumer sees this advertisement and understands JD Bank is a viable option for a home loan.

Decoding occurs when the message reaches one or more of the receiver's senses. Consumers both hear and see television ads. Other consumers handle (touch) and read (see) a coupon offer. It is even possible to "smell" a message. A well-placed perfume sample might entice a buyer to purchase both the magazine containing the sample and the perfume being advertised. Hungry people tend to pay closer attention to advertisements and other information about food.

Quality marketing communication takes place when customers (the **receivers**) decode or understand the message as it was intended by the sender. In the case of the JD Bank advertisement shown in this section, effective marketing communications depend on receivers encountering the right message and responding in the desired fashion, such as obtaining a home loan or refinancing a home's current mortgage.

Chick-fil-A's approach to social media provides an example of a successful communication strategy that integrates the web with both online and offline advertising to build a loyal customer base.[3] Before launching a social media site, Chick-fil-A's third-party digital agency discovered that more than 500 Facebook profiles mentioned Chick-fil-A and that one particular fan page had 25,000 "fans." Engaging consumers constituted the social media program's goal. John Keehler, director of interactive strategy at ClickHere, noted that, "One of the mistakes we'd seen is brands would gather a lot of friends but wouldn't get people to interact with them."

The Facebook page allows fans to network with Chick-fil-A. The company holds a "Cow Appreciation Day" each July that encourages

- Talking on the phone during a commercial on television
- Driving while listening to the radio
- Looking at a sexy model in a magazine ad and ignoring the message and brand
- Scanning a newspaper for articles to read
- Talking to a passenger as the car passes billboards
- Scrolling past internet ads without looking at them
- Becoming annoyed by ads appearing on a social media site
- Ignoring tweets on Twitter because they are not relevant
- Being offended by the message on a flyer for a local business

◀ **FIGURE 2**
Examples of Communication Noise

customers to dress like cows and post their photos on Facebook. To build the base of members, coupons have been offered as part of a "Chicken Wave" during the kickoff of the college football season. Other promotions through Twitter and Facebook resulted in a Facebook community with more than 1 million members. Currently, the company announces any new Chick-fil-A store opening on Facebook first, and customers are invited to visit the restaurant and participate in grand-opening festivities.

A compatible offline program represents one key to the social media utilization. Successfully-integrated communications employ multiple channels providing a consistent message. Many Chick-fil-A commercials feature cows urging people to "Eat Mor Chikin." All advertising and promotional venues present the same tagline and theme, thereby increasing the chances that consumers will encounter and perceive the same message. A stronger brand presence has been the result.

In the communication process, **feedback** takes the form of the receiver's response to the sender. In marketing communications, feedback includes purchases, inquiries, complaints, questions, store visits, blogs, and website hits.

Noise consists of anything that distorts or disrupts a message, including marketing communications. It might occur at any stage in the communication process, as shown in Figure 1. **Clutter** remains the most common form of noise affecting marketing communications. Figure 2 provides examples of noise that can affect the advertising messages.

The marketing professionals involved in the communication process pay attention to each aspect of the communications model to ensure that all audiences encounter a consistent message. They try to make sure the message can cut through noise and clutter. In the case of quick-serve chicken restaurants, common objectives marketing teams seek to achieve include an increase in market share, sales, and brand loyalty.

Communicating with consumers and other businesses requires more than creating attractive advertisements. The upcoming section describes the nature of integrated marketing communications. An effective program integrates all marketing activities into a complete package.

Donald E. Baack

▲ A Chick-fil-A contest winner.

Integrated Marketing Communications

The communications model provides the foundation for an advertising and marketing program. **Integrated marketing communications (IMC)** is the coordination and integration of all marketing communication tools, avenues, and sources in a company into a seamless program designed to maximize the impact on customers and other stakeholders. The program covers all of a firm's business-to-business, market channel, customer-focused, and internally-directed communications.[4]

objective 2
What is an integrated marketing communications program?

▶ **FIGURE 3**
Components of Promotion

▶ **FIGURE 3**
Components of Promotion

Before further examining an IMC program, consider the traditional framework of marketing promotions. The **marketing mix**—price, product, distribution, and promotions—provides the starting point. For years, the view was that promotional activities included advertising, sales promotions, and personal selling activities. This approach has expanded to incorporate digital marketing, social media, and alternative methods of communication. It also includes activities such as database marketing, direct response marketing, personal selling tactics, sponsorships, and public relations programs (see Figure 3).

A complete IMC plan combines every element of the marketing mix: products, prices, distribution methods, and promotions. While this text primarily deals with the promotions component, note that, in order to present a unified message, the other elements of the marketing mix should be blended into the program.

An Integrated Marketing Communications Plan

A strategic marketing plan forms the basis for integrated marketing communications. The plan coordinates every component of the marketing mix in order to achieve harmony in the messages and promotions relayed to customers and others. Figure 4 lists the steps required to complete a marketing plan.

A *current situational analysis* process involves examination of the firm's ongoing market situation. Next, marketers conduct a *SWOT analysis* by studying the factors in the organization's internal and external environments. SWOT identifies internal company strengths and weaknesses along with the marketing opportunities and threats present in the external environment.

Defining primary *marketing objectives* establishes targets such as higher sales, an increase in market share, a new competitive position, or desired customer actions, such

- Current situational analysis
- SWOT analysis
- Marketing objectives
- Target market

- Marketing strategies
- Marketing tactics
- Implementation
- Evaluation of performance

▶ **FIGURE 4**
Steps of a Marketing Plan

PERFECT LANDING

VISIT *South Walton*
FLORIDA
FIND YOUR PERFECT BEACH.
VISITSOUTHWALTON.COM

Visit South Walton

◀ Matching marketing objectives with the key target market is an important step in developing the "Visit South Walton (Florida)" campaign.

as visiting the store and making purchases. Marketing objectives are paired with key target markets. A comprehensive understanding of these markets helps the marketing team prepare an effective integrated marketing communications program.

Based on the marketing objectives and target market, the team develops *marketing strategies*. These strategies apply to every ingredient in the marketing mix and include all positioning, differentiation, and branding strategies. Based on the strategies, *marketing tactics* guide the day-by-day activities necessary to support marketing strategies. The final two steps in the marketing plan consist of stating how to *implement* the plan and specifying methods to *evaluate performance*.

The steps of the strategic marketing plan help pull together all company activities into one consistent effort. The steps provide guidance to company leaders and marketing experts as they coordinate the firm's overall communications package.

Emerging Trends in Marketing Communications

Many forces impact the field of marketing communications. Financial pressures have caused the company leaders who hire advertising agencies to conclude that they cannot pay out unlimited dollars for marketing programs. Competition, both domestically and globally, forces company leaders to examine their communications plans to ensure maximum effectiveness. The internet and emerging social trends impact marketing messages and means of communicating with consumers and businesses. Figure 5 highlights the current trends that have an impact on marketing communications.

Emphasis on Accountability and Measurable Results

Company leaders expect advertising agencies to produce tangible outcomes. They spend promotional dollars carefully. Any coupon promotion,

objective 3

What trends are affecting marketing communications?

- Emphasis on accountability and measurable results
- Explosion of the digital arena
- Integration of media platforms
- Shift in channel power
- Increase in global competition
- Increase in brand parity
- Emphasis on customer engagement

▲ **FIGURE 5**

Trends Affecting Marketing Communications

This app for Gulf Coast Seafood illustrates the rapid explosion of digital media.

Gulf Coast Seafood

contest, rebate program, or advertising campaign should yield measurable gains in sales, market share, brand awareness, customer loyalty, or other observable results to be considered successful.

The increasing emphasis on accountability and measurable results has been driven by chief executive officers (CEOs), chief financial officers (CFOs), and chief marketing officers (CMOs). According to Martyn Straw, chief strategy officer of the advertising agency BBDO Worldwide, corporate executives and business owners are tired of "funneling cash into TV commercials and glossy ads" that keep increasing in cost while appearing to do less and less.

Many companies rely less on 30-second television spots and instead pursue digital and alternative communication venues. Marketing messages can be tied to special events in which names, profiles, and addresses of prospective customers are collected and tracked. Straw suggests that marketing should not be viewed as an expense, but rather as an investment in which promotional dollars generate sales and profits.[5]

Explosion of Digital Media

Internet-based marketing communications have evolved from individual web advertisements to interactive websites, blogs, and social networks. Smartphones, tablets, and text-messaging systems have created a new landscape and, in some cases, nearly a new language. Ingenious digital marketing techniques seek to create experiences with a brand rather than mere purchases with little or no emotional attachment. Notice the advertisement for the smartphone app in this section. The app was created for Gulf Coast Seafood. It offers a recipe along with a GPS function that assists consumers in locating the nearest Wild Gulf Seafood.

Many companies have cut traditional media expenditures, moving the dollars to digital media. Procter & Gamble (P&G), AT&T, Johnson & Johnson, Kraft Foods, Verizon, and Toyota are a few of the many companies that have reduced company television advertising budgets to expand use of various forms of digital media. Unilever recently increased its digital spending by 15 percent.[6] As a General Motors executive noted, "Some 70 percent of consumers who shop for a new car or truck do web research."[7] The same holds true for many other products.

With social media and the internet, consumers enjoy access to a wealth of information about companies, products, and brands. They can communicate with each other, sending favorable or unfavorable ratings and information. Messages travel almost instantaneously. Digital marketing cannot be considered as an option for companies but rather as a mandatory ingredient. Marketers now seek to engage a brand with all current and prospective customers in order to achieve success.

Advances in digital technology allowed self-styled makeup maven Lauren Luke to sell cosmetics around the world. She started by offering them on eBay and then began posting videos that she recorded in her bedroom on YouTube. The videos have been viewed 50 million times. Her YouTube channel now contains more than 250,000 subscribers. It is not just entrepreneurs such as Lauren Luke who have taken advantage of the opportunities present in today's information and technology-rich environment. In just six months, Dell generated $1 million in sales from individuals who contacted the firm using Twitter.[8]

Integration of Media Platforms

Today's consumers spend an average of five hours and 16 minutes in front of a screen that does not involve television. When combined with television (which consumers watch for an additional four hours and 31 minutes per day), the total becomes more than 10 hours per day examining some kind of screen, whether it is a computer, tablet, mobile

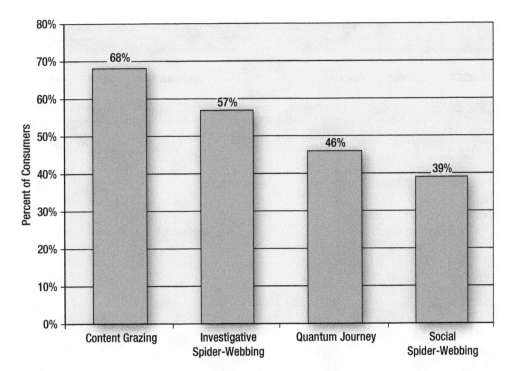

◀ **FIGURE 6**

Pathways Consumers Use to Interact Across Media Devices

Source: Based on Mark Walsh, "Microsoft Highlights Usage Across Device Pathways," *Online Media Daily*, March 14, 2013, www.mediapost.com/publications/article/195786

phone, or television.[9] Understanding how consumers integrate these multiple devices into their daily lives is important to marketers as they devise ways to reach these individuals. Research by Flamingo Research and Ipsos OTX indicates four ways consumers interact across these multiple media formats (see Figure 6).[10]

Content grazing involves looking at two or more screens simultaneously to access content that is not related. It may be someone watching TV and texting a friend at the same time or checking on football game scores on his smartphone. *Investigative spider-webbing* occurs when a consumer pursues or investigates specific content across multiple platforms. It may be someone watching a football game and accessing stats for various players on her PC or mobile phone. *Quantam journey* focuses on completing a specific task, such as when a consumer looks for a Chinese restaurant using a PC to locate one in the area, then obtains consumer reviews of the units close by on a smartphone, and finally employs a map app to locate the restaurant or to place an order. The fourth pathway, *social spider-webbing*, takes place when consumers share content or information across multiple devices. Posting pictures on Facebook from a laptop then texting friends to go check them out would be an example.

To reach consumers, marketers understand that today's consumers use multiple devices in multiple ways. An individual television ad or banner ad will likely go unnoticed. Advertisers try to find ways to engage consumers with a brand through portals such as their tablets and mobile phones. That same ad or message delivered across all of the platforms in various formats increases the chances it will be heard and assimilated by consumers.

Changes in Channel Power

A marketing channel consists of a producer or manufacturer vending goods to wholesalers or middlemen, who, in turn, sell items to retailers who offer the items to consumers. Recent technological developments alter the levels of power held by various members of the channel.

Retailers seek to maintain channel power by controlling shelf space and purchase data that allows them to determine which products and brands are placed on store shelves. Through checkout scanners, retailers know which products and brands are selling. Many retailers share the data with suppliers and require them to ensure that store

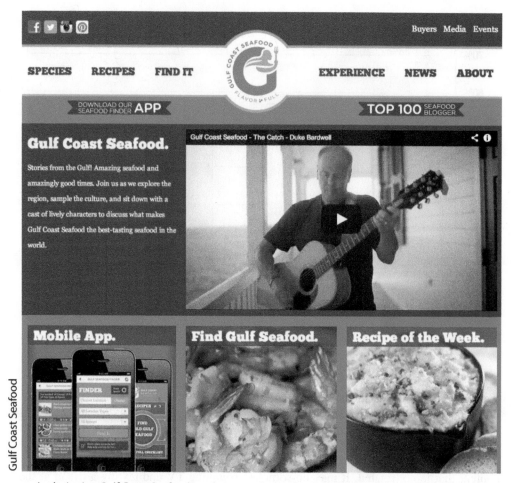

In designing Gulf Coast Seafood's website, marketers for the brand understand that consumers integrate various media platforms and desire an experience with the brand.

shelves remain well stocked. The size and power of mega-retailers mean manufacturers and suppliers have no choice but to follow the dictates of "mega" stores.

At the same time, the growth of internet usage along with other methods of communication has shifted some channel power to consumers.[11] Consumers obtain information about goods and services and purchase them using the internet. Internet-driven sales have risen at a tremendous rate. According to Forrester Research, online retail sales have grown from $31 billion in 2001 to $252 billion in 2013 and are projected to reach $327 billion by 2016. Currently, online purchases account for about eight percent of all retail purchases.[12]

Consumer relationships with brands have changed. Individuals wield tremendous power. Social media allows dissatisfied customers to instantly vent about bad experiences to enormous audiences, where little forgiveness of mistakes takes place. Fifty-seven percent of consumers say they will not buy a particular brand after just one negative experience and 40 percent are likely to tell others not to purchase that brand.[13] Previously held positive feelings about a company are quickly forgotten.

The same principles apply to business-to-business purchasing activities. Buyers who shop on behalf of organizations and other company members seeking business-to-business products also are quick to use social media to lament about brands that did not deliver. Consequently, a similar shift in channel power has taken place in the business-to-business sector.

Fortunately, the environment is not completely negative. Approximately 50 percent of consumers share positive experiences with a brand. Consumers often seek the opinions of friends and relatives concerning products. As a result, approximately 70 percent of consumers say friends and families are a primary source of information regarding various brands.[14]

Understanding these shifts in channel power has become essential. Marketers know they cannot rely solely on mass media advertising. They must incorporate social media and engage consumers with their brands.

Increases in Global Competition

Advances in information technology and communication means competition no longer takes place with just the company down the street—it may be from a firm 10,000 miles away. Consumers desire high quality along with low prices. The company that delivers the best value of quality and price makes the sale, often regardless of location. Advancements in delivery systems make it possible for purchases to arrive in a matter of days from anywhere in the world.

Advances in information and communication technology have created global competition for goods and services.

Doritos' marketing team recognized that new communication technologies and social media have made the world smaller. Consumers travel and communicate with each other. As a result, Doritos launched its first global campaign by updating packaging and the company's logo to give a consistent look across 37 countries in which its products are sold. Before this global effort, Doritos offered 25 different package designs and utilized a number of different marketing approaches. The global campaign, called "For the Bold," included digital and TV spots in the United States, Mexico, England, Canada, Spain, and Turkey as well as digital and social media initiatives. The global campaign provided a venue to connect fans worldwide, a consistent storyline, and the same look and feel for the Doritos brand across multiple countries. Today, Doritos remains the largest tortilla/corn chip brand in the world with a 39 percent market share.[15]

Increase in Brand Parity

Many currently available products offer nearly identical benefits. When consumers believe that various brands provide the same set of attributes, **brand parity** results. When it occurs, shoppers select from a group of brands rather than one specific brand.[16] Brand parity means quality becomes less of a concern because consumers perceive only minor differences between brands. Consequently, other criteria—such as price, availability, or a specific promotional deal—impact purchase decisions. The net effect becomes a steady decline in brand loyalty.[17]

A recent survey revealed that consumers are willing to switch brands in most product categories because they do not have one specific brand they must buy or believe is significantly superior.[18] In response to this trend, marketing teams have created messages that suggest the ways a company's products are different. Although these messages were designed to convince consumers that the company's brand was superior and not the same as the competition, they often did not move consumers from the perception of brand parity. As a result, some companies have changed to new and innovative marketing tactics to connect consumers with the brand.

Emphasis on Customer Engagement

The expanding number of available brands perceived to be roughly equivalent leads to another response. To build loyalty, many marketing efforts have been made to engage customers with the brand at every contact point. Any place where customers interact with or acquire additional information about a firm constitutes a **contact point**. Customer engagement programs often utilize digital and social media and have become part of the total integrated marketing approach.

Salvation Army of San Diego

WE COMBAT NATURAL DISASTERS WITH ACTS OF GOD.

When catastrophe strikes, your generosity strikes back. Thanks to your help, The Salvation Army serves disaster survivors from the moment of impact until the healing is complete. Proving that while disasters may be unpredictable, the good of people is not. Thank you for your continued giving at 1-800-SAL-ARMY or at salvationarmyusa.org.

DISASTER RELIEF   EMERGENCY RESPONSE   REHABILITATION   HUMAN TRAFFICKING ABOLITION   YOUTH SERVICES   EVANGELISM

DOING THE MOST GOOD

▲ Nonprofits, such as the Salvation Army, must understand how to engage donors to ensure sufficient funds when disasters strike.

An effective contact provides a setting for two-way communication. Engagement can be built by offering incentives and reasons for the consumer to communicate with the company. For customers to take advantage of these initiatives, however, they must develop emotional commitments to the brand and have feelings of confidence, integrity, pride, and passion toward it.[19] The brand, in turn, must deliver on its promises and provide reasons for consumers to continue to interact with the company.

The Restaurant Industry

Technomic Consumer Brand Metrics monitors 120 restaurants across 60 attributes. The company published a white paper entitled "Perceptions of Restaurant Advertising." In the study, the researchers asked 78,743 respondents to evaluate restaurants on three advertising metrics:

- Has memorable advertising
- Has advertising I can relate to
- Has advertising that makes me hungry

The scores were then tabulated on a percent basis. Figure 7 presents the composite score of the top 10 restaurants. The study reveals that while some restaurants tended to scored high on the metric "advertising makes me hungry" they did not fare as well on "advertising I can relate to" and "memorable advertising."[20]

Subway's high score can be partially attributed to the organization's real-life spokesperson, Jared Fogle, who has been the face of the company for 15 years. Jared's weight gain of 40 pounds in 2010 was documented in the press and created a potentially

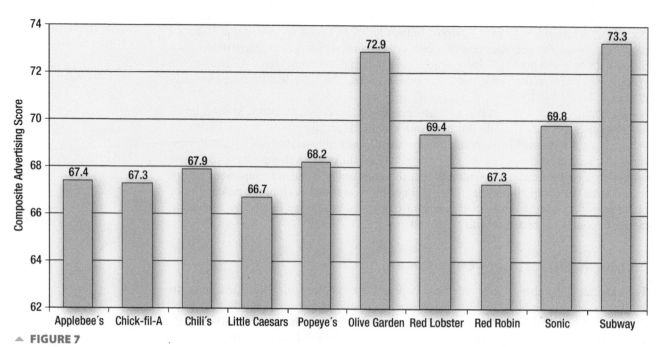

▲ **FIGURE 7**

Composite Scores of Top Ten Restaurants on Advertising Perceptions

Source: Based on Colleen Rothman and Gina Gapp, "Perceptions of Restaurant Advertising," *Technomic* white paper, Issue 3, September 2013.

damaging effect on Subway's advertising program. The company's marketing team learned, however, that Jared's struggle resonated with consumers because he represented what many real people face—difficulty with weight control. Subway's leaders remained loyal to Jared and encouraged him to train and enter the New York City marathon. Another factor contributing to Subway's top ranking was that the marketing messages were delivered in newer formats and social media. Subway features strong online content and has 24 million Facebook fans and 1.5 million Twitter followers. Subway was named a top brand in terms of social currency, which measures the extent to which consumers include a brand in their status updates, videos, and image posts.

Many of the examples of integrated marketing communications in this text will be drawn from the restaurant and food industries. These examples will help provide a better understanding of the concepts and theories presented.

International Implications

objective 5

What does the term *GMIC* mean?

The same trends that exist among advertising agencies in the United States occur in the international arena. Instead of IMC, international programs are called *GIMC*, or *globally integrated marketing communications programs*.[21] The goal remains the same: to coordinate marketing efforts across all platforms. The challenges become greater due to larger national and cultural differences in target markets.

Marketers employ two different strategies for global companies. **Standardization**, in which a company features a uniform product and message across countries, represents one option. The approach involves generating economies of scale in production while creating a global product using a more universal promotional theme. The language may be different, but the basic marketing message stays the same.

The second approach, **adaptation**, results in the creation of products and marketing messages designed for and adapted to individual countries. The manner in which a product is marketed in Mexico will differ from the methods used in Italy, India, or Australia.

The standardization method may be easier to apply; however, GIMC principles can and should be used with either adaptation or standardization.[22] To reduce costs, careful coordination of marketing efforts should occur across countries. Even when a firm uses the adaptation strategy, marketers from various countries learn from each other. Synergies take place between countries and regions. More importantly, learning can occur.

Recently, Adrian Hallmark, global brand director of Jaguar, commented that "for too many luxury consumers, there is awareness of the Jaguar brand, but not consideration and modern relevance." To restore its iconic status, Jaguar's marketing group launched a multinational ad campaign created by Spark 44, a London ad agency. The campaign debuted on websites JaguarUSA.com, Facebook, and YouTube with a 45-second version of a 30-second TV ad. Jaguar then introduced print, digital, and outdoor advertising in the United States, Austria, Spain, France, Germany, Italy, Russia, Korea, Japan, Australia, and South Africa. The campaign included an 18-city road show in the United States to allow prospective buyers to try the new Jaguar. The ads were adapted to individual markets in each country using the central theme of the campaign "How alive are you?" which was featured in every print, digital, outdoor, television, and video ad.[23]

Photocreo Bednarek/Fotolia

▲ In developing global communication campaigns, firms must decide the best approach, standardization, or adaptation.

Summary

Communication consists of transmitting, receiving, and processing information. It represents a two-way street in which a sender establishes a connection with a receiver. Effective communication forms the basis for a solid and successful marketing program. The components of the communication process include the sender, an encoding process, the transmission device, the decoding process, and the receiver. Noise is anything that distorts or disrupts the flow of information from the sender to the receiver.

In the marketing arena, senders are companies seeking to transmit ideas to consumers, employees, other companies, retail outlets, and others. Encoding devices provide the means of transmitting information and include advertisements, public relations efforts, press releases, sales activities, promotions, and a wide variety of additional verbal and nonverbal cues sent to receivers. Transmission devices are the media and spokespersons that carry the message. Decoding occurs when the receivers (customers or retailers) encounter the message. Noise takes many forms in marketing, most notably the clutter of an overabundance of messages in every available channel.

Integrated marketing communications (IMC) takes advantage of the effective management of the communications channel. Within the marketing mix of products, prices, distribution systems, and promotions, firms that speak with one clear voice are able to coordinate and integrate all marketing tools.

The fields of advertising, promotions, and marketing communications have experienced several new trends. Marketing departments and advertising agencies, as well as individual account managers, brand managers, and creatives, encounter strong pressures. They are held accountable for expenditures of marketing communications dollars. Company leaders expect tangible results from promotional campaigns and marketing programs.

IMC plans are vital to achieving success. The explosion of digital media, new information technologies, and social media strongly influences IMC programs. Marketing professionals seek to find ways to integrate all media platforms together to present a consistent message. Channel power has shifted in many ways. Company leaders adjust in order to maintain a strong market standing, and IMC programs can assist in this effort. New levels of global competition drive marketers to better understand customers and be certain that those end users hear a clear and consistent message from the firm.

As consumers develop a stronger sense of brand parity, wherein consumers perceive no real differences in product or service quality, marketers seek to create situations in which a company or brand develops a distinct advantage over others. This may be difficult because consumers collect and integrate information about products from a wide variety of sources, including the internet and social media. Quality IMC programs help maintain the strong voice a company needs to ensure customers hear its message through an emphasis on customer engagement in all marketing activities.

When a firm conducts business internationally, a GIMC, or globally integrated marketing communications system, can be of great value. By developing one strong theme and then adapting that theme to individual countries, the firm conveys a message that integrates international operations into a more coherent marketing package.

This text explains the issues involved in establishing an effective IMC program. The importance of business-to-business marketing efforts is noted because many firms market items as much to other companies as they do to consumers. Successful development of an IMC program should help firms remain profitable and vibrant, even when the complexities of the marketplace make these goals more difficult to attain.

Key Terms

communication Transmitting, receiving, and processing information

senders The person(s) attempting to deliver a message or idea

encoding The verbal (words, sounds) and nonverbal (gestures, facial expressions, posture) cues that the sender utilizes in dispatching a message

transmission devices All of the items that carry a message from the sender to the receiver

decoding What occurs when the receiver employs any of his or her senses (hearing, seeing, feeling) in an attempt to capture a message

receivers The intended audience for a message

feedback The information the sender obtains from the receiver regarding the receiver's perception or interpretation of a message

noise Anything that distorts or disrupts a message

clutter What exists when consumers are exposed to hundreds of marketing messages per day, and most are tuned out

integrated marketing communications (IMC) The coordination and integration of all marketing communication tools, avenues, and sources in a company into a seamless program designed to maximize the impact on customers and other stakeholders

marketing mix The elements of a marketing program, including products, prices, places (the distribution system), and promotions

brand parity What occurs when there is the perception that most goods and services are essentially the same

contact point Any place where customers interact with or acquire additional information about a firm

standardization A program in which a firm features uniform products and market offerings across countries with the goal of generating economies of scale in production while using the same promotional theme

adaptation What takes place when products and marketing messages are designed for and adapted to individual countries

MyMarketingLab
Go to **mymktlab.com** to complete the problems marked with this icon ⭐.

Review Questions

1. Define communication. How does it play a crucial role in marketing and business?

2. What are the parts of an individual communications model?

3. Who are the typical senders in marketing communications? Who are the receivers?

4. Name the transmission devices, both human and non-human, that carry marketing messages.

5. Define clutter. Name some of the forms of clutter in marketing communications.

6. Define integrated marketing communications (IMC).

7. What are the four parts of the marketing mix?

8. What steps are required to write a marketing plan?

9. What trends were given to explain the growth in importance of IMC plans in this chapter?

10. How has the explosion of the digital arena impacted marketing communications?

11. Identify and describe the four ways consumers interact with multiple media formats.

12. What is channel power? How has it changed in the past few decades?

13. What is brand parity? How is it related to successful marketing efforts?

14. What is a contact point? How do marketers link contact points to customer engagement?

15. What are the components of an integrated marketing communications program, as outlined in this text?

16. What is a GIMC? Why is it important for multinational firms?

17. What is the difference between standardization and adaptation in GIMC programs?

Critical Thinking Exercises

DISCUSSION QUESTIONS

⭐ 18. Do you use Miracle Whip? Ask five people how they feel about the product. Using YouTube and the website highlighted in this chapter, view the 2011 campaign. Evaluate its impact and explain whether you believe the campaign was a good idea. Defend your answer.

⭐ 19. The marketing director for a furniture manufacturer is assigned the task of emphasizing the furniture's natural look in the company's integrated marketing communications program. Discuss the problems the director might encounter while developing this message and

in ensuring that consumers understand the message correctly. Refer to the communication process outlined in the chapter for ideas. Explain how noise or clutter interferes with the communication process.

⭐ 20. What do you typically do during commercials on television? What percentage of the time do you watch commercials? What makes you watch? Ask these same questions of five other people. What type of activities do people engage in during commercials?

21. Examine the four ways consumers interact across multiple media formats. Which best describes you? Explain why.

22. The use of social media has exploded during the last decade. Discuss your personal use of social media. Which social media platforms do you use? Why did you select those particular ones? How do you use social media?

23. Brand parity has become a major issue for companies. Identify three product categories where the brand you purchase is not very important. Why is the brand not important? Identify three product categories where the brand is important. What brand or brands do you typically purchase in each category?

24. The marketing director for a manufacturer of automobile tires has been asked to integrate the company's global marketing program. Should the director use a standardization or adaptation approach? How could the company be certain that its marketing program will effectively be integrated among the different countries in which it sells tires?

Integrated Learning Exercises

25. Access the website of Chick-fil-A at **www.chickfila.com**. Access the websites of Chick-fil-A's competitors: KFC (**www.kfc.com**), Popeye's (**www.popeyes.com**), Church's Chicken (**www.churchschicken.com**), and Bojangles (**www.bojangles.com**). Which sites have a link to Facebook, Twitter, or other social media sites? Compare and contrast the information available and the design of each company's website. Which website did you like the best? Why? Which one did you like the least? Why?

26. Figure 7 identified the top 10 restaurants based on a composite score of advertising perceptions from a survey by Technomic Consumer Brand Metrics. Pick one of the restaurants and access the company's website. Go to YouTube and locate at least three ads for the restaurant. Is the company's advertising effective?

Why or why not? From the website, describe how the restaurant utilizes social media. In your opinion, does the restaurant integrate all of its marketing messages? Why or why not?

27. Information is one key to developing a successful integrated marketing communications program. Access each of the following websites. Describe the type of information and news available on each site. How would this information help in developing an integrated marketing campaign?

    a. *Adweek* (**www.adweek.com**)

    b. *Interbrand* (**www.interbrand.com**)

    c. *Media Industry Today* (**www.media.einews.com**)

    d. *Branding Asia* (**www.brandingasia.com**)

Blog Exercises

Access the authors' blog for this text at the URLs provided to complete these exercises. Answer the questions that are posed on the blog.

28. Chick-fil-A campaign, **http://blogclowbaack.net/2014/04/24/chick-fil-a-chapter-1/**

29. Subway advertising, **http://blogclowbaack.net/2014/04/24/subway-chapter-1/**

30. Integrated marketing, **http://blogclowbaack.net/2014/04/24/imc-chapter-1/**

Student Project

CREATIVE CORNER

Executives at Red Robin Gourmet Burgers have decided to open a restaurant near your campus. You have been chosen as a marketing intern to help the firm establish this restaurant. Examine the company's website at http://www.redrobin.com. Read the "About Us" section of the website in order to fully understand the Red Robin brand. When you have a good feel for Red Robin, prepare a newspaper ad for your student newspaper about a grand opening near your campus. Next, examine the company's social media presence on Facebook, Twitter, YouTube, and LinkedIn by accessing these pages from the restaurant's website. Write a report that discusses whether you believe social media will be effective in reaching students at your college. Cite specific examples from the company's social media pages.

CASE 1 — WAKE UP CALL FOR 8:00

Any longstanding product runs the risk of becoming stale in the eyes of consumers. Eight O'Clock Coffee's marketing team recently decided that the company's entire brand and promotion program was in need of rejuvenation. The net result was an entire "refresh" marketing effort.[24]

Eight O'Clock Coffee has been available to consumers since 1859. To combat recent sluggish sales, company leaders began with a rejuvenation of the product itself, creating new flavors such as Dark Chocolate Cherry, Cinnamon Bun, and others. The new items were complemented with updated packaging that was slimmer and brandished a bright red color.

To launch these innovations, the marketing program began with a redesigned website that highlighted a major event. The campaign included a social-media driven sweepstakes that was incorporated into Fashion Week in New York. Participants in the fashion show were offered red bags. The theme, "The Red Bag Collection in Support of Dress for Success" was featured, which added a cause-related tie-in to the refresh rollout. Individuals involved in the fashion event were encouraged to "Spot the Red Bag" in order to win prizes. They accessed the company through the hash tag "#SpottheRedBag" to post photos of their discoveries. The photos of red bags were posted on the company's Facebook page.

Beyond the social media and fashion show elements, the company added more traditional advertising during the Emmy awards on television. The tagline "put coffee first" punctuated these messages. The campaign was then extended to other programs in many of the company's major markets.

These marketing efforts for Eight O'Clock Coffee stress the value of a multifaceted approach to enticing, exciting, and engaging customers and potential customers. Use of new

▲ Eight O-Clock Coffee's marketing team understood that it must engage consumers with the brand to obtain long-term loyalty.

methods such as social media combined with more traditional marketing programs (sweepstakes, television advertising) indicates the wave of the future for integrated marketing communications.

31. What coffee brands would constitute Eight O'Clock Coffee's primary competition?

32. Would you characterize coffee consumption as a situation in which brand parity or brand loyalty exists? Why?

33. Who is the target market for Eight O'Clock Coffee's brand refresh program? Will the campaign be effective in reaching the right audience? Why or why not?

34. Evaluate the value of using social media for this type of marketing communications effort. Is it necessary or helpful? Why or why not?

CASE 2 — A NEW SALSA SENSATION

Hector Fernandez created a salsa that became legendary within just a few years. Hector operated a successful restaurant, El Casa Grande, in Taos, New Mexico, for many years. A new chapter in his life opened when he was approached by two of his best customers, who offered to help him produce and market his salsa throughout the state, with the goal of reaching regional distribution in five years.

As a first step, Hector located the home office of a major advertising agency in Albuquerque. The agency positioned itself as being a "full-service" organization. Hector wondered exactly what that meant. He was introduced to Matt Barnes, who was to serve as his marketing and promotions consultant.

Matt's first questions were about Hector's salsa: "What makes your salsa better?" and "Is there a way we can convince people of the difference?" Hector responded that his customers often commented about both the taste and the texture of the salsa. He had a secret formula that had a few unusual seasonings that made his salsa burst with flavor. Hector also believed that it was less "runny" than others.

The next item the two discussed was potential customers. Hector noted that Tex-Mex was a popular form of dining in New Mexico as well as across the country. He believed that his salsa would appeal to a wide variety of people who enjoy Tex-Mex cuisine.

▲ Hector had a great salsa, but no brand name and no marketing communications plan.

Matt's next question was simple: "Who do you think are your major competitors?"

Hector responded, "That's easy, Pace and Old El Paso."

Matt then asked what Hector thought of the two companies and their products. He suggested an investigation on both a personal and competitive basis. For example, Matt asked, "What do you think of when you hear the name Pace? How about Old El Paso?" He noted that both brands were solid and that Hector's company would need a compelling brand in order to compete.

The next step was a visit to the website of each company (www.pacefoods.com and www.oldelpaso.com). They noticed that the two companies offered some products that were the same and others that were not.

Matt asked Hector what he thought about the advertising and promotions for each company and its products. Hector replied, "Well, to tell you the truth, I only remember one television ad. It said something about one of the two companies was located in New York City instead of near Mexico, but I can't remember which was which." They concluded that it was possible that these companies do not engage in a great deal of traditional media advertising or that Hector was simply too busy with his own company to notice. Hector noted that he used a DVR to watch television and that he listened to satellite radio in both his restaurant and his car.

Matt suggested that Hector should look in Sunday papers for the past several weeks to see if either company was offering price-off coupons or other promotions, such as a contest or sweepstakes. He told Hector it would be a good idea to attend events where salsa was being sampled or sold, such as at county fairs, Mexican heritage events, and at ballparks and other sports stadiums where nachos were on the menu.

The two then discussed a crucial issue: How could Hector's new company convince grocers and others to designate some shelf space for his salsa, thereby taking space away from some other product?

Finally, Matt handed Hector a package of materials (see Figure 9). He asked Hector to consider how to reach every possible type of customer for his product, including grocery stores, other restaurants, and individual consumers shopping for salsa. He suggested that Hector would need to think about what type of sales tactics to use, which promotional programs were most important, and how the company should look—from its logo, to its letterhead, to the business cards handed out by sales representatives. Remember, Matt stated, "Everything communicates."

35. Can you think of a brand name that could be used not only for salsa, but for any other product related to salsa that Hector's company might sell?

36. How can Hector's company compete with Pace and Old El Paso? Is there a market niche the company can locate?

37. What kinds of advertising and promotions tactics should the company use? Will the tactics be the same in 5 years?

38. How can the company utilize social media to gain fans and stimulate sales?

- Company logo
- Product brand name and company name
- Business cards
- Letterhead
- Carry home bags (paper or plastic)
- Wrapping paper
- Coupons
- Promotional giveaways (coffee mugs, pens, pencils, and calendars)
- Design of booth for trade shows
- Advertisements (billboards, space used on cars and busses, television, radio, magazines, and newspapers)
- Toll-free 800 or 888 number
- Company database
- Cooperative advertising with other businesses
- Personal selling pitches
- Characteristics of target market buyers
- Characteristics of business buyers
- Sales incentives provided to salesforce (contests, prizes, bonuses, and commissions)
- Internal messages
- Company magazines and newspapers
- Statements to shareholders
- Speeches by company leaders
- Public relations releases
- Sponsorship programs
- Website

◀ **FIGURE 9**

Items to Be Included in an IMC Program

MyMarketingLab

Go to **mymktlab.com** for Auto-graded writing questions as well as the following Assisted-graded writing questions:

39. For years, Nike's advertising tagline was "Just do it." What meaning was conveyed by the tagline? Do you think this conveys a clear message about the company's operations?

40. Find each of the following companies on the internet. For each company, discuss how effective its website is in communicating an overall message. Also, discuss how well the marketing team integrates the material on the website. How well does the website integrate the company's advertising with other marketing communications?

   a. Revlon (**www.revlon.com**)

   b. J.B. Hunt (**www.jbhunt.com**)

   c. JD Bank (**www.jdbank.com**)

   d. Red Lobster (**www.redlobster.com**)

Endnotes

1. Based on T. L. Stanley (2011). Miracle Whip ads: Love Them or Hate Them? *Adweek*, February 24, http://www.adweek.com/adfreak/miracle-whip-ads-love-them-or-hate-them-127028, accessed February 20, 2012.

2. Donald Baack, "Communication Processes," *Organizational Behavior* (Houston: Dame Publications, Inc., 1998), pp. 313–37.

3. Brian Morrissey, "Chick-fil-A's Strategy: Give Your Fans Something to Do," *Brandweek* 50, no. 35 (October 5, 2009), p. 40.

4. James G. Hutton, "Integrated Marketing Communications and the Evolution of Marketing Thought," *Journal of Business Research* 37 (November 1996), pp. 155–62.

5. Diane Brady, "Making Marketing Measure Up," *BusinessWeek* (December 13, 2004), pp. 112–13; "Top 10: Issues Facing Senior Marketers in 2007," *Advertising Age* 78, no. 17 (April 23, 2007), p. 23.

6. "Unilever Cuts Agency, Production Spending Even as Ad Costs Rise," *Advertising Age*, February 2, 2012, http://adage.com/print/232485.

7. Andrew McMains, "Ad Spending Trends Reveal No Surprises," *Adweek* 48, no. 44 (December 3, 2007), p. 9.G14

8. Alison Circle, "Marketing Trends to Watch," *Library Journal* 134, no. 16 (October 1, 2009), pp. 26–29.

9. Katherine Rosman, "In Digital Era, What Does Watching TV Even Mean?" October 8, 2013, *http://online.wsj.com/news/articles/SB10001424052702303442004*.

10. Mark Walsh, "Microsoft Highlights Usage Across Device Pathways," *Online Media Daily*, March 14, 2013, *www.mediapost.com/publications/article/195786*.

11. Lauren Keller Johnson, "Harnessing the Power of the Customer," *Harvard Management Update* 9 (March 2004), pp. 3–5; Patricia Seybold, *The Customer Revolution* (London: Random House Business Books, 2006).

12. Lauren Indvik, "U.S. Online Retail Sales to Reach $327 Billion by 2016, http://mashable.com/2012/02/27/ecommerce-327-billion-2016-study, accessed March 9, 2012.

13. Katy Keim, "Don't Be Fooled: Social-Media Consumers Aren't in a Relationship with You," *Advertising Age*, May 29, 2013, *http://adage.com/print241722*.

14. Ibid.

15. "Doritos Launches First Global Campaign," *Advertising Age*, March 6, 2013, *http://adage.com/print/240173*.

16. M. N. Tripathi, "Customer Engagement—Key to Successful Brand Building," *The XIMB Journal of Management* 6, no. 1 (March 2009), pp. 131–40.

17. Jean-Noel Kapferer, "The Roots of Brand Loyalty Decline: An International Comparison," *Ivey Business Journal* 69, no. 4 (March–April 2005), pp. 1–6.

18. Debbie Howell, "Today's Consumers More Open to Try New Brands," *DSN Retailing Today* 43, no. 20 (October 25, 2004), pp. 29–32.

19. Jana Lay-Hwa Bowden, "The Process of Customer Engagement: A Conceptual Framework," *Journal of Marketing Theory & Practice* 17, no. 1 (Winter 2009), pp. 63–74.

20. "Study: Subway's Advertising Most Effective in Restaurant Space," *Advertising Age*, October 16, 2013, *http://adage.com/print/244761*; Colleen Rothman and Gina Gapp, "Perceptions of Restaurant Advertising," *Technomic* white paper, Issue 3, September 2013.

21. Stephen J. Gould, Dawn B. Lerman, and Andreas F. Grein, "Agency Perceptions and Practices on Global IMC," *Journal of Advertising Research* (January–February 1999), pp. 7–26.

22. Ibid.

23. Jane L. Levere, "A Campaign from Jaguar to Show its Wild Side," *The New York Times*, February 26, 2012, http://www.nytimes.com/2012/02/27/business/media/jaguar-ad-campaign.

24. Karlene Lukovitz, "Eight O'Clock Coffee Ups Marketing for Brand Refresh," *Marketing Daily,* August 16, 2013, http://www.mediapost.com/publications/article/206930/eight-oclock-coffee-ups-marketing-for-brand-refre.html. Eight O'Clock Coffee, 2013, http://www.eightoclock.com/. Daily Coffee News, "Eight O'Clock Coffee Unveils Brand Redesign, Marketing Plans," August 14, 2013, http://dailycoffeenews.com/2013/08/14/eight-oclock-coffee-unveils-brand-redesign-marketing-plans/.

Advertising
Campaign
Management

Advertising Campaign Management

Chapter Objectives

After reading this chapter, you should be able to answer the following questions:

1 Why is an understanding of advertising theories important in the advertising management process?

2 What is the relationship of advertising expenditures to advertising effectiveness?

3 When should a company employ an external advertising agency rather than completing the work in-house?

4 How do companies choose advertising agencies?

5 What are the primary job functions within an advertising agency?

6 What are the advertising campaign parameters that should be considered?

7 How does a creative brief facilitate effective advertising?

8 What are the implications of advertising management in the global arena?

MyMarketingLab™

⭐ **Improve Your Grade!**

Over 10 million students improved their results using the Pearson MyLabs. Visit **mymktlab.com** for simulations, tutorials, and end-of-chapter problems.

Overview

The average person encounters more than 600 advertisements per day, delivered by an expanding variety of media. Television and radio have long been the advertising staples, along with newspapers, magazines, and billboards. More recently, internet advertisements, social networks, and mobile phones apps offer additional venues to contact and interact with customers.

Today's marketers face several challenges. A company simply cannot afford to prepare advertisements for every medium. Further, each message should create a marketing advantage in a highly cluttered world in which people are increasingly adept at simply tuning ads out. **Advertising campaign management** is the process of preparing and integrating a specific advertising program in conjunction with the overall IMC message. One advertising agency that has achieved success in advertising campaign management is Zehnder Communications. Some of the agency's ads are featured in this text.

ZEHNDER COMMUNICATIONS

Zehnder Communications provides a variety of services, including strategic planning, creative, web and application development, media, public relations, and social media. The company also provides research and analytics services for clients. As stated on the company's website, "We have a unique situation at Zehnder in that we are a full-service agency that continually challenges traditional thinking."

Zehnder's client list includes Visit South Walton (Florida), Visit Baton Rouge, Burger King, Community Trust Bank, Gulf Seafood Marketing Coalition, NOLA.com/The Times Picayune, along with many others. The firm specializes in the Advocacy, Attractions/Entertainment, Automotive, Energy Services, Financial Services, Food and Beverage, Healthcare, Hospitality/Tourism, and Insurance industries.

Zehnder states, "As experts, it's not enough that we remain well versed in new media trends. We owe it to our clients to remain at the forefront of innovation, dedicated to developing new ways to reach the consumer. That's what it all comes down to—connecting with your audience through all available

Courtesy of Zehnder Communications

▲ Lobby of Zehnder Communications.

means. Innovation and campaign integration mean nothing unless you can make that connection which changes perception and ultimately behavior."

Zehnder has been listed as a "best place to work" in the area for more than 12 consecutive years. One innovation developed by founder Jeffrey Zehnder is the VAN ("Vacation as Needed") system. The firm allows employees to take time off when they feel it is appropriate, so long as doing so does not interfere with or slow down the activities of other employees. The sense of freedom and empowerment that results helps build morale over time.

Advertising management consists of several important activities. First, those involved decide on an advertising

▼ Zehnder has been listed as a "best place to work" for more than 12 consecutive years.

Courtesy of Zehnder Communications

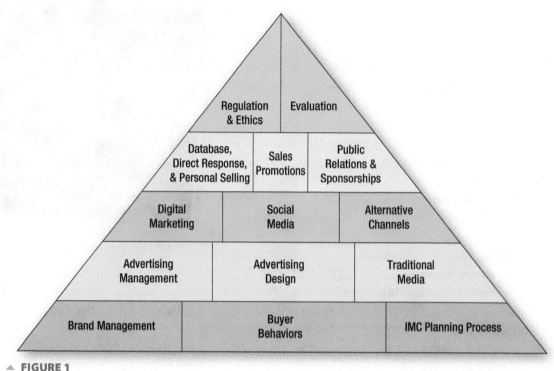

▲ **FIGURE 1**

Overview of Integrated Marketing Communications

theory or approach to guide the process. Next, company leaders develop guidelines that help everyone understand the relationship of advertising to eventual success. Then, the company's management team decides whether to complete advertising work as an in-house activity or in conjunction with an advertising agency. Advertising parameters are generated to help control the process. A creative brief will then be prepared to direct the actual design of the advertising campaign. This chapter concludes with an examination of the international implications of these activities.

Advertising Theory

objective 1

Why is an understanding of advertising theories important in the advertising management process?

In developing an advertising campaign, two theoretical approaches provide a solid foundation. The hierarchy of effects model and a means–end chain can assist in developing effective campaigns. Advertisers also consider the mix of visual and verbal elements in a commercial or advertisement.

Hierarchy of Effects

The **hierarchy of effects model** helps to clarify the objectives of an advertising campaign. The model outlines six steps a consumer or a business buyer moves through when making a purchase:

1. Awareness
2. Knowledge
3. Liking
4. Preference
5. Conviction
6. The actual purchase

These steps are sequential. The model suggests that a consumer spends a period of time at each one before moving to the next. Thus, before a person develops a liking for a product, she must first know about the product. Once the individual has the knowledge and develops liking for the product, the advertiser tries to influence the consumer to favor a particular brand or company.

The hierarchy of effects approach enjoys the benefit of allowing marketers to identify common steps consumers and businesses take when making purchases. Building brand loyalty requires all six steps. Logically, a customer cannot be loyal to a brand without first being aware of it. The customer typically will not develop loyalty to a brand without sufficient knowledge. Then, the purchaser must like the brand and build a strong preference for it. Finally, the customer experiences the conviction that the particular brand is superior to the others on the market. The components of the hierarchy of effects approach highlight the responses that advertising or marketing communication should stimulate in both consumers and business-to-business customers.

The hierarchy of effects model features similarities with theories regarding attitudes and attitudinal change, including the concepts of cognitive, affective, and conative elements. The cognitive component refers to the person's mental images, understanding, and interpretations of the person, object, or issue. The affective component contains the feelings or emotions a person has about the object, topic, or idea. The conative component consists of the individual's intentions, actions, or behavior. The most common sequence that takes place when an attitude forms is:

Cognitive → Affective → Conative

The sequence parallels the six-step hierarchy of effects process. As a general guideline, cognitive-oriented ads work best for achieving brand awareness and brand knowledge. Affective-oriented advertisements are better at inspiring liking, preference, and conviction. Conative ads are normally best suited to facilitating product purchases or other buyer actions.

Although the hierarchy of effects approach may help a creative understand how a consumer reaches a purchase decision, recent literature suggests that some of the theory's assumptions may be questioned. For one, these six steps might not always constitute the route taken by a consumer. A person may make a purchase (such as an impulse buy) and then later develop knowledge, liking, preference, and conviction. Also, a shopper could purchase products with little or no preference involved, because a coupon, discount, or purchase incentive caused him to choose one brand instead of another. The introductory

Kadmy/Fotolia

▲ When making high-involvement purchases, such as with a 35 mm digital camera, consumers will typically go through all six hierarchy of effects steps.

▲ This introductory price may spur a consumer to make a purchase without going through the first five steps of the hierarchy of effects model.

Flavors to Savor

7 Different Flavors to Choose From:
* Original
* Jalapeño Cilantro
* Roasted Garlic
* Spicy Avocado
* Roasted Red Pepper
* Kalamata Olive
* Spinach & Artichoke

www.chickmehummus.com

Introductory Price
$3.59

*Chick*me Hummus

Taylor Kemp

▶ **FIGURE 2**
Personal Values

- Comfortable life
- Equality
- Excitement
- Freedom
- Fun, exciting life
- Happiness

- Inner peace
- Mature love
- Personal accomplishment
- Pleasure
- Salvation
- Security

- Self-fulfillment
- Self-respect
- Sense of belonging
- Social acceptance
- Wisdom

We both need *Calcium*

DRINK MILK

© Igor Mojzes/Fotolia

▲ A milk advertisement based on the means–end chain.

price of \$3.59 in the newspaper ad for Chickme hummus on the previous page may spur a consumer to purchase the product with no prior knowledge of or preference for the brand. At other times, the individual might not even remember the name of the brand purchased previously. This may be the case with commodity products such as sugar or flour or even some clothing purchases such as socks and shirts. Even with these criticisms, however, the framework remains as a popular approach to the development of advertising messages and campaigns.

Means–End Theory

The second theoretical approach available to creatives, a **means–end chain**, suggests that an advertisement should contain a message, or *means*, that leads the consumer to a desired end state. These *end* states are personal values (see Figure 2). A means–end chain should start a process in which viewing the advertising message leads the consumer to believe that using the product will help achieve a personal value.

Means–end theory forms the basis of the **Means–End Conceptualization of Components for Advertising Strategy (MECCAS)** model.[1] The MECCAS model explains ways to move consumers from product attributes to personal values by highlighting the product's benefits. Advertisers can link the attributes of the product to specific benefits consumers can derive. These benefits, in turn, lead to the attainment of a personal value. Using the elements in Figure 3, the product benefit of healthy bones. The personal value the consumer obtains from healthy bones may be feeling wise for using the product or a comfortable life. The milk ad shown in this section highlights the use of a means–end chain.

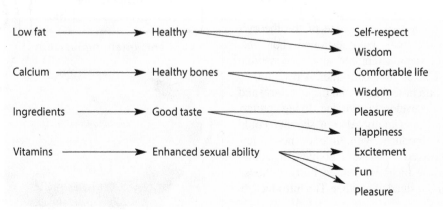

Low fat	→ Healthy	→ Self-respect
		→ Wisdom
Calcium	→ Healthy bones	→ Comfortable life
		→ Wisdom
Ingredients	→ Good taste	→ Pleasure
		→ Happiness
Vitamins	→ Enhanced sexual ability	→ Excitement
		→ Fun
		→ Pleasure

▶ **FIGURE 3**
Means–End Chain for Milk

Internet ———————▶ Robust samples ———————▶ Job security

Speed ———————▶ Quicker results ———————▶ Self-fulfillment

Expertise ———————▶ Actionable information ◀———▶ Wisdom

Social acceptance

Experience ———————▶ Reliability ———————▶ Job security

◀ **FIGURE 4**
B-to-B Means–End Chain for
Marketing Research Services

The MECCAS approach can be applied to business-to-business advertisements. Members of the buying center may be influenced by personal values, organizational values, and corporate goals. Consider the advertisement for ReRez shown in this section and the means–end chain provided in Figure 4. Each attribute in the ad leads to the benefits business customers can obtain. Although not explicitly stated, the personal values of members of the buying center choosing ReRez might include job security for making good decisions, self-fulfillment, wisdom, and social acceptance by other members of the buying group that believe ReRez offers quality marketing research.

Verbal and Visual Images

Most major forms of advertising contain visual and verbal or written elements. A visual ad places the greatest emphasis on a picture or the optical element of the presentation. A verbal or written ad places more emphasis on the copy. Visual and verbal elements should work together to create an advertisement that meets the desired stage of the hierarchy-of-effects model or the attribute-benefit-personal value chosen from a means–end chain.

Visual images often lead to more favorable attitudes toward both the advertisement and the brand. Visuals tend to be more easily remembered than verbal copy. They are stored in the brain as both pictures and words. This dual-coding process makes it easier for people to recall the message. Further, verbal messages tend be stored in the left side of the brain only; images are usually stored in both the left and right sides of the brain. The advertisement for OIB Reward Plus on the next page illustrates the power of visual imagery. Created by the Newcomer, Morris and Young advertising agency, the visual image of the child immediately garners attention and is more likely to be remembered than an ad that only uses copy.

Visual images range from concrete and realistic to highly abstract. A concrete visual displays something recognizable such as a person, place, or thing. In an abstract image, the subject becomes more difficult to recognize. Concrete pictures instill a higher level of recall than abstract images because they allow the image to be stored in the brain with both visual and verbal elements. Viewers process an advertisement with a picture of spaghetti as both a picture and as a verbal representation of the restaurant. Ads with concrete images also tend to lead to more favorable attitudes than those with no pictures or abstract pictures.[2]

Radio advertisers often seek to create visual images for the audience. Pepsi produced a radio commercial in which listeners could hear a can being opened, the soft drink being poured, and the sizzle of the carbonation—an excellent example of creating a visual image. If consumers visualize a picture in their imaginations, the effect may be greater than actually viewing a visual. A visual image requires less brain activity than using one's imagination. The secret is getting the person to think beyond the advertisement and picture the scene being simulated.

Visual Esperanto Advertisers often use visual imagery in international marketing. Global advertising agencies try to create **visual Esperanto**, the universal language that makes global advertising possible for any good or service. *Visual Esperanto* advertising

▲ A ReRez business-to-business advertisement for marketing research that illustrates the use of the means–end chain.

An advertisement for OIB (Ouachita Independent Bank) with a strong visual image.

recognizes that visual images are more powerful than verbal descriptions and can transcend cultural differences.[3]

To illustrate the power of a visual image compared to a verbal account, think of the word *exotic*. To some, exotic means a white beach in Hawaii with young people in sexy swimsuits. To others, it may be a small cabin in the snow-capped mountains of Switzerland. To others still, exotic may be a close-up of a tribal village in Africa. The word "exotic" can vary in meaning. At the same time, a picture of a couple holding hands in front of Niagara Falls has practically the same meaning across all cultures, because the image conveys a similar emotional experience in multiple settings.

Finding the appropriate image constitutes the most important challenge in creating *visual Esperanto*. The creative looks for the image that conveys the intended meaning or message. Brand identity can be emphasized using visuals rather than words. Then the creative uses words to support the visual image. For example, the creative may decide that a boy and his father at a sports event illustrate the priceless treasure of a shared family moment. In Mexico, the setting could be a soccer match instead of a baseball game in the United States. The specific copy (the words) can then be adapted to another country. Identifying an image that transcends cultures represents the most difficult part of inspiring *visual Esperanto*. Once a universal image has been found, creatives in each country represented take the image and modify it to appeal to the local target audience.

While the meaning "exotic" may vary across cultures, the visual created in this photo can transcend cultures through *visual Esperanto*.

Lulia Sokolovska/Fotolia

Business-to-Business   In the past, creatives designing business-to-business advertisements relied heavily on the verbal or written element rather than on visuals. The basis of this approach was the belief that business decisions are made in a rational, cognitive manner. In recent years, more business ads have incorporated strong visual elements to heighten the emotional aspects of making purchases.

In summary, the two theoretical models, along with concepts regarding visual and verbal messages, provide useful ideas for the advertising creative. Each suggests key concepts to be followed in developing an advertising campaign. The endpoint will be reached when the viewer remembers the products, thinks favorably about it, and looks for that product when making a purchase decision.

The Impact of Advertising Expenditures

In developing advertising campaigns, unrealistic assumptions concerning the relationship of advertising budgets to effectiveness may occur. For instance, a manager may believe that a direct relationship exists between expenditures on advertising communications and subsequent sales revenues. A common concept was that a 10 percent increase in advertising would lead to a two percent increase in sales. Unfortunately, recent studies indicate that the increase might be closer to one percent, although the actual amount varies widely.[4] Figure 5 displays a more realistic conceptualization of the relationship between marketing expenditures and advertising. The factors present in the relationship include:

- The communications goal
- Threshold effects
- Diminishing returns
- Carryover effects
- Wear-out effects
- Decay effects

objective 2

What is the relationship of advertising expenditures to advertising effectiveness?

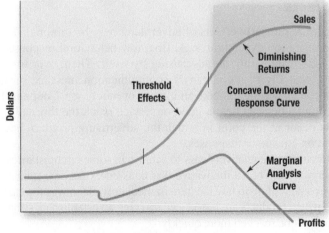

An unrealistic assumption about the relationship between promotional expenditures and sales

◄ FIGURE 5

Relationships between Advertising and Marketing Expenditures and Sales and Profit Margins

Communications goals differ depending on the stage in the buying process. The hierarchy of effects model suggests that prior to making a purchase, a consumer goes through the stages of awareness, knowledge, liking, preference, and conviction. The communications objective and stage in the hierarchy of effects model influence the advertising goal, budget, and message to be sent. For example, an early advertising campaign for the Sun Life Financial company highlighted the fact that people had not heard of the company, but would. Several humorous commercials helped develop awareness of the brand. Over time, the company prepared advertisements featuring other aspects of the company's services and comparative advantages. The entire campaign began at one place (awareness) and ended at another (encouraging action). It would not be logical to expect that early marketing expenditures would create a high sales yield when the primary objective was to create awareness.

Threshold Effects

As shown in Figure 5, the early effects of advertising may be minimal. The same holds true for all communication expenditures. At first, few behavioral responses occur, especially when only companies rely on advertising by itself. Then, over time, a consumer who is exposed repeatedly to a company's communication message recalls the brand and eventually becomes willing to make an inquiry or purchase.[5] Coupons, free samples, and other marketing tactics can help a good or service reach the threshold point sooner. **Threshold effects** occur at the point in which the advertising program begins to have a significant impact on consumer responses.

Threshold effects may be relatively easy to achieve in some circumstances. For instance, a new good or service may be so innovative that consumers become quickly aware of its advantages and become willing to buy the item immediately. Such was the case with the first iPhone. Also, when new products are introduced carrying an established, strong brand name, the threshold point will be reached more quickly.

Diminishing Returns

Eventually, a circumstance will be reached in which a promotional campaign has saturated the market, which indicates a point of **diminishing returns**. At that instant, further expenditures produce a minimal impact. The S-shaped curve displayed in Figure 5 represents a *sales-response function curve* and the diminishing returns from additional advertising expenditures. Diminishing returns are part of the *concave downward function*, in which incremental increases in expenditures in advertising result in smaller and smaller increases in sales. A *marginal analysis* reveals that further advertising and promotional expenditures adversely affect profits, because sales increases are less than what the company spends on the marketing or advertising.

Carryover Effects

Consumers purchase many products only when they are needed, such as washing machines and refrigerators. Promotions for these products should be designed to create brand recall. Recall occurs when the consumer has been exposed to the company's message for so long that when the time comes to buy, the individual remembers the key company, which indicates the presence of **carryover effects**. In other words, when a washing machine breaks down and requires a replacement, remembering Maytag brand will be the company's goal. Consequently, the consumer remembers Maytag's products and the advertisements have effectively carried over.

Wear-Out Effects

An additional complication to the advertising campaign may emerge. At a certain point, an advertisement or particular campaign simply becomes "old" or "boring." Consumers tend to ignore the advertisement or tune it out.[6] Some consumers may even develop negative attitudes toward the brand if they become annoyed at the marketing communication and believe the advertisement should be discontinued. This indicates **wear-out effects**.

Research regarding advertising campaigns over the last 50 years indicates that about half of all campaigns last too long and experience wear-out effects. On the other hand, the same research suggests that the long-term effect of advertising remains twice as high as the short-term effect. As a result, marketers try to continue a campaign long enough to capture that long-term effect but not so long that wear-out sets in.[7] Discovering the balance between wear-out and long-term impact remains challenging.

Decay Effects

When a company stops advertising, consumers begin to forget the message, which indicates **decay effects** (see Figure 6). In some instances, a dramatic degree of decay takes place. In others, the carryover effects are strong enough that some time can lapse before the brand drops out of the consumer's consciousness. The presence of decay effects means that companies should continue to engage in some form of marketing communications to keep the brand in people's minds.

◀ The concept of carryover effects applies to this advertisement for St. Francis Medical Center.

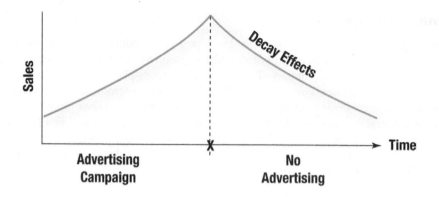

▶ **FIGURE 6**
A Decay Effects Model

In-House Versus External Advertising Agencies

objective 3

When should a company employ an external advertising agency rather than completing the work in-house?

When beginning an advertising program, deciding whether to use an in-house advertising group or an external advertising agency constitutes the first issue. Figure 7 compares the advantages of an in-house facility to an outside agency.

With tightening marketing budgets, more companies are deploying in-house advertising resources. Recently, Apple significantly expanded its in-house department from 300 to more than 500 employees. A study conducted by the Association of National Advertisers revealed that 58 percent of the association's members now utilize in-house advertising resources, compared to 42 percent five years ago. [8]

In-house advertising may help create several advantages. First, marketing managers may believe the approach lowers costs and retains better control of the message, which can be aligned with the brand and other company communications. The CEO can work closely with the marketing team to make sure this occurs. Consequently, members of the marketing department may conclude they have a better understanding of the firm's products and mission and more quickly produce advertisements. An in-house program will be more consistent, because of a lower turnover rate in the creative team.

While companies may use in-house resources, many will outsource specific functions such as writing, filming, recording, and editing advertisements. Most utilize media companies to plan and purchase media time (on television and radio) and space (in magazines, in newspapers, and on billboards).

An outside agency often reduces costs when compared to less efficient in-house facilities. This occurs when in-house employees spend more time on campaigns and ad designs than an agency would. The agency provides greater expertise and may have access to top talent in the industry. Advertising agencies offer an outside perspective not influenced by internal corporate politics and personal biases. Agency professionals often have a better understanding of consumers and trends because they work with a number of clients over an array of products. Knowledge gained from one product can often be transferred to other, even unrelated products.

Advantages of In-House	Advantages of Outside Agency
• Lower costs	• Reduce costs
• Consistent brand message	• Greater expertise
• Better understanding of product and mission	• Outsider's perspective
• Faster ad production	• Access to top talent
• Works closer with CEO	
• Lower turnover rate in the creative team	

▶ **FIGURE 7**
Advantages of In-House Versus
External Agencies

Advertising agencies provide a variety of options. All sizes and types of agencies exist. At one end of the spectrum, highly specialized, boutique-type agencies offer one specific service (e.g., making television ads) or serve one type of client. G+G Advertising of Albuquerque, New Mexico, specializes in advertising to Native Americans—a market of an estimated 10 million people.[9]

At the other end of the spectrum, full-service agencies such as mcgarrybowen, Zehnder Communications, and The Richards Group provide every type of advertising and promotional activity. These companies offer advice and assistance in working with other components of the IMC program, including consumer and trade promotions, direct-marketing programs, digital programs, and alternative media (see Figure 8).

Some agencies provide specialized services. For instance, *media service companies* negotiate and purchase media packages (called *media buys*) for companies. *Direct-marketing agencies* handle every aspect of a direct-marketing campaign through telephone orders (800 numbers), internet programs, and direct mail. Some companies focus on *consumer promotions, trade promotions*, or both. These companies assist in developing promotions such as coupons, premiums, contests, and sweepstakes. A new group of agencies specializes in developing *digital services*. Boxcar Creative designs *interactive websites* and widgets that can be used on multiple sites. Other companies offer *social media services* to reach consumers and businesses through a wide array of social media techniques. *Public relations* firms provide experts to help companies and brands develop positive public images and for damage control responses when negative publicity arises.

Budget Allocation Considerations

The size of the account affects the choice between an in-house team versus an external advertising agency. A small account may not be attractive to an advertising agency, because it generates lower revenues. If the agency charges a higher fee to compensate, it becomes too costly for the small firm. Smaller accounts create other challenges. Less money can be spent on media time and space purchases because the company spends the majority of the advertising budget on production of the advertisement.

One rule of thumb marketers consider, the 75–15–10 breakdown, suggests that 75 percent of the money to be spent on advertising should be used to purchase media time or space, 15 percent to the agency for the creative work, and 10 percent for the actual production of the ad. In contrast, for smaller accounts, the breakdown may be 50–30–20. Only 50 percent of expenditures are for media purchases; the other 50 percent of the funds goes to the creative and production work.

Unless the majority of the company's advertising budget can be used to pay for media purchases, it may be wise either to perform the work in-house or to develop contracts with smaller specialty firms to prepare various aspects of an advertising campaign.

▲ Skyjacker is one of a number of firms that perform all advertising functions in-house.

- Advice about how to develop target markets
- Specialized services for business markets
- Suggestions about how to project a strong company image and theme
- Assistance in selecting company logos and slogans
- Preparation of advertisements
- Planning and purchasing media time and space

◀ **FIGURE 8**
Services Provided by Full-Service Agencies

Stakhov/Fotolia

▲ Crowdsourcing of creative materials involves fans and can generate considerable buzz for the brand.

Crowdsourcing

Crowdsourcing involves outsourcing the creative aspect of an advertisement or campaign to the public. It offers an alternative to creating commercials in-house or hiring an external advertising agency. Crowdsourcing can create a viral buzz as users view advertisements online, recommend or send favorites to friends, and post links.

Doritos has used crowdsourcing to create Super Bowl ads. Fans were invited to submit ideas for ads. Doritos ads have been voted as some of the best of the Super Bowl. Although it may seem that crowdsourcing would be a cheaper method of creating a Super Bowl commercial, in reality the total cost stays about the same as for hiring a professional agency. The costs of running the contest, paying prize money, creating the microsite to host the contest, and producing the commercial combined with the time spent by Doritos and the agency in choosing from the thousands of entries are nearly equal to what would have been spent on an agency. Crowdsourcing, however, yields the advantage of involving fans and generating the subsequent buzz that surrounds the contest for the consumer-generated advertisement.[10]

Harley-Davidson employs an extreme approach to crowdsourcing. The company obtains all creative work through crowdsourcing with agencies only responsible for producing the ads. According to Harley-Davidson CMO Mark-Hans Richer, "We made a decision to turn over the major creative to owners because we have a passionate customer base who wants to engage with us." The creative comes through Facebook. Harley-Davidson has about 3 million Facebook fans. About 8,000 signed up to be part of the Fan Machine, the creative forum for Harley. The Fan Machine group reviews advertising briefs, submits ideas, and votes on ideas from members. While the company offers some branded products, according to Richer "it's really about the spirit and creativity and passion of the brand than the financial reward." A recent project received 300 idea submissions, with 20,000 votes for the best ideas. "What really shocked me was how good the ideas actually were. There were a lot of surprising insights. It's like a focus group and creative wrapped into one," he said.

Recent research regarding consumer-generated advertising produced several key findings. First, consumer-generated advertising works best when targeted to current customers and customers who have high levels of brand loyalty. Consumers with lower levels of brand loyalty are likely to be more skeptical of the ad creation and the campaign overall. Second, sharing background information about the ad creator increases the persuasiveness of the consumer-generated ad by establishing credibility and showing similarities between the ad creator and consumers. The social media and public relations components of crowdsourcing constitute important ingredients in successfully using this approach to advertising. Consequently, while consumer-generated ads may be effective at generating customer retention, they are not as successful for increasing a customer base. [11]

Critics of crowdsourcing argue that while the approach may lead to innovative and eye-catching advertisements, no consistent message or theme results over time. The commercials may or may not reinforce the brand's major selling points or elements. Stan Richards of The Richards Group suggests that without a strategic approach, key components of the overall communications effort can be lost.

Choosing an Agency

Choosing an agency begins with the development of quality selection criteria. The choice of an agency represents a key component of the advertising management process for many companies. Figure 9 lists the steps involved in selecting an agency.

objective 4

How do companies choose advertising agencies?

Goal Setting

Prior to making any contact with an advertising agency, company leaders identify and prioritize corporate goals. The goals provide a sense of direction and prevent personal biases from affecting selection decisions. Goals guide company leaders by providing a clear idea of what the company seeks to accomplish. They also help the marketing team as they make requests for proposals for campaigns.

Kraft Foods recently changed agencies for 20 of the company's iconic brands, including Maxwell House, Crystal Light, Kraft Singles, Cadbury, Fig Newtons, Planters, Oreo, and Kraft Macaroni & Cheese. Dana Anderson, Senior VP of Marketing Strategy and Communications stated that, "More than ever, we're focusing on contemporizing and making our iconic brands more relevant to today's consumers. We're raising the bar with our agencies in order to deliver more creative and engaging campaigns. Our ultimate goal is to heighten the profile and performance of Kraft Foods brands." By determining the goal in advance, Kraft's marketing team was able to select the best agency for each of the brands under review.[12]

Selection Criteria

Even firms with experience set selection criteria in advance in order to reduce any biases that might affect decisions. Emotions and other feelings can lead to poor choices. Figure 10 identifies some of the major issues to be considered during the process. The list can be especially useful during the initial screening, when the field narrows to the top five (or fewer) agencies.

Agency Size As noted earlier, the size of the agency should be considered, most notably as it compares to the size of the company hiring the agency. A good rule of thumb to follow is that the account should be large enough for the agency so that it is important to the agency but small enough that, if lost, the agency would not be badly affected.

Relevant Experience When an agency has experience in a given industry, the agency's employees are better able to understand the client firm, its customers, and the

1. Set goals.
2. Select process and criteria.
3. Screen initial list of applicants.
4. Request client references.
5. Reduce list to two or three viable agencies.
6. Request creative pitch.

◀ **FIGURE 9**
Steps in Selecting an Advertising Agency

- Size of the agency
- Relevant experience of the agency
- Conflicts of interest
- Creative reputation and capabilities
- Production capabilities
- Media purchasing capabilities
- Other services available
- Client retention rates
- Personal chemistry

◀ **FIGURE 10**
Evaluation Criteria in Choosing an Advertising Agency

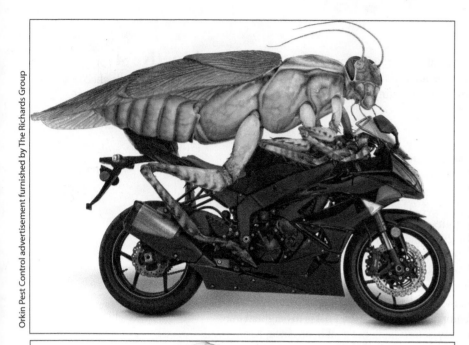

Orkin Pest Control advertisement furnished by The Richards Group

Orkin Pest Control advertisement furnished by The Richards Group

▲ Orkin Pest Control is just one of the many accounts handled by The Richards Group.

structure of the marketing channel. At the same time, the client company makes sure the agency does not have any *conflicts of interest*. An advertising firm hired by one manufacturer of automobile tires would experience a conflict of interest if another tire manufacturer attempted to hire the agency.

An advertising agency can have relevant experience without representing a competitor. Such experience can be gained when an agency works for a similar company operating in a different industry. For example, when an agency has a manufacturer of automobile batteries as a client, the experience will be relevant to selling automobile tires.

The agency should also have experience with the business-to-business program, so that retailers, wholesalers, and any other channel party are considered in the marketing and advertising of the product. A number of advertisements in this text were created by The Richards Group. In addition to the Orkin advertisements in this section, The Richard's Group's clients include Motel 6, Home Depot, Sub-Zero, and Bridgestone. Note that the list does not include competing firms within the same industry.

Creative Reputation and Capabilities
One method of assessing an agency's creativity would include asking for a list of awards the company has received. Although awards do not always translate into creating effective advertisements, in most cases a positive relationship exists between winning awards and writing effective ads. Most creative awards are given by peers. As a result, they represent effective indicators of what others think of the agency's creative efforts.

Production and Media-Purchasing Capabilities   Agency capabilities should be examined when production and media-purchasing services are needed. A firm that needs an agency to produce a television commercial and also buy media time should check on these activities as part of the initial screening process. Many agencies either employ subsidiary companies to perform the media work or subcontract it to a media firm. The advertising agency does not necessarily need to make media buys, but it should have the capacity to make sure they are made to fit with the ads being designed.

Other Criteria   The final three selection criteria—*other services available, client retention rates*, and *personal chemistry*—are utilized during the final steps of selection. These criteria help make the final determination in the selection process.

Creative Pitch

When the company reduces the list to two or three finalists, the selection team asks each for a creative pitch. The advertising agencies chosen to compete provide a formal presentation that addresses a specific problem, situation, or set of questions—a process also called a *shootout*. The presentations reveal how each agency would deal with specific issues that might arise during preparation of a campaign. The process helps a client company choose the agency that best understands the issues at stake and offers a comprehensive approach to solving the problem or issue. For instance, after Bank of America suffered several years of corporate crises and publicity missteps, it put its $380 million account up for review. Agencies were asked "to create a new positioning for Bank of America" that would signal to its audiences that the bank was addressing its challenges.[13]

▲ During a creative pitch, an agency presents ideas on the problem or campaign posed by the potential client.

Monkey Business/Fotolia

Preparing a pitch takes time and creates expenses for advertising agencies; therefore, they only want to prepare pitches that have a decent chance of acceptance. When an agency spends time preparing a presentation only to find out later that the company had no desire to switch agencies, but were told by upper management to solicit pitches, it becomes frustrating.[14] A company seeking to retain an advertising agency should provide sufficient time for the competing finalists to prepare the pitch. Pink Jacket Creative's Bill Breedlove reports, "I would prefer at least 30 days to prepare a pitch. Even 45 to 60 days would be wonderful sometimes, and for some companies."

Recently, Oscar Mayer, a brand under the Kraft umbrella, sought ways to unify its portfolio of products and contemporize its image with consumers. The mcgarrybowen agency demonstrated how Oscar Mayer could contemporize the brand and build emotional ties with customers. The agency's ideas were fresh, contemporary, and had the emotional spark the organization desired.[15]

When Kraft launched its Oscar Mayer Deli Creations sandwiches, the initial print ad developed by the brand's previous agency depicted a woman in a suit, standing with her arm bent eating one of the Deli Creation sandwiches. Karen Adams, senior director of advertising at Kraft Foods, stated, "People don't eat sandwiches that way." Instead, new ads were created showing real people in real-life situations eating sandwiches.[16]

Successful creative pitches result from hard work and thorough planning. Figure 11 highlights some of the "do's" and "don'ts" for advertising agencies in making pitches.

- Do listen. Allow the client to talk.
- Do your preparation. Know the client and its business.
- Do make a good first impression. Dress up, not down.
- Do a convincing job of presenting. Believe in what you are presenting.
- Don't assume all clients are the same. Each has a unique need.
- Don't try to solve the entire problem in the pitch.
- Don't be critical of the product or the competition.
- Don't overpromise. It will come back to haunt you.
- Don't spend a lot of time pitching credentials and references.

◀ **FIGURE 11**
Pitching Do's and Don'ts

Agency Selection

During the presentation phase, company marketers meet with agency creatives, media buyers, account executives, and other people who will work on the account. *Chemistry* between employees of the two different firms becomes critical. The client company's leaders should be convinced that they will work well together. Chemistry can break or make the final decision.[17]

After completing the selection process, the agency and the company will work together to prepare the advertising campaign. Those who did not win the account are also notified, in order to maintain more positive relations with them over time. The account executive, account planner, and advertising creative all play key roles in the process.

Roles of Advertising Personnel

objective 5

What are the primary job functions within an advertising agency?

Advertising agency employees perform a wide variety of roles. In small agencies, an individual may carry out multiple roles. In a large agency, multiple individuals will be employed in the various departments and perform similar functions. The primary roles within the agency consist of the account executives, creatives, traffic managers, and account planners.

Account Executives

The account executive serves as the go-between for the advertising agency and the client company. In some agencies, the executive will be actively involved in soliciting the account, finalizing details of the contract, and working with personnel within the agency to make sure the advertisements meet the client's specifications. In other agencies, especially larger firms, account executives do not solicit accounts, but rather manage the relationship and work that the agency performs for the brand. The account executive often helps the company define the theme of the overall IMC program and how advertising fits into the brand's marketing strategy.

Creatives

▼ Account executives work with creatives, traffic managers, and account planners to develop advertising campaigns for clients.

Creatives develop and design advertisements. They are either members of advertising agencies or freelancers. Some smaller agencies provide only creative advertising services without becoming involved in other marketing programs and activities. Creatives may appear to hold the "glamour" jobs in agencies, because they get to actually create ads and marketing materials. At the same time, creatives work long hours and face enormous pressures to design effective advertisements that produce tangible results.

Monkey Business/Fotolia

Traffic Managers

The traffic manager works closely with the advertising agency's account executive, creatives, and production staff. The manager's responsibilities include scheduling the various aspects of the agency's work to make sure it is completed on time. During production, the traffic manager assumes the responsibility of making sure props, actors, and other items needed have been ordered and are in place at the time of the filming or recording.

Account Planners

The account planner provides the voice and serves as the advocate for the consumer within the advertising agency. The planner makes sure the creative team understands the consumer (or business). Account planners interact with the account executive and the client to understand the target audience of the ad campaign. The planner then works to make sure creative messages reach the right customers.

The account planner assists the client in developing long-term communication strategies and provides direction for individual advertising campaigns. In small agencies, the role may be performed by the account executive. Larger firms employ separate individuals and/or departments to conduct the account planning role.

Advertising Campaign Parameters

Producing effective advertising campaigns requires the joint efforts of the account executive, creative, account planner, and media planner. Working independently might produce some award-winning ads, but often they may not achieve the client's objectives. Advertising agencies seek to produce campaigns that stand out among the competing messages. Creating effective campaigns requires attention to the advertising campaign parameters listed in Figure 12.

Advertising Goals

Advertising goals are derived from the firm's overall communication objectives. Figure 13 identifies the most common advertising goals. These goals should be consistent with the marketing communication objectives and other components of the integrated marketing communications plan.

Build Brand Awareness   A strong global brand often constitutes a key advertising goal, especially for larger companies. Building a brand's image begins with developing brand awareness. *Brand awareness* means the consumers recognize and remember a particular brand or company name when they consider purchasing options. Advertising offers an excellent venue to increase brand awareness.

Successful brands possess two characteristics: the top of mind and the consumer's top choice. When consumers are asked to identify brands that quickly come to mind from a product category, one or two particular brands are nearly always mentioned. These names are the **top-of-mind brands**. For example, when asked to identify fast-food hamburger restaurants, McDonald's and Burger King almost always head the list. The same may be true for Nike and Reebok athletic shoes and may be the case in the United States as well as in other countries.

The term **top choice** suggests what the term implies: A top-choice brand is the first or second pick when a consumer reviews her evoked set of possible purchasing alternatives. Many products become top-of-mind or top choice due to brand equity. Advertising can strengthen brand equity.

Provide Information   Advertising can achieve other goals such as providing information to both consumers and business buyers. Typical information for consumers includes

▲ The account planner represents the consumer's viewpoint so that a creative can design effective advertisements such as this one for Maxwell House coffee.

objective 6

What are the advertising campaign parameters that should be considered?

- Advertising goals
- Media selection
- Tagline
- Consistency
- Positioning
- Campaign duration

▲ **FIGURE 12**
Advertising Campaign Parameters

▼ **FIGURE 13**

Advertising Goals

- To build brand awareness
- To inform
- To persuade
- To support other marketing efforts
- To encourage action

a retailer's store hours, business location, or sometimes more detailed product specifications. Information may make the purchasing process appear to be simple and convenient, which can entice customers to travel to the store to finalize a purchase.

Persuasion   When an advertisement convinces consumers of a particular brand's superiority, persuasion has taken place. Changing consumer attitudes and convincing them to consider a new purchasing choice can be challenging. Advertisers can utilize several persuasion methods. One involves showing consumers the negative consequences of failing to buy a particular brand. Persuasive advertising more often targets consumers rather than business-to-business prospects.

Supporting Marketing Efforts   Advertising supports other marketing functions. Manufacturers use advertising to accompany trade and consumer promotions such as theme packaging or combination offers. Contests, such as the McDonald's Monopoly game, require additional advertising to be effective.

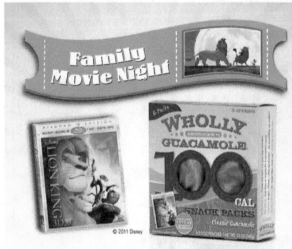

Retailers also advertise to support marketing programs. Any type of special sale (white sale, buy-one-get-one-free, pre-Christmas sale) requires effective advertising to attract customers to the store. Manufacturers and retail outlets both run advertisements in conjunction with coupons or other special offers.

Encouraging Action   Many firms set behavioral goals for advertising programs. A television commercial encouraging viewers to take action by dialing a toll-free number to make a quick purchase serves as an example. Everything from ShamWow to Snuggies has been sold using action tactics. Infomercials and home shopping network programs rely heavily on immediate consumer purchasing responses.

Action-oriented advertising can be used in the business-to-business sector. Generating leads becomes the primary goal. Many business advertisements provide web addresses or

▲ This advertisement supports a brand alliance between Wholly Guacamole and Disney.

telephone numbers buyers can use to request more information or make a purchase.

The five advertising goals of building image, providing information, being persuasive, supporting other marketing efforts, and encouraging action are not separate from each other. They work together in key ways. For instance, awareness and information are part of persuasion. The key is to emphasize one goal without forgetting the others.

Media Selection

Selecting the appropriate media requires an understanding of the media usage habits of the target market and then matching that information with the profile of each medium's audience. Volkswagen positioned the Tiguan crossover as a fun vehicle aimed at young, active individuals who love the outdoors. Although the campaign featured television commercials, the more unique component of the campaign was the outdoor segment. The theme "people want an SUV that parks well with others" was featured in a series of outdoor ads placed at bike racks and trail heads at 150 national parks and resorts. Brian Martin, CEO of Brand Connections Active Outdoor, which placed the ads, noted that more than 30 million impressions were made with hikers, bikers, and other outdoor lovers.[18]

The advertising team identifies the media favored by a target market. Teenagers surf the web and watch television. Only a small percentage reads newspapers and news magazines. Various market segments exhibit differences in when and how they view various media. Older African Americans watch television programs in patterns that differ from those of older Caucasians. Males watch more sports programs than females, and so forth.

In business-to-business markets, knowing the trade journals or business publications that various members of the buying center most likely read assists in the development of a print advertising campaign. Engineers, who tend to be the influencers, often have different media viewing habits than vice presidents, who may be the deciders.

Although media buys are guided by the advertising agency and the client company, media companies typically make the purchases. A trend toward involving media companies at an earlier stage in the campaign process has evolved in recent years. Previously, most media companies were contacted after a campaign became ready or was nearly complete, with the specific task of purchasing media space or time. Now, companies such as Procter & Gamble, Johnson & Johnson, Clorox, Kimberly-Clark, Verizon, and HP enlist media companies as strategic partners in developing advertising and marketing campaigns.[19] Agencies invite media companies to participate in the strategy development stage because many have quality insights regarding the target audience. They are able to provide valuable information to the creative staff about how to best reach the client's target market employing the primary media that target consumers favor.

In some cases, media companies actually create commercials. Joe Kuester, senior brand manager for Kimberly-Clark, stated, "It doesn't matter to us where the idea comes from or who champions that idea." That statement was in response to Kimberly-Clark's media company, Mindshare Entertainment, creating a series of webisodes involving Whoopi Goldberg for its Poise brand. Another media company, MEC Entertainment, worked with its client Ikea to produce a campaign for A&E called "Fix this Kitchen." This trend to involve media companies in all facets of advertising campaign development is quickly gaining momentum with companies.[20]

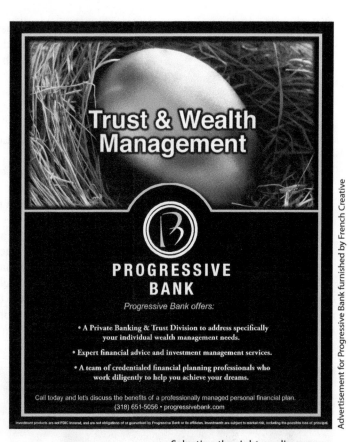

▲ Selecting the right media ensures that the consumers who are the most likely to use Progressive Bank for trust and wealth management will see this advertisement.

Taglines

The key phrase in an advertisement, the **tagline**, should be something memorable that identifies the uniqueness of a brand or conveys some type of special meaning. "Just Do It" has been Nike's tagline for many years. Figure 14 identifies other well-known taglines.

- American Express—"Don't leave home without it."
- Avis—"We try harder."
- Bounty—"The quicker picker-upper."
- Capital One—"What's in your wallet?"
- CNN—"The most trusted name in news"
- Energizer—"It keeps going, and going, and going."
- Hallmark—"When you care enough to send the best."

- John Deere—"Nothing runs like a Deer."
- Maxwell House—"Good to the last drop."
- Nokia—"Connecting people"
- Office Depot—"Taking care of business."
- Target—"Expect more. Pay less."
- UPS—"What can Brown do for you?"
- Wal-Mart—"Save money. Live better."

◀ **FIGURE 14**
Taglines Used by Various Brands

Taglines provide consistency across various advertising platforms. Consumers often remember taglines and identify them with specific brands. A catchy tagline identifies a brand and then stays with it over successive campaigns. In order to bring freshness to a campaign, company marketers occasionally tweak or modify a tagline every few years. With shorter attention spans, taglines have been shrinking from short sentences to just two or three words. L'Oreal Paris has used the shortened tagline "Because I'm Worth It" for more than 40 years. Other taglines that have been shortened include BMW's "ultimate driving machine," Lucozade"s (British energy drink) "Yes" and Wal-Mart's "Save money, live better."

In other instances, a completely new version may be developed. To make the Oscar Mayer brand more contemporary, the company's marketing personnel and its agency, mcgarrybowen, created a new tagline. Oscar Mayer was known for trust, nostalgia, heritage, jingles, bologna, hot dogs, and kids. The image needed to be freshened, made more contemporary, and reach adults as well as kids. The Oscar Mayer marketing team wanted to take the brand to a place that was energetic, culturally relevant, and that captured the spirit of everyday food making people feel good. Real joy, real moments, real friendship, real emotion, and real people were at the forefront. The idea was that Oscar Mayer is "good mood food." One Oscar Mayer ad conveys the good mood feeling that resulted from marketing brainstorming sessions and music collaborations and led to the campaign tagline "It doesn't get better than this."[21]

▼ This advertisement for JD Bank, combined with the one on the next page, use variability theory concepts to create consistency within the campaign.

Consistency

Repeatedly seeing a specific visual image, headline, copy, or tagline helps to embed a brand into a person's long-term memory. Visual consistency becomes especially important because most customers spend very little time viewing an advertisement. In most cases, an individual makes just a casual glance at a print advertisement or a cursory glimpse at a television commercial. Visual consistency leads the viewer to move the message from short-term to long-term memory. Logos, taglines, and headlines that remain consistent across ads and campaigns aid in this process.

Repetition helps increase consumer ad recall as well as brand recall. While mere repetition of the same ad may accomplish this goal, varying the ad appears to have better results. Some advertisers emphasize the principles present in **variability theory,**[22] which suggests that variable encoding occurs when a consumer sees the same advertisement in different environments. These varied environments increase recall and effectiveness by encoding it into the brain through various methods. Creatives can generate the effect by varying the situational context of a particular ad. For example, Capital One campaigns use various settings to convey the same basic message, "What's in your wallet?" Changing the context of the ad increases recall and offers an effective method for overcoming competitive ad interference.[23]

Selecting two media to convey a message generally can be more effective than repeating an advertisement in the same medium. An advertisement placed in more than one medium reduces competing ad interference. In other words, a message presented on television and in magazines works better than one that appears only on television. Consumers seeing an advertisement in a different medium are more likely to recall the ad than when it appears in only one medium.

Whether across different media or modifications of ads within the same media, consistency constitutes the key to effectiveness. Consistency reduces wearout effects and maintains interest in the advertising campaign. It aids in providing carryover effects when the consumer is in the purchase state.

Positioning

Maintaining consistent product positioning throughout a product's life makes it more likely that a consumer will place the product in a cognitive map. When the firm emphasizes quality in every advertisement, it becomes easier to tie the product into the consumer's cognitive map than if the firm stresses quality in one ad, price in another, and convenience in a third campaign. Inconsistency in positioning makes the brand and company more difficult to remember. Consistent positioning avoids ambiguity, and the message stays clear and understandable.

JD Bank

Campaign Duration

The length or duration of a campaign should be identified. Using the same advertisement for an appropriate period of time allows the message to embed in the consumer's long-term memory. Account executives consider how long to run an advertisement. It should be changed before it becomes stale and viewers lose interest; however, changing ads too frequently impedes retention. Creating new campaigns also increases costs.

Typical campaigns last about six months, but there are exceptions. Some last for years. The criterion that typically determines when it is time to change a campaign is the wear-out effect. When consumers ignore ads and it no longer is producing results, it becomes time to launch a new campaign.

The Creative Brief

When an advertising agency prepares a document to guide in the production of an advertising campaign or for a specific commercial, the document is called a *creative strategy* or **creative brief**. Although various forms exist, the basic components of a standard creative brief are displayed in Figure 15. The creative takes the information provided to produce

objective 7

How does a creative brief facilitate effective advertising?

▼ **FIGURE 15**

The Creative Brief

- The objective
- The target audience
- The message theme
- The support
- The constraints

▼ An advertisement targeted to human resource individuals within businesses.

advertisements and use it to convey the desired message. A quality creative brief, when prepared properly, saves the agency considerable time and effort and results in a stronger advertising campaign for the client.

Ineffective communications between agencies and clients sometimes occurs when those involved do not properly prepare a brief. A survey of senior executives of advertising agencies indicated major problems with creative briefs, and most agencies voiced some level of frustration. The most common problem cited was a lack of focus. Fifty-three percent of the executives said the briefs were complete, but lacked focus and 27 percent said they were both incomplete and inconsistent. Only 20 percent said they were complete and focused most of the time. Not one, zero percent, said they were complete and focused all of the time.[24]

The Objective

A creative brief identifies the objective of the advertising campaign such as those common objectives noted in the previous section. The creative reviews the main objective (or goal) before designing specific ads or the advertising campaign. The objectives guide the advertising design and the choice of execution. For instance, for an increased brand awareness goal, the name of the product will be prominently displayed in the advertisement or repeated several times in a television ad. Building brand image normally results in the actual product being more prominently displayed in the ad.

The Target Audience

A creative then examines the target audience. An advertisement designed to persuade a business to inquire about new computer software differs from a consumer advertisement created for the same company. The business advertisement focuses on the type of industry and a specific member of the buying center. The more detail available regarding the target audience, the easier it becomes for a creative to design an effective advertisement. The LUBA Worker's Comp ad in this section targets individuals who work in human resource departments within companies.

Overly general target market profiles are not helpful. Rather than specifying "males, ages 20 to 35," more specific information will be needed, such as "males, ages 20 to 35, college educated, and professionals." Other information, including hobbies, interests, opinions, and lifestyles, make it possible to more precisely develop an advertisement.

The Message Theme

The message theme presents an outline of key idea(s) that the advertising program conveys. The message theme represents the benefit or promise the advertiser uses to reach consumers or businesses. The promise, or unique selling point, describes the major benefit the good or service offers customers. A message theme for an automobile could be oriented toward luxury, safety, fun, fuel

NOT THINKING ABOUT OUR WORKERS' COMP

LUBA Workers' Comp

Luckily, it gets our undivided attention.
888.884.5822 • LUBAwc.com   Rated A- Excellent by A.M. Best.

LUBA Workers' Comp

efficiency, or driving excitement. A message theme for a hotel could focus on luxury, price, or unusual features, such as a hotel in Paris, France, noting the ease of access to all of the nearby tourist attractions. The message theme matches the medium selected, the target market, and the primary IMC message.[25]

Message themes can be oriented toward either rational or emotional processes. A "left-brain" advertisement oriented toward the logical, rational side informs individuals using numbers, letters, words, and concepts. Left-brain advertising features a logical, factual, rational appeal. A number of logical features (size, price, special features) influence the decision to buy a car. At the same time, many consumers purchase cars for emotional reasons. The right side of the brain contains emotions. It works with abstract ideas, images, and feelings. An automobile may be chosen for its color, sportiness, or other less rational reasons.

Most advertising targets either the right brain or the left brain. Advertising can also be effective by balancing the two sides. Rational, economic beings have difficulty defending the purchase of an expensive sports car such as a Porsche. Many product purchases are based on how a person feels about the good or service, combined with rational information.[26]

The Support

Support should be provided in the fourth component of the creative strategy. **Support** takes the form of facts that substantiate the message theme. When Aveeno products won "Best of Beauty" awards from *Allure* magazine, its "Best of Beauty" seal was placed on the company's products. Company advertising mentioned the award to support Aveeno's claims of superiority.

In this section, the advertisement for St. Francis Medical Center shows three Best Regional Hospital awards by *US News* and two Best Employers awards. This type of support indicates to patients the high quality of care they will receive from St. Francis.

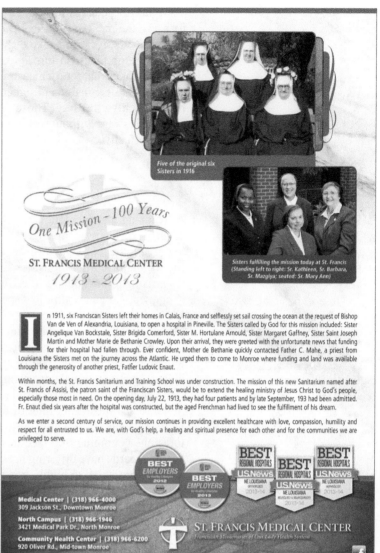

▲ An advertisement for St. Francis Medical Center showing the awards the institution has received.

Newcomer, Morris and Young Inc.

The Constraints

Constraints include any legal and mandatory restrictions placed on advertisements. Constraints spell out legal protections for trademarks, logos, and copy registrations. Constraints also establish all disclaimers about warranties, offers, and claims. For warranties, a disclaimer specifies the conditions under which they will be honored. Tire warranties, for example, often state that they apply under normal driving conditions with routine maintenance. A person cannot ignore tire balancing and rotation and expect to get free new tires when the old ones quickly wear out. Disclaimer warranties notify consumers of potential hazards associated with products. Tobacco advertisements contain statements and images regarding the dangers of smoking and chewing tobacco. Disclaimers about marketing offers specify the terms of financing agreements as well as when bonuses or discounts apply. Claims identify the exact nature of the statement made in the advertisement. This includes nutritional claims as well as statements about serving sizes and other information describing the product.

After these steps have been completed, the creative brief is ready. From this point forward, the message and the media match, and actual advertisements can be produced. Effective creative briefs take the overall IMC message and tailor it to a specific advertising campaign. This, in turn, gives the company a better chance of reaching customers with messages that return measurable results and help guarantee success. Recent research suggests that campaigns designed in two months or less have the greatest likelihood of being "highly effective." Those that take longer tend not to be as effective. Marketers try to move forward without rushing. A campaign designed in two weeks or less is also likely to be ineffective.[27]

International Implications

objective 8

What are the implications of advertising management in the global arena?

Advertising management now involves major expenditures overseas. The top 100 global advertisers spent an average of 62 percent of advertising budgets outside the United States. Figure 16 compares the non-U.S. advertising budget to non-U.S. sales revenue for six major corporations. As illustrated, Coca-Cola spends 83.5 percent of company advertising dollars outside the United States, where 74.9 percent of its total revenues are generated. Colgate-Palmolive spends 85.6 percent of its advertising dollars on non-U.S. ads and generates 76.7 percent of its revenues outside the United States. Data for Ford, Mattel, McDonald's, and Procter & Gamble are also provided.[28]

Two major differences emerge when considering advertising management in an international perspective. The first is in regard to the process itself. The second concerns preparing international advertising campaigns.

The general processes used to prepare advertising campaigns remain fairly uniform. Some of the most important differences are in the areas of availability of qualified advertising agencies and how those agencies are selected. For example, in many Asian cultures, the beginning of a face-to-face meeting would include an exchange of gifts. Also, business cards have differing uses and meanings across cultures. In some countries, cards are only presented to highly trusted allies. In others, they are freely passed out. The marketing team in any company should carefully study the nuances of business meetings,

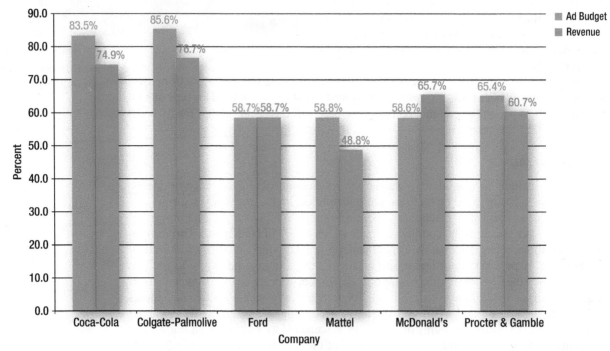

▲ **FIGURE 16**

Non-U.S. Ad Budgets and Sales Revenue Comparisons for Major Brands including the use of formal titles, eye contact, who speaks first, and other variables, before beginning a relationship with an advertising agency in another country.

Agencies in other countries might not follow typical procedures such as a shootout or the preparation of a creative brief. Forms of preplanning research may also vary. In some countries, it is not possible to conduct the same types of research as in the United States and other Western cultures.

Advertising campaigns designed for an international audience require an understanding of the various languages and cultures that might be involved. In Europe, French, Spanish, Portuguese, Italian, and other languages need translation and back-translation of advertising themes and messages to make certain the idea can be clearly presented in various countries. Media selection processes may also require adjustment; some countries have state-run television networks and others place restrictions on what can be shown in an advertisement.

Summary

This chapter reviews the advertising campaign management process. Effective advertising occurs when the firm has a well-defined mission statement and targets its energies in the direction of creating goods or services to meet the needs of a target market.

Quality advertising begins with an understanding of various advertising theories that explain consumer purchasing processes. The hierarchy of effects model, a means–end analysis or MECCAS model can be combined with an analysis of the visual and verbal elements needed to create an effective method provide marketers with quality guidelines for creating marketing messages. *Visual Esperanto* is a universal language that makes global advertising possible.

Advertisers should also understand the impact of advertising expenditures. The relationships between marketing expenditures and eventual success can be modeled using concepts such as threshold effects, diminishing returns, carryover effects, wear-out effects, and decay effects. Such an analysis assists in the design of advertisements as well as in assessing levels of effectiveness.

Advertising management continues with the decision to employ an in-house department to develop advertisements or whether an external advertising agency should be retained. When choosing an external agency, the company's leaders establish clear steps to lead to the selection of the optimal agency. The steps include spelling out and prioritizing organizational goals, establishing quality selection criteria, screening firms based on those criteria, requesting references from firms that are finalists, requesting creative pitches, making on-site visits to get to know those in the agencies, and offering and finalizing a contract.

Common selection criteria used in selecting agencies include the size of the agency matching the size of the company, relevant experience, no conflicts of interest, production capabilities, quality creative capabilities, suitable media-purchasing skills, other services that can be rendered as needed, client retention rates, and a good chemistry between those in the company and those in the agency. Carefully utilizing these criteria increases the odds of a successful match between the company and the agency, which increases the chance of success.

Within the advertising agency, the account manager performs the functions of soliciting accounts, finalizing contracts, and selecting creatives to prepare advertising campaigns. Account executives are go-betweens who mediate between the agency and the client company and aid client organizations in refining IMC messages and programs. Traffic managers help to schedule various aspects of the agency's work. Account planners serve as the voice and advocate for the consumer within the advertising agency.

Creating effective advertising campaigns requires attention to various parameters. Advertising goals are derived from the firm's overall communication objectives and include building brand awareness, providing information, generating persuasion, supporting other marketing efforts, and encouraging action. Then media selection can commence. Advertisers seek to develop quality taglines that express something memorable and unique about the brand or convey a special meaning. Another key advertising parameter, consistency, assists in recall of the advertisement. Variability theory suggests that variable encoding can help build strong campaigns. Advertisers also pay attention to quality positioning and seek to understand the best duration for the campaign.

Creatives who prepare advertisements are guided by the creative brief. The document spells out the objective of the promotional campaign, the target audience, the message theme, the support, and the constraints. The message theme presents an outline of the key idea(s) that the program seeks to convey. The constraints include logos, warranties, disclaimers, or legal statements that are part of various advertisements. These processes are carried out by domestic U.S. agencies as well as by advertisers around the world.

Key Terms

advertising campaign management The process of preparing and integrating a company's advertising efforts with the overall IMC message

hierarchy of effects model A method advertisers use to help clarify the objectives of an advertising campaign

means–end chain A conceptual model that shows how a message, or means, can lead consumers to a desired end state

Means–End Conceptualization of Components for Advertising Strategy (MECCAS) A model that explains ways to move consumers from product attributes to personal values by highlighting the product's benefits

visual Esperanto A form of universal language that makes advertising possible for any good or service

threshold effects What occurs at the point in which an advertising program begins to have a significant impact on consumer responses

diminishing returns A point at which a promotional campaign has saturated the market and further advertising and promotional expenditures adversely affect profits

carryover effects An instance in which an individual becomes ready to buy a product and remembers a key company due to the effectiveness of its marketing program

wear-out effects An instance in which consumers ignore or even develop negative attitudes toward a brand because the campaign has become "old" or "boring"

decay effects What occurs when a company stops advertising and consumers begin to forget the message

crowdsourcing The process of outsourcing the creative aspect of an advertisement to the public

top-of-mind brands The brands that quickly come to mind when consumers are asked to identify brands from a product category

top choice The first or second pick when a consumer reviews his or her evoked set of possible purchasing alternatives

tagline A key, memorable phrase in an advertisement that conveys some type of special meaning

variability theory A theory that suggests variable encoding will be more effective as consumers view advertisements in differing environments

creative brief A document that guides in the production of an advertising campaign or for a specific commercial

support The facts that substantiate the unique selling point of a creative brief

constraints The company, legal, and mandatory restrictions placed on advertisements which include legal protection for trademarks, logos, and copy registrations

---

MyMarketingLab

Go to **mymktlab.com** to complete the problems marked with this icon .

Review Questions

1. Define advertising campaign management.
2. What are the six stages of the hierarchy of effects model? Do they always occur in that order? Why or why not?
3. How are the three components of attitudes related to the hierarchy of effects model?
4. In a means–end chain, what are the means? The ends? How do they affect advertising design?
5. Why are visual elements in advertisement important? What is the relationship between visual and verbal elements? Can there be one without the other?
6. What is *visual Esperanto*?
7. What are threshold effects? Diminishing returns? Carryover effects?
8. What are the differences between wear-out effects and decay effects?
9. What factors influence the decision of whether to use an in-house advertising group or an external advertising agency?
10. Besides advertising agencies, what other types of organizations play roles in the communication process?
11. What is crowdsourcing? What are its advantages and disadvantages?
12. What steps should be taken in selecting an advertising agency?
13. What evaluation criteria should be used in selecting an advertising agency?
14. What is a creative pitch?
15. Describe the various roles within an advertising agency.
16. What advertising campaign parameters were described in this chapter?
17. Describe the terms top-of-mind and top choice.
18. What is a tagline, and what role does a tagline play in an advertisement?
19. Explain how variability theory can be used to create consistency in an advertising campaign.
20. What elements are included in a creative brief?

Critical Thinking Exercises

DISCUSSION QUESTIONS

⭐ **21.** Identify five recent commercials that you have seen or watched that you believe are effective. Identify the part of the hierarchy of effects model that the advertisement targets, noting the specific step in the model. Explain your answer.

22. Pick one of the following brands. Develop a means–ends chain similar to the two that are shown in this chapter.

    a. St. Francis Medical Center

    b. JD Bank

    c. Orkin Pest Control

    d. Maxwell House Coffee

⭐ **23.** Think about recent advertisements you have seen or watched. For each of the concepts listed, give an example of an advertisement you believe illustrates the concept. Explain why you believe the ad fits the category.

- Threshold effects
- Diminishing returns
- Carryover effects
- Wear-out effects
- *Visual Esperanto*

24. Look through the ads in this chapter. Which ad do you like the best? Why? Which ad is the least appealing to you? Why? Discuss the relationship between the visual and verbal elements. Locate one ad you believe displays the characteristic of *visual Esperanto*. Explain why.

25. Review the responsibilities of each of the jobs under "Roles of Advertising Personnel." Which one most appeals to you? Why? Which is least appealing? Why?

26. Choose one of the following products. Use the information in this chapter to prepare a creative brief. You can pick a brand from within the product category.

    a. Energy drink

    b. Frozen apple juice

    c. Fast-food restaurant

    d. Museum

    e. Dress shoes

Integrated Learning Exercises

27. Making the decision to use an external advertising agency as opposed to an in-house program for advertising or some other aspect of the advertising function can be difficult. Access the American Association of Advertising Agencies website at **www.aaaa.org**. What type of information is available at this website? How would it benefit companies looking for an advertising agency? Explain your answer. How would it benefit advertising agencies? Explain your answer.

28. A number of agencies assist business organizations with integrated marketing communications programs. Whereas some firms try to provide a wide array of services, others are more specialized. Access the following association websites. What type of information is available on each site? How would the information provided be useful in building an IMC program?

    a. International Social Media Association (**www.ismaconnects.org**)

    b. Brand Activation Association (**www.bbalink.org**)

    c. Outdoor Advertising Association of America (**www.oaaa.org**)

    d. Direct Marketing Association (**www.the-dma.org**)

    e. Digital Marketing Association (**www.digital marketingassoc.com**)

29. Part of an advertising management program includes understanding the media usage habits of consumers and their attitudes toward various media. An excellent source of information in Canada is the Media Smarts Program at **www.mediasmarts.ca**. Review the types of information available at the website. Examine the news articles. What type of information is available at this website, and how could it be used in developing an advertising campaign?

⭐ **30.** Many advertisers direct ads toward the right side of the brain and develop advertisements based entirely on emotions, images, and pictures. Companies often advertise auto parts and tools with a scantily clad woman to attract the attention of men. The woman has nothing to do with the product, but garners attention. The rationale for using a sexy woman is that if consumers like her, they will like the product and then purchase that brand. Effective advertisements integrate elements from both the left side of the brain as well as the right. They contain elements that appeal to emotions but also have rational arguments. A laundry detergent can be advertised as offering the rational benefit of getting clothes cleaner but also contain the emotional promise that your mother-in-law will think of you more favorably. For each of the following websites, discuss the balance of left-brain versus right-brain advertising appeal.

    a. Pier 1 Imports (**www.pier1.com**)

    b. Pig O' My Heart Potbellies (**www.potbellypigs.com**)

c. Volkswagen of America (**www.vw.com**)

d. Popeyes Louisiana Kitchen (**www.popeyes.com**)

e. Backcountry.com (**www.backcountry.com**)

31. You have been asked to select an advertising agency to handle an account for Red Lobster, a national restaurant chain. Your advertising budget is $30 million. Study the websites of the following advertising agencies. Follow the selection steps outlined in the chapter. Narrow the list down to two agencies and justify your decision. Then choose between the two agencies and justify your choice.

a. The Richards Group (**www.richards.com**)

b. Leo Burnett (**www.leoburnett.com**)

c. DDB (**www.ddb.com**)

d. Lucas Design & Advertising (**www.aladv.com**)

e. mcgarrybowen (**www.mcgarrybowen.com**)

f. Zehnder Communications (**www.z-comm.com**)

32. A marketing manager has been placed in charge of a new sporting goods chain of stores to be introduced into the market. The company's corporate headquarters are in Atlanta, and the firm's management team has already decided to use one of the local advertising agencies. The primary objective in choosing an agency is that the firm must have the capability to develop a strong brand name. Type "advertising agencies in Atlanta" into a search engine. Identify an initial list of six ad agencies. Follow the steps outlined in the chapter to narrow the list to two agencies. Discuss the steps you used in choosing the two agencies and why you selected them. Then design a project for the agencies to prepare as part of an oral and written presentation to the company's marketing team.

Blog Exercises

Access the authors' blog for this text at the URLs provided to complete these exercises. Answer the questions that are posed on the blog.

33. Oreo Cookies: **http://blogclowbaack.net/2014/05/07/oreo-cookies-chapter-5/**

34. John Deere: **http://blogclowbaack.net/2014/05/07/john-deere-chapter-4/**

35. Advertising Agencies: **http://blogclowbaack.net/2014/05/07/advertising-agencies-chapter-5/**

Student Project

CREATIVE CORNER

Use the following creative brief for this exercise.

Product:	Porsche
Objective:	To change consumers view that the Porsche can be driven every day
Target Audience:	30- to 55-year-old consumers, slightly more male, college educated, with annual incomes of approximately $100,000. Psychographically, the targeted market is a group known as individualists. They tend not to buy mainstream products. In automobile selection, they place greater emphasis on design elements, distinctiveness, and utility. Social status is important.
Background Information:	Market research found that potential customers balked at the idea of buying a car just to sit around. When asked what kept them from driving the car every day, they said, "I don't feel comfortable driving in city traffic. It doesn't have the technology that I need to manage my everyday life. It doesn't have space for passengers."
Message Theme:	The Porsche can be driven every day for normal activities. It does not have to sit in the garage and be driven only on weekends. It has the newest technology and can comfortably carry passengers.
Constraints:	All ads must contain the Porsche logo.

36. As an account executive for an advertising agency, discuss the creative brief in terms of the completeness of the information provided and whether the objective is realistic. What additional information should Porsche provide before a creative can begin working on the account?

37. The media planner for the Porsche account suggests a media plan consisting of cable television, print advertising, internet ads, and network advertising on *Family Guy*, *CSI*, *Monday Night Football*, *Big Bang Theory*, and *American Idol*. Evaluate this media plan in light of the creative brief's objectives. Can these shows reach the target audience? What information does a creative and the account executive want from the media planner before starting work on actual commercials?

38. Using the information provided in the creative brief, prepare a magazine advertisement. Which magazines might match the target audience? Why?

CASE 1 > CLASSIC CRYSTAL

Every day, most people in developed countries will use a glass or cup as part of their routines. Glassware is sold in a variety of stores, from large discount retailers such as Wal-Mart and Target to small specialty stores. Customers purchasing glassware range from individuals seeking the simplest, most economical versions to brides making choices at various registries, to bars, restaurants, and hotels requiring vessels to hold drinks of all types.

Glasses can be made from plastic, actual glass, crystal, and other elements. Designs can be nonexistent to exotic. Some glasses are round; others square or in more unusual shapes. Some are dishwasher safe and even designed for heavy-duty use. Arcoroc sells "drinkware" in conjunction with flatware and silverware, giving various businesses such as restaurants the option of purchasing an entire dinner setting that meshes together. In its marketing materials, Arcoroc stresses the durability of it products. At the other extreme, heavy duty glassware can also be found in some Army surplus stores.

Other glassware forms are dainty and can only be hand washed or should at least be handled with a great deal of care. Novica offers hand-blown drinkware that the company describes as "our artisan crafted treasures." Two popular products include "Amber Feast" with a light amber tint and "Night Sky," which is a dark, cobalt blue.

Glassware is often designed to match the fluid it will hold and the setting it will serve. Wine glasses tend to have stems and seek to enhance the aroma of the drink. Some are created to generate "snob appeal." Beer mugs tend to be sturdy and feature handles. Milk glasses for children are short, round, and stout. Dinner glasses assume a variety of forms.

Advertising campaign management for glass manufacturers would feature all of the elements described in this chapter. Advertising theories would help explain how a product is chosen and why. Advertising expenditures should be managed to achieve the highest levels of effectiveness. The manufacturer will decide on an in-house or agency-based approach to marketing. When an agency is chosen, the campaign parameters will be outlined and a creative brief should be developed to guide the advertising process.

39. Using the internet, identify a glassware brand and/or manufacturer that interests you. Based on the information provided for the brand, choose a particular type of glassware. Explain why you chose this particular brand. In your explanation, include the brand's website address and a screenshot of its main page.

Nataliya Dvukhimenna/Fotolia

▲ Drinkware comes in a variety of shapes and sizes.

40. Develop a means–end chain that explains the purchasing process for the brand's specific products.

41. Using the internet, identify five advertising agencies in your area. Evaluate each advertising agency in terms of its ability to handle an advertising campaign for your company. Choose one of the five to handle your account and explain why it was chosen. (Include each agency's URL in your response).

42. Develop a creative brief for an advertising campaign that you believe would best fit your glassware company.

43. Design a print ad that fits the creative brief you developed.

CASE 2 ADVERTISING JEANS TO TEENS

If there is one nearly common denominator among teens around the world, it may be the desire to impress peers and potential romantic partners. A variety of enticing adornments assist in the process, including choices regarding hair style, cosmetics, jewelry, and clothing. In many cultures, designer jeans allow younger consumers to look sleek and sassy.

In the United States, top name designer jeans include Citizens of Humanity, Rockstar, Bluelab, Superfine, Dylan George, Stitch's, Current/Elliot, Red Engine, Rich and Skinny, Chip & Pepper, Mavi, Monarchy, HA-67, and Diesel. These companies compete with more established Lee and Levi jeans. In Brazil, Butt Lift products have gained an edge in the marketplace, competing with Moleton and Blue Monster. French products include 2Leep and German companies sell Trewano.

The market for jeans remains lucrative. Teens with disposable income may spend a great deal of time and effort choosing the brand they will wear. Influences include the price and fit, but also social and peer pressure, jeans worn by celebrities, and parental limitations. Social media allows them to consider a variety of brands, discussing the options with friends while seeking to discover the most popular new hot item.

Each year, jean styles change. The elements in jeans may move from looking old and torn, to those stitched with special designs, and then to multifabric entries. Length can be Capri, full, straight-legged, or flared. Pockets may be small or large. They may be closed using zippers or buttons. Trendsetters dictate the new fads and fashions.

To complicate matters further, jeans may be worn for style or for work. Besides teenagers, young children and older adults also buy these items. Some marketers, such as Levi and Lee, try to develop brands and lines with staying power. Others focus solely on one segment such as young women or work jeans for older men.

▲ Teens are an attractive market for brands of jeans.

44. Select one of the brands of jeans in this case or another brand you like. Access the brand's website. Explain why you chose this particular brand. In your response, include the brand's website address and a screenshot of its main page.

45. Develop a means–ends chain that explains the purchasing process for the brand of jeans.

46. Using the internet, identify five advertising agencies in your area. Evaluate each advertising agency in terms of its ability to handle an advertising campaign for your company. Choose one of the five to handle your account and explain why it was chosen. (Include each agency's URL in your response).

47. Develop a creative brief for an advertising campaign that you believe would best fit the brand of jeans you selected.

48. Design a print ad that fits the creative brief you developed.

MyMarketingLab

Go to **mymktlab.com** for Auto-graded writing questions as well as the following Assisted-graded writing questions:

49. Look through the ads in this chapter. Which ad to you like the best? Why? Which ad is the least appealing to you? Why? Discuss what makes a print ad appealing and what creates the opposite effect.

50. You have been asked to select an advertising agency to handle an account for Red Lobster, a national restaurant chain. Your advertising budget is $30 million. Study the websites of the following advertising agencies. Follow the selection steps outlined in the chapter. Narrow the list down to two agencies and justify your decision. Then choose between the two agencies and justify your choice.

　a. The Richards Group (**www.richards.com**)

　b. Leo Burnett (**www.leoburnett.com**)

　c. DDB (**www.ddb.com**)

　d. Lucas Design & Advertising (**www.aladv.com**)

　e. mcgarrybowen (**www.mcgarrybowen.com**)

　f. Zehnder Communications (**www.z-comm.com**)

Endnotes

1. Jerry Olson and Thomas J. Reynolds, "Understanding Consumers' Cognitive Structures: Implications for Advertising Strategy," *Advertising Consumer Psychology*, L. Percy and A. Woodside, eds. (Lexington, MA: Lexington Books, 1983), pp. 77–90; Thomas J. Reynolds and Alyce Craddock, "The Application of the MECCAS Model to Development and Assessment of Advertising Strategy," *Journal of Advertising Research* 28, no. 2 (1988), pp. 43–54.

2. Laurie A. Babin and Alvin C. Burns, "Effects of Print Ad Pictures and Copy Containing Instructions to Imagine on Mental Imagery That Mediates Attitudes," *Journal of Advertising* 26, no. 3 (Fall 1997), pp. 33–44.

3. Marc Bourgery and George Guimaraes, "Global Ads: Say It with Pictures," *Journal of European Business* 4, no. 5 (May–June 1993), pp. 22–26.

4. Gerard J. Tellis, "Study: Advertising Half as Effective as Previously Believed," *Advertising Age*, June 26, 2011, http://adage.com/print/228409.

5. Margaret Henderson Blair, "An Empirical Investigation of Advertising Wearin and Wearout," *Journal of Advertising Research* 40, no. 6 (November–December 2000), pp. 95–100.

6. Ibid.

7. Gerard J. Tellis, "Study: Advertising Half as Effective as Previously Believed," *Advertising Age*, June 26, 2011, http://adage.com/print/228409.

8. "Leaner Ad Budgets Mean More Marketers Rely on In-House Agencies," *Advertising Age*, http://adage.com/print/243976, September 5, 2013.

9. G+G Advertising (**www.gng.net**, accessed January 16, 2010); "G&G Advertising," *Agency Compile* (**www.agencycompile.com/factsheet/factsheet.aspx?agency_id=7823**, accessed January 16, 2010).

10. Bruce Horovitz, "Amateur Doritos Ad Maker Could Win $1M… and a Job," *USA Today, Money*, accessed November 27, 2011, www.usatoday.com/money/media/story/2011-09-26.

11. Prashant Malaviya, "Consumer-Generated Ads: Good for Retention, Bad for Growth," *Forbes*, www.forbes.com/sites/onmarketing/2013/07/02/consumer-generated-ads-good-for-retention-bad-for-growth, July 2, 2013.

12. E.J. Schultz and Rupal Parekh, "Behind Kraft's Seismic Shift: Why It's Shaking Up Its Shops," *Advertising Age*, November 15, 2010, http://adage.com/print?article_id=147105.

13. Suzanne Vranica and Daniel Fitzpatrick, "BofA Reviews Ad Strategy," *Wall Street Journal*, January 12, 2012, http://online.wsj.com/article/SB10001424052970204257504 5771550.

14. Heather Jacobs, "How to Make Sure Your Pitch Is Heard," *B&T Weekly* 57, no. 2597 (February 8, 2007), pp. 14–16.

15. Interview with Jane Hilk, Senior Vice President of Marketing, Oscar Mayer, January 28, 2010.

16. Emily Bryson York, "Behind Kraft's Marketing Makeover: From New Ad Agencies to New Attitude," *Advertising Age* (http://adage.com/article?article_id=141943), February 8, 2010.

17. Jacobs, "How to Make Sure Your Pitch Is Heard."

18. Steve Miller, "VW Is Going Outdoors, Literally," *Brandweek.com* (http://brandweek.com/VW+IS+Going+Outdoor), June 23, 2008.

19. Jack Neff, "The Newest Ad Agencies: Major Media Companies," *Advertising Age* (http://adage.com/print?article_id=140712), November 3, 2008.

20. "Media Agencies Make Mark as Content Creators," *Advertising Age*, April 24, 2011, http://adage.com/print/227163.

21. Interview with Jane Hilk, Sr. Vice President of Marketing, Oscar Mayer, January 28, 2010.

22. H. Rao Unnava and Deepak Sirdeshmukh, "Reducing Competitive Ad Interference," *Journal of Marketing Research* 31, no. 3 (August 1994), pp. 403–411.

23. Naveen Donthu, "A Cross-Country Investigation of Recall of and Attitudes Toward Comparative Advertising," *Journal of Advertising* 27, no. 2 (Summer 1998), pp. 111–21.

24. "Survey: Clients Must Improve Quality of Briefs to Agencies if They Want Better Work," *Advertising Age*, http://adage.com/print/241065, April 24, 2013.

25. Henry A. Laskey and Richard J. Fox, "The Relationship Between Advertising Message Strategy and Television Commercial Effectiveness,"*Journal of Advertising Research* 35, no. 2 (March–April 1995), pp. 31–39.

26. Herbert E. Krugman, "Memory Without Recall, Exposure Without Perception," *Journal of Advertising Research* 40, no. 6 (November–December 2000), pp. 49–55; David Kay, "Left Brain Versus Right Brain," *Marketing Magazine* 108, no. 36 (October 27, 2003), p. 37.

27. "Picking Up the Pace," *Marketing News* 36, no. 7 (April 1, 2002), p. 3.

28. Laurel Wentz and Bradley Johnson, "Top 100 Global Advertisers Heap Their Spending Abroad," *Advertising Age* (http://adage.com/print?article_id=140723), November 30, 2009.

Advertising Design

From Chapter 6 of *Integrated Advertising, Promotion, and Marketing Communications,* Seventh Edition. Kenneth E. Clow, Donald Baack.

Advertising Design

Chapter Objectives

After reading this chapter, you should be able to answer the following questions:

1 How are message strategies used in designing effective advertisements?

2 What are the seven main types of advertising appeals?

3 What role does the executional framework play in advertising design?

4 How are sources and spokespersons decisions related to advertising design?

Overview

Which advertising message made the biggest impression on you in the past five years? Was it funny, sexy, or emotional? Did it appear during the Super Bowl? In a recent *Adweek* Media and Harris Interactive survey, the majority of consumers (55 percent) said that advertisements were somewhat or very interesting. Only 13 percent replied that ads were not interesting at all. When making purchase decisions, six percent of the respondents reported that advertisements were "very influential" and 29 percent viewed them as "somewhat influential." Contrary to popular belief, advertising does influence younger consumers. Nearly half of 18- to 34-year-olds in the survey stated that they were influenced in some way by advertising, compared to 37 percent for 35- to 44-year-olds and 28 percent for consumers age 45 and older.[1]

This poll emphasizes the importance of designing a compelling and influential advertising campaign. Doing so can be one of the most challenging elements of an integrated marketing communications program. A successful advertising campaign results when people do more than merely enjoy what they see; it also changes their behaviors and attitudes. At the least, viewers should remember the good or service. One advertising agency with a strong track record of success in advertising design is mcgarrybowen.

MCGARRYBOWEN

In 2002, three partners came together to form a new competitor in the advertising and communications world, the mcgarrybowen agency. John P. McGarry, Jr., Gordon Bowen, and Stewart Owen designed a company that would be "gracious" and "tenacious" at the same time. Instead of one distinct style with a predetermined media solution, the agency delivers a strategic approach focused on the client's business and brand.

Mcgarrybowen Chicago

◀ Chicago office of mcgarrybowen.

Mcgarrybowen Chicago

Mcgarrybowen Chicago

The agency's impressive client list includes Chevron, Canon, Disney, J. P. Morgan, Kraft, Marriott, Oscar Mayer, Pfizer, Sharp, *The Wall Street Journal*, and Verizon. Specific products advertised and marketed through mcgarrybowen include 7UP, Advil, Miracle Whip, Snapple, and Viagra. Most recently, the firm recaptured the Reebok account and added several new clients, including Sears, Burger King, United Airlines, and Bud Light. *Advertising Age* named mcgarrybowen Agency of the Year in 2009, #2 on its A-List in 2010, and Agency of the Year in 2011.

The mcgarrybowen agency's full service approach covers nearly every marketing and communications activity. Among them, advertising, brand strategies, digital messages, mobile, social networks, data analytics, direct marketing, sponsorships, entertainment marketing, media planning, and multicultural marketing are featured. Company leaders emphasize collaboration. The net result is a motivated and inspired work force that delivers high-quality, creative solutions for clients.

A creative at mcgarrybowen noted, "We pride ourselves on storytelling. The foundations of those stories come out as a product truth." Another employee noted, "Our account planning has more fluidity. Planning becomes most crucial when strategy is the first chapter of the story. The premise of our brand strategy is how we are going to connect the brand story on a human level." In essence, storytelling involves "getting to a single insight that interprets the brand and makes a personal connection."

Account executives lead advertising agencies by working with creatives, media planners, and media buyers. This chapter turns the focus to message design. The work will be completed by the agency's staff based on the creative brief that was prepared by the client in conjunction with the account executive.

The first three topics in this chapter are message strategies, appeals, and executional frameworks. These elements of advertising design are similar to what takes place when developing a movie or television program. The message strategy resembles what the actor says—the verbal message. The appeal represents the manner in which a message is conveyed; through a serious tone, laughter, or sexual cues. The executional framework is comparable to the plot or story of the movie in which the action takes place.

The final topic in the chapter is a discussion of sources or spokespersons. These individuals present the message verbally and visually through the various media used in the advertising program. Agencies and companies carefully consider who will become the "face" of the company and its products.

Message Strategies

objective 1

How are message strategies used in designing effective advertisements?

The message theme outlines the key idea in an advertising campaign and becomes the central part of the creative brief. The message theme helps the advertising team derive a **message strategy**—the primary tactic or approach used to deliver the message theme. The three broad categories of message strategies include cognitive, affective, and conative approaches.[2] The categories represent the components of attitudes. Figure 1 identifies the various forms or approaches from each category.

- Cognitive
  - Generic
  - Unique selling proposition
  - Hyperbole
  - Comparative
- Affective
  - Resonance
  - Emotional
- Conative

▶ **FIGURE 1**
Message Strategies

Cognitive Message Strategies

A **cognitive message strategy** presents rational arguments or pieces of information to consumers. The ideas require cognitive processing. The advertising message seeks to describe the product's attributes or benefits customers can obtain by purchasing the product.[3]

A cognitive message strategy advertisement influences a person's beliefs and/or knowledge structure by suggesting one of a variety of potential product benefits. Foods may be described as healthy, pleasant tasting, or low calorie. Marketers can depict a tool as durable, convenient, or handy to use. The five major forms of cognitive strategies are generic messages, preemptive messages, unique selling propositions, hyperbole, and comparative advertisements.

Generic Messages An advertisement that directly promotes the product's attributes or benefits without any claim of superiority transmits a **generic message**, which works best for a brand leader firm or one that dominates the industry. A generic message makes the brand synonymous with the product category. Campbell's can declare "Soup is good food" without making any claim to superiority. The company leads the industry. When most consumers think of soup, they think of Campbell's, which sells 69 percent of all cans sold each year.[4] Nintendo employs a similar approach because the company dominates the game-console category with a 47 percent market share.[5] In the business-to-business arena, Intel can deploy the generic message strategy "Intel inside" because it controls 80 percent of the microchip market.[6]

Generic message strategies help stimulate brand awareness. The advertiser may try to develop a cognitive linkage between a specific brand name and a product category, such as Sketchers and sporty footwear. The advertisement might contain little information about the product's attributes. Instead, it attempts to place the brand in a person's cognitive memory and cognitive map.

Preemptive Messages A claim of superiority based on a product's specific attribute or benefit with the intent of preventing the competition from making the same or a similar statement is a **preemptive message**. Crest toothpaste's reputation as "the cavity fighter" preempts other companies from making similar claims, even though all toothpastes fight cavities. An effective preemptive strategy occurs when the company states the advantage first. Competitors saying the same thing become viewed as "me too" brands or copycats.

Unique Selling Proposition An explicit, testable claim of uniqueness or superiority that can be supported or substantiated in some manner is a **unique selling proposition**. In the advertisement for P & S Surgical Hospital shown in this section, the company claims to have the best smaller-sized hospital. Substantiation of these claims comes through being rated #1 in Louisiana by CareChex and receiving a 5-star rating by HealthGrades.

An advertisement for Community Trust Bank featuring a cognitive message strategy stating checks can be deposited anytime and anywhere.

An advertisement for P & S Surgical Hospital using a unique selling proposition message strategy.

Karns Quality Foods

▲ This advertisement for Karns Quality Foods features a hyperbole message strategy.

Hyperbole An *untestable* claim based on some attribute or benefit is **hyperbole**. When NBC states that it has America's favorite comedies, the claim is hyperbole. It does not require substantiation, which makes this cognitive strategy quite popular. The hyperbole approach often uses puffery terms, such as *best* or *greatest* such as in the ad for Karns Foods shown here.

Comparative Advertising The final cognitive message strategy, a **comparative advertisement**, allows an advertiser to directly or indirectly compare a product to the competition on some product attribute or benefit. The advertisement may or may not mention the competitor by name. An advertiser can simply present a make-believe competitor with a name such as "Brand X."

Comparative ads offer the advantage of capturing the consumer's attention. When comparisons are made, both brand awareness and message awareness increase. Consumers tend to remember more of what was said about a brand than when a non-comparative format presents the same information.

Low believability and negative consumer attitudes represent the potential downside of comparative ads. Many consumers consider comparative ads to be less believable. They view the information about the sponsor brand as exaggerated and conclude that the advertisement probably mis-states information about the comparison brand to make the sponsor brand appear superior. This in turn can lead to negative consumer attitudes toward a brand.

Another danger with comparative ads occurs when consumers experience negative attitudes toward the advertisement, which can then transfer to the sponsor's product. This becomes more likely when the sponsor runs a *negative comparative ad* about the competition's product. Research suggests that negative comparative ads typically result in lower believability of the advertising claim and may result in less favorable attitudes toward the brand.[7] In psychology, the concept of *spontaneous trait transference* suggests that when a comparative advertisement criticizes the competition's brand based on a particular attribute, it may lead viewers to also attribute the deficiency to the sponsor brand. The transference becomes more likely when the consumer purchases the comparative brand, not the sponsored brand.[8]

At times, negative ads can succeed. One negative comparative campaign that achieved the desired results was the "Scroogled" campaign by Microsoft's search engine, Bing. The campaign presents negative information about Google, such as invasive ads in Gmail, sharing data with app developers, and exploiting private data to maximize Google's advertising profits. Most of the ads do not mention Bing until the very end when the voiceover says "For honest results, try Bing." Ad effectiveness research indicated that 53 percent of viewers said they would look at Bing after viewing the ads.[9]

Company leaders carefully choose an appropriate comparison firm and use caution when using a negative comparison format. The comparison brand must be viewed as a viable competing brand. Comparisons consisting of hype and opinion with no substantial differences are less likely to succeed. Misleading comparisons may cause the Federal Trade Commission (FTC) to investigate. The majority of complaints filed with the FTC are concerned with potentially misleading comparison advertisements.

Comparing a brand with a low market share to the market leader works well, because viewers concentrate more carefully on the advertisement's content and message. Such was the case in a recent campaign for the Kindle Fire, which was compared to the iPad. The commercials argue that the Kindle Fire has better quality product attributes and a lower price. Comparing a high-market share brand with another high-market share brand may not be as effective. In these cases, a better strategy may be to simply make the comparison without naming the competitor.

The five cognitive message strategies are based on rational logic. Advertisers design messages that lead consumers to pay attention to the ad and take the time to cognitively process the information. In terms of attitudes, the sequence of *cognitive → affective → conative* represents the rational approach. The cognitive message strategy first presents consumers with rational information about a good, service, or company and then leads them to develop positive feelings about the same product or company.

Affective Message Strategies

Advertisements trying to evoke feelings or emotions and match those feelings with the good, service, or company feature **affective message strategies**. These messages attempt to enhance the likeability of the product, recall of the appeal, or comprehension of the advertisement. Affective strategies should elicit emotions that in turn lead the consumer to act, preferably by buying the product and subsequently by affecting the consumer's reasoning process.

Resonance   Connecting a brand with a consumer's experiences in order to develop stronger ties between the product and the consumer is resonance affective advertising. The use of music from the 1980s takes Echo Boomers back to that time. Any strongly held memory or emotional attachment becomes a candidate for resonance advertising.

Subaru's advertising team designed a resonance approach for an online marketing effort that attempted to tap into a person's nostalgia for his first car. The program included an animation generator at a microsite called FirstCarStory.com where consumers could recreate the look and feel of their first cars. The program's technology transferred words into custom images. Alan Bethke, director of marketing communications at Subaru, noted, "The First Car Story campaign provides a creative outlet for reliving those unique, funny, unforgettable experiences anyone who had a first car can relate to."[10]

A new form of resonance advertising, **comfort marketing**, emerged when marketers looked for ways to encourage consumers to purchase branded products rather than generic versions. The approach reassures consumers looking for value that a branded product stands the test of time. Comfort marketing involves bringing back vintage

◁ This advertisement for visit South Walton (Florida) presents an affective message strategy through the headline "Make Connections."

Visit South Walton

Kraft Foods, Inc
© 2012 Kraft Foods

If you could hold onto any moment in time,

which?

pheel the moment

PHILADELPHIA
REGULAR

▲ An advertisement for Philadelphia Cream Cheese using an emotional message strategy through the image and tagline "pheel the moment."

characters, themes, and jingles from the past to evoke fond memories when times were better. To ensure the brand does not look old-fashioned, most refresh the mascot, music, taglines, and other aspects of the ad to the twenty-first century. Brands that have employed this approach include StarKist, Alka-Seltzer, Bacardi, Doritos, Dr. Pepper, Pepsi-Cola, and Planters. Robert Furniss-Roe of Bacardi North America, said, "People, particularly in this environment, are looking for substance and authenticity."[11]

Emotional The **emotional affective approach** attempts to elicit powerful emotions that lead to product recall and choice. Many emotions can be connected to products, including trust, reliability, friendship, happiness, security, glamour, luxury, serenity, pleasure, romance, and passion. Companies incorporate emotional appeals into both consumer-oriented and business-to-business advertisements. Members of the buying center in a business are human. They make purchasing decisions based on more than simple rational thought processes. Emotions and feelings also affect choices. When an advertisement presents products' benefits in an emotional framework, it will normally be more effective, even in business-to-business ads.[12]

Many creatives believe affective strategies help build a stronger brand name. Affective advertisements guide consumers to like the brand, develop positive feelings toward it, and eventually purchase the item. Cognitive beliefs about the brand then follow. This approach relies on the attitude development sequence of *affective → conative → cognitive*. For some products, affective advertisements succeed because few real tangible differences among brands actually exist. The St. Francis Medical Center advertisement in this section features an affective strategy by depicting a warm mother/daughter relationship.

Conative Message Strategy

Conative message strategies seek to lead directly to a consumer response. They can support other promotional efforts, such as coupon redemption programs, cash-back rebates, or encourage consumers to access a website. Advertisements that seek to persuade viewers to call a toll-free number to purchase DVDs or other merchandise contain the goal of

▶ An advertisement for St. Francis Medical Center featuring an emotional message strategy.

Newcomer, Morris and Young

My first and only choice.

✝ ST. FRANCIS
MEDICAL CENTER
Future of Healing. Tradition of Caring.

Franciscan Missionaries of Our Lady Health System   stfran.com

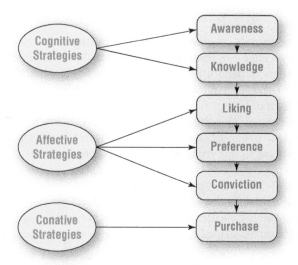

◀ **FIGURE 2**
The Hierarchy of Effects Model
and Message Strategies

▼ This advertisement for Skyjacker
Suspensions offers a cash-back
rebate.

eliciting behaviors. Conative ads typically encourage quick action by stating that the item cannot be purchased in stores and will be available for only a limited time.

With conative advertising, cognitive knowledge of the brand or affective liking of the product may come later (after the actual purchase) or during product usage. For instance, a point-of-purchase display can be designed (sometimes through advertising tie-ins) to cause people to make *impulse buys*. Making the sale constitutes the goal, with cognitive knowledge and affective feelings forming as the product is used. The attitude sequence for conative message strategies becomes *conative → cognitive → affective*.

Cognitive, affective, and conative strategies can be matched with the hierarchy of effects approach, which suggests that consumers pass through a series of stages, from awareness to knowledge, liking, preference, conviction, and, finally, to the purchase. As shown in Figure 2, each message strategy highlights a different stage of the hierarchy of effects model.

Choosing the right message strategy remains a key ingredient in creating a successful advertising program. To be effective, the message strategy should match the message to the appeal and executional framework. These should mesh with the media to be utilized. The creative and the account executive remain in constant contact throughout the process to be certain all of these advertising ingredients remain consistent.

Types of Advertising Appeals

Throughout the years, advertisers have employed numerous advertising approaches. Of these, seven **advertising appeals** have achieved the most success. Normally, one or a combination of these types of appeals will be featured in an advertisement (see Figure 3).

The type of appeal chosen will be based on a review of the creative brief, the objective of the campaign, the means–end chain to be conveyed, and the message strategy. Advertisers consider a number of factors, including the product being sold, the target market of the campaign, and the personal preferences of the advertising agency and client.

objective 2

What are the seven main types of advertising appeals?

▲ **FIGURE 3**
Types of Appeals

Fear Appeals

Advertisements featuring fear appeals are commonplace. Life insurance companies focus on the consequences of not having a life insurance policy when a person dies. Shampoo and mouthwash ads invoke fears of dandruff and bad breath, which can make a person a social outcast. Advertisements feature fear more often than most realize.

Advertisers employ fear appeals because they work. Fear increases viewer interest in an advertisement and can enhance the ad's persuasiveness. Many individuals remember commercials with fear appeals better than they do warm, upbeat messages.[13] Consumers pay greater attention to ads using fear and are more likely to process the information they present, which makes it possible to accomplish an advertisement's main objective.

The *behavioral response model* displayed in Figure 4 illustrates the ways fear works in advertising.[14] As shown, various incidents can lead to negative or positive consequences, which then affect future behaviors.

Severity and Vulnerability When developing fear advertisements, the creative includes as many aspects of the behavioral response model as possible. A business-to-business advertiser offering internet services tries to focus on the **severity** of downtime if a company's internet server goes down or is hacked. Another ad describes the firm's **vulnerability** by showing the probability that a company's server will crash or can be hacked into and customer data stolen. The ReRez advertisement for marketing research services shown on the next page features a picture of a man hanging to illustrate the danger of poor marketing research. The advertisement attempts to cause business leaders to believe low quality decisions would result from inadequate research. ReRez can help them identify these potential problems before they turn into disasters.

Rewards to Response Efficacy To further understand the behavioral response model, consider a young smoker who sees an ad for the Nicoderm CQ patches, which help a person quit. The man considers three things in evaluating the advertisement and making a decision to purchase Nicoderm CQ.

Intrinsic and extrinsic rewards are the first factor. Intrinsic rewards come from gaining social acceptance by quitting and feeling healthier. Extrinsic rewards may include savings on the cost of cigarettes as compared to the price for Nicoderm CQ.

The smoker then considers the second factor, *response costs*. When smoking leads to peer acceptance it becomes rewarding, which means there is a lower incentive to quit,

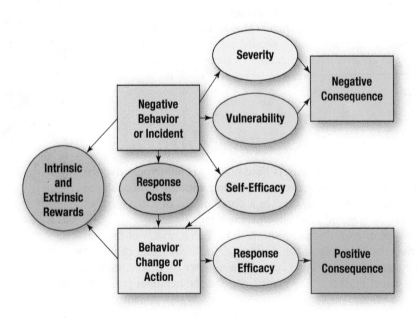

▶ **FIGURE 4**
The Behavioral Response Model

◀ This business-to-business advertisement for ReRez features a fear appeal.

because smoking creates intrinsic value, making quitting more difficult. A man who quits smoking becomes more likely to gain weight and lose the friends who continue to smoke. The higher the perceived costs, the less likely the decision to quit smoking becomes.

Self-efficacy constitutes the third factor. In this situation, self-efficacy relates to the man's confidence in his ability to stop smoking. Many individuals have tried and failed. Thus, they have little hope Nicoderm CQ will work. The smoker must believe that Nicoderm CQ can truly help him quit before he will purchase it.

The combination of intrinsic and extrinsic rewards, response costs, and the degree of self-efficacy contribute to the smoker's *response efficacy*. The decision to purchase Nicoderm CQ with the idea of stopping smoking will be based on the conclusion that doing so will lead to net positive consequences. The person concludes he will fit in with family and friends, feel better, improve his health, and believe that he is capable of quitting smoking.

Appeal Strength   When using fear, the strength of the appeal constitutes another key factor. Most advertisers believe a moderate level of fear will be the most effective. A low level of fear may not be noticed and the fear level may not be convincing in terms of severity or vulnerability. An advertisement containing a fear level that is too strong can also backfire, because the message only generates feelings of anxiety. This leads the viewer to avoid watching the commercial by changing the channel or muting the sound.[15] Consequently, a fear appeal should be powerful enough to capture a viewer's attention and to influence her thinking but not so scary that she avoids the advertisement.

Humor Appeals

Clutter presents a significant problem in every advertising medium. Capturing a viewer's attention continues to be difficult. Even after grabbing the audience's attention, keeping it becomes even more challenging. Humor has proven to be one of the best

Himchenko/Fotolia

▲ Marketers use humor in advertising because people like to laugh.

techniques for cutting through clutter, by getting attention and keeping it. Consumers, as a whole, enjoy advertisements that make them laugh. A funny message offers intrusive value and attracts attention.[16]

Humor appears in about 30 percent of television and radio advertisements.[17] Humorous ads often win awards and tend to be favorites among consumers. In a *USA Today* consumer survey of the most likeable advertising campaigns, humor was a key ingredient.[18]

Humorous ads achieve success for three reasons. Humor causes consumers to: watch, laugh, and, most important, remember. In recall tests, consumers most often recall humorous ads. The best results occur when the humor connects directly with the product's benefits. The advertisement should link the product's features with the advantage to customers and personal values in a means–end chain.

Advertising research indicates that humor elevates people's moods. Happy consumers often associate a good mood with the advertiser's products. In essence, humor helps fix the brand in the consumer's cognitive structure with links to positive feelings. Figure 5 summarizes the primary reasons for using humor.

Although a funny advertisement can capture the viewer's attention, cut through clutter, and enhance recall, humorous ads can also go wrong. A Snickers commercial that ran during a recent Super Bowl featured two mechanics eating from opposite ends of the same candy bar until they accidentally ended up kissing. The two men responded in disgust by ripping out their own chest hairs. The outcry from some groups was loud enough that it was immediately pulled.[19]

Advertisers should not allow the humor to overpower the message. Humor fails when consumers remember the joke but not the product or brand. In other words, the advertisement was so funny that the audience forgets or does not catch the sponsor's name.

Using humor with global campaigns can create difficulties. Humor rooted in one culture may not transfer to another. Further, not all audiences experience a humorous ad in the same way. To avoid these potential problems, the humor in an advertisement should focus on a component of the means–end chain. The humor can relate to a product's attributes, a customer benefit, or the personal value obtained from the product. The most effective ads are those in which the humor incorporates all three elements.

▶ **FIGURE 5**
Reasons for Using Humor in Ads

- Captures attention.
- Holds attention.
- Often wins creative awards.
- High recall scores.
- Consumers enjoy ads that make them laugh.
- Evaluated by consumers as likeable ads.

Sex Appeals

Advertisers use sexual appeals to break through clutter. Advertisements in the United States and other countries contain more visual sexual themes than ever. Nudity and other sexual approaches are common. Sexual themes in ads, however, do not always work. Sex no longer has shock value. Today's teens grow up in societies immersed in sex. One more sexually-oriented ad captures little attention. Currently, many advertisers prefer more subtle sexual cues, suggestions, and innuendos.[20] Figure 6 lists the ways marketers employ sexuality in advertisements.

Subliminal Approach   Placing sexual cues or icons in advertisements in an attempt to affect a viewer's subconscious is the subliminal approach. In an odd paradox, truly subliminal cues are not noticed, which means they do not create any effects. Consumers already pay little attention to ads. A subliminal message that registers only in the viewer's subconscious will not be effective. If it worked, there would be no need for stronger sexual content in advertising.

Sensuality   Some women respond more favorably to a sensual suggestion than an overtly sexual approach. An alluring glance across a crowded room can be sensual and draw attention to a product. Many view sensuality as being more sophisticated, because it relies on the imagination. Images of romance and love can be more enticing than raw sexuality.

Sexual Suggestiveness   A sexually suggestive advertisement hints that sex is about to take place. Recently, Pine-Sol included suggestiveness to advertise a household cleaner. In several television ads, shirtless, muscular men are shown mopping the floor while the female watches or fantasizes. Diane Amos, who has been featured in Pine-Sol ads for the last 16 years and appears in this new series of ads featuring men, says, "We would all like our husbands to mop. It can be fun, it can be sexy, and women like it clean."[21]

Nudity or partial nudity   Products that contain sexual connotations or elements, such as clothing, perfume, and cologne, may feature a degree of nudity. Some ads are designed to solicit a sexual response. Others are not. In 1987, underwear companies were first allowed to use live models in television advertisements. The first commercials were modest and informational, emphasizing the design or materials used in the undergarment. The first Playtex bra commercials with live models drew strong criticism from organizations such as the American Family Association. Currently, advertisements for undergarments go much further and involve superstars, such as actress Jennifer Love Hewitt who appeared in television and print ads for the Hanes All-Over Comfort Bra and the Perfect Panty. The campaign even included an online element with footage from the photo shoots, a "bad bra toss" game, and a blog about bad bra moments.[22]

- Subliminal techniques
- Sensuality
- Sexual suggestiveness
- Nudity or partial nudity
- Overt sexuality

▲ **FIGURE 6**
Sexuality Approaches Used in Advertising

▼ A milk advertisement using a sex appeal.

Is milk part of your daily routine?

Soft drinks and energy drinks did not create this body. It was milk, exercise, and basketball with the big boys.

Milk has the calcium my body needs for healthy bones. That same milk reduces my chances of developing bone problems, the osteoporosis my mom now lives with daily. Watching her suffer is my motivation to stay fit.

© Dash/Fotolia

Tuzyra/Fotolia

▲ Live models are now featured in lingerie ads with sexual appeal.

Overt Sexuality Using overt sexuality in ads for sexually-oriented products is normally accepted, but it often becomes controversial when used for other types of products. When Procter & Gamble launched a television advertising campaign for Dentyne, eyebrows were raised. The commercial showed two teens in a living room. The girl pops a piece of Dentyne Fire bubble gum into her mouth and then rips off her blouse and jumps on her boyfriend. At first, the parents stare in shock. Then, the mom tries a piece of Dentyne Fire and promptly jumps on the dad. The controversy centered on whether the ad promoted teenage sexuality by suggesting that parents should openly display sexual feelings and desires.[23]

Decorative Models One common sexual approach involves placing **decorative models** into advertisements. These individuals adorn products as sexual or attractive stimuli. They serve no other purpose than to attract attention. In the past, commercials for automobiles, tools, and beer often used female models dressed in bikinis standing by the products. Marketers conducted a number of studies in order to determine the effectiveness of decorative models. Figure 7 provides some basic conclusions regarding this tactic.[24]

Effectiveness of Sex Appeals Numerous studies have examined the effectiveness of sexual appeals and nudity in advertising. Almost all of them conclude that sex and nudity do increase attention. At the same time, brand recall tends to be lower than advertisements with other types of appeals. It appears that although people watch the advertisement, the sexual theme distracts them from noticing the brand name.[25]

Observers often rate sexually-oriented advertisements as more intriguing. Both males and females rate ads deemed to be highly controversial in terms of sexual content as more interesting. The paradox, however, is that although such ads are more interesting, they fail to increase the transmission of information. Respondents are less likely to remember any more about the message.[26]

Advertisements featuring overt sexual stimuli or containing nudity produce higher levels of physiological arousal responses. These arousal responses have been linked to

- The presence of female (or male) decorative models improves ad recognition, but not brand recognition.
- The presence of a decorative model influences emotional and objective evaluations of the product among both male and female audiences.

- Attractive models produce a higher level of attention to ads than do less attractive models.
- The presence of an attractive model produces higher purchase intentions when the product is sexually relevant than if it is not sexually relevant.

▶ **FIGURE 7**
Factors to Consider Before Using Decorative Models

the formation of both affective and cognitive responses. If the viewer is male and the sexual stimulus is female, such as a nude female in an ad for cologne, then the viewer tends to develop a strong feeling (affective) toward the ad based on the arousal response his body experiences. Female viewers of male nudity in an advertisement often experience the same type of response, although the arousal response may not be as strong. The cognitive response depends on whether the viewer sees the advertisement as pleasant or offensive. When the viewer likes the ad, it results in a positive impression of the brand. When the viewer thinks the ad exhibits poor taste, negative feelings and beliefs about the brand often emerge.[27]

Societal Trends   When an advertising team determines the level of sex appeal to feature in an advertisement, they consider society's views and prevalent levels of acceptance.[28] Just as economies go through cycles, attitudes toward sex in advertising experience acceptance fluctuations.

The use of and approval of sexual themes in advertising had swung to a high level of tolerance in the early part of the 2000s, until the Super Bowl of 2004. The public reaction to Janet Jackson's breast-baring halftime show sent ripples all the way to Madison Avenue. Shortly afterward, Victoria's Secret dropped its TV lingerie fashion show. Abercrombie & Fitch killed the company's quarterly catalog, which had been strongly criticized for featuring models in sexually suggestive poses. Anheuser-Busch dropped some of its risqué ads.[29]

The pendulum has now begun swinging back toward greater acceptance of sexually-oriented ads, but it has not reached the pre-2004 level yet. A recent Calvin Klein ad featuring actress Eva Mendes in the nude in a provocative pose for its Secret Obsession fragrance was rejected by the major networks in the United States but accepted by television stations in Europe. A less-provocative version was created for the United States, although it was not shown until after 9:00 p.m.[30]

Coka/Fotolia

▲ Sexually-oriented images in advertisements stimulate physiological responses in both males and females.

Criticisms of Sex Appeals   One common criticism of sexually based advertising is that it perpetuates dissatisfaction with one's body. Often, thin females adorn print and television advertisements. The prevailing idea seems to be "the thinner the better." As advertising models have gotten thinner, body dissatisfaction and eating disorders among women have risen. Research indicates that many women feel unhappy about their own bodies and believe they are too fat after viewing advertisements showing thin models. Dove's recent "Campaign for Real Beauty" included a series of advertisements and social media posts highlighting this criticism. Still, ads featuring thin models are more likely to convince women to purchase a product.[31] With men, the reverse is true. Many men worry they are not muscular enough and are too thin or too fat to buy the item. It does not make any difference whether the male views a male model or a female model in advertisements.[32]

Luanateutzi/Fotolia

▲ One of the criticisms of sex appeals is that they perpetuate dissatisfaction with one's body.

Music Appeals

Music often adds an important ingredient to an advertisement. A musical theme connects with emotions, memories, and other experiences. Music can be intrusive; it gains the attention of someone who previously was not listening to or watching a program. It may provide the stimulus that ties a particular musical arrangement, jingle, or song to a certain brand. As soon as the tune begins, consumers recognize the brand being advertised because they have been conditioned to tie the product to the music.

Music gains attention and increases the retention of information when it becomes intertwined with the product. Even when a consumer does not recall the ad message argument, music can lead to a better recall of an advertisement's visual and emotional aspects. Music can increase the persuasiveness of an argument. Subjects who compared ads with music to identical ads without music almost always rated those with music higher in terms of persuasiveness.[33] Several decisions are made when selecting music for commercials, including the following:

- What role will music play in the ad?
- Will a familiar song be used, or will something original be created?
- What emotional pitch should the music reach?
- How does the music fit with the message of the ad?

Music plays a variety of roles in advertisements. Sometimes music will be incidental. In others, it becomes the primary theme. An important decision involves selecting a familiar tune as opposed to creating original music. Writing a jingle or music specifically for the advertisement occurs more often and has become the current trend. Background or mood-inducing music is usually instrumental, and advertisers often pay musicians to write music that matches the scenes in the ad. A number of advertising agencies have formed in-house recording labels for the sole purpose of writing jingles, songs, and music for ads.[34]

In the 2000s, using a well-known song in an advertisement was common. A popular, well-known song creates certain advantages. The primary benefit is that consumers already have developed an affinity for the song. Brand awareness, brand equity, and brand loyalty become easier to develop when consumers are familiar with the music. This occurs when consumers transfer an emotional affinity for the song to the product. Some companies purchase an existing song and adapt the ad's verbiage to the music.[35] Using popular songs may be expensive. The price for the rights to a popular song can be in the range of six to seven figures.[36] The internet company Excite paid $7 million for the rights to Jimi Hendrix's song "Are You Experienced," and Microsoft paid about $12 million for the Rolling Stones' "Start Me Up."[37]

An alternative method of developing music has emerged, primarily because of the internet. Greater cooperation now exists between musicians and marketers. Some musicians view advertisements as a way to get their songs heard. Marketers see an opportunity to tie a new, exciting song to a product.

When a commercial only plays part of a song, many firms place entire tunes on company websites or on YouTube so that individuals can download them. Occasionally, a song written for a commercial will crack Billboard's Top 100 list. Jason Wade, a singer in the band Lifehouse, had never written a song for a commercial before. After viewing a copy of the 60-second commercial for Allstate Insurance produced by Leo Burnett Agency, Wade wrote a song entitled "From Where You Are." The commercial promoted Allstate's safe-driving program for teenagers. After the commercial aired, the song was made available on iTunes. Within two weeks, sales were high enough for the song to reach number 40 on Billboard's charts.[38]

Rational Appeals

A rational appeal follows the hierarchy of effects stages of awareness, knowledge, liking, preference, conviction, and purchase. A creative designs the advertisement for one of the six steps. An ad oriented to the knowledge stage transmits basic product information. In the preference stage, the message shifts to presenting logical reasons that favor the brand, such as the superior gas mileage of an automobile. A rational advertisement should lead to a stronger conviction about a product's benefits, so that the consumer eventually makes the purchase.

Rational appeals rely on consumers actively processing the information presented in the advertisement. The consumer must pay attention to the commercial, comprehend the message, and compare the information to knowledge embedded in a cognitive map. Messages consistent with the current concepts in a person's cognitive map strengthen key linkages. New messages help the individual form cognitive beliefs about the brand and establish a new linkage from her current map to the new product. As a result, print media and the internet offer the best outlets for rational appeals. Television and radio commercials are short, which makes it harder for viewers to process message arguments.

Marketers feature rational appeals in many business-to-business advertising campaigns. A business customer who sees a Kinko's advertisement about videoconferencing services already may have the company in his cognitive structure. The customer may have used Kinko's in the past but was not aware that the company offers videoconferencing. When Kinko's has been established in this person's cognitive map, creating a new linkage to entice the customer to try its videoconferencing services becomes easier.

In general, rational appeals succeed when potential customers have high levels of involvement and are willing to pay attention to the advertisement. Message arguments, product information and benefits should be placed in the copy. A rational appeal works best when individuals have a particular interest in the product or brand. Otherwise, people tend to ignore rational appeal ads.

Emotional Appeals

Emotional appeals are based on three ideas (see Figure 8). First, consumers ignore most advertisements. Second, rational appeals go unnoticed unless the consumer is in the market for a particular

▲ Music can be an integral part of a broadcast advertisement.

▲ This advertisement for Crowe Horwath features a rational appeal targeting the construction industry.

- Consumers ignore most ads.
- Rational appeals generally go unnoticed.
- Emotional appeals can capture attention and foster an attachment.

▲ **FIGURE 8**
Reasons for Using Emotional Appeals

This is where fall drapes summer in a blanket of gold

Where the forecast calls for morning sun and afternoon strolls

Where the view from down valley is rivaled by the view downtown

And the road less traveled is the best road in town

COLORADO

Explore fall getaways and order a guide at colorado.com

Colorado Tourism Office

▲ This advertisement for Colorado features visual elements that create the emotional appeal of serenity and peace.

product at the time it is advertised. Third and most important, emotional advertising can capture a viewer's attention and create an emotional attachment between the consumer and the brand.

Most creatives view emotional advertising as the key to brand loyalty. Creatives want customers to experience a bond with the brand. Visual cues in advertisements are key components of many emotional appeals. The visual elements in the ad for Colorado shown in this section help contribute to a feeling or mood of serenity. Although individuals develop perceptions of brands based largely on visual and peripheral stimuli, this does not happen instantly. With repetition, perceptions and attitudinal changes emerge. Figure 9 displays some of the more common emotions presented in advertisements.

Godiva employed an emotional appeal in its latest advertising campaign entitled "the golden moment." Created by Lipman Agency, the campaign focused on the emotional appeal of giving, sharing, or eating Godiva chocolates. Laurie Len Kotcher, Chief Marketing Officer and Senior Vice President for Global Brand Development of Godiva Chocolatier, said, "When you give the gold box, receive the gold box, eating something from the gold box, there is something special about that moment."[39]

While advertisements for many consumer products feature emotional appeals, the approach has begun to appear more frequently in business-to-business advertising. In the past, only five to ten percent of all business-to-business ads featured emotional appeals. Today, the figure has risen to nearly 25 percent. A magazine advertisement created by NKH&W Advertising Agency for a product to treat racehorses switched from a rational appeal to an emotional appeal. The target market was veterinarians. In the past, an advertisement would have opened with such ad copy as "For swelling in joints use…" The emotional ad shows the horse thinking, "I will prove them wrong. I will run again. I will mend my spirits."[40]

Television remains one of the best medium to present emotional appeals, because it offers advertisers intrusion value and can utilize both sound and sight. Models in the ads can be real people. Facial expressions convey emotions and attitudes. Consumers learn about a particular brand and develop attitudes based on these experiences. Television ads also are more vivid, lifelike, and often create dynamic situations that pull viewers in. Music can be incorporated to make the commercial more dramatic. Peripheral cues constitute important components of emotional appeals. The cues, such

- Trust
- Reliability
- Friendship
- Happiness
- Security
- Glamour-luxury

- Serenity
- Anger
- Protecting loved ones
- Romance
- Passion

- Family bonds
  - with parents
  - with siblings
  - with children
  - with extended family members

▶ **FIGURE 9**
Emotions Used in Advertisements

as music and background visuals, help capture the viewer's attention.

Emotions are often tied with humor, fear, music, and other appeals to make a compelling case for a product. The same ad can influence a consumer both emotionally and rationally. The creative selects the most appropriate emotional appeal for the product and company.

Scarcity Appeals

Scarcity appeals urge consumers to buy a particular product because of a limitation. It can be a limited number of the products available or that the product will be made available for only a limited time. When consumers believe only a finite supply of a product will be available, the perceived value of the product might increase. For the Olympics, General Mills introduced USA Olympic Crunch cereal and Betty Crocker Team USA desserts for a limited time.[41] McDonald's, Wendy's, and Burger King offer sandwiches (McRib, Hot N' Spicy Chicken, Dollar Whoppers) for limited-time periods throughout the year. The scarcity concept applies to musical compilations, encouraging consumers to buy a CD because of its restricted availability. By making sure it is not available in retail stores, marketers increase its scarcity value. Notice in the advertisement for Wholly Guacamole shown in this section that the company's guacamole is only free on one day, March 20, and only at Schlotzsky's.

Executional Frameworks

An **executional framework or execution** signifies the manner in which an ad appeal will be presented and a message strategy conveyed. Figure 10 displays the various frameworks. Each will be matched with the type of appeal and message strategy as part of the overall advertising design process.

Animation Executions

Animation has become an increasingly popular executional framework, and its use has risen dramatically. The growing sophistication of computer graphics programs makes new and exciting animation technologies available. Successful animated movie films such as *Up*

- Animation
- Slice-of-life
- Storytelling
- Testimonial
- Authoritative
- Demonstration
- Fantasy
- Informative

▲ **FIGURE 10**
Executional Frameworks

▲ This advertisement for DuPage Medical Group utilizes an emotional appeal.

▲ This advertisement uses a scarcity appeal because Wholly Guacamole is free at Scholotzky's only on March 20.

objective 3

What role does the executional framework play in advertising design?

and *Dr. Seuss' The Lorax* continue to generate interest in animation advertising, which can be featured in television spots, on the internet, and in movie trailers. Single shots of animated characters, such as *Dora the Explorer*, are placed in print ads.

The *rotoscoping* process facilitates digitally painting or sketching figures into live sequences, which makes it possible to present both live actors and animated characters in the same frame.[42] The creative can also merge or modify various live scenes. Advertising executive Stan Richards noted, "The opportunities are great, because we are at a point where anything that we can think of, we can do. We've never had that before. There is a cost consequence. A lot of that digital production is expensive, but those costs are coming down. Within a few years, those costs will be half of what they are now."[43]

For years, marketing professionals rarely used animation in business-to-business advertisements. Many marketers viewed it negatively, believing animation appealed to children but not to businesspeople. These opinions have changed. Business ads shown on television now take advantage of high-quality graphics to illustrate a product's uses with animation.

Pink Jacket Creative: A Creative Factory

▲ This advertisement created by Pink Jacket Creative for the Snoring Center uses animation combined with a slice-of-life execution.

Slice-of-Life Executions

In slice-of-life commercials, advertisers provide solutions to the everyday problems consumers or businesses face. Proctor & Gamble made this format famous during the early days of television advertising in the 1950s. Slice-of-life commercials depict the common experiences, especially the problems people encounter, and introduce the brand to solve the problem. The most common slice-of-life format contains four components: encounter, problem, interaction, and solution (see Figure 11). In some ads, the actors portray the dilemma or problem and solve the problem themselves. In others, a voiceover explains the benefits or solution to the problem that the good, service, or company provides.

Business-to-business advertisements often utilize the slice-of-life method because it allows the advertiser to highlight the ways a brand can meet business needs. A typical business-to-business ad begins with a routine problem, such as a sales manager making a presentation to the board of directors. Then, a projector being used does not have a clear picture. The ad offers the solution: a projector from Sony. The presentation resumes with great clarity, and the board of directors accepts the

▶ **FIGURE 11**

Components of a Slice-of-life Execution

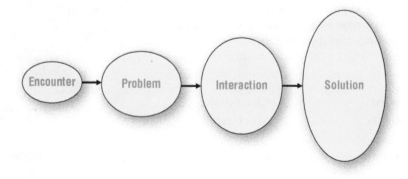

customer's bid for the account. As with all slice-of-life commercials, a disaster has been avoided and a happy ending results instead.

Storytelling Executions

Many advertisers use a new execution format: storytelling. Storytelling does not include an encounter where a brand solves a problem faced by a consumer or business, such as in the slice-of-life approach. Instead, a storytelling execution resembles a 30-second movie with a plot or story suggesting the brand is more at the periphery rather than at the center of the ad. In contrast to a "hard-sell" approach in which the ad directly presents a brand's benefits or features; the storytelling format allows the viewer to draw his own conclusions about the product. In a recent ad for Subaru, the commercial depicts a loving dad handing his daughter the car keys for the first time. He still sees her as his little girl, but now she is a teenager. The Subaru brand does not appear in the ad until the end. The story focuses on a little girl growing up and the dad trusting his beloved daughter with a Subaru. Many of the Super Bowl ads now feature the storytelling approach. Budweiser developed ads showing a small calf and colt growing up together and developing a strong bond. Another Budweiser ad features a dog that keeps returning to a farm because he developed a relationship with one of the horses.

Testimonial Executions

Advertisers have achieved success with a testimonial type of execution for many years, especially in the business-to-business and service sectors. A customer relating a positive experience with a brand offers a testimonial. In the business-to-business sector, testimonials from current customers add credibility to the claims. Most buyers believe what others say about a company more than they believe what a company says about itself. Testimonials generate greater credibility than self-proclamations.

Testimonials offer an effective method for promoting services. Services are intangible; they cannot be seen or touched and consumers cannot examine them before making decisions. A testimony from a current customer provides a succinct description of the benefits or attributes of the service. Choosing a dentist, an attorney, or an automobile repair shop employee often leads customers to ask friends, relatives, or coworkers. A testimonial advertisement simulates this type of word-of-mouth recommendation.

Testimonials can enhance company credibility. Endorsers and famous individuals do not always have high levels of credibility, because consumers know they are being paid for their endorsements. The same holds true for paid actors who look like everyday consumers. The most believable testimonies come from everyday people, actual customers. Retailer Stein Mart featured real customers talking about their favorite merchandise in a recent TV campaign. Marketers recruited customers through the company's Facebook page. The TV spots encouraged customers to create videos about their favorite merchandise at Stein Mart and upload them to the website. The goals

▼ An advertisement featuring a testimony execution.

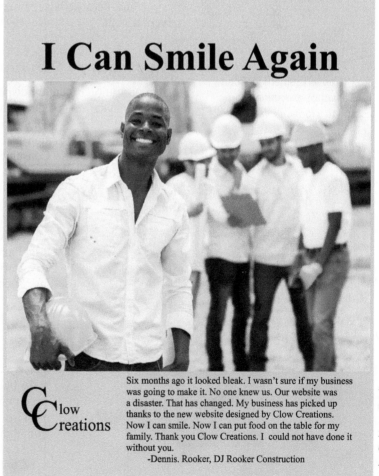

I Can Smile Again

CClow
Creations

Six months ago it looked bleak. I wasn't sure if my business was going to make it. No one knew us. Our website was a disaster. That has changed. My business has picked up thanks to the new website designed by Clow Creations. Now I can smile. Now I can put food on the table for my family. Thank you Clow Creations. I could not have done it without you.
-Dennis. Rooker, DJ Rooker Construction

© Andres Rodriguez/Fotolia

were to reach a younger target market, women between 35 and 55, and to create an online community of avid customers who found something they love at Stein Mart.[44]

Authoritative Executions

When using the authoritative execution, the advertiser seeks to convince viewers regarding a brand's superiority. *Expert authority* constitutes one form. The ads employ a physician, dentist, engineer, or chemist to state the particular brand's advantages compared to other brands. Firms also can feature less recognized experts such as automobile mechanics, professional house painters, and aerobics instructors. These individuals talk about the attributes or benefits of the product that make the brand superior.

Many authoritative advertisements include scientific or survey evidence. Independent organizations such as the American Medical Association undertake a variety of product studies. Quoting the results generates greater credibility. Survey results may be less credible. Stating that four out of five dentists recommend a particular toothbrush or toothpaste may not be as effective, because consumers do not have details about how the survey was conducted or even how many dentists were surveyed (5 or 500). In contrast, an American Medical Association statement that an aspirin a day reduces the risk of a second heart attack will be highly credible. Bayer can take advantage of the finding by including the information in the company's ads. The same holds true when a magazine such as *Consumer Reports* ranks a particular brand as the best.

The authoritative approach assumes consumers and business decision makers rely on cognitive processes when making purchase decisions and that they will pay attention to an ad and carefully think about the information conveyed in it. The approach works well in print ads, because buyers take the time to read the claim or findings presented in the advertisement.

Demonstration Executions

A demonstration execution displays how a product works. It provides an effective way to communicate the product's benefits to viewers. Recent advertisements for Swiffer demonstrated the product's multiple uses by cleaning a television screen, a wooden floor, a saxophone, and light fixtures. Consumers were shown how to use the product while at the same time hearing about its advantages.

Business-to-business ads often present demonstrations. These allow a business to illustrate how a product meets the specific needs of another business. For example, GoldTouch, Inc. can demonstrate the InstaGold Flash System, which deposits a bright and uniform gold surface finish on products, such as jewelry, through a nonelectrical current process of immersion plating. Such demonstrations can be presented via television ads or flash media ads on the internet.

Fantasy Executions

Fantasy executions lift the audience beyond the real world to a make-believe experience. Some are meant to be realistic. Others are completely irrational. Viewers often more clearly recall the most irrational and illogical ads. Fantasies can deal with anything from a dream vacation spot or cruise ships to a juicy hamburger or an enticing DiGiorno pizza.

Common fantasy themes include sex, love, or romance. Some marketing experts believe sex and nudity in advertising have lost their impact. Instead, advertisers feature a softer, more subtle presentation. Fantasy fits with target audiences that

▼ This advertisement for Biltmore uses a fantasy execution of an escape to a romantic castle.

have a preference for a tamer presentation. Instead of raw sexuality, fantasy takes them into a world of romantic make-believe.

The perfume and cologne industries often employ fantasy executions. In the past, a common theme was that splashing on the cologne caused women to flock to a man. For women, the reverse was suggested. Although used extensively, these ads were not particularly effective because people did not believe them. Currently, perfume advertisers tend to portray the product as enhancing a couple's love life or making a man or woman feel more sensuous.

Informative Executions

Informative advertisements present information to the audience in a straightforward manner. Agencies prepare informative messages extensively for radio commercials, where only verbal communication takes place. Informative ads are less common in television and print, because consumers tend to ignore them. With so many ads bombarding the consumer, it takes more than just the presentation of information to capture someone's attention. The Philadelphia Cream Cheese ad shown here has an excellent chance of being noticed for two reasons: it utilizes an eye-catching image, and it provides a recipe with instructions on how to prepare the cheesecake bars.

Consumers who are highly involved in a particular product category pay attention to an informational ad. Business buyers in the process of gathering information for either a new buy or a modified rebuy will notice an informative commercial. When a business does not need a particular product, buying center members often pay less attention to the advertisement. Thus, informative ads tend to work best in high-involvement situations. Many advertisers believe that business buyers desire detailed information in order to make intelligent buying decisions. As a result, the informative framework continues to be a popular approach for business-to-business advertisers.

Correct placement of an informative advertisement is vital. An informative advertisement about a restaurant placed on a radio station just before noon will be listened to more carefully than one that runs at 3:00 p.m. An informative ad about a diet product in an issue of *Glamour* that has a special article on weight control or exercising will be noticed more than if it is placed in the fashion section of the magazine. An informative business ad featuring a new piece of industrial equipment works well next to an article about the capital costs of equipment.

Beyond these executional frameworks, the creative selects the other ingredients, including music, copy, color, motion, light, and the size of a print ad. Almost any of these executions can be used within the format of one of the various appeals and message strategies. A slice-of-life can depict a fear appeal and cognitive message strategy. Informative ads may be humorous, but so can animations. Testimonials or demonstrations are rational or emotional, and can deploy any of the three message strategies. As the advertising campaign comes together, one element remains, finding the face or voice for the product.

pheel
triumphant

Philadelphia Vanilla Mousse Cheesecake

Makes 16 servings:
40 NILLA Wafers, crushed (about 1½ cups)
3 Tbsp. butter or margarine, melted
4 pkg. (8 oz. each) PHILADELPHIA Cream Cheese, softened, divided
1 cup sugar, divided
1 Tbsp. plus 1 tsp. vanilla, divided
3 eggs
1 tub (8 oz.) COOL WHIP Whipped Topping, thawed

HEAT oven to 325°F. Mix wafer crumbs and butter; press onto bottom of 9-inch springform pan.

BEAT 3 pkg. cream cheese, ¾ cup sugar and 1 Tbsp. vanilla with mixer until well blended. Add eggs one at a time, mixing on low speed after each just until blended. Pour over crust.

BAKE 50 to 55 min. or until center is almost set. Run knife around rim of pan to loosen cake; cool completely in pan.

BEAT remaining cream cheese, sugar and vanilla with mixer in large bowl until well blended. Whisk in COOL WHIP; spread over cheesecake. Refrigerate 4 hours. Remove rim of pan before serving cheesecake. Garnish with fresh berries if desired.

© 2012 Kraft Foods

PHILADELPHIA   pheel the moment

Kraft Foods, Inc.

▲ An advertisement for Philadelphia Cream Cheese using an informative execution.

Sources and Spokespersons

When creating a commercial or ad, the final issue facing the creative, the company, and the account executive will be the choice of the **source or spokesperson**, who delivers an advertising message visually and/or verbally. Selection of this individual often constitutes a critical choice. Consider, for example, the impact of the spokesperson Flo in

objective 4
How are sources and spokespersons decisions related to advertising design?

▲ FIGURE 12

Types of Sources and Spokespersons

Progressive Insurance ads, or The Most Interesting Man in the World in commercials for Dos Equis beer. Both have greatly enhanced the visibility of the products they represent. Figure 12 identifies four types of sources and spokespersons.

Celebrity Spokespersons

Of the four types, celebrity spokespersons are the most common, even though their appearances in ads have been declining. The research firm Millward Brown noted that only around six percent of advertisements feature celebrity endorsements.[45] The high cost of celebrity endorsements represents a primary reason for the decline. Many ask for millions of dollars and want multiyear deals. Others may sign on for only one campaign. It cost the high-end fashion label Louis Vuitton $10 million for actress Angelina Jolie's appearance in a single advertising campaign.[46]

An advertiser employs a celebrity endorser when the person's stamp of approval enhances the brand's equity. Celebrities can also help create emotional bonds with brands. Transferring the bond that exists between the celebrity and the audience to the product being endorsed is the objective. A bond transfer will often be more profound for younger consumers. A MediaEDGE survey revealed that 30 percent of 18- to 34-year-olds would try a brand promoted by a celebrity. The survey also indicated that younger people are 50 percent more likely than older consumers to recommend a celebrity-endorsed product to others. Older consumers are less likely to be influenced by celebrity endorsements. Fewer than 14 percent reported that they would try a celebrity-endorsed product. Still, many advertisers believe that celebrity endorsements improve brand awareness and help define the brand's personality.[47]

Athletes constitute a significant component of the celebrity endorsers. Some, such as Danica Patrick, earn more from endorsements than they do from their sports. Top athletic endorsers include Phil Mickelson, Roger Federer, Lebron James, David Beckham, Cristiano Ronaldo, Alex Rodriguez, and, until recently, Tiger Woods. The top two female athletic endorsers are Danica Patrick and Maria Sharapova.[48]

Agencies also feature celebrities to help establish a brand "personality." The objective is to tie the brand's characteristics to those of the spokesperson. A brand personality

▶ Interstate Batteries features NASCAR driver Kyle Busch in some advertisements.

emerges after the brand has been established. The celebrity helps to define the brand more clearly. Using celebrities for new products does not always work as well as it does for established brands.

Additional Celebrity Endorsements Four additional variations of celebrity endorsements include unpaid spokespersons, celebrity voiceovers, dead person endorsements, and social media endorsements. *Unpaid spokespersons* are celebrities supporting a charity or cause by appearing in advertisements. These types of endorsements are highly credible and can entice significant contributions to a cause. Politicians, actors, musicians, and athletes all appear in these ads. A few years ago, a campaign featured a number of musicians plus former Presidents Bush and Clinton in an effort to raise money for Haiti after its devastating earthquake.

Celebrities may provide *voiceovers* for television and radio ads without being shown or identified. Agencies may use a voiceover because the celebrity provides a quality voice to the advertisement, even when individuals listening to the ad do not recognize the voice. Advertising executive Stan Richards noted, "We use Hollywood actors quite a bit. It's largely not for their celebrity; we're not interested in that. Our voice for Home Depot is Ed Harris, who is a terrific actor. I don't think anybody in the world knows it's him, but he can take a script and bring it to life."[49] One negative of voiceovers is that they can be a distraction if the consumer becomes focused on identifying the speaker rather than hearing the content of the ad.

A *dead person endorsement* occurs when a sponsor uses an image or past video or film featuring an actor or personality who has died. Dead person endorsements are somewhat controversial but are becoming more common. Bob Marley, Marilyn Monroe, John Wayne, John Lennon, Elvis Presley, and many others have appeared in ads and have even become spokespersons for products after dying.

The newest form of endorsements is through *social media*. Firms now pay celebrities to send promotional tweets for them. Most of these tweets are not cheap, costing between $200 and $10,000 per message. Snoop Dog was recently paid to tweet about the Toyota Sienna, which he called a "swagger wagon." Kathy Ireland has been hired by Therapedic International to endorse the company's mattresses through social media and Twitter.[50]

CEO Spokespersons

Instead of celebrities, advertisers can employ a CEO as the spokesperson or source. Michael Dell has appeared as the spokesperson for Dell. A highly visible and personable CEO can become a major asset for the firm and its products. Many local companies succeed, in part, because their owners are out front in small-market television commercials. They then begin to take on the status of local celebrities.

Experts

Expert sources include physicians, lawyers, accountants, and financial planners. These experts are not celebrities or CEOs. Experts provide backing for testimonials, serve as authoritative figures, demonstrate products, and enhance the credibility of informative advertisements.

▼ Showing the partners, Ronquillo and Godwin, in this advertisement for litigation services adds credibility.

Gosdwin Ronquilo PC

▲ An advertisement for Richland State Bank using typical persons.

Typical Persons

Typical persons are one of two types. The first includes paid actors or models that portray or resemble everyday people. The second is actual, typical, everyday people. Wal-Mart has featured store employees in freestanding insert advertisements. Agencies also create "man-on-the-street" types of advertisements. For example, PERT shampoo recently prepared ads showing an individual asking people if they would like to have their hair washed. Dr. Scholl's interviews people about foot problems that might be resolved with cushioned shoe inserts.

Real people sources are becoming more common. One reason may be the overuse of celebrities. Many experts believe that consumers have become bored by celebrity endorsers and that the positive impact today will be less than in the past. One study conducted in Great Britain indicated that 55 percent of the consumers surveyed reported that a famous face was not enough to hold their attention.[51]

Source Characteristics

In evaluating sources, most account executives and companies consider several characteristics. The effectiveness of an advertising campaign that utilizes a spokesperson depends on the degree to which the person has one or more of the characteristics listed in Figure 13.

Credibility The composite of attractiveness, similarity, likeability, trustworthiness, and expertise creates credibility, which in turn affects the receiver's acceptance of the spokesperson and message.[52] People believe credible sources. Most sources do not score highly on all five attributes, yet they need to score highly on multiple characteristics to be viewed as credible. Celebrities may be more likely to possess at least an element of all characteristics. A CEO, expert, or typical person probably lacks one or more of them.

Attractiveness Two forms of attractiveness include physical and personality characteristics. Physical attractiveness contributes an important asset for an endorser. Advertisements with physically attractive spokespersons fare better than advertisements with less attractive people, for both male and female audiences. The attractiveness of the spokesperson's personality will also be important to many consumers, because it helps viewers form emotional bonds with the spokesperson. When the spokesperson exhibits a sour personality, even if physically beautiful, consumers become less likely to develop an emotional bond with the individual and the product.

Similarity Closely related to attractiveness is similarity. Consumers are more inclined to be influenced by a message delivered by a similar person. A "stay-at-home" mom may be more influenced by an advertisement that starts out with a woman saying, "Since

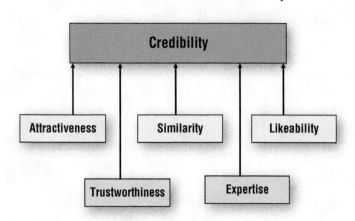

▲ **FIGURE 13**

Characteristics of Effective Spokespersons

◀ Attractiveness remains an important source characteristic even for children in ads, such as this one for Ouachita Independent Bank.

▼ Terry Bradshaw's high degree of likeability makes him an excellent choice to be the spokesperson for Community Trust Bank.

I made the decision to stop working and care for my family full-time...." Similarity leads the viewer to identify with the spokesperson. Dove recently launched a series of ads featuring male athletes, but the focus was on them and their families, not sports. Individuals such as Magic Johnson, Drew Brees, and Shaquille O'Neal talk about being "comfortable in their own skin."

At other times, *identification* comes from the belief that the source has similar beliefs, attitudes, preferences, or behaviors or faces the same or a similar situation as the customer. Female fans are able to identify with female jockey Anna Roberts as the "new face of horse racing" because many females have enjoyed horseback riding and have dreamed of winning a famous horse race. Identification was also gained because most jockeys are males. Anna Roberts immediately gained similarity and identification with female fans.

Likeability   Attractiveness and similarity are closely linked to likability. Consumers respond positively to spokespersons they like. Viewers may like an actor or the character played by the actor in a movie. La-Z-Boy signed a multiyear agreement with Brook Shields to serve as its celebrity spokesperson. The campaign targeted females ages 35 to 64 who report a high degree of likeability for her.[53] Terry Bradshaw is one the most well-known and well-liked retired athletes and hosts of football telecasts.

1. Betty White
2. Denzel Washington
3. Sandra Bullock
4. Clint Eastwood
5. Tom Hanks
6. Harrison Ford
7. Morgan Freeman
8. Kate Middleton
9. Will Smith
10. Johnny Depp

▲ **FIGURE 14**
The 10 Most Trusted Celebrities

▼ Willie Robertson, star of reality TV show *Duck Dynasty*, has a high level of expertise for truck suspension and lift kits.

Choosing him as a spokesperson for Community Trust Bank was easy, because he is also one of the bank's customers.

Consumers who do not like a particular spokesperson are inclined to transfer that dislike to the brand. This explains why many companies who retained Tiger Woods quickly dropped him as an endorser in 2010 after his extramarital affairs became public. The worry was that his endorsement would result in a negative impact on attitudes toward the brand. In other situations, it may not be an automatic transfer because consumers recognize that endorsers are paid spokespersons.

Trustworthiness   A celebrity may be likeable or attractive but may not be viewed as trustworthy. Trustworthiness represents the degree of confidence or the level of acceptance consumers place in the spokesperson's message. A trustworthy spokesperson helps consumers believe the message. Likeability and trustworthiness are connected. People who are liked tend to be trusted, and people who are disliked tend not to be trusted. A Reuters/Ipsos survey revealed that celebrities ranking the highest in terms of trustworthiness included Betty White, Denzel Washington, Sandra Bullock, and Clint Eastwood (see Figure 14 for a complete list). The most unpopular personalities included Paris Hilton, Charlie Sheen, Britney Spears, Arnold Schwarzenegger, and Tiger Woods.[54]

Expertise   Spokespersons exhibiting higher levels of expertise become more believable. Kyle Bush and Jeff Gordon are experts when advertising automobile products and lubricants. Willie Robertson, star of reality TV show *Duck Dynasty*, is viewed as an expert for off-road vehicles.

Often when a commercial requires expertise, the advertising agency opts for the CEO or a trained or educated expert in the field. American Express features Maria Barraza, a small-business owner and designer, to promote its Small Business Services. Expertise can be valuable in persuasive advertisements designed to change opinions or attitudes. Spokespersons with high levels of expertise are more capable of persuading an audience than someone with zero or low expertise.[55]

Matching Source Types and Characteristics

The account executive, ad agency, and corporate sponsor, individually or jointly, may choose the type of spokesperson. They can choose a celebrity, CEO, expert, or typical person, and the specific individual should have the key source characteristics.

In terms of trustworthiness, believability, persuasiveness, and likeability, celebrities tend to score well. These virtues increase when the match between the product and celebrity consists of a logical and proper fit. Phil Mickelson endorsing golf merchandise offers a good fit. Some celebrities have become almost as famous for their

Skyjacker Suspensions

advertising appearances as for an acting or athletic career. Danica Patrick has signed endorsement contracts with Honda, Secret, Boost Mobile, Pepsi, and Go Daddy, possibly gaining as much notoriety from endorsements as she has from competing in races.[56]

Two dangers exist when using celebrities. First, any negative publicity about a celebrity caused by inappropriate conduct may damage credibility. Michael Vick's arrest and conviction for dog fighting created considerable negative press. A second danger of using celebrities occurs when they endorse too many products. Advertising research indicates that when a celebrity endorses multiple products, it tends to reduce likeability as well as consumer attitudes toward the brand.[57]

A CEO or other prominent corporate official may or may not possess the characteristics of attractiveness and likeability. CEOs should, however, appear to be trustworthy, have expertise, and maintain a degree of credibility. A CEO is not a professional actor or model. It might be difficult for the CEO to come across well in a commercial.

First and foremost, experts should be credible. The advertising agency seeks an attractive, likeable, and trustworthy expert. Experts are helpful in promoting health care products and other high-involvement types of products. Recent research indicates that experts are more believable than celebrities for high-technology products. As a result, the use of an expert reduces a consumer's level of perceived risk in purchasing the brand, which means they are the most helpful when consumers or businesses perceive high levels of risk involved in a purchase.[58]

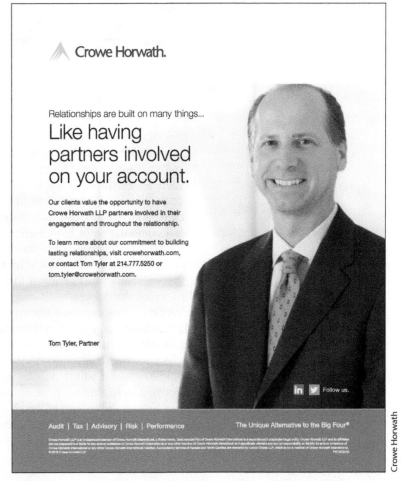

▲ Showing Tom Tyler, a partner in the firm, presents the source characteristics of trustworthiness, expertise, and credibility.

Advertisements with typical persons are sometimes difficult to prepare, especially when they employ real persons. Typical person sources do not have the name recognition of celebrities. Consequently, advertisers often feature multiple sources within one advertisement to build credibility. Increasing the number of sources makes the ad more effective. Hearing three people talk about a good dentist will be more believable than hearing it from only one person. By using multiple sources, viewers are motivated to pay attention and process its arguments.[59]

Real person ads present a double-edged sword. On the one hand, trustworthiness, similarity, and credibility rise for a bald or overweight source or someone with other physical imperfections. This can be especially valuable when the bald person promotes a hair replacement program or the overweight source talks about a diet program. On the other hand, attractiveness and likeability may be lower.

For the first time in its history, Pizza Hut decided to go with servers, bartenders, and franchise executives in their advertisements rather than celebrities. Dan Howard, a marketing professor at Southern Methodist University, noted, "With an actor, there's an inherent loss of persuasiveness because they are paid. Employees are not viewed in the same way as paid actors. They have greater credibility." One of the employees, 28-year-old Ashlie Marquez, who was featured in an ad further stated, "We're real employees who know what the customer likes and we can talk more passionately about it." Many viewers see employees as credible. Featuring employees in ads has also generated a positive effect on the company's culture, because the company recognizes that employees make a difference and celebrates their work.[60]

In general, the advertising agency wants to be certain that the source or spokesperson has the major characteristics the advertisement requires. Likeability would be important when creating a humorous appeal. In a rational or informational ad, expertise and credibility are crucial, especially in business-to-business ads. In each case, trying to include as many of the characteristics as possible when retaining a spokesperson will be the goal.

International Implications

Many of the international implications of advertising design have already been described in this chapter. Message strategies, advertising appeals, and executions should be adapted to cultural differences. As a small example, fear of body odor often sells products in the United States. In other cultures, body odor does not carry the same meaning. Sexual appeals should be adjusted to fit the laws and customs of a region. Advertisers should seek to understand these differences before designing advertising messages. For example, a combination of humor and sex would not be advisable in a commercial designed for a French audience. The French culture, while quite comfortable with overt sexuality and nudity, does not find sex to be funny.

Care should also be given to language and translation. For example, Sega recently discovered that its product's name is slang for "masturbation" in Italian, after a major advertising campaign had started. Marketers make great efforts to avoid such mistakes. Musical tastes vary, as do perceptions of rationality and scarcity. Emotions may be stronger in some cultures, whereas in others people are much more reserved.

An international company or a firm seeking to expand into additional countries should adapt and adjust the message strategy, appeal, and execution in order to create effective advertisements. Sources and spokesperson may have differing levels of success, depending on the culture of the country involved. Finally, finding universal themes, such as *visual Esperanto,* may be of great help to the international advertising creative.

Summary

A message strategy represents the primary tactic or approach used to deliver an advertisement's message theme. Three categories of message strategies include cognitive, affective, and conative approaches. Cognitive message strategies present rational arguments of pieces of information to consumers. Cognitive approaches include generic messages, preemptive messages, unique selling propositions, hyperbole, and comparative advertisements. Affective message strategies seek to invoke feelings or emotions that match those feelings with a good or service. Affective approaches include resonance advertising, comfort marketing, and emotional methods. Conative message strategies seek to lead directly to a consumer response. Each message exhibits specific advantages and disadvantages. Marketing teams seek to match the strategy with the message to be delivered.

Advertising creatives form advertising messages using one (or more) of the seven major appeals: fear, humor, sex (through sensual, suggestive, nudity-based, or overt formats), music, rationality, emotions, or scarcity. Logical combinations of these appeals for various messages can be utilized. Often, music provides the backdrop for messages invoking fear, humor, sex, and emotions. Humor can be linked with

sex, music, rationality (by showing how being illogical is silly or funny), and scarcity. Rationality combines with fear in many commercials. Creatives seek to design message arguments that take advantage of the various characteristics of these appeals, break through clutter, and convince the audience to buy the item.

Executional frameworks constitute the manner in which an advertising appeal will be presented and the message strategy will be conveyed. Executions include animation, slice-of-life, testimonial, authoritative, demonstration, fantasy-based, and informative approaches. These methods can be used to enhance the effectiveness of an advertisement.

Sources or spokespersons present the advertising message visually and/or verbally. Celebrities, CEOs, experts, and typical persons can serve as sources. Advertisers seek to enhance the quality of the message by relying on the credibility, attractiveness, similarity, likeability, trustworthiness, and expertise of the spokesperson.

The process of designing ads for international markets is similar to that for domestic ads. The major difference is careful consideration of local attitudes and customers, with due care given to the language, slang, and symbols of the area.

Key Terms

message strategy The primary tactic or approach used to deliver a message theme

cognitive message strategy A strategy used to present rational arguments or pieces of information to consumers

generic message An advertisement that directly promotes a product's attributes or benefits without any claim of superiority

preemptive message An advertising claim of superiority based on a product's specific attribute or benefit with the intent of preventing the competition from making the same or a similar statement

unique selling proposition An explicit, testable claim of uniqueness or superiority in an advertisement

hyperbole An untestable advertising claim based on some attribute or benefit

comparative advertisement The direct or indirect advertising comparison with a competitor based on some product attribute or benefit

affective message strategies Advertisements trying to evoke feeling or emotions that match those feelings with the good, service, or company

comfort marketing A form of resonance advertising designed to encourage consumer to purchase branded

product rather than generic versions because the branded product has stood the test of time

emotional affective approach An advertising method that attempts to elicit powerful emotions that will lead to product recall and choice

conative message strategy An advertising approach designed to lead directly to a consumer response

advertising appeals Advertising approaches to reaching consumers with ads, featuring an element of fear, humor, sex, music, rationality, emotions, or scarcity

severity The part of the fear behavioral response model that leads the individual to consider how strong certain negative consequences of an action will be

vulnerability The part of the fear behavioral response model that leads the individual to consider the odds of being affected by the negative consequences of an action

decorative models Individuals in advertisements whose primary purpose is to adorn the product as a sexual or attractive stimulus without serving a functional role

source or spokesperson The individual who delivers an advertising message visually and/or verbally

MyMarketingLab

Go to **mymktlab.com** to complete the problems marked with this icon .

Review Questions

1. What is a message strategy?

2. Describe a cognitive message strategy and identify the five major forms advertisers can use.

3. What is spontaneous trait transference in comparison advertising?

4. Describe an affective message strategy and identify the primary forms it can take in an advertisement.

5. What is comfort marketing?

6. What is the attitude sequence present in a conative message strategy advertisement?

7. What are the seven most common types of advertising appeals?

8. What are the advantages and disadvantages of fear appeals in advertising?

9. When does humor work in an ad? What pitfalls should companies avoid in using humorous appeals?

10. What types of sexual appeals can advertisers use?

11. When are sexual appeals most likely to succeed? To fail?

12. Name the different ways music can play a role in an advertisement. Explain how each role should match individual appeals, media, and other elements in the design of the ad.

13. Compare the advantages and disadvantages of rational appeals to emotional appeals.

14. What types of execution frameworks can be used when developing an advertisement?

15. Describe how each of the executional frameworks can be used in ad development.

16. What four types of sources or spokespersons can be used by advertisers?

17. What are the most desirable characteristics of a source or spokesperson?

Critical Thinking Exercises

DISCUSSION QUESTIONS

18. Select five advertisements from a magazine. Identify the message strategy, appeal, and executional framework used. Did the creative select the right combination for the advertisement? What other message strategies or executions could have been used?

19. Studies involving comparative advertisements versus noncomparative ads produced the following findings. Discuss why you think each statement is true. Try to think of comparative ads you have seen that substantiate these claims.

   a. Message awareness was higher for comparative ads than for noncomparative ads if the brands are already established brands.

   b. Brand recall was higher for comparative ads than for noncomparative ads.

   c. Comparative ads were viewed as less believable than noncomparative ads.

   d. Attitudes toward comparative ads were more negative than toward noncomparative ads.

20. Watch one of your favorite television shows. Record all of the television commercials in one commercial break (at least seven ads). Identify the appeal used in each one. Were the ads effective? Why or why not?

21. Locate a print ad or television ad that features a fear appeal. Using the behavioral response model shown in this chapter, identify various elements in the ad that correspond with the components in the model. Some of the elements will require thinking beyond what is visually or verbally present in the ad itself.

22. Locate five television commercials on YouTube or find five print advertisements that use sex appeals. Identify which of the four ways sexuality was used. Evaluate each ad in terms of the appropriateness and effectiveness of the sex appeal.

23. Identify an advertisement that uses each of the following executional frameworks. Evaluate the advertisement in terms of how well it is executed. Also, did the appeal and message strategy fit well with the execution? Was the ad memorable? What made it memorable?

   a. Animation
   b. Slice-of-life
   c. Testimonial
   d. Authoritative
   e. Demonstration
   f. Fantasy
   g. Informative

24. Find a copy of a business journal such as *Business Week* or *Fortune* or a trade journal. Also locate a copy of a consumer journal such as *Glamour, Time, Sports Illustrated*, or a specialty magazine. Look through an entire issue. What differences between the advertisements in the business journal and consumer journals are readily noticeable? For each of the concepts listed below, discuss specific differences you noted between the two types of magazines. Explain why the differences exist.

   a. Message strategies
   b. Appeals
   c. Executional frameworks
   d. Sources and spokespersons

25. A manager from a resort in Florida wants to develop an advertisement highlighting scuba diving lessons. The target market will be college students. Identify the best combination of message strategy, appeal, and execution. Justify your choice. What message strategy, appeal, and execution would you use if the target market was families with children? Justify your choice. Choose one of the target markets. Design a print ad using the design combination you selected.

26. Name three influential spokespersons. For each one, discuss the five characteristics used to evaluate spokespersons and their overall level of credibility. Next, make a list of three individuals who are poor spokespersons. Discuss each of the five evaluation characteristics for each of these individuals. What differences exist between an effective and a poor spokesperson?

Integrated Learning Exercises

27. Current as well as past Super Bowl ads are available at **www.superbowl-ads.com**. Access the site and compare Super Bowl ads over the last several years. What types of message strategies were used? What types of appeals were used? What types of executions were used? Who and what types of endorsers or spokespersons were used? Compare and contrast these four elements of ads over the last three years of Super Bowl ads.

28. Most advertising agencies provide examples of advertisements on company websites. The goal is to display the agency's creative abilities to potential clients. Using a search engine, locate three different advertising agencies. Locate samples of their work. Compare the ads produced by your three agencies in terms of message strategies, appeals, executions, and spokespersons. What similarities do you see? What differences do you see? Which agency, in your opinion, is the most creative? Why?

29. Visit the following websites. Identify the primary message strategy, appeal, and execution used. Evaluate the quality of the website based on message strategy, appeal, and execution. Do the sites utilize a spokesperson? If so, who is it and which type is he or she? Evaluate the spokesperson in terms of the components of credibility.
    a. Johnson & Johnson (**www.jnj.com**)
    b. Hyundai Motors, USA (**www.hyundaiusa.com**)

    c. Skechers (**www.skechers.com**)
    d. Bijan Fragrances (**www.bijan.com**)
    e. Applebee's (**www.applebees.com**)

30. Visit the following websites. Identify the primary message strategy, appeal, and execution used. Evaluate the quality of the website based on message strategy, appeal, and execution. Do the sites utilize a spokesperson? If so, who is it and which type is he or she? Evaluate the spokesperson in terms of the components of credibility.
    a. Ruby Tuesdays (**www.rubytuesday.com**)
    b. Bonne Bell (**www.bonnebell.com**)
    c. MessageMedia (**www.message-media.com**)
    d. Jantzen (**www.jantzen.com**)
    e. Jockey International (**www.jockey.com**)

Student Project

CREATIVE CORNER

It is time to try your creativity with a television advertisement. Borrow a camcorder and develop a 30- or 45-second television spot for one of the following products, using the suggested appeal. Before designing the ad, decide on the message strategy and execution you will use. Justify your decision. If you do not have access to a camcorder, then develop a magazine advertisement.

a. Denim skirt, sex appeal
b. Tennis racket, humor appeal
c. Ice cream, emotional appeal
d. Vitamins, fear appeal
e. Golf club, rational appeal
f. Spring break trip package, scarcity appeal
g. Restaurant, music appeal

Blog Exercises

Access the authors' blog for this text at the URLs provided to complete these exercises. Answer the questions that are posed on the blog.

31. Television ads, set 1 - **http://blogclowbaack.net/2014/05/08/television-ads-set-1-chapter-6/**
32. Television ads, set 2 - **http://blogclowbaack.net/2014/05/08/television-ads-set-2-chapter-6/**
33. Television ads, set 3 - **http://blogclowbaack.net/2014/05/08/television-ads-set-3-chapter-6/**
34. Television ads, set 4 - **http://blogclowbaack.net/2014/05/08/television-ads-set-4-chapter-6/**

CASE 1 ▸ PEERLESS MARKETING

In the United States, the majority of homes have indoor plumbing. Sinks, faucets, toilets, and other pieces of hardware are largely taken for granted. Only in two circumstances are they prominently in the minds of customers. The first is when a plumbing product is purchased for the first time, such as when a home is built or an area is refurbished. The second is when an item is defective and must be replaced.

The challenge to manufacturers is to make certain that a company's brand is remembered by consumers and preferred by builders and plumbers. The products must be placed in stores such as Home Depot or Lowes in ways that make them easy to find and always accessible.

One of the major players in the plumbing fixture marketplace is Delta Faucet Company. A strange path brought the company to prominence. In the 1920s, an immigrant named Alex Manoogian founded Masco Company, which provided auto parts. Twenty-five years later, Manoogian was contacted by an inventor who had created the first washerless faucet. Although it was not related to his current business, Manoogian saw the potential and refined the item, which was first sold out of the trunks of salesmen's cars, as the first Delta Faucet. The name was chosen because a key part of the product resembled the shape of the Greek letter delta.

The Delta Faucet Company became a separate part of the original Masco Company and relocated. Over the next two decades, it expanded quickly to an entire line of products. Currently, Delta Faucet Company is a multinational firm with four primary locations: Indianapolis, Indiana; Jackson, Tennessee; London Ontario, Canada; and Panyu, China. It sells more than one million faucets per month. The overall Masco Company now sells door hardware and locks, cabinets, and glass products in addition to faucets.

The Delta line includes two other names: Brizo and Peerless. Brizo is the high-end line of faucets, Delta is the flagship and primary brand, and Peerless is the lower-end line of items.

The primary advertising challenges appear to exist in four main areas. First, company leaders must make sure that one brand does not cannibalize the others. The brands must remain as distinct products offered to separate sets of consumers. Second, the brands must be viewed as the primary choices and must be remembered by consumers when the time comes to buy a plumbing fixture. Third, there cannot be brand confusion. Builders and plumbers must believe that the fixtures are distinct along several lines, including quality and durability, ease of installation, and strong warranties, but they must also be

yo/Fotolia

▲ Delta Faucet Company offers a wide variety of faucets for the consumer market.

perceived as being fashionable. Fourth, innovation has become a new part of the plumbing fixture industry. A wide variety of options exist. Delta's products must compete with all the new faucet variations and retain its position as one of the premier manufacturers.

Complications occur due to differences in markets and customers. Many contractors and builders are simply looking for a low-cost option, especially when lower-end rental properties and similar units are being developed. Plumbers may be willing to install a wide variety of products. They will consider the costs of a product but also want something that will be easy to install and that will be durable. Individual consumers are the most likely to be interested in other product qualities such as novel features and the look of the product.

35. What type of message strategy should Delta Faucet Company utilize? Should it be the same for all of the brands and in all of the markets (builders, plumbers, consumers)?

36. What type of advertising appeal makes the most sense for Delta Faucet Company advertising to individual consumers? To contractors, builders, and plumbers? How does the appeal you selected match the message strategy chosen in Question 1?

37. What types of executional framework should be used in traditional advertisements aimed at each of the target audiences: consumers, contractors, builders, and plumbers? Explain how it fits with the message strategies and appeals you have already selected.

38. Should the company use a spokesperson? If so, which one of the four types should be used? Justify your answers. Discuss how the individual you selected will possess the characteristics of spokespersons described in the chapter.

Source: www.deltafaucet.com (accessed April 20, 2012).

CASE 2 ▸ BLACK-EYED MARKETING

If Black Eyed Peas band member will.i.am wasn't in music, "He'd be the best ad executive on Madison Avenue," says Randy Phillips, president and CEO of the concert promoter AEG Live. "I've never seen anyone more astute at dealing with sponsors' and companies' needs and understanding their brands." The Black Eyed Peas have been able to move beyond the status as a high-energy band into the world of corporate sponsorship without missing a beat.

Marketers love the Black Eyed Peas for the diverse ethnicity of the band's members, writes the *Wall Street Journal*. The band's corporate backers include Coors, Levi's, Honda, Apple, Verizon, and Pepsi. The advertisement featuring the group's song "Hey Mama" and dancing silhouettes that was used to help launch Apple's iTunes store gained almost iconic status.

What makes this group of musicians such an effective set of spokespeople? Part of the appeal is the group's global fan base and the Pea's fetching party anthems, with powerful dance beats, crazy special effects, and repetitive hooks that are integrated into numerous party mixes. As one critic noted, the band achieves the nearly impossible—making both kids and their parents feel cool at the same time.

Beyond the glitz and glitter of the shows, the group gives careful thought to its marketing. Oftentimes, will.i.am pitches concepts to corporate sponsors himself, using "decks" that sum up the Peas' package, frequently in PowerPoint form. He reports, "I consider us a brand. A brand always has stylized decks, from colors to fonts. Here's our demographic. Here's the reach. Here's the potential. Here's how the consumer will benefit from the collaboration."

There was a time when rock and roll was nearly synonymous with rebellion. Bands with corporate ties would be

▲ The Black Eyed Peas use marketing to enhance the band's image and presence.

viewed as sell outs. For some companies, such a move would seem too risky, especially if the band's fans felt betrayed. Over the years, music has become less threatening, as Baby Boomers near retirement age.

The economics of music have also changed. Downloading and pirating CDs is commonplace. Bands can no longer count on record sales to make money. Many younger bands now look for other sources of income and publicity. The Peas were among the fastest learners of the industry's new math. Even now, however, the band hears complaints that they are merely shills. "You have to take the criticism, and sometimes it hurts a lot," says band member Stacy Ferguson, who is also known as Fergie.

Currently, many top-name musicians and groups have corporate sponsors. Cooperative advertisements promote the brand, the band, and often a tour. The Rolling Stones began the movement when the group's "Tattoo You" tour was sponsored by Jovan Musk cologne. Even groups that at first resolutely avoided corporate tie-ins, such as U2, have changed. U2 developed a relationship with Apple that included commercials featuring the song "Vertigo." The band helped with BlackBerry commercials and had a sponsored tour with the brand.

The Black Eyed Peas continues to expand its corporate connections. A concert in Times Square that promoted Samsung's new line of 3-D televisions led to a meeting with *Avatar* director James Cameron, who agreed to direct a feature film about the Peas. The 3-D film incorporates concerts, travel footage, and narrative themes about technology, dreams, and the brain.

According to will.i.am, all corporate partnerships are equally important. The band lends its music at relatively small charges in exchange for exposure. "It wasn't about the check," says former manager Seth Friedman.

The efforts have paid off. The Black Eyed Peas have performed at an NFL season-kickoff show, New Year's Eve in Times Square, the Grammys, a Victoria's Secret fashion show, and the season opener for *The Oprah Winfrey Show*, for which they summoned a flash mob of synchronized dancers to downtown Chicago. As will.i.am puts it, "I get the credit from the brands. They know. I used to work with the marketing people and the agencies, now I work with the CEOs of these companies."

39. Discuss each of the source characteristics in terms of the Black Eyed Peas serving as a spokesperson for a product. Would it make a difference as to what type of product the Black Eyed Peas were endorsing? Explain.

40. What types of brands or products are best suited to endorsements by the Black Eyed Peas? By rock bands in general? What about country music artists? What about hip-hop artists?

41. If you were going to design a television advertisement for a concert for the Black Eyed Peas, who would be your target market? What message strategy, appeal, and executional framework would you use? Why? Describe your concept of an effective television ad.

42. Suppose the Black Eyed Peas were contracted to perform at your university. Design a print ad for your local student newspaper. Discuss the message strategy, appeal, and execution you used and why you used it.

Source: John Jurgensen, "The Most Corporate Band in America," *Wall Street Journal Online* (www.wsj.com, accessed April 14, 2010).

MyMarketingLab

Go to **mymktlab.com** for Auto-graded writing questions as well as the following Assisted-graded writing questions:

43. Watch one of your favorite television shows. Record all of the television commercials in one commercial break (at least seven ads). Identify the appeal used in each one. Were the ads effective? Why or why not?

44. Hardee's and Carl's Jr. recently used a television commercial featuring a schoolteacher dancing on top of her desk while a room full of guys performed a rap song entitled "I Like Flat Buns." The song seemed appropriate because the ad was for the Patty Melt on a flat bun. Instead, the ad received considerable flack because the sexy blonde schoolteacher was wearing a short, tight skirt. Teachers' associations complained that it was inappropriate because it was a "sexually exploitive assault" on teachers, students, and schools. Which type of sex appeal is being used? Discuss the appropriateness of this ad in terms of the concepts presented in the chapter in the "Sex" appeal section. What makes it effective? What makes in ineffective?

Endnotes

1. Mark Dolliver, "Assessing the Power of Ads," *Adweek .com* (http://adweek.com/aw/content_display/news/agency/e3i34e2ede5adb7e1e8aa21d1f4fa3b2d0b), June 22, 2009.

2. Henry A. Laskey, Ellen Day, and Melvin R. Crask, "Typology of Main Message Strategies for Television Commercials," *Journal of Advertising* 18, no. 1 (1989), pp. 36–41.

3. David Aaker and Donald Norris, "Characteristics of TV Commercials Perceived as Informative," *Journal of Advertising Research* 22, no. 2 (1982), pp. 61–70.

4. **www.campbellsoupcompany.com/atw_usa.asp** (accessed January 12, 2008).

5. Wolfgang Gruener, "Nintendo Wii Surrenders Market Share in Weak Game Console Market," *TG Daily* (**www.tgdaily.com/trendwatch-features/43289**), July 17, 2009.

6. Tony Smith, "Intel Extends Market Share Gains," *Register Hardware* (**www.reghardware.co.uk/2007/04/20/intel_vs_amd_q1_07/print.html**), April 20, 2007.

7. Shailendra Pratap Jain and Steven S. Posavac, "Valenced Comparisons," *Journal of Marketing Research* 41, no. 1 (February 2004), pp. 46–56.

8. Dhruv Grewal and Sukumar Kavanoor, "Comparative Versus Noncomparative Advertising: A Meta-Analysis," *Journal of Marketing* 61, no. 4 (October 1997), pp. 1–15; Shailendra Pratap Jain and Steven S. Posavac, "Valenced Comparisons," *Journal of Marketing Research* 41, no. 9. (February 2004), pp. 46–56.

9. "Microsoft's Google-Bashing Try Campaign Is Actually Working," *Advertising Age*, http://adage.com/print/244691, October 15, 2013.

10. Aaron Baar, "Subaru Taps Nostalgia for the First Car," *Marketing Daily*, February 26, 2012, www.mediapost.com/publications/article/168531.

11. Stuart Elliott, "In New Ads, Stirring Memories of Commercials Past," *The New York Times*, January 12, 2012, www.nytimes.com/2012/01/13/business/media/stirring-memories-of-commercials-past.

12. Joanne Lynch and Leslie de Chernatony, "The Power of Emotion: Brand Communication in Business-to-Business Markets," *Journal of Brand Management* 11, no. 5 (May 2004), pp. 403–420.

13. Based on Rosemary M. Murtaugh, "Designing Effective Health Promotion Messages Using Components of Protection Motivation Theory," *Proceedings of the Atlantic Marketing Association* (1999), pp. 553–57; R. W. Rogers and S. Prentice-Dunn, "Protection Motivation Theory," *Handbook of Health Behavior Research I: Personal and Social Determinants,* D. Gochman, ed. (New York: Plenum Press, 1997), pp. 130–32.

14. Ibid.

15. Michael S. Latour and Robin L. Snipes, "Don't Be Afraid to Use Fear Appeals: An Experimental Study," *Journal of Advertising Research* 36, no. 2 (March–April 1996), pp. 59–68.

16. Martin Eisend, "A Meta-Analysis of Humor Effects in Advertising," *Advances in Consumer Research–North American Conference Proceedings* 34 (2007), pp. 320–23.

17. James J. Kellaris and Thomas W. Cline, "Humor and Ad Memorability," *Psychology & Marketing* 24, no. 6 (June 2007), pp. 497–509.

18. Theresa Howard, "Windex Birds Make Clean Sweep as Most-Liked Ads," *USA Today* (December 18, 2006), p. 7B (Money).

19. Matthew Creamer, "Marketing's Era of Outrage," *Advertising Age* 78, no. 7 (February 12, 2007), pp. 1, 26.

20. "Sex Doesn't Sell," *The Economist* 373, no. 8399 (October 30, 2004), pp. 62–63.

21. Andrew Adam Newman, "Selling a Household Cleaning Product on Its...Sex Appeal?" *The New York Times* (**www.nytimes.com/2009/11/13/business/media/13adco.html**), November 13, 2009.

22. Sandra O'Loughlin, "Hanes Shows Some 'Love' in Battle for Intimates," *Brandweek* 48, no. 9 (February 26, 2007), p. 11.

23. Bob Garfield, "Dentyne Spot Makes It Seem That Naysayers Have a Point," *Advertising Age* 76, no. 5 (January 31, 2005), p. 41.

24. Based on G. Smith and R. Engel, "Influence of a Female Model on Perceived Characteristics of an Automobile," *Proceedings of the 76th Annual Convention of the American Psychological Association* 15, no. 3 (1968), pp. 46–54; Leonard Reid and Lawrence C. Soley, "Decorative Models and the Readership of Magazine Ads," *Journal of Advertising Research* 23 (April–May 1983), pp. 27–32; R. Chestnut, C. LaChance, and A. Lubitz, "The Decorative Female Model: Sexual Stimuli and the Recognition of Advertisements," *Journal of Advertising* 6 (Fall 1977), pp. 11–14.

25. Jessica Severn, George E. Belch, and Michael A. Belch, "The Effects of Sexual and Non-Sexual Advertising Appeals and Information Level on Cognitive Processing and Communication Effectiveness," *Journal of Advertising* 19, no. 1 (1990), pp. 14–22.

26. Tom Reichart, "Sex in Advertising Research: A

Review of Content, Effects, and Functions of Sexual Information in Consumer Advertising," *Annual Review of Sex Research* 13 (2002), pp. 242–74; D. C. Bello, R. E. Pitts, and M. J. Etzel, "The Communication Effects of Controversial Sexual Content in Television Programs and Commercials," *Journal of Advertising* 3, no. 12 (1983), pp. 32–42.

27. "Note to Chrysler: Gutter Humor Has No Place in Ads," *Automotive News* 78, no. 6064 (October 27, 2003), p. 12.

28. Tom Reichart, "Sex in Advertising Research: A Review of Content, Effects, and Functions of Sexual Information in Consumer Advertising," *Annual Review of Sex Research* 13 (2002), pp. 242–74; Andrew A. Mitchell, "The Effect of Verbal and Visual Components of Advertisements on Brand Attitude and Attitude Toward the Advertisement," *Journal of Consumer Research* 13 (June 1986), pp. 12–24.

29. Bruce Horovitz, "Risqué May Be Too Risky for Ads," *USA Today* (April 16, 2004), p. 1B.

30. Julie Naughton and Amy Wicks, "Eva's Seduction: Calvin Klein Stirs Controversy with Mendes Ads," *Women's Wear Daily* 196, no. 25 (August 4, 2008), p. 1.

31. Kate Lunau, "Study Finds Real Women Don't Sell," *Maclean's* 121, no. 33 (August 25, 2008), p. 34.

32. Howard Levine, Donna Sweeney, and Stephen H. Wagner, "Depicting Women as Sex Objects in Television Advertising," *Personality and Social Psychology Bulletin* 25, no. 8 (August 1999), pp. 1049–58.

33. Steve Oakes, "Evaluating Empirical Research into Music in Advertising: A Congruity Perspective," *Journal of Advertising Research* 47, no. 1 (March 2007), pp. 38–50.

34. Andrew Hampp, "A Reprise for Jingles in Madison Avenue," *Advertising Age*, September 6, 2010, http://adage.com/pring?article_id=145744.

35. Felicity Shea, "Reaching Youth with Music," *B&T Weekly* 54, no. 2491 (October 1, 2004), pp. 16–17.

36. Brian Steinberg, "The Times Are a-Changin' for Musicians and Marketers," *Advertising Age* 78, no. 43 (October 29, 2005) p. 43.

37. Nicole Rivard, "Maximizing Music," *SHOOT* 48, no. 4 (February 23, 2007), pp. 17–21.

38. Douglas Quenqua, "What's That Catchy Tune? A Song for Car Insurance Makes the Charts," *The New York Times* (**www.nytimes.com/2007/12/31/business/media/31allstate.html**), December 31, 2007.

39. Stuart Elliott, "Godiva Rides in a New Direction," *The New York Times* (**www.nytimes.com/2009/11/16/business/media/16adnewsletter1.html**), November 16, 2009.

40. Joanne Lynch and Leslie de Chernatony, "The Power of Emotion: Brand Communication in Business-to-Business Markets," *Journal of Brand Management* 11, no. 5 (May

2004), pp. 403–20; Karalynn Ott, "B-to-B Marketers Display Their Creative Side," *Advertising Age's Business Marketing* 84, no. 1 (January 1999), pp. 3–4.

41. Stephanie Thompson, "Big Deal," *Mediaweek* 7, no. 44 (November 24, 1997), p. 36; Judann Pollack, "Big G Has Special Cheerios for Big '00," *Advertising Age* (June 14, 1999), pp. 1–2.

42. Jim Hanas, "Rotoscope Redux," *Creativity* 10, no. 1 (February 2002), pp. 40–41.

43. Interview with Stan Richards by Donald Baack and Kenneth E. Clow, January 20, 2010.

44. Aaron Baar, "For Stein Mart, It's Love at First Find," *Marketing Daily*, September 10, 2011, www.mediapost.com/publications.

45. Matthew Warren, "Do Celebrity Endorsements Still Work?" *Campaign (UK)* 44 (November 2, 2007) p. 13.

46. "Angelina Joli to be $10m face of Louis Vuitton," *Marketing*, www.marketingmagazine.co.uk/news/1067170, accessed May 3, 2011.

47. "Highest Paid Athletes," *Buzzle.com*, www.buzzle.com/articles/highest-paid-athletes.htmil, accessed April 16, 2012.

48. Jonathan Wexler, "Who Is the Athlete With the Most Endorsements?" Playing Field Promotions (**www.playingfieldpromotions.com/blog/438/who-is-the-athlete-with-the-most-endorsements**), June 9, 2009.

49. Interview with Stan Richards by Donald Baack and Kenneth E. Clow, January 20, 2010.

50. Laura Petrecca, "Small Companies Seek Publicity from Celebrities," *USA Today*, www.usatoday.com/cleanprint/?1296061644796, accessed January 26, 2011.

51. Claire Murphy, "Stars Brought Down to Earth in TV Ads Research," *Marketing* (January 22, 1998), p. 1.

52. Kamile Junokaite, Sonata Alijosiene, and Rasa Gudonaviciene, "The Solutions of Celebrity Endorsers Selection for Advertising Products," *Economics & Management* 12, no. 3 (2007), pp. 384–90.

53. Stuart Elliott, "La-Z-Boy, Meet Brooke Shields," *The New York Times*, November 29, 2010, www.nytimes.com/2010/11/29/business/media/29adnewsletter1.html.

54. "Betty White Voted America's Most Trusted Celebrity: Poll," *Reuters*, August 18, 2011, www.reuters.com/assets/print?aid=USTRE77H2WE20110818.

55. Roobina Ohanian, "Construction and Validation of a Scale to Measure Celebrity Endorsers' Perceived Expertise," *Journal of Advertising* 19, no. 3 (1990), pp. 39–52.

56. Kenneth Hein, "Danica Patrick Talks GoDaddy, Pepsi," *Brandweek* (**www.brandweek.com/bw/content_display/news-and-features/direct/e3i7a35e791d5c**), November 30, 2009.

57. Dipayan Biswas, Abhijit Biswas, and Neel Das,

"The Differential Effects of Celebrity and Expert Endorsements on Consumer Risk Perceptions," *Journal of Advertising* 35, no. 2 (Summer 2006), pp. 17–31.

58. David J. Moore and John C. Mowen, "Multiple Sources in Advertising Appeals: When Product Endorsers Are Paid by the Advertising Sponsor," *Journal of Academy of Marketing Science* 22, no. 3 (Summer 1994), pp. 234–43.

59. Raymond R. Burke and Thomas K. Srull, "Competitive Interference and Consumer Memory for Advertising," *Journal of Consumer Research* 15 (June 1988), pp. 55–68.

60. Karen Robinson-Jacobs, "With Employees in Ads, Pizza Hut Goes for Slices of Life," *The Dallas Morning News*, November 17, 2010, www.dallasnews.com/sharedcontent/dws/bus/stories.

Traditional Media Channels

From Chapter 7 of *Integrated Advertising, Promotion, and Marketing Communications,* Seventh Edition. Kenneth E. Clow, Donald Baack.

Traditional Media Channels

Chapter Objectives

After reading this chapter, you should be able to answer the following questions:

1 What is a media strategy?

2 What elements and individuals are involved in media planning?

3 How do the terms used to describe advertising help the marketing team design effective campaigns?

4 What are some of the primary advertising objectives?

5 What are the advantages and disadvantages associated with each traditional advertising medium?

6 How can the marketing team use the media mix to increase advertising effectiveness?

7 What are the key issues associated with media selection for business-to-business markets?

8 What issues are associated with media selection in international markets?

Overview

If a tree falls in the forest and no one is present, does it make a sound? This philosophical question has been posed for many years and even recently appeared in a Geico Insurance commercial. Unfortunately, in the world of advertising, far too many "trees" fall as unheard and unseen advertisements. Successful marketing involves identifying target markets and finding the media that reach the members of those markets. Once the advertising team identifies the right media, creatives can design clever, memorable, exciting, and persuasive advertisements. When an advertising campaign succeeds, it may not only reach customers in traditional ways (television, magazines, radio), but in the new world of digital media it will be passed along and shared via the internet and in other ways.

WONDERFILLED OREOS

In 2013, Oreo cookies celebrated their 100th birthday. In honor of the event, the Virginia-based Martin Agency created the Wonderfilled Oreos campaign. Using animation, the campaign was driven by the theme, "Celebrate the Kid Inside." Television commercials served as the anchor for the campaign. They were combined with print advertising. Oreo-themed events took place across the country, in print advertisements, and were supported by a strong social media presence.

A special music piece was performed by the group Chitty Bang to pull the events together, called the "Wonderfilled Anthem." *Adweek* magazine labeled the music a "branded pop song cover." Sam Thielman from *Adweek* noted, "The loose-limbed Adventure Time-y animation seems to be getting a lot of traction with viewers on YouTube. At least one commenter proclaimed the original version 'the only YouTube ad that I'll sit through…'"[1]

The musical television campaign included commercials suggesting that eating Oreos will make bad things good, such as a vampire wanting milk to go with the cookies rather than stalking another victim. Another ad implies that Oreos would cause a shark to make friends with baby seals and squid. Oreo's advertising team then adapted the commercials to individual markets in other countries, creating an entertaining international campaign that gained significant traction in the world of social media.[2]

Traditional media continue to play an important role in developing a fully integrated marketing program. This chapter explains the various traditional media channels. It begins with

BlueSkyImages/Fotolia

an analysis of the media strategy as well as media planning processes. Next, common advertising terms are explained followed by an examination of advertising objectives. These processes lead to media choices and selection targeted to specific consumers, businesses, and customers in other countries.

Advertising agencies design a campaign within the framework of the overall integrated marketing communications program. Client companies depend on effective advertisements to attract customers and entice them into purchasing various goods and services. This helps build the firm's image and creates a larger customer base. Advertising media selection remains an important element in the process.

The Media Strategy

A **media strategy** involves analyzing and choosing media for an advertising and marketing campaign. The average consumer examines only nine of the more than 200 consumer magazines on the market. A radio listener usually tunes in to only three of the stations available in an area. Television viewers on average watch fewer than eight of the stations available via cable or satellite. Network prime-time ratings have declined by more than 30 percent over the last decade. Consequently, choosing the optimal media to speak to potential customers creates challenges.

To make the account executive and media buyer's jobs more difficult, prices for advertising time and space have risen. Client budgets for advertising have not gone up as quickly,

objective 1
What is a media strategy?

even as stronger demands for results and accountability emerged. The marketing team faces difficulties in locating cost-effective media outlets. After developing a media strategy, other aspects of media selection can proceed.

Media Planning

objective 2

What elements and individuals are involved in media planning?

Media planning commences with an analysis of the target market. It involves understanding the processes customers use in making purchases and what influences their final decisions. One method of addressing media planning starts with a study of the media choices that members of a specific, defined target market might make at different times during the course of a day (see Figure 1).

Details of the type shown in Figure 1 become valuable when developing a media strategy. Demographics such as age, sex, income, and education do not explain the media habits of consumers. Information about the listening and viewing patterns of groups helps the marketing team design appealing messages. These can then be shown at the best times and in the best places. No two media plans are alike. The components of a media plan include the elements identified in Figure 2.

A marketing analysis provides a comprehensive review of the marketing program. It includes a statement about current sales, current market share, and prime prospects to be solicited (by demographics, lifestyle, geographic location, or product usage). These elements should reflect a compatible pricing strategy based on the product, its benefits and distinguishing characteristics, and an analysis of the competitive environment.

An advertising analysis states the primary advertising strategy and budget to be used to achieve advertising objectives. The media strategy spells out the media to be used and the creative considerations. The media schedule notes when ads will appear in individual vehicles. The justification and summary outlines the measures of goal achievement. It also explains the rationale for each media choice.[3]

Several individuals take part in media planning. In addition to account executives, account planners, and creatives, most agencies utilize media planners and media buyers. In smaller agencies, the media planner and media buyer may be the same person. In larger companies, they are usually different individuals. Some agencies employ media firms to handle media planning and buying or hire a subsidiary agency.

Media Planners

The **media planner** formulates a media program stating where and when to place ads. Media planners work closely with creatives, account executives, account planners, agencies, and media buyers. The creative should know which media will be used to help design effective messages. Creatives construct television ads in different ways than for radio or newspaper.

Media planners provide valuable services and are in high demand. The issue of accountability for advertising results combined with the need to create a return on investment on marketing dollars has led the media buying side of an agency to hold greater power.

▼ Understanding consumer media choices is important for newspapers, such as *The Times-Picayune* of New Orleans.

- A favorite wake-up radio station or one listened to during the commute to work
- A favorite morning news show or newspaper
- Trade or business journals examined while at work
- A radio station played during office hours at work
- Favorite computer sites accessed during work

- Favorite magazines read during the evening hours
- Favorite television shows watched during the evening hours
- Internet sites accessed during leisure time
- Shopping, dining, and entertainment venues frequented

◀ **FIGURE 1**

Examples of Times Consumers Are Exposed to Advertisements

- Marketing analysis
- Advertising analysis
- Media strategy
- Media schedule
- Justification and summary

▲ **FIGURE 2**

Components of a Media Plan

▼ The media planner will locate the best medium for this advertisement for JD Bank.

Media planning has an impact on strategic planning. Marketing experts at companies such as Procter & Gamble and Unilever consider media planning to be at the heart of a communications strategy. In both companies, setting brand priorities and objectives constitutes the first step.[4] The task media buyers in this environment undertake, according to Carl Fremont of the media services company Digitas, will be "to integrate marketing messages across a range of media, and sometimes this involves working with several agencies to accomplish the client's goals."[5]

The media planner conducts research to help match the product with the market and media. If JD Bank's executives decide to run a print campaign directed to farmers who may need loans for tractors, the media planner researches the best media to place the ads. The media planner matches the target market with the venues that farmers would most likely watch or view.

The media planner gathers information about various media. This includes newspaper and magazine circulation rates along with the characteristics of those who read them. The audience for a television show may be different from those of a radio station or a magazine. Quality research improves the chances of selecting the appropriate media.

Media Buyers

After the media are chosen, the **media buyer** purchases the space and negotiates rates, times, and schedules for the ads. Media buyers remain in contact with media sales representatives. They know a great deal about rates and schedules. Media buyers watch for special deals and tie-ins between media outlets (e.g., radio with television, magazines with the same owner, etc.).

Placement in a television show or magazine continues to be an important consideration, both in terms of price and effectiveness. Recently, the Pink Jacket Creative advertising agency purchased magazine space for The Snoring Center consisting of the outer sides of adjacent pages containing an article. The slender ads on the edges of the two pages bracketed the article. As individuals read the article, they first noticed the ad on the left side of the article and the second half on the right side as they held the magazine open. The cost of the ad space was lower and it turned out to be more effective in conveying the two-part message.

JD BANK
JD gets me

JD Gets Me going

Whether buying business equipment or your dream car, we're here for life's big moments as well as your everyday needs. As a community bank committed to making loans to qualified applicants, our personalized service, low interest rates, and flexible term options make it easy to keep you moving.

CHECKING | SAVINGS | LOANS | MORTGAGES | BUSINESS

MEMBER FDIC   1.800.789.5159
jdbank.com

JD Bank

I said for better or worse...

▲ These ads for the Snoring Center were placed strategically on a two-page article spread on the outer edges.

objective 3

How do the terms used to describe advertising help the marketing team design effective campaigns?

Some research indicates that little connection exists between the size of an advertising firm and the prices it can negotiate. Differences in media costs are based on the time of the actual purchase (closer to the day the ad is to run) rather than the size of the agency.[6] A media plan costing one firm $10 million can cost another $12 million. Other major factors in cost differences are knowledge of the marketplace and the ability to negotiate package deals.

A **spot ad** is a one-time placement of a commercial in a medium. Rates are negotiated individually by the number of times the ads appear. Spot television prices fluctuate by as much as 45 percent for the same time slot. Radio time slot prices vary by as much as 42 percent and national print ads by as much as 24 percent.[7] Negotiation skills affect media purchase outcomes.

The quality of media choices, creativity, financial stewardship, the agency's culture and track record, and the relationship between the agency and the medium's sales representative lead to differences in the effectiveness of various advertising campaigns. The quality of the media selections made combined with the advertisement's content determines eventual levels of success.

Advertising Terminology

As with many subjects, advertising has its own unique set of terms and measures (see Figure 3). **Reach** represents the number of people, households, or businesses in a target audience exposed to a media vehicle or message schedule at least once during a given time period, which normally consists of four weeks. In other words, how many targeted buyers did the ad reach at least once during a four-week period?

Frequency

The average number of times an individual, household, or business within a particular target market is exposed to a particular advertisement within a specified time period, again, usually four weeks, constitutes **frequency**. It specifies how many times the person encountered the ad during a campaign. A regular viewer will see the same ad shown daily on *Wheel of Fortune* more frequently than she views an ad shown once on *CSI*, even though the *CSI* program has a greater reach.

Opportunities to See

In media planning, instead of frequency, buyers can use **opportunities to see (OTS)** or the cumulative exposures achieved in a given time period. When a company places two ads on a weekly television show, eight OTS (four shows × two ads per show) occur during a four-week period.

Not for snoring!

Make bedtime better for your better half.

Do something nice for yourself, too. If you snore you're probably getting less sleep, less sex and less out of life.

We're not marriage counselors, but we have helped thousands of relationships. Call or visit us online today.

SNORINGCENTER.COM

- Reach
- Frequency
- Opportunities to see (OTS)
- Gross rating points (GRP)
- Cost per thousand (CPM)

- Cost per rating point (CPRP)
- Ratings
- Continuity
- Gross impressions

▶ **FIGURE 3**
Advertising Terminology

Gross Rating Points

Gross rating points (GRPs) measure the impact or intensity of a media plan. Advertisers calculate gross rating points by multiplying a vehicle's rating by the OTS, or number of insertions of an advertisement. GRPs provide the advertiser with a better idea of the odds that members of the target audience actually viewed the commercial. By increasing the OTS or frequency, the chances of a magazine reader seeing the advertisement rise. An advertisement featured in each weekly issue of *People* during a four-week period is more likely to be seen than one appearing in a monthly periodical.

Cost

Cost measures the overall expenditures associated with an advertising program or campaign. To see how cost-effective one medium or ad placement is compared to another, the **cost per thousand (CPM)** figure can be calculated. CPM identifies the dollar cost of reaching 1,000 members of the media vehicle's audience. Marketers calculate CPM using the following formula:

$$\text{CPM} = (\text{Cost of media buy}/\text{Total audience}) \times 1{,}000$$

Figure 4 displays cost and readership information for a campaign for a 35 mm digital camera. The first three columns of the figure provide the name of the magazine, the cost of a four-color full-page advertisement, and the magazine's paid and verified circulation. The fourth column contains a measure of the CPM of each magazine. The CPM for *Better Homes and Gardens* is $66.21 and has a circulation of 7.6 million. *Sports Illustrated* has a smaller circulation, 3.2 million, but the CPM is $122.69. In terms of cost per thousand readers, *Reader's Digest* offers the best buy, at $26.04 per thousand.

if you can dream it, you can dip it.

new

Made with real Belgian chocolate blended with PHILADELPHIA Cream Cheese spread, it's a new kind of chocolate for a new kind of chocolate lover. Also available in milk and white chocolate.

pheel the moment

Philadelphia Cream Cheese

▲ Opportunities to see measures the number of times consumers have an opportunity to see this advertisement for Philadelphia Cream Cheese.

Publication	4C Base Rate	Total Paid & Verified Circulation	CPM	Target Market (20 Million)			
				Percent of Readers Fit Target Market	Number of Readers Fit Target Market	Rating (Reach)	Cost per Rating Point (CPRP)
Better Homes and Gardens	$506.380	7,648,600	$566.21	13.51%	1,033,000	5.2	$97,381
Glamour	$219,190	2,320,325	$94.47	24.65%	572,000	2.9	$76,640
Good Housekeeping	$387,055	4,652,904	$83.19	10.81%	503,000	2.5	$153,899
National Geographic	$225,455	4,495,931	$50.15	26.96%	1,212,000	6.1	$37,204
Reader's Digest	$185,300	7,114,955	$26.04	18.62%	1,325,000	6.6	$27,970
Southern Living	$198,800	2,855,973	$69.61	10.57%	302,000	1.5	$131,656
Sports Illustrated	$392,800	3,201,524	$122.69	16.77%	537,000	2.7	$146,294
Time	$320,100	3,376,226	$94.81	18.60%	628,000	3.1	$101,943

▲ **FIGURE 4**

Hypothetical Media Information for a 35 mm Digital Camera

Ratings and Cost per Rating Point

Consider the target market's profile when a company seeks to advertise a 35 mm digital camera. The number of readers that fit the target market's profile becomes the key goal. **Ratings** measure the percentage of a firm's target market exposed to a television show or the number of readers of a print medium. In order to compare media, a measure called the **cost per rating point (CPRP)** may be used. The cost per rating point formula that measures the relative efficiency of a media vehicle relative to a firm's target market is:

$$\text{CPRP} = \text{Cost of media buy}/\text{Vehicle's rating}$$

Assume there are 20 million potential buyers of 35 mm digital cameras. The figure shows the rating for *Better Homes and Gardens* is 5.2, which means that 5.2 percent of the defined target market for 35 mm digital cameras read *Better Homes and Gardens*. Backing up a step, 13.51 percent, or 1.033 million, of *Better Homes and Gardens'* readership fits the target profile for the 35 mm digital camera. The 5.2 rating is then obtained by dividing the 1.033 million *Better Homes and Gardens* readers that fit the target profile by the 20 million total for the target market. The CPRP for *Better Homes and Gardens* becomes $98,041. It specifies the average cost for each rating point, or of each 1 percent of the firm's target audience (35 mm digital camera buyers) that can be reached through an advertisement in *Better Homes and Gardens*. Not all readers of a magazine are part of the firm's target market. The CPRP more accurately measures an advertising campaign's efficiency than does CPM. Notice that the CPRP is the lowest for *National Geographic* and *Reader's Digest*. It is the highest for *Good Housekeeping*.

CPRP provides a relative measure of reach exposure in terms of cost. It costs $37,204 to reach 1 percent, or 200,000, of the 20 million in this firm's target market using *National Geographic*. It costs $146,294 to reach 1 percent, or 200,000, using *Sports Illustrated*. To reach 1 percent, or 200,000, using *Reader's Digest* costs only $27,970. *Reader's Digest* is the most efficient, which raises the question, "Why wouldn't a media planner just do all of the advertising in that magazine?" The answer lies in *Reader's Digest*'s rating. Advertising in only that magazine reaches just 6.6 percent (or 1,325,000) of the target audience; 93.4 percent of the target market does not read *Reader's Digest* and would not see the ad. Another magazine or media outlet is needed to reach them. This explains why diversity in media is essential to reach a large portion of a firm's target market.

An alternative method of determining whether an ad has reached the target market efficiently is a **weighted (or demographic) CPM** value, which can be calculated as:

$$\text{Weighted CPM} = \frac{\text{Advertisement cost} \times 1,000}{\text{Actual audience reached}}$$

Referring to Figure 5, the cost of an advertisement in *Good Housekeeping* is $387,055. Although it has a circulation of 4,652,904, only 503,000 of the readers fit the target profile for the 35 mm digital camera. Using the formula for weighted CPM, the

▼ **FIGURE 5**
Calculating Weighted (or Demographic) CPM

| Publication | 4C Base Rate | Total Paid & Verified Circulation | CPM | Target Market (20 Million) | | |
				Percent of Readers Fit Target Market	Number of Readers Fit Target Market	Weighted (Demographic) CPM
Better Homes and Gardens	$506,380	7,648,600	$66.21	13.51%	1,033,000	$490.20
Glamour	$219,190	2,320,325	$94.47	24.65%	572,000	$383.20
Good Housekeeping	$387,055	4,652,904	$83.19	10.81%	503,000	$769.49
National Geographic	$225,455	4,495,931	$50.15	26.96%	1,212,000	$186.02
Reader's Digest	$185,300	7,114,955	$26.04	18.62%	1,325,000	$139.85
Southern Living	$198,800	2,855,973	$69.61	10.5%	302,000	$658.28
Sports Illustrated	$392,800	3,201,524	$122.69	16.77%	537,000	$731.47

cost to reach 1,000 readers of *Good Housekeeping* that fit the target profile is $769.49. As with CPRP, marketers can compare the various magazines to determine which offer the best buy in terms of reaching the target demographic. The difference in the numbers is that CPRP measures the cost of reaching 1 percent of the target market, whereas the weighted CPM measures the cost of reaching 1,000 members of the target market.

Continuity

The exposure pattern or schedule used in a campaign signifies its **continuity**. The three types of patterns are continuous, pulsating, and discontinuous. A *continuous campaign* uses media time in a steady stream. Home construction companies such as Buford Hawthorne would use a continuous schedule, because individuals making decisions to build homes do not follow any consistent time frame for when they will be ready to buy. Consequently, media buyers would look for ad space in specific magazines for a period of one to two years. By using different ads and rotating them, readers will not get bored, because they will see more than one advertisement for the same product.

A retailer such as JCPenney might feature a *pulsating schedule* by placing ads in various media throughout the entire year, but then increasing the number of advertisements in small, short bursts around holidays, including Christmas, Thanksgiving, Memorial Day, Labor Day, Mother's Day, Father's Day, and Easter. Pulsating advertising should reach consumers when they are most likely to make purchases or buy special merchandise, such as during the holidays. A Barnes & Noble advertisement just prior to Christmas can encourage consumers to purchase gift cards.

A *flighting* (or *discontinuous*) *campaign* schedule, in which advertisements run at only certain times of the year, differs from the first two approaches. It would be more likely to be used by a ski resort that runs ads during the fall and winter seasons but none during the spring and summer.

▲ In terms of continuity, a continuous schedule is a logical choice for home construction firm Buford Hawthorne.

Buford Hawthorne

Impressions

The final advertising term is impressions. The number of **gross impressions** represents the total exposures of the audience to an advertisement. It does not account for the percentage of the total audience that sees the advertisement. Figure 5 indicates that *National Geographic*'s total circulation is approximately 4.6 million. If six insertions were placed in *National Geographic*, multiplying the insertions by the readership would yield a total of 27.6 million impressions.

Achieving Advertising Objectives

Advertisers consider the number of times a person will be exposed to an advertisement before it creates an impact. Most agree that a single exposure will not be sufficient. The actual number inspires a great deal of debate. Some argue it takes three. Others say as many as 10 or more.

objective **4**

What are some of the primary advertising objectives?

From Cassina - Mex Cube sofa and island by Piero Lissoni and LC3 chair by Le Corbusier, Pierre Jeanneret and Charlotte Perriand

YOUR EX DESERVED THAT PAIR OF COLONIAL SIDE TABLES.

Scott and Cooner Inc.

SCOTT + COONER

Dallas 214.748.9838   Austin 512.480.0436   scottcooner.com

▲ Based on recency theory, a person looking for designer home furnishings would be more likely to notice this advertisement.

The Three-Exposure Hypothesis

Most media planners believe an advertisement requires a minimum of three exposures for an advertisement to be effective. The three-exposure hypothesis, as developed by Herbert Krugman, states that an advertisement can make an impact on an audience regardless of individual needs or wants.[8] Further, the **intrusion value** of an advertisement represents the ability of a medium or an advertisement to capture the attention of a viewer without her voluntary effort. This reasoning suggests that it takes at least three exposures to capture a viewer's attention.

Recency Theory

Currently, many advertisers believe that clutter has diminished the viability of the three-exposure hypothesis. Another concept, **recency theory**, notes that a consumer exhibits selective attention and focuses on personal needs and wants as he considers advertisements.[9] When a consumer pays attention to messages that might meet his needs or wants, the closer an exposure to a commercial is to the purchase decision, the more powerful the ad becomes. Further, when a consumer contemplates a future purchase of the product being advertised, the consumer becomes more likely to notice and react favorably toward an ad. A member of a buying center from a business in the market for a new copier will more readily notice copier advertisements. Someone who is not in the market for a copier ignores the same ad. The same holds true in consumer markets: An individual desiring a new pair of jeans notices clothing ads, especially ones that feature jeans.

Recency theory proposes that *one ad exposure* may actually be enough to affect an audience when that person or business needs the product being promoted. Additional exposures may not be necessary. Therefore, companies should advertise almost continually to ensure an advertisement reaches a buyer when she thinks about making a purchase.

The advertising approach that matches recency theory would be to spread the message around using a variety of media, each type providing limited exposure per week or time period. In the case of selling supplemental health insurance to the elderly, magazines such as *Senior Living*, television spots on local news and weather programs, and newspaper ads can quickly reach the target audience in a cost-effective manner. This method, which maximizes reach, accomplishes more than increasing frequency.

In the business-to-business arena, recency theory suggests that advertisements should appear in a number of outlets and over a longer period of time rather than running a series of ads in one trade journal. Many times, buying centers consist of several members, each with differing responsibilities. Making sure each one sees an advertisement would mean placing ads in every journal that might be read by buying center members. To facilitate the purchasing process for a company seeking to acquire an audio-conferencing system, the media buyer purchases space in trade journals, human resource journals, sales journals, and business journals. This increases the odds that the message will reach buying center members. One exposure might be enough for each, because the member actively looks for information and is ready to make a decision.

Effective Reach and Frequency

Seeking to discover the minimum number of exposures needed to be effective may be based on two concepts: effective frequency and effective reach. **Effective reach** identifies the *percentage of an audience* that must be exposed to a particular message to achieve a specific objective. **Effective frequency** refers to the *number of times* a target audience

◀ Effective reach and effective frequency are important considerations in reaching the target market for Office Furniture.

must be exposed to a message to achieve a particular objective. The effective frequency concept implies that a minimum number of exposures will be needed.

Effective frequency and effective reach provide crucial guidelines. Too few exposures means the advertiser might fail to attain its intended objectives. In contrast, too many exposures waste resources. Discovering the optimal reach and frequency mix to accomplish the intended objectives without experiencing diminishing returns from extra ads should be the goal. The optimal mix for an objective dealing with brand recognition will be different than when brand recall serves as the objective.

Other elements can also enhance effective frequency and effective reach. They include the size and placement of an advertisement. A small magazine advertisement does not create the same impact as a larger ad. If a firm uses 15-second television ads, effective frequency may require six exposures. In comparison, a longer 45-second spot may require only four exposures to be remembered. In television advertising, a spot in the middle of an ad sequence usually has less of an impact than the ads shown at the beginning and end of the series.

The number of different media used in an advertising campaign also influences effectiveness. In general, a campaign featuring ads in two types of media, such as television and magazines, will generate greater effective reach than a campaign in only one medium, such as magazines only.

In recent years, numerous media companies have designed computer models to optimize reach and frequency, including Nielsen SAVE and Adware. These programs are based on probability theory. They help a marketing team effectively allocate advertising dollars. The interaction between an attention-getting television commercial and a magazine ad with copy explaining the product's features may create a more potent synergistic effect than either ad would generate by itself.

Brand Recognition

Brand recognition requires an emphasis on the visual presentation of the product and/or logo. Strengthening or creating links between the brand and other nodes of information that exist in the person's knowledge structure becomes the goal. Rather than leading the individual to recall the brand name from memory, the advertiser wants the person to recognize the brand name and logo at the retail store or in the advertisement. Media that are effective at maximizing reach include television, billboards, magazines, the internet, and direct mail.[10]

▶ Billboards offer an excellent medium for achieving brand recognition objectives for Ouachita Independent Bank.

▶ **FIGURE 6**
Brand Recognition Versus Brand Recall

Objective	Brand Recognition	Brand Recall
Goal	Create or strengthen mental linkages	Place brand in evoked set
Method	Increase reach	Increase frequency (repetition)
Best media	Television	Television
	Billboards	Radio
	Magazines	Newspapers
	Internet	Internet
	Direct mail	

Brand Recall

To increase brand recall, frequency becomes more important than reach. Repetition helps embed a brand in the consumer's cognitive memory. Repetition makes it more likely that a particular brand will come to mind. When a 30-second commercial repeats the name of a restaurant seven times, it becomes easier to remember than when it is stated only once or twice. In terms of media selection, television, radio, newspapers, and the internet offer the potential for higher frequency.[11] Figure 6 compares brand recall with brand recognition.

Once the media buyer, media planner, account executive, and company leaders agree to basic objectives of the advertising campaign, they select the actual media, seeking to identify logical media combinations. The next section examines traditional advertising media.

Media Selection

objective 5

What are the advantages and disadvantages associated with each traditional advertising medium?

Effectively mixing advertising media constitutes a vital element in the design of a quality advertising campaign. To do so, marketing professionals consider the advantages and disadvantages of each individual medium.

Television

Deloitte Research recently noted that 71 percent of Americans still rate television as their favorite medium. In terms of impact on buying decisions, 86 percent stated that TV advertising exerts the greatest influence.[12] While the power of television has declined,

▶ This banner advertisement for "Visit Baton Rouge" should help increase brand recall.

Advantages	Disadvantages
• High reach	• High level of clutter
• High frequency potential	• Low recall due to clutter
• Low cost per contact	• Channel surfing during ads
• High intrusion value	• DVRs skipping ads
• Quality creative opportunities	• Short amount of copy
• Segmentation through cable	• High cost per ad

◀ **FIGURE 7**
Television Advertising

for many brands and companies it remains a viable advertising option. At the same time, advertisers should be aware that television viewing has changed. It now occurs on a tablet or laptop computer rather than a regular television screen. Figure 7 lists the pros and cons of television advertising.

Advantages of Television Advertising   Television provides the most extensive coverage and highest reach of any medium. A single advertisement can reach millions. Television offers a low cost per contact, which justifies spending as much as $4 million for a 30-second spot on the Super Bowl, where a vast audience of more than 110 million households and nearly one billion people may be watching. The cost per person reached by the commercial is low.

Television provides intrusion value. Commercials featuring a catchy musical tune, sexy content, or humor can quickly capture a viewer's attention. Television offers opportunities to be creative in designing advertisements. Visual images and sounds can be incorporated in a commercial. Advertisers are able to demonstrate products and services on television in a manner not possible in print or using radio advertisements. Segmentation may be achieved by targeting specialty shows and networks such as *The Food Channel* or *ESPN*.

Disadvantages of Television Advertising   Clutter continues to be the primary problem for television advertising. Many programs include 31 commercials per hour and they take as long as 19 minutes to run. Four- and five-minute commercial breaks are common.[13] As a result, many viewers switch channels during commercial breaks. Often, low recall exists, especially for commercials placed in the middle of an advertising segment. Messages at the beginning or near the end of the break have a better chance to be recalled. Also, ads near the beginning of a television show or during the last commercial break have a higher recall, because individuals want to catch the start of the show and make sure they see the last part of a show for its climax or conclusion.

Some viewers cope with clutter by using a DVR, recording favorite programs and watching them later. Advertisers fear the DVR users will skip over the commercials. Recent research indicates, however, that fewer than half fast-forward through commercials. Also, the majority watches the television show the same day it is recorded, and 75 percent have viewed it by the end of the next day. This means that time-sensitive ads are seen close to when they first were run. Consequently, the fear that DVRs cause viewers to skip commercials may be somewhat unjustified.[14]

Television airtime is expensive, as are the costs of producing ads. The average cost of production for a 30-second national ad is $358,000. Production fees account for the largest portion of the cost, an average of $236,000. Other costs include director fees ($23,000), fees for editing and finishing the ad ($45,000), and creative/labor fees and music ($34,000).[15]

Ratings   To gain a sense of how well an advertisement fared in terms of reaching an audience, a given program's rating can be calculated. The typical ratings formula is:

$$\text{Rating} = \frac{\text{Number of households tuned to a program}}{\text{Total number of households in a market}}$$

▷ A storyboard illustrating a television commercial for Interstate Batteries.

Interstate Battery Systems International, Inc.

In the United States, approximately 109.7 million households own television sets. To calculate the rating of an episode of *American Idol*, if the number of households tuned to the season finale was 17.8 million, the rating would be:

$$\text{Rating} = \frac{17,800,000}{109,700,000} = 16.2$$

Next, if the advertiser were interested in the percentage of households that actually were watching television at that hour, the program's share could be calculated. Assuming 71 million of the 109.7 million households had a television turned on during the hour in which *American Idol* aired, the share would be:

▼ Ratings measure how many households are tuned to a particular television program.

$$\text{Share} = \frac{\text{Number of households tuned to } American\ Idol}{\text{Number of households with a television turned on}} = \frac{17,800,000}{71,000,000} = 25$$

A 16.2 rating would mean that 16.2 percent of all televisions in the United States were tuned to *American Idol*. A 25 share means 25 percent of the households with a television actually turned on were watching the program. Ratings do not guarantee viewers saw the commercial. Ratings and shares only indicate of how well the television program fared.

C3 Ratings Some advertisers have began to adopt a new system—the commercial C3 rating—which calculates a rating for the actual commercial time slot rather than the television program. It computes a commercial's rating plus any viewing of the commercial three days after the original ad ran. Many firms now use the C3 rating to determine national television

Tatyana Gladskih/Fotolia

American Idol	$467,617
Sunday Night Football	$415,000
Glee	$272,694
Family Guy	$259,289
The Simpsons	$253,170
House	$226,180
Grey's Anatomy	$222,113
The Office	$213,617
Desperate Housewives	$210,064

◀ **FIGURE 8**

Cost of 30-second advertisements based on C3 Ratings

advertising rates. Marketers calculate the C3 rating by computing the average rating of all commercials within a particular pod or commercial segment. Various advertisers have criticized the system, claiming that not all ads within a pod receive equal exposure. For instance, the first position in a pod generates 28 percent higher awareness than ads in the middle of the commercial sequence. Thus, the position of a particular ad in the commercial break and the length of the pod have no impact on the rates being charged.

Nielsen intends to expand the C3 rating system to correct this problem. Called "On Demand C3" the new system will produce a rating for each commercial. It will include the show's live telecast viewing along with three-day post viewing period via DVRs.[16]

Figure 8 provides the costs of 30-second ads using the C3 system. The higher a show's rating over time, the more that can be charged. The highest costs are for *American Idol* at $467,617 and *Sunday Night Football* at $415,000.[17]

Ratings Providers   ACNielsen continues to be the primary organization that calculates and reports ratings and shares. The company provides information regarding shares of stations in local markets known as *designated marketing areas* (DMAs). Data-gathering techniques used by ACNielsen include diaries written by viewers who report what they watched, audience meters that record what is being shown automatically, and people meters that track the viewing habits of individual members of families. Nielsen augments TV ratings with information about viewing from tables and smartphones, because the number of individuals using these alternative screens to watch television programming continues to grow, especially among younger consumers.

These numbers can be further refined to help advertisers understand whether an advertisement reached a target market. Within rating and share categories, viewers can be subdivided by certain demographics, such as age, income, gender, educational level, and race or ethnic heritage. Organizations that prepare this information include Nielsen Media Research; Starch INRA; Hooper, Inc.; Mediamark Research, Inc.; Burke Marketing Research; and Simmons Market Research Bureau. Psychographic information can be then be added, such as whether outdoor enthusiasts watch certain programs. This gives the advertiser a sense of whether the program provides the best audience for an advertisement or campaign.

Local and Regional Television Advertising   For local and regional companies, spot TV may be the best television advertising option. In many cases, national brands supplement national commercials with spot TV purchases in select markets. Media planners use this approach primarily due to the high cost of national ad time and because 75 to 80 percent of prime-time slots are sold out during the spring, shortly after they go on the market. By selecting local early news, late news, and local prime access, a media planner generates higher GRP at a lower cost than if only national ad time has been purchased.

Denver local pizza operation Anthony's Pizza & Pasta switched from 90 percent out-of-home billboard advertising to 90 percent television. The company used a concentrated flighting schedule during the first and fourth quarters to build awareness and

Monkey Business/Fotolia

▲ Through dynamic advertising, DirecTV targeted Spanish-speaking consumers in select markets.

drive traffic to the restaurants. Spots were run in Denver on all of the national broadcast networks and 14 cable channels including ESPN, Comedy Central, Cartoon Network, Food Network, and AMC. The spots featured the key message/tagline "authentic, New York-style pizza." Five spots focused on the crafting of the pizza, and six spots utilized humor. During the six months when no ads were run, the company used social media, especially Facebook, to maintain contact with customers.[18]

Dynamic Advertising   TV networks, cable, and satellite TV companies have introduced a new technology that helps advertisers zero in on specific target markets. **Dynamic advertising** allows a company such as DirecTV to obtain consumer information from marketing research firms and combine it with the company's data to send targeted ads to its subscribers that meet specific criteria and live in targeted areas. It can be Spanish-speaking consumers, individuals who want to lose weight, or who are early adopters of technology. Toyota used dynamic advertising to target ads to DirecTV customers who were identified as tech-savvy early adopters who live in San Francisco, Los Angeles, and San Diego. No other DirecTV subscribers saw the ads.[19]

Social Media and Television   The rise of social media and the internet has led some advertisers to become concerned that television provides less of an impact. While many consumers watch less TV as they spend more time online, for others the opposite takes place. Social media, mobile, and the internet can be used to enrich television viewing experiences and actually drive consumers to watch more programs. Individuals who spend considerable time with social media tend to watch more TV, although some of it may be on tablets and other portable devices. Adam Rossow of iModerate notes that these individuals "love the social interaction and frequently add shows to their viewing lineup due to social chatter. More time is spent on social networks and more hours watching television." A Deloitte Research study revealed that 75 percent of consumers multitask while watching TV—42 percent are online, 29 percent are talking on phones, and 26 percent are sending text messages.[20] Research by Nielsen's SocialGuide service suggests that the heaviest Twitter activity occurs during television shows, not during commercial breaks.[21]

The interaction between social media and television viewing caused the marketing team for Bluefin Labs to examine online buzz about brands and television shows. People who commented online about Wal-Mart also tweeted or commented about television shows *America's SuperNanny, Dallas Cowboys Cheerleaders, Wife Swap, Cell Block 6: Female Lockup*, and *America's Most Wanted*. In contrast, social media comments about Target were tied to online comments and tweets about *Top Secret Recipe, My Yard Goes Disney, HGTV'd, Fashion Hunters*, and *Free Agents*.[22]

As people spend greater amounts of time on social media, the amount of online buzz about television shows will also rise. By monitoring this type of online chatter, advertising professionals and their clients can gain better perspectives regarding the television shows that provide the best matches for placing ads.

YouTube and Television   Many companies and advertising agencies post television commercials on YouTube. Some of the ads are placed on the site simultaneously with the TV launch (called *in-stream*) while others are be submitted to YouTube prior to the national launch (called *pre-roll*). For the Super Bowl, part of the ad, a teaser, appears on YouTube prior to the game.

Google and Ipsos research indicates that YouTube pre-roll of TV ads as well as in-streaming of TV ads result in higher recall. Individuals who watched the commercial on

YouTube and on TV had a 200 percent higher recall than individuals who saw the ad only on TV. Those who saw the ad online on YouTube only had a 150 percent higher recall. More than 3 billion consumers watch videos on YouTube daily.[23]

Super Bowl Advertising The Super Bowl offers the biggest television advertising event of the year. Many of the 110 million viewers tune in to see new ads as much as to watch the game. Recent research indicated that 39 percent of the viewers stated the new commercials were their favorite part of the game, and 73 percent consider Super Bowl advertisements to be entertainment. These findings reinforce the statement by Paul Chibe, vice president of marketing at Anheuser-Busch, that, "the Super Bowl is a huge brand-building opportunity."[24]

In the past, ads were kept under wraps until the moment they appear during the game. The rise of social media changed this approach. Many Super Bowl commercials first appear on YouTube, Facebook, the company's website, or on the agency's site prior to the game. As noted, pre-roll teaser ads entice viewers to watch the entire commercial during the game. Pre-rolling ads generates excitement and allows viewers to see, share, and discuss the ads before, during, and after the game. Many companies and agencies now spend as much time developing a marketing plan for the pre-roll as they do for the actual Super Bowl commercial.

▲ The Super Bowl has become a showcase for advertisers.

Further, another new approach involves the release of extended versions of advertisement with more content or additional information about the ad spot on the website.

One pre-roll teaser ad for Volkswagen released to YouTube three weeks prior to the Super Bowl was viewed 11 million times. Then, an extended version of the sequel was uploaded to YouTube the week prior to the Super Bowl and was viewed over 1.3 million times. A Super Bowl commercial for the Chevrolet Camaro went online 17 days before the Super Bowl. Brian Sharpless, chief executive of HomeAway, stated that, "Because social media can build buzz for Super Bowl commercials before, during, and after the game, if you don't take advantage of all that, you're not getting the most bang for your buck."[25]

Super Bowl advertising results in nearly immediate feedback. A number of companies run various types of ad meters during the game and monitor social media buzz to determine the best ads and those that missed the mark. Stan Richards of the Richards Group commented, "You get quick feedback. I have to tell you, when you go to bed right after the Super Bowl, your last thought is, 'What is it going to say in *USA Today* tomorrow morning?'"[26]

Radio

Despite CDs, iPods, audio books, and other types of audio devices, the vast majority of Americans, approximately 80 percent, still listen to the radio daily.[27] Adverting professional Mary Price stated that, "Right now, on a weekly basis terrestrial radio still reaches 93 percent of everybody. It used to be 96 or 97, but it's still up there. As long as they can create a following for local personalities and local events, you can't get that off an iPod. If you want some kind of commentary about the music you're listening to ... you can't get that on a pre-recorded iPod."[28]

While radio may not seem as glamorous as television, it remains an effective advertising medium (see Figure 9). A well-placed, clever commercial results in a one-on-one message (announcer to driver in a car stuck in traffic). Many smaller local companies rely heavily on radio advertising. Most radio ads are produced locally and with small budgets.

Richard Kane/Fotolia

▶ **FIGURE 9**
Radio Advertising

Advantages	Disadvantages
• Recall promoted	• Short exposure time
• Narrower target markets	• Low attention
• Ad music can match audience	• Difficult to reach national audiences
• High segmentation potential	• Target duplication with several stations using the same format
• Flexibility in making ads	• Information overload
• Modify ad to local conditions	
• Intimacy with DJs	
• Mobile – listen anywhere	
• Creative opportunities with sound and music	

Advantages of Radio Advertising Quality radio advertisements cause the listener to remember the message by creating powerful images to visualize and by employing repetition. These actions move the information from the consumer's short-term to long-term memory. Sound effects and lively tunes can assist in the process. Through repetition a person hears an advertisement often enough to generate recall.

A radio station reaches definable target markets based on its format, such as talk radio, lite mix, oldies, or country. A firm can advertise on a specific type of station across the country. Radio advertisers can examine the rating and share of a program as well as the estimated number of people listening. Arbitron calculates these numbers for local stations. Radio's All-Dimension Audience Research (RADAR) reports ratings for national radio networks.

Radio can create intimacy. Listeners often feel personally close to DJs and radio personalities. The attachment grows over time. Listening to the same individual becomes more personal and intimate, especially if the listener has a conversation with the DJ during a contest or when requesting a song. The bond or intimacy level gives the radio personality a higher level of credibility and an edge to goods and services the radio celebrity endorses.

Beachbody, a fitness brand based in Santa Monica, California, used radio as the prime medium to promote its P90X, a home exercise system that promised total body improvements within 90 days. Robinson Radio from Virginia was contracted to develop and manage the radio campaign. Robinson realized the best approach was to use "radio's secret weapon," the DJs, who used the product, documented their successes, and then described their progress on the air. The DJs also posted their photos on the company's website, created chat rooms for listeners, and asked listeners to share their success stories. Early in the campaign, it became clear that the micro website was a key component of the radio campaign, because it allowed communications between the listeners, customers of the product, and the DJs. The other advantage of emphasizing radio was that it was easy and inexpensive to make changes to ads as the campaign progressed. The campaign was highly successful in California. Beachbody expanded the campaign nationally within a few months.[29]

▼ Radio is an important component of an integrated advertising campaign.

Fotolia/ra2 studio

Disadvantages of Radio Advertising Short exposure time creates one problem for radio. Most commercials last 15 or 30 seconds. Listeners involved in other activities, such as driving or working on a computer, may not pay attention. Further, people often use radio as a background to drown out other distractions, especially at work.

For national advertisers, covering a large area with radio advertisements can be difficult. To place a national advertisement requires contacting a large number of companies. Few large radio conglomerates means contacts must be made with multiple stations. Negotiating rates with individual stations based on volume may be difficult. Local businesses can often negotiate better rates than national advertisers because of the local company's relationships with the radio stations.

The four main national radio networks in the United States are Westwood One, ABC, CBS, and Unistar. These are joined by a few other strong networks, such as ESPN radio and CNN. Nationally syndicated programs such as those on the Fox radio network offer some opportunities to national advertisers.

In large metropolitan areas, duplication presents another problem. Several radio stations may try to reach the same target market. Chicago has several rock stations. Advertising on each one may not be financially feasible, yet reaching everyone in that target market might not be possible unless all rock stations are included.

Radio enjoys the advantage of intimacy with the local DJ.

© WavebreakmediaMicro/Fotolia

Opportunities for Radio Radio advertising offers a low-cost option for a local firm. Ads can be placed at ideal times and adapted to local conditions. Careful selection of stations, times, and quality construction of the advertisement will be the keys. Radio allows local businesses to present remote broadcasts. Remotes may be used to attract attention to a new business (restaurants, retail stores, etc.) or to a company trying to make a major push for immediate customers. Advertisers often combine radio promotions with other media (local television or newspapers) to send more integrated messages.

For business-to-business advertisers, radio provides the opportunity to reach businesses during working hours, because many employees listen to the radio during office hours. Radio often reaches businesspeople while in transit to or from work. Both radio and television usage has increased for business-to-business marketing.

Out-of-Home Advertising

Billboards along major roads continue to be the most common form of out-of-home (OOH) advertising; however, there are others. Signs on cabs, buses, park benches, and fences of sports arenas are other types of outdoor advertising. A blimp flying above a major sporting event constitutes another form of out-of-home advertising.

This billboard was part of a highly successful campaign for the Snoring Center.

Courtesy of Pink Jacket Creative: A Creative Factory

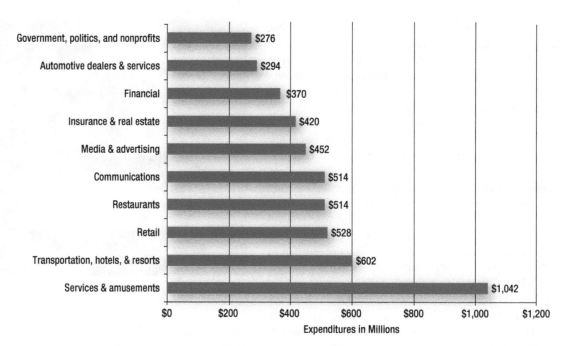

▶ **FIGURE 10**
Expenditures on Out-of-Home Advertising

Government, politics, and nonprofits $276
Automotive dealers & services $294
Financial $370
Insurance & real estate $420
Media & advertising $452
Communications $514
Restaurants $514
Retail $528
Transportation, hotels, & resorts $602
Services & amusements $1,042

Expenditures in Millions

In the past, many company leaders seldom considered outdoor advertising as part of the planning process for an integrated marketing communications program or the development of the media plan; however that has now changed. Advances in technology have dramatically improved OOH advertising. Annual expenditures on outdoor advertisements total more than $5.5 billion. Global positioning systems, wireless communications, and digital display technology have transformed outdoor advertising. LED technology creates animated videos in locations such as Times Square in New York and the Strip in Las Vegas. It can present static messages and visuals that change electronically. Figure 10 provides a breakdown of outdoor spending by categories.

The Firehouse Agency of Dallas created a unique billboard campaign for Stripes Convenience Stores. The signs invited customers of Stripes to tweet about tacos sold at the convenience stores. The tweets were then streamed into digital billboard displays located near traffic lights in eight different Texas cities where vehicles would stop for a red light. According to Ian Dallimore of Lamar Advertising, "Stripes wanted to do something more than just change the copy a few times a day. It wanted to create the sense of a conversation, and make people feel involved. The idea is to get people more engaged with outdoor advertising and arouse curiosity about the tacos." The tweets ran from lunchtime until midnight daily.[30]

Advantages of Out-of-Home Advertising Billboard advertising offers long life. For local companies, billboards can be an excellent advertising medium, because the message will primarily be seen by residents. It also provides a low-cost medium in terms of cost per impression. Out-of-home advertising features a broad reach and a high level of frequency when advertisers purchase multiple billboards or venues. Every person who travels past a billboard or sees an advertisement on a taxi has been exposed to the message. Many out-of-home companies feature rotation packages in which an ad moves to different locations throughout an area during the course of the year, thereby increasing its reach. Digital boards and signs deliver higher resolution graphics as well as capabilities of changing messages on demand or on a routine schedule. Figure 11 lists the advantages and disadvantages of out-of-home ads.

Disadvantages of Out-of-Home Advertising Short exposure time remains the major drawback of out-of-home advertising. Drivers must pay attention to the traffic as they travel by a billboard. As a result, advertisers keep messages short. Pedestrians often

Advantages	Disadvantages
• Select key geographic areas	• Short exposure time
• Accessible for local ads	• Brief messages
• Low cost per impression	• Little segmentation possible
• Broad reach	• Clutter
• High frequency on major commuter routes	
• Large visuals possible	
• Digital capabilities	

get only a quick look at an advertisement placed on a vehicle. Most either ignore outdoor ads or give them just a casual glance. Ironically, in large cities along major arteries the cost of billboard spots has increased. The reason: traffic jams. People stuck in slow-moving traffic spend more time looking at billboards. Another option is to purchase billboard locations where traffic stops for signals or at stop signs.

Print Media

Printed outlets remain an important component of traditional media. A growing number of print magazines and newspapers have developed digital versions of materials that can be viewed on computers, tablets, and smartphones. In some cases, the digital format will be identical to the print version. In others, the site includes additional or different content. Just as websites became essential for businesses, print media companies now must develop digital components to compete effectively. This chapter covers traditional print media.

Magazines

For many advertisers, magazines represent a secondary choice in media buying. Recent research indicates, however, that magazines often deliver a quality option. An Affinity Research study suggests that half of readers either take action, such as accessing a website, after seeing an ad in a magazine. Others develop more favorable opinions about magazine advertiser companies. Several studies conclude that magazines are a strong driver of purchase intentions and boost the effectiveness of other media.[31] Figure 12 identifies some potential advantages and disadvantages of magazines.

Advantages of Magazine Advertising Magazines create high levels of market segmentation by topic area. Even within certain market segments, such as automobiles, a number of magazines exist. High audience interest constitutes another advantage. An individual who subscribes to *Modern Bride* has an attraction to weddings.

▼ Print advertising is a valuable IMC component for LUBA Workers' Comp.

LUBA Workers' Comp

▶ **FIGURE 12**
Magazine Advertising

Advantages	Disadvantages
• High market segmentation	• Declining readership
• Targeted audience by magazine	• Clutter
• Direct-response techniques	• Long lead time
• High color quality	• Little flexibility
• Long-life	• High cost
• Read during leisure—longer attention to ads	
• Availability of special features	

People reading magazines also tend to view and pay attention to advertisements related to their needs and wants. Often, readers linger over an ad for a longer period of time because they read magazines in waiting situations, such as in a doctor's office, or during leisure time. The high level of interest, segmentation, and differentiation, when combined with high-quality color, are ideal for products with well-defined target markets.

Trade and business journals represent the primary choice for business-to-business marketers. Businesses target advertisements to buying center members. The ad's copy can deliver a greater level of detail about products. Interested readers take more time to study the information provided in the advertisement. Ads often contain toll-free telephone numbers and website addresses so that interested parties can obtain further information.

Magazines have long lives that reach beyond an immediate issue. An avid magazine reader may examine a particular issue several times and spend a considerable amount of time with each issue. Advertisers know the reader will be exposed to the ad more than once and might be more likely to pay attention. Other individuals may also review the magazine. In the business-to-business sector, trade journals are often passed around to several individuals or members of the buying center. As long as the magazine lasts, the advertisement is still available to be viewed.

In addition to the standard sniff-patches that can be placed in magazines for perfume and cologne, advertisers can now add QR codes or special mobile apps. DirecTV partnered with *Sports Illustrated* to create a free Android and IOS app for *SI*'s annual swimsuit edition. Individuals who downloaded the app to their smartphones could hold the phone over the swimsuit models in the *SI* magazine and watch videos of the model's picture shoot. The magazine had 19 embedded videos, each approximately 30 seconds in length.[32]

Disadvantages of Magazine Advertising
While overall readership of magazines has declined, the trend is less evident among "influential Americans." Individuals with incomes of $100,000 or more read an average of 15.3 publications, and individuals with incomes over $250,000 read an average of 23.8.[33] Magazine

▼ Magazines offer an excellent medium for GE Café to reach its target audience.

THE CHEF'S COMPLEMENT

GE Café™ appliances give builders and remodelers a unique opportunity to attract homeowners who love to live in the kitchen. With inspired aesthetics and impressive power that mimics great restaurants, GE Café helps you create kitchens that aspiring and seasoned cooks would give anything to own.

Café™

Factory Builder Stores	Capital Distributing	Ferguson Enterprises	Builder Sales & Service
512 E Dallas Road #500	2910 N Stemmons Fwy.	All Locations DFW	2201 E Loop 820 South
Grapevine, TX 76051	Dallas, TX 75247		Fort Worth, TX 76112
817-410-8868	214-638-2681		817-457-7900

For additional information, check online at www.geappliances.com

GE Café

advertisements require a great deal of lead time and are expensive to prepare. They may be less viable for more general consumption products such as basic necessities.

At the same time, magazines still provide an effective advertising medium. In both consumer and business markets, it appears that magazines, used in conjunction with other media, can enhance the effectiveness of an advertising campaign.

Newspapers

When *USA Today* was launched, few believed a national daily newspaper could succeed. At the same time, news reporting has changed. Many small local papers no longer exist and conglomerates, such as Gannett, own most major city newspapers. Still, daily readership continues in some segments.

For many smaller local firms, newspaper ads, billboards, and local radio programs provide the most viable advertising options. Newspapers are distributed daily, weekly, or in partial form as the advertising supplements found in the front sections of grocery stores and retail outlets.

Advantages of Newspaper Advertising   As noted in Figure 13, many retailers rely on newspaper because it offers geographic selectivity (local market access). Promoting sales, retail hours, and store locations is easier. Short lead time permits retailers to quickly change ads and promotions. Such flexibility presents the advantage of allowing advertisers the ability to keep ads current, and the ads can be modified to meet competitive offers or to focus on recent events.

Newspapers retain high levels of credibility. Readers rely on newspapers for factual information. Newspaper readers hold high interest levels in the articles as well as advertisements. Greater audience interest permits advertisers to provide more copy detail in ads. Newspaper readers take more time to read copy unless an advertiser jams too much information into a small space. A recent survey of shoppers revealed that newspapers were the most trusted source of information for purchase decisions.[34]

Recognizing a match between newspaper readers and its customer base, Starbucks launched a unique newspaper campaign designed by the agency Wieden + Kennedy

▲ Newspapers provide an ideal medium for advertising local businesses, such as Baxter Printing, which offers high-end home and commercial painting and decorating.

Advantages	Disadvantages
• Geographic selectivity	• Poor buying procedures
• High flexibility	• Short life span
• High credibility	• Clutter
• Strong audience interest	• Poor quality reproduction
• Longer copy	• Internet competition
• Cumulative volume discounts	• Aging readership
• Coupons and special-response features	

◄ **FIGURE 13**
Newspaper Advertising

▲ Newspapers remain an excellent medium for local businesses to advertise, such as Fiesta Nutrition Center.

of Portland, Oregon. Starbucks invited coffee drinkers to stop at a local Starbucks for a free cup of coffee on March 15. Four-page full-color ads were placed in daily newspapers of 11 major markets, including New York, Los Angeles, Chicago, Boston, and Dallas. The ads were placed in the newspapers the week before the giveaway and again the day before. Then, on the day of the giveaway, Starbucks hired street vendors to pass out free copies of the newspapers that contained the Starbucks ad. The newspapers were banded with the distinctive Starbucks' coffee cup sleeve. The campaign cost $545,000, but resulted in a half-million customers going into a Starbucks store. Lines wrapped around the block in some locations. Starbucks estimated the newspaper campaign resulted in 12 million impressions.[35]

Disadvantages of Newspaper Advertising

Newspapers cannot be easily targeted to specific market segments, although sports pages carry sports ads, entertainment pages contain movie and restaurant ads, and so forth. Newspapers have short lives. Once read, a newspaper will be cast aside, recycled, or destroyed. If a reader does not see an advertisement during the first pass through a newspaper, it may go unnoticed. Readers rarely pick up papers a second time. When they do, it is to continue reading, not to reread or rescan a section that has already been viewed.

Newspaper readers continue to age. Younger consumers obtain news either through the internet or from television; few read a print newspaper. The average age of those who read printed papers is 51 compared to 44 for those who read the digital version. Digital readers are younger, better educated, and are often more affluent than the print readers.[36]

Media Mix

Selecting the proper blend of media outlets for advertisements is crucial. As they prepare campaigns, advertisers make decisions regarding the appropriate mix of media. Media planners and media buyers are excellent sources of information regarding the most effective type of mix for a particular advertising campaign. Figure 14 displays the media mix in the United States for Coca-Cola. Total U.S. spending for advertising by Coca-Cola was $752 million; 63.4 percent went to television advertising. Coca-Cola spent far less on the other media.[37]

Recent studies by Millward Brown and ACNielsen highlight the benefits of combining media.[38] The Millward Brown report indicates that ad awareness became strongest when consumers were exposed to an advertisement on television and in a magazine. Ad awareness was considerably lower for only those who read the magazine ad and even less for those who only saw the television commercial.

The **media multiplier effect** suggests that the combined impact of using two or more media will be stronger than using either medium alone. The British insurance company Churchill discovered that 62 percent of consumers who saw the company's TV commercial and heard its radio ad planned to look into Churchill Insurance, compared to 49 percent who only saw only the television advertisement.[39]

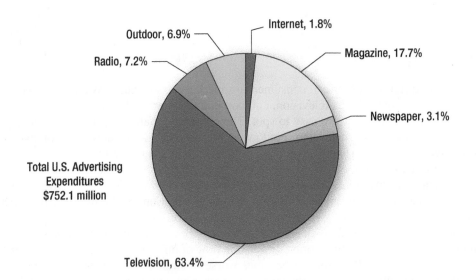

Internet, 1.8%

Outdoor, 6.9%

Magazine, 17.7%

Radio, 7.2%

Newspaper, 3.1%

Total U.S. Advertising
Expenditures
$752.1 million

Television, 63.4%

◀ **FIGURE 14**
U.S. Advertising Expenditures
by Media for Coca-Cola

▼ The campaign for Ouachita
Independent Bank utilized
multiple media, such as television,
radio, newspapers, internet, and
billboards.

Newcomer, Morris and Young Inc.

The media multiplier effect is equally useful for business-to-business advertisers. In a survey conducted by American Business Media, 89 percent of the business respondents indicated that an integrated marketing approach raised their awareness of a company or brand. Seeing advertisements in more than one medium led the company or brand name to become top-of-mind. It also resulted in more businesses making purchases.[40] Finding effective combinations of media will be the key to utilizing the media multiplier effect. Figure 15 displays the process for choosing the best media for a particular advertising message. Media experts decide which go best together for individual target markets, goods and services, and advertising messages.

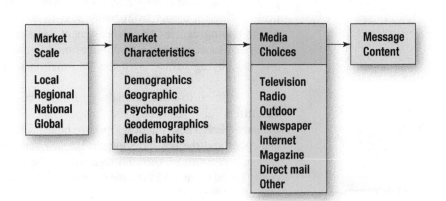

Market Scale	Market Characteristics	Media Choices	Message Content
Local Regional National Global	Demographics Geographic Psychographics Geodemographics Media habits	Television Radio Outdoor Newspaper Internet Magazine Direct mail Other	

◀ **FIGURE 15**

Developing Logical Combinations
of Media

Media Selection in Business-to-Business Markets

objective 7

What are the key issues associated with media selection for business-to-business markets?

Identifying differences between consumer ads and business-to-business ads has become more difficult, especially on television, outdoor, and the internet. In the past, business-to-business advertisements were easy to spot. The content was aimed at another company. Marketers seldom used television, outdoor, or the internet. Now, however, companies spend over half of all business advertising dollars on nonbusiness venues.[41]

Several explanations have been offered regarding the shift to nonbusiness media. First, business decision makers also consume goods and services. The same psychological techniques used to influence and gain consumer attention can be used for business decision makers.

Second, reaching business decision makers at work can be hard. Gatekeepers (secretaries, voice mail systems, etc.) often prevent the flow of information to users, influencers, and decision makers. The problem becomes worse in straight rebuy situations in which orders are routinely placed with the current vendor. Any company other than the chosen vendor finds it difficult to make contact with buying center members. Consequently, some business-to-business vendors try to reach them at home, in the car, or in some other nonbusiness setting.

Third, clutter among the traditional business media makes it more challenging to get a company noticed. Business advertisers recognize that a strong brand name can be a major factor in making a sale. Taking lessons from major giants such as Nike, Kraft Foods, and Procter & Gamble, business marketers seek to develop strong brands because the name helps a company gain the attention of members of the buying center.

In the past, many business ads were fairly dull. Currently, business ads are more likely to resemble those aimed at consumers. Ads feature creative appeals and the use of music, humor, sex, and fear. The boldest business ads sometimes include nudity or other more risqué materials.

Figure 16 identifies the ways business-to-business advertising expenditures are divided among the various media. In the past, business publications accounted for most of the expenditures, often half of the dollars. Business publications now represent about one-fourth of the more than $14 billion spent annually on business-to-business advertising. As more dollars are shifted to nonbusiness types of media, the amount being spent on television, newspapers, and consumer magazines has steadily increased.[42]

Although the use of business publications has decreased, trade journals still present an excellent opportunity to contact members of the buying center whom salespeople cannot reach. Gatekeepers do not prevent trade journals from being sent to members of the buying center. An advertisement has the best chance of success when a firm makes modified rebuy and the buying center is in the information search stage.

In addition to trade journals, business-to-business advertisers also use business magazines such as *BusinessWeek*. These publications have highly selective audiences and the ads have longer life spans in print. Business decision makers and members of the buying center spend more working time examining print media than any other medium.

▼ In business-to-business advertising, print remains an important medium for companies such as ReRez.

ReRez

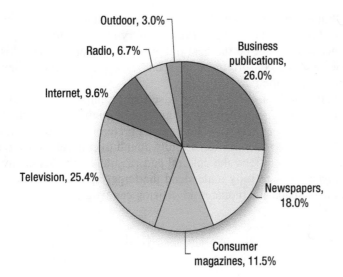

◀ **FIGURE 16**
Business-to-Business Advertising
Expenditures

Many goals in business-to-business advertisements are the same as those devoted to consumers. Most of the variables shown in Figure 15 apply equally well to business advertising.

International Implications

Understanding media viewing habits in international markets constitutes an important part of a successful advertising program. In Japan, television provides a major advertising tool; in other countries, it is not as prevalent. In Europe, a good way to reach consumers is through print media, such as magazines and newspapers.

For several years, reports have surfaced that teenagers are watching less TV and spending more time on the internet. A Forrester Research study contradicted that notion, at least in Europe. Thousands of teenagers in Europe were surveyed about their media usage.[43] The general conclusions of the Forrester study are that:

- European teens spend more time watching TV than they do with any other medium, averaging 10.3 hours per week.
- Average personal time on the internet is 9.1 hours per week.
- Europeans ages 10 to 17 spend less time on the internet than individuals 18 and older.
- Only 41 percent of European teens visit social networks at least once a week.
- Teenagers like to multitask—watching TV while texting friends or playing video games while listening to music or TV.
- Younger European teens love video games, playing twice as much as individuals 18 and older.
- Most teenagers do not read the paper. They get news from TV or the internet.

Although a large number of media buying agencies operate throughout the world, nearly three-quarters of all media buying is conducted by only six large global agencies or their holding agencies. The largest global media company is the WPP Group, which holds 22 percent of the market share.[44] To combat these large media networks, a global media consortium has been formed. The consortium consists of a number of smaller independent agencies and offers services in Europe, North America, the Russian Federation, and Asia. Central offices are located in New York and London to serve business clients and to pitch for regional and national accounts.[45]

Large global media agencies have faced some criticism in recent years from marketing managers. They complain about the inability to provide effective media buys

objective 8

What issues are associated with media selection in international markets?

throughout all the countries where the clients operate. Although a few agencies do cover the world, it is difficult to be strong in every country in which an agency has a presence. The global agency may not be the best option in every country. For this reason, local media agencies and the consortium of independent agencies believe they have a better opportunity to increase their market shares.

In general, the tactics used to develop advertising campaigns and choose appropriate media in the United States apply to other countries throughout the world. What differs is the nature of the target markets, consumer media preferences, and the processes used to buy media. Company representatives carefully attend to cultural mores to make sure the buying process does not offend the cultural and religious attitudes in any given region. Agency employees seek to fully understand the target market as a company purchases advertising time or space and prepares advertising campaigns.

INTEGRATED campaigns in action

The Snoring Center

In the past decade, the Pink Jacket Creative advertising agency, led by co-owners Bill Breedlove and Elena Baca, helped develop a highly successful advertising program for a medical company—The Snoring Center. According to Breedlove, "When we first started working with The Snoring Center, a physician had an office here in Dallas. He decided he wanted to start treating snoring and sleep apnea. Did you know that 46 percent of adults snore? 25 percent snore habitually? Of that, 23 percent of married couples regularly sleep apart because of sleep apnea."

To develop brand awareness for The Snoring Center, the central component of the advertising program was billboards, with television and print ads as support media. Bill Breedlove recalls, "It was a really simple outdoor campaign. We put up branded billboards that said simply, 'Snoring Kills …,' and then underneath it would have something that it kills, such as 'it kills careers' or 'it kills your love life,' or 'it kills your mojo,' or 'your morning quickies,' or 'your afternoon delight,' and so on.

Within a year and a half, the physician shut his ENT practice down and had two locations of The Snoring Center. Within 24 months, The Snoring Center became the world's leading provider of minimally invasive snoring treatment. The company now performs more procedures than any other provider in the world.[46]

The Snoring Center campaign is located at the Pearson Instructor's Resource Center (www.pearsonhighered.com). The campaign has a PowerPoint presentation outlining the details of the campaigns and examples of the collaterals developed by Pink Jack Creative. Also available is video of the creative minds behind the campaign, Bill Breedlove and Elena Baca.

Courtesy of Pink Jacket Creative: A Creative Factory

◀ Billboard ads were the central component of the campaign for The Snoring Center.

Summary

In traditional advertising, the roles of media planners and media buyers have grown in importance. Bob Brennan, chief operating officer of Chicago-based Leo Burnett Starcom USA, stated that in the past "Ninety-five percent of your success was great creative and 5 percent was great media. Now it's much closer to 50–50."[47]

A media strategy is the process of analyzing and choosing media for an advertising and promotions campaign. Media planners and buyers complete much of this work. The media planner formulates a program stating where and when to place advertisements. Media planners work closely with creatives and account executives. Media buyers purchase the space, and they negotiate rates, times, and schedules for the ads.

The goals of reach, frequency, opportunity to see, gross rating points, effective rating points, cost, continuity, and gross impressions drive the media selection process. Reach identifies the number of people, households, or businesses in a target audience exposed to a media vehicle or message schedule at least once during a given time period. Frequency represents the average number of times an individual, household, or business within a particular target market is exposed to a particular advertisement within a specified time period. Gross rating points (GRPs) measure the impact or intensity of a media plan. Cost per thousand (CPM) is one method of finding the cost of the campaign by assessing the dollar cost of reaching 1,000 members of the media vehicle's audience. Cost per rating point (CPRP), a second cost measure, assesses the efficiency of a media vehicle relative to a firm's target market. Ratings measure the percentage of a firm's target market exposed to a show on television or an article in a print medium. Continuity sets the schedule or pattern of advertisement placements within an advertising campaign period. Gross impressions are the number of total exposures of the audience to an advertisement.

The three-exposure hypothesis suggests that a consumer must be exposed to an ad at least three times before it has the desired impact; other experts believe even more exposures are necessary. In contrast, recency theory suggests that ads truly reach only those wanting or needing a product and that the carryover effects of advertising diminish rapidly. It is necessary, therefore, to advertise on a continuous basis to ensure that the message is noticed by consumers as they make purchase decisions.

In addition to these basic concepts, advertising experts often utilize the concepts of effective frequency and effective reach. Effective frequency states the number of times a target audience must be exposed to a message to achieve a particular objective. Effective reach identifies the percentage of an audience that must be exposed to a particular message to achieve a specific objective.

In seeking advertising goals, marketing experts, account executives, and others assess the relative advantages and disadvantages of each individual advertising medium. Thus, television, radio, out-of-home, magazines, and newspapers should all be considered as potential ingredients in a campaign. Other new media can be used to complement and supplement the more traditional media outlets. Logical combinations of media should be chosen.

In business-to-business settings, companies can combine consumer media outlets with trade journals and other business venues (trade shows, conventions, etc.) to attempt to reach members of the buying center. In many cases, enticing ads using consumer appeals such as sex, fear, and humor have replaced dry, dull, boring ads with an abundance of copy.

International advertising media selection is different in some ways from that which takes place in the United States, because media buying processes differ as do media preferences of locals in various countries. At the same time, the process of media selection is quite similar. Marketing experts choose media they believe will reach the target audience in an effective manner.

Key Terms

media strategy The process of analyzing and choosing media for an advertising and promotions campaign

media planner The individual who formulates the media program stating where and when to place advertisements

media buyer The person who buys the media space and negotiates rates, times, and schedules for the ads

spot ad A one-time placement of a commercial on a local television station

reach The number of people, households, or businesses in a target audience exposed to a media vehicle or message schedule at least once during a given time period

frequency The average number of times an individual, household, or business within a particular target market is exposed to a particular advertisement within a specified time period

opportunities to see (OTS) The cumulative exposures to an advertisement achieved in a given time period

gross rating points (GRPs) A measure of the impact or intensity of a media plan

cost per thousand (CPM) The dollar cost of reaching 1,000 members of the media vehicle's audience

ratings A measure of the percentage of a firm's target market exposed to a show on television or an article in a print medium

cost per rating point (CPRP) A measure of the efficiency of a media vehicle relative to a firm's target market

weighted (or demographic) CPM A measure used to calculate whether an advertisement reached the target market effectively

continuity The schedule or pattern of advertisement placements within an advertising campaign period

gross impressions The number of total exposures of the audience to an advertisement

intrusion value The ability of media or an advertisement to intrude upon a viewer without his or her voluntary attention

recency theory A theory suggesting that consumer attention is selective and focuses on individual needs and wants and therefore has selective attention to advertisements

effective reach The percentage of an audience that must be exposed to a particular message to achieve a specific objective

effective frequency The number of times a target audience must be exposed to a message to achieve a particular objective

dynamic advertising A research method that allows a company to obtain consumer information from marketing research firms and combine it with the company's data to send target ads to consumers

media multiplier effect The combined impact of using two or more media is stronger than using either medium alone

---

MyMarketingLab

Go to **mymktlab.com** to complete the problems marked with this icon ⭐.

Review Questions

1. What is a media strategy? How does it relate to the creative brief and the overall IMC program?

2. What does a media planner do?

3. Describe the role of media buyer in an advertising program.

4. What is reach? Give examples of reach in various advertising media.

5. What is frequency? How can an advertiser increase frequency in a campaign?

6. What are gross rating points? What do they measure?

7. What is the difference between CPM and CPRP? What costs do they measure?

8. What is continuity?

9. Describe the three-exposure hypothesis.

10. How does recency theory differ from the three-exposure hypothesis?

11. What is effective frequency? Effective reach?

12. What are the major advantages and disadvantages of television advertising?

13. What are the major advantages and disadvantages of radio advertising?

14. What are the major advantages and disadvantages of outdoor advertising?

15. What are the major advantages and disadvantages of magazine advertising?

16. What are the major advantages and disadvantages of newspaper advertising?

17. Is the strong intrusion value of television an advantage? Why or why not?

18. What special challenges does media selection present for businesses? What roles do gatekeepers play in creating those challenges?

19. What special challenges does media selection present for international advertising campaigns? What differences and similarities exist with U.S. media selection processes?

Critical Thinking Exercises

DISCUSSION QUESTIONS

⭐ 20. To be effective, multiple media should be chosen and integrated carefully. Individuals exposed to advertisements in combinations of media selected from television, radio, magazines, newspapers, and outdoor are more inclined to process the information than when a message appears in only a solitary medium. For each of the media, what is the probability of being exposed to an advertisement? The percentages should add up to 100 percent. Discuss which media are most effective in reaching you.

21. Billboard advertising in Times Square has become so popular that space has already been sold for the next 10 years. Coca-Cola, General Motors, Toshiba, ⭐ Prudential, NBC, Budweiser, and *The New York Times* pay rates in excess of $100,000 per month to hold these spaces. Why would companies pay so much for outdoor advertising? What are the advantages and disadvantages of purchasing billboards at Times Square?

22. The Super Bowl is the most watched program on television. Many tune in just to watch the ads. Discuss the concepts of effective reach, effective frequency, ratings, gross rating points, brand recognition, brand recall, and opportunities to see as it relates to Super Bowl advertising. What are the advantages for a brand to advertise on television during the Super Bowl? What are the disadvantages?

23. Xerox offers a color printer that sells for $1,200. The goal is to market it to business buyers. What media mix would you suggest for a $5 million advertising campaign? Justify your answer.

24. Complete the following table by calculating the missing values. Based on the values you calculated, identify two magazines and two television shows for advertising sports equipment. Support your answer with specific data from the table.

| Publication | 4C Base Rate or 30-second Ad | Circulation or Audience | CPM | Target Market (30 million) | | | | |
				Percent of Readers Fit Target Market	Number of Readers Fit Target Market	Rating (Reach)	Cost per Rating Point (CPRP)	Weighted (Demographic) CPM
Magazines								
Allure	$165,554	1,080,000		12.2%				
Ebony	$81,167	1,170,000		16.1%				
Men's Health	$215,850	1,900,000		22.7%				
Road & Track	$119,421	720,000		28.4%				
Sports Illustrated	$412,500	3,170,000		7.8%				
Television Shows								
NCIS	$180,264	19,700,000		6.3%				
2 Broke Girls	$175,506	9,000,000		4.2%				
Big Bang Theory	$316,912	20,000,000		10.8%				
Criminal Minds	$119,052	10,400,000		12.5%				
Modern Family	$281,961	9,100,000		17.8%				

▲ **FIGURE 17**

25. Use the internet or phone directory to identify all of the radio stations in your area. What type of format does each have (i.e., talk, country, hip hop, rock, ⭐ etc.)? Is radio a good advertising medium to reach college students at your university? Why or why not? Which of the radio stations on your list would be the most effective in reaching college students?

⭐ 26. As you drive to school (or home) make a list of all of the billboards and outdoor advertising you see. Which are the most effective? Why? Which are the least effective? Why? How effective are billboards at reaching you with an advertising message?

27. Pick three different magazines on a wide range of topics. For each, describe the types of ads and the number of ads in the issue. Did you see any business-to-business ads? What similarities did you see in the ads across the five magazines? What differences did you notice? Which would be most effective at reaching people in your demographic?

Integrated Learning Exercises

28. Go to the Life Section of *USA Today* (**www.usatoday .com/life**) and locate the Nielsen ratings. What were the top 10 television shows last week? What other information is available at the website about the top TV shows?

29. In Canada, a valuable source of information is BBM (Bureau of Broadcast Measurement). Access this website at **www.bbm.ca**. What type of information is available on the site? What media does the BBM cover? How can it be used to develop a media plan for Canada?

30. A trade organization for magazines is the Magazine Publishers of America. Access the association's website at **www.magazine.org**. What type of information is available? How could it be used by a company wanting to advertise in magazines?

31. Two websites important for radio advertising are the Radio Advertising Bureau at **www.rab.com** and the top 100 radio sites at **www.100topradiosites.com**. Access both sites. What information is available on each site? Discuss how the information can be used to develop an advertising plan using radio.

32. A major company for outdoor advertising is Lamar Advertising Company. Access its website at **www .lamar.com**. Access the outdoor advertising component of the company and locate the rates for your area or another area of interest to you. What type of outdoor advertising is available? What other products does Lamar offer? What services does Lamar offer? Write a short report on what types of advertising Lamar can provide for a company.

33. An excellent source of information for business advertisers is at *Entrepreneur*. Access the advertising section of *Entrepreneur* at **http://www.entrepreneur .com/advertising**. What type of information is available at this website? How can it be used by a small business?

34. The Newspaper Association of America is a trade association for newspaper. Access the website at **http:// www.naa.org**. What type of information is available? How could this information be used by your local newspaper to increase business?

Blog Exercises

Access the authors' blog for this text at the URLs provided to complete these exercises. Answer the questions that are posed on the blog.

35. Duracell Batteries - **http://blogclowbaack.net/2014/ 05/08/duracell-chapter-7/**

36. Geico Insurance - **http://blogclowbaack.net/2014/05/ 08/geico-chapter-7/**

37. Media - **http://blogclowbaack.net/2014/05/08/media-chapter-7/**

Student Project

CREATIVE CORNER

Horse racing has struggled to maintain attendance at some race tracks. The majority of serious fans of horse racing are older, white males. One challenge in drawing new fans to horse racing is to help them understand this complex sport. Recognizing which horse won a race is easy; however, after that it becomes very complex and difficult to grasp horse racing stats. A steep learning curve that requires thoughtful and complex analysis is needed. Many potential fans do not want to invest the time or energy to learn. According to Tim Capps, a professor at the University of the Louisville College of Business, horse racing "has been run more for itself than for its fans. One thing racing has to do is make participation in our sport easier for fans, because the fan has not come first in our industry." He further adds "people don't want to go to school. They want to be entertained."

While all agree there is a need to attract new fans, wide disagreement exists regarding the type of fan it should be. Do you market to the individuals who are already going to the track, or do you go after new individuals? Do you go after young people, middle-age individuals, or work harder to reach baby boomers? Which gender—male or female—do you seek?

First, choose the target audience for an advertising campaign. Defend your choice. Second, select the media that would be most appropriate. Third, design a magazine ad for the target market chosen. Fourth, develop a billboard or outdoor ad to accompany the magazine ad.

TRUST YOUR POWER

SUDIO 1ONE/Fotolia

▲ Derrick Coleman's ad and story are an inspiration to many youth that they can succeed.

Designing television commercials that will be powerful and create a long-lasting impact is a key goal for many companies and advertising agencies. At times, inspiration comes from unusual places and circumstances. The New York-based Saatchi and Saatchi agency recently developed an inspiring advertisement for Duracell batteries.

Professional football player Derrick Coleman is the first legally deaf person to make an NFL roster, the Seattle Seahawks. Coleman made the team even though he was not a draft pick. His ability to read lips combined with new hearing aid technology helped in the process. In 2014, he was asked to tell his story as part of a commercial for Duracell. As fortune would have it, the Seahawks moved into the NFC Championship game just as the spot was aired.[48]

As reported by *Adweek*, "Bravely narrating the ad himself, Coleman tells his own story of being picked on as a kid, being told he could never make it—and being passed over by the NFL draft. 'They didn't call my name, told me it was over,' he says. 'But I've been deaf since I was 3, so I didn't listen.' That's a great line. The tagline: "Trust the power within.'"

The buzz was immediate. Within a short period of time, the commercial had been viewed by more than 2 million people on YouTube. Yahoo! asked, "Want goosebumps? Watch this commercial." The site adds: "That might just be another victory Coleman adds to his amazing list.[49] Other sites, such as BleacherReport, chimed in with similar praise and a story about the ad appeared in *USA Today*. Twitter and other social media outlets also picked up on the story. Coleman's response was, "I just hope to inspire people, especially children, to trust the power within and achieve their dreams."[50]

38. Go to Duracell's YouTube channel (**www.youtube.com/user/OfficialDuracell**) and watch the advertisement for Durcell featuring Derrick Coleman. What was your reaction? Do you think Coleman's story could overpower the brand being advertised? Why or why not?

39. As a media planner, how would you evaluate this type of advertisement? In which television shows would you place this ad? Why?

40. Explain the roles that reach, frequency, and opportunities to see would play in the release of this ad. For Durcell, which would be more important—brand recognition or brand recall? Justify your answer.

41. Besides television, which media would support this message and campaign? Explain why.

42. Explain the media you would choose to present this advertisement to men. Explain which media you would choose to present this advertisement to women. Provide support for your answers.

CASE 2 ▸ AFTER UNLEASHING

Dog owners constitute a large target market. Most members share something in common: the desire to let the pet run free and unfettered. If other friendly dogs are nearby and want to play—all the better. The Unleashed Dog Park was created to meet this need.

Out-of-home advertising can be the critical component of an IMC program and, in some cases, the primary medium. To help launch the new business venture, The Pink Jacket Creative advertising agency created a feeling of expectancy and mystery with its "Unleashed Dog Park" campaign, which featured the three successive billboards shown in this section.

The first billboard displays a dog on a leash. The unfinished nature of the image helps capture interest. Next, the dog, now with an unfastened leash, moves to the center of the billboard, and "unleash" appears in the top-right corner. In the final billboard, the dog is on the right side of the billboard, the leash is gone, and the message "Unleashed indoor dog parks" appears. It also displays the services offered, the website address of the park, and the location of the facility. In addition to billboards, street kiosks and bus wraps were used to get the message out.

The early results of the campaign were positive. Many dog owners became aware of the new indoor dog park. What followed represent common challenges in marketing communications: sustaining initial interest, moving consumers to action, and building repeat business.

In this next phase, dog owners needed to be encouraged to try the facility. They should be led to believe that the price of entry was a value. Then, over time, they can be enticed to make return visits and to offer word-of-mouth referrals to other pet owners. Only if these objectives can be attained will the initial success of the Unleashed campaign become validated.

43. Define the marketing goals for the second phase of the Unleashed Dog Park promotional efforts.

44. How would the three-exposure hypothesis or recency theory apply to this advertising program in its initial stages? What about the second campaign after consumers are aware of the dog park?

45. Which traditional advertising media should the marketing team use for the second campaign? Discuss the pros and cons of each in terms of the Unleashed Dog Park campaign and the desire to stimulate trial usage.

46. How could social media and nontraditional media be used to supplement a traditional media campaign in this circumstance?

47. Design a newspaper ad and an outdoor ad that will be placed at little league baseball parks in the area.

▲ A series of ads for the Unleashed Dog Park was created by Pink Jacket Creative to gain the attention of motorists, causing them to wonder what the total message would be.

Pink Jacket Studio

MyMarketingLab

Go to **mymktlab.com** for Auto-graded writing questions as well as the following Assisted-graded writing questions:

48. The Super Bowl is the most watched program on television. Many tune in just to watch the ads. Discuss the concepts of effective reach, effective frequency, ratings, gross rating points, brand recognition, brand recall, and opportunities to see as it relates to Super Bowl advertising. What are the advantages for a brand to advertise on television during the Super Bowl? What are the disadvantages?

49. An excellent source of information for business advertisers is at *Entrepreneur*. Access the advertising section of *Entrepreneur* at **http://www.entrepreneur.com/advertising**. What type of information is available at this website? How can it be used by a small business?

Endnotes

1. Sam Thielman, "Ad of the Day: Is Chiddy Bang's Version of Oreo's Wonderfilled Song the Best Yet?, *Adweek*, July 31, 2013, http://www.adweek.com/news/advertising-branding/ad-day-oreo-gets-edge-chiddy-bangs-version-wonderfilled-151561, retrieved January 14, 2014.

2. Creative Blog: Top 35 TV Commercials, Oreos, http://www.creativebloq.com/3d/top-tv-commercials-12121024, retrieved January 14, 2014.

3. Mickey Marks, "Millennial Satiation," *Advertising Age* 14 (February 2000), p. S16; J. Thomas Russell and W. Ronald Lane, *Kleppner's Advertising Procedure,* 15th ed. (Upper Saddle River, NJ: Prentice Hall), 2002, pp. 174–75.

4. Larry Percy, John R. Rossiter, and Richard Elliott, "Media Strategy," *Strategic Advertising Management* (2001), pp. 151–63.

5. Kate Maddox, "Media Planners in High Demand," *BtoB* 89, no. 13 (November 8, 2004), p. 24.

6. Arthur A. Andersen, "Clout Only a Part of Media Buyer's Value," *Advertising Age* 70, no. 15 (April 5, 1999), p. 26.

7. Ibid.

8. Herbert E. Krugman, "Why Three Exposures May Be Enough," *Journal of Advertising Research* 12, no. 6 (1972), pp. 11–14.

9. Erwin Ephron and Colin McDonald, "Media Scheduling and Carry-over Effects: Is Adstock a Useful Planning Tool," *Journal of Advertising Research* 42, no. 4 (July–August 2002), pp. 66–70; Laurie Freeman, "Added Theories Drive Need for Client Solutions," *Advertising Age* 68, no. 31, p. 18.

10. Larry Percy, John R. Rossiter, and Richard Elliott, "Media Strategy," *Strategic Advertising Management* (2001), pp. 151–63.

11. Ibid.

12. Jack Loechner, "TV Advertising Most Influential," *Media Post Research Brief*, March 23, 2011, www.mediapost.com/publications/?fa=articles.printfriendly&art_aid=147033.

13. Diane Holloway, "What's On? Ads, Ads, and Maybe a TV Show," *Austin American Statesman* (**www.austin360.com/tv/content/movies/**television/2005/10/11tvcolumn.html, accessed January 17, 2008), October 11, 2005.

14. Jack Neff, "Future of Advertising? Print, TV, Online Ads," *Advertising Age* (**www.adage.com/print?article_id=136993**), June 1, 2009; Gregory Solman, "Forward Thought: Ads A-Ok on DVRs," *Hollywood Reporter* (http://hollywoodreporter.com), December 27, 2007.

15. Steve McClellan, "Audit Finds Nielsen's C3 Ratings Hurt Advertisers," *Media Daily News*, September 19, 2011, www.mediapost.com/publications/article/158818.

16. Brian Steinberg, "Simon Who? Idol Spots Still Priciest in Prime Time," *Advertising Age*, October 18, 2010, http://adage.com/pring/146495.

17. Adapted from Brian Steinberg, "Sunday Night Football Remains Costliest TV Show," *Advertising Age* (http://adage.com/article?article_id=139923), October 26, 2009; "List of Top 20 Prime-time Programs in the Nielsen Ratings for Sept. 28–Oct. 4," *Entertainment Daily* (http://blog.taragana.com/e/2009/10/06/list-of-top-20-prime-time-programs-in-the-nielsen-ratings-for-sept28-oct4), October 6, 2009.

18. Karlene Lukovitz, "Regional Gain Uses TV to Take On Big Pizza Brands," *Marketing Daily*, November 15, 2011, www.mediapost.com/publications/article/162392.

19. Andy Fixmer, Ian King, and Cliff Edwards, "DirecTV Upends Ad Model with Toyota Spots of Auto Geeks," *Bloomberg Businessweek* www.businessweek.com/printer/articles/596492, September 23, 2013.

20. Gavin O'Mally, "Social Media Chatter Ups Live TV Stats," *MediaPost News*, March 22, 2012, www.

mediapost.com/publications/articl/170743; Jack Loechner, "TV Advertising Most Influential," *Media Post Research Brief*, March 23, 2011, www.mediapost.com/publications/?fa=articles.printfriendly&art_aid=147033.

21. Anthony Crupi, "Commercial Breaks Aren't Twitter Breaks," *Adweek*, www.adweek.com/news/advertising-branding/commercial-breaks-arent-twitter-breaks, September 18, 2013.

22. Ki Mae Heussner, "Social Data Uncovers Brand, TV-Show Affinity," *Adweek*, December 22, 2011, www.adweek.com/print/137243.

23. Susan Kuchinsakas, "Brands Increase Recall with TV/Digital Mix, Google Says," *ClickZ*, December 6, 2011, www.clickz.com/print_article/clikz/stats/2130484.

24. Gabriel Beltrone, "Ads Trump Football in Super Bowl Survey," *Adweek*, www.adweek.com/news/advertising-branding/ads-trump-football-in-super-bowl-survey, January 24, 2013; Stuart Elliott, "Mainstays Will Reappear in the Big Game Again," *The New York Times*, January 27, 2012, www.nytimes.com/2012/01/27/business/media/mainstays-will-reappear-in-the-big-game-once-again.

25. Stuart Eliioott, "Before the Toss, Super Bowl Ads," *The New York Times*, February 2, 2012, www.nytimes.com/2012/02/03/business/media/before-the-toss-super-bowl-ads; Stuart Elliott, "Before Sunday, A Taste of the Bowl," *The New York Times*, February 3, 2012, www.nytimes.com/2011/02/04/business/media/04adco.html. G28

26. Interview with Stan Richards, The Richards Group, February 4, 2010; Rupal Parekh, "Behind the Scenes of Bridgestone's Super Bowl Spots," *Advertising Age*, February 8, 2010, pp. 4–5.

27. Doug McPherson, "Into Thin Air," *Response* 18, no. 5 (February 2010), pp. 40–45.

28. Interview with Mary Price by Donald Baack and Kenneth E. Clow, January 20, 2010.

29. Doug McPherson, "Into Thin Air," *Response* 18, no. 5 (February 2010), pp. 40–45.

30. Sarah Mahoney, "Taco Tweets Fuel Texas C-Store's Advertising," *Media Post News, Marketing Daily*, February 9, 2011, www.mediapost.com/publications/?fa=Articles.print_aid=144522.

31. Morianna Morello, "Why Print Media—and Why Now?" *Response* 17, no. 8 (May 2009), p. 77.

32. Edward C. Baig, "DirecTV Takes the Dive with SI's Swimsuit Issue," *USA Today Money*, February 1, 2012, www.usatoday.com/money/media/story/2012-02-01/directv-takes-the-dive-with-sis-swimsuit-issue.

33. Nat Ives, "If You're Rich, You Still Have Time to Read," *Advertising Age* (**www.adage.com/print?article_id=130685**), September 2, 2008.

34. Erik Sass, "Newspaper Ads Still Guide Shopping," *Media Daily News*, April 13, 2011, www.mediapost.com/publications/?fa=Articles=148632.

35. Bill Gloede, "Best Use of Newspapers," *Adweek* 48, no. 25 (June 18, 2007), pp. SR22–23.

36. Erik Sass, "Newspaper's Digital Audience Skews Younger, More Affluent," *Media Daily News*, December 13, 2011, www.mediapost.como/publications/article/164161.

37. *Marketer Trees 2009* (http://adage.com/marketertres09), December 28, 2009.

38. Lindsay Morris, "Studies Give 'Thumbs Up' to Mags for Ad Awareness," *Advertising Age* 70, no. 32 (August 2, 1999), pp. 16–17; Rachel X. Weissman, "Broadcasters Mine the Gold," *American Demographics* 21, no. 6 (June 1999), pp. 35–37.

39. Stacey Pratt, "Planning Casebook," *Mediaweek*, no. 1230 (October 20, 2009), p. 17.

40. "ABM Releases Harris Study Data: B2B Advertising Highly Effective," *Min's B2B* 9, no. 26 (June 26, 2006), p. 8.

41. Kate Maddox, "Top 100 B-to-B Advertisers Increased Spending 3% in '06," *BtoB* 92, no. 11 (September 10, 2007), pp. 25–30.

42. Ibid.

43. Eric Pfanner, "TV Still Has a Hold on Teenagers," *The New York Times* (**www.nytimes.com/2009/12/14/business/media/14iht-cache14.html**), December 14, 2009.

44. Joe Mandese, "Power Shift," *Broadcasting & Cable* 135, no. 53 (December 12, 2005), p. 12.

45. Martin Croft, "Media Indies Take on Networks with Consortium," *Marketing Week* 29, no. 28 (July 13, 2006), p. 13.

46. Interview with Bill Breedlove by Donald Baack and Kenneth E. Clow, January 21, 2010.

47. Jack Neff, "Media Buying & Planning." *Advertising Age* 70, no. 32 (August 2, 1999), pp. 1–2.

48. Alison Smith, Duracell Releases Ad Featuring Deaf Seahawks Fullback Derrick Coleman: Urges People to Use Your Power, NFL.com http://nesn.com/2014/01/duracell-releases-ad-featuring-deaf-seahawks-running-back-derrick-coleman-urges-to-trust-your-power-video/, retrieved January 14, 2014.

49. Yahoo! Sports. Want Goosebumps? Watch this commercial featuring deaf Seahawks fullback Derrick Coleman, January 14, 2014, http://sports.yahoo.com/blogs/nfl-shutdown-corner/want-goosebumps-watch-commercial-featuring-deaf-seahawks-fullback-173222906—nfl.html, retrieved January 14, 2014.

50. Tim Nudd, Deaf NFL Player Derrick Coleman Tells His Story in a Terrific Duracell Ad, *Adweek*, January 13, 2014, http://www.adweek.com/adfreak/deaf-nfl-player-derrick-coleman-tells-his-story-terrific-duracell-ad-154952, retrieved January 14, 2014.

Digital Marketing

From Chapter 8 of *Integrated Advertising, Promotion, and Marketing Communications,* Seventh Edition. Kenneth E. Clow, Donald Baack.

Digital Marketing

Chapter Objectives

After reading this chapter, you should be able to answer the following questions:

1 What is digital marketing?

2 How has the transition to Web 4.0 affected the field of marketing communications?

3 How can e-commerce programs and incentives build a stronger customer base and overcome consumer concerns at the same time?

4 How do mobile marketing systems enhance digital marketing programs?

5 What digital strategies do marketing professionals employ?

6 What types of web advertising can companies use to reach consumers?

7 What is a search engine optimization strategy?

8 How can companies successfully conduct digital marketing programs in international markets?

Overview

Developing quality advertising and communications programs has become increasingly complex over the past decade. The essential ingredients of a marketing communications program: traditional media programswork in combination with other elements of the promotions mix. Thus, a television–radio—magazine campaign would incorporate coupons, discounts, personal selling techniques, sponsorships, and other ingredients to create a strong, coherent message.

Today's marketers and advertising professionals recognize that these efforts, while necessary, do not constitute a complete program. This text explains the additional elements needed to fully reach a target market and all potential customers. The activities to be added include the digital marketing programs detailed in this chapter; social media messages, and the additional alternative marketing channels. Companies and marketers that effectively combine these ingredients with other communications efforts have the best chance at succeeding in today's complex and challenging marketing environment.

Digital marketing combines all of the components of e-commerce, internet marketing, and mobile marketing. It includes anything with a digital footprint. Today's consumers and businesses rely on the internet to research products, make comparisons, read comments by other consumers, interact with other consumers and businesses, and make product purchases. One such company that helps create effective digital marketing programs is Marketing Zen.

Imagine a situation in which a person walking down a busy street is suddenly handed a bullhorn. The person may or may not have been encouraged to say something and has no idea what to say. In essence, many companies face this dilemma. In the past decade, new megaphones named Facebook, Twitter, Yahoo!, Google, YouTube, MySpace, the blogosphere, and others emerged. Many company leaders wondered how to effectively use these new tools.

Marketing Zen offers solutions to digital marketing complexities. What at first was primarily a consulting business has evolved into a full-service company. The organization grew from 4 to more than 20 employees in less than a year. Founder and owner Shama Kabani has been acclaimed one of the "10 Most Influential and Powerful Women in Social Media." She notes, "We take over online marketing for companies; we handle everything from soup to nuts. We handle their website, their SEO (search engine optimization), their social media, their email marketing, everything. We are their online marketing department. About 80 percent of our business is essentially taking over online marketing and handling that department for them."

Digital marketing goes beyond a company presenting a message to potential customers. Any new client of Marketing Zen is advised to make sure a bona fide reason exists for becoming involved with digital marketing and social media. In fact, Shama has written and published an article about the 10 reasons why a company should not use the forum. She says, "You use social media when you have something to say. It is a means to an end. If all your customers are on the web, or people are looking for you on the web…then you should be on the web."

The company features two types of metrics to assess the effectiveness of a digital marketing program. "There is a quantitative metric and a qualitative metric," Shama reports. "Often the qualitative can be heavier, because you're looking at what people are saying about the company, and what are they saying about the brand. How are they responding? Are they talking to their friends about it? It's being on the internet to see what people are saying about them."

"The quantitative metrics really depend on what the goals were. We measure things like traffic to the website and new visitors. Because social media is a great tool to attract people, we try to send them to the website. We try to send them to the hub of what's going on. You look at visitors; you look at how

Courtesy of Shama Hyder Kabani

▲ Shama Hyder Kabani.

Marketing Zen Group

▲ Shama's book *The Zen of Social Media Marketing.*

much time they spend on the site. You look at Twitter followers; you look at Facebook fans, and any other tool that we can utilize. We look at how many people left comments on the blog; we look at how many bloggers are talking about them."

In the end, the bottom line should be greater traffic to a company's website, longer visits while on the site, and ultimately making sales while building loyalty. Marketing Zen stays with a client to update and improve digital marketing efforts over time. Shama notes, "Our business is more than sales. It's relationship-building and networking and marketing and follow up and keeping in touch." By keeping true to its principles, Shama believes Marketing Zen has a bright future, even as the internet, social media, and other forms of communication continue to evolve.[1]

objective 1
What is digital marketing?

Clearly, the internet has changed the ways individuals communicate and how the world conducts business. It presents an open environment. A buyer can locate numerous sellers offering practically the same merchandise at comparable prices and with similar offers at any time. Currently, the internet offers more than a method to conduct business transactions: It serves as a communication highway.

This chapter presents the various concepts related to digital marketing. The first section of the chapter examines the evolution to Web 4.0. Next, e-commerce programs, including the incentives used to attract customers as well as consumer concerns with internet shopping, are presented. Then, the explosion in the use of smartphones also leads to an examination of mobile marketing techniques. Digital strategies designed to maximize a company's reach are described. Also, web advertising programs receive attention along with search engine optimization (SEO) techniques. Finally, international implications of these activities are drawn.

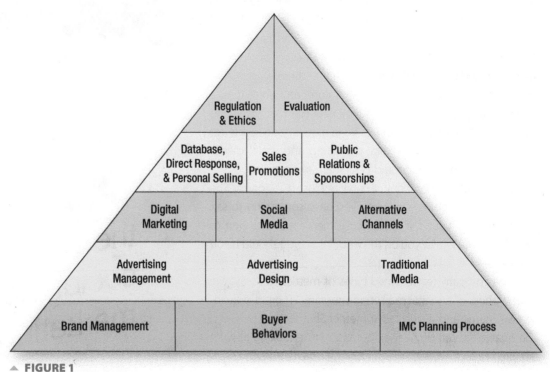

▲ FIGURE 1

Overview of Integrated Marketing Communications

objective 2
How has the transition to Web 4.0 affected the field of marketing communications?

Web 4.0

A recent study revealed that many companies have slashed traditional media marketing budgets and moved the funds to online communications. Many marketing experts believe that online searches, email, social media conversations, digital

- Web 1.0
  - Static content provided by creator
  - Dominated by institutions and businesses
  - Commercially and technically based
- Web 2.0
  - Content is socially based and audience generated
- Web 3.0
  - Content driven by online metrics
  - Integration of content and communications
  - Instant real-time communications
- Web 4.0
  - Customer engagement
  - Cloud operating systems
  - Web participation a necessity

◀ **FIGURE 2**
Primary Characteristics of
Web 1.0 to 4.0

ads, and mobile marketing will soon constitute a significant portion of marketing expenditures. The transition from Web 1.0 to Web 4.0 changed the ways consumers communicate and interact with companies. Figure 2 displays the characteristics of Web 1.0 to Web 4.0.

In the 1990s, the internet (Web 1.0) was typified by static content provided by a site's creator. Businesses and institutions included little consumer involvement on websites. These commercially and technically based organizations created sites that were crude, simple, and designed to accomplish one specific function.

As Web 2.0 dawned, content became more socially based and audience-oriented. Social networking sites such as Facebook and MySpace emerged. People wrote blogs. E-commerce expanded and consumers could purchase almost anything online. Sites became more appealing and customer-focused as competition drove web designers to create customer-friendly experiences.

Integration, online metrics, and real-time instant communications characterize Web 3.0. As marketers realized the wealth of online metrics available and the ability to track browser behavior on the web, content on sites became metric driven. Individuals searching on a site for hiking supplies found that the next time they logged onto the site, hiking-related supplies would be prominently promoted on the main page. With online metrics came integration of the web with every aspect of a company's marketing program, both online and offline. The things consumers viewed online matched what they encountered offline.

Web 3.0 online channels pushed companies into "real-time" communications. Instant communication meant consumers demanded improved customer service through live chats and instant messaging. Consumers also expect immediate responses to negative events. When an internet video showed two Domino's employees doing disgusting things to food, Twitter lit up with chatter and demands that the company address the matter. When Ford's legal department sent a legal notice to a Ford Ranger blogger to surrender his URL, Scott Monty, Ford's social media leader, jumped in and quickly resolved the issue before it went viral.[2]

Now Web 4.0 has emerged, with key characteristics of customer engagement, cloud operations, and web participation as necessities. Companies cannot just sell products to individuals and then allow customers to post reviews. Engagement constitutes the primary business model for Web 4.0. Companies that succeed use the web to connect customers with the brand through various venues such as social media, blogs, and Twitter. With the rise of smartphones and tablets, consumers have access to thousands of apps and ability to operate using the cloud. They can access brands anywhere, at any time.

▶ This Visit Baton Rouge website encourages interaction and engagement with site visitors.

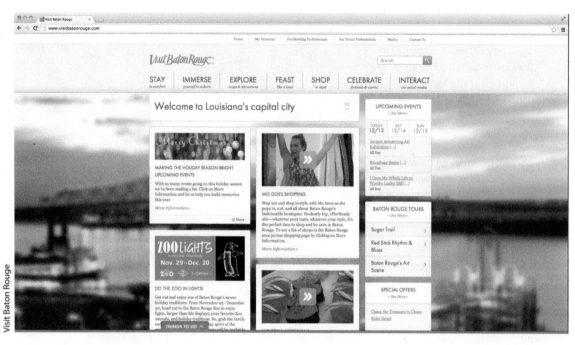

Visit Baton Rouge

E-Commerce

objective 3

How can e-commerce programs and incentives build a stronger customer base and overcome consumer concerns at the same time?

E-commerce focuses on selling goods and services over the internet. Many types of e-commerce businesses exist, ranging from click-only operations that sell entirely online to bricks-and-clicks that supplement physical store operations with an online presence. E-commerce involves both businesses selling to consumers (B2C) and businesses selling to other businesses (B2B). Mega-retailers such as Wal-Mart as well as mom-and-pop operations offering merchandise from home engage in e-commerce. Online sales account for nearly eight percent of all retail activity.[3]

Many consumers that make purchases at retail stores first use the internet to collect information or read reviews. A Pew Research Center survey revealed that 80 percent of Americans have researched a product online before making a purchase.[4] In Australia, half of the consumers first conduct online research.[5]

Building a Successful E-Commerce Site

E-commerce includes real-time communication and engagement with customers necessitated by Web 4.0. Figure 3 offers suggestions for developing successful e-commerce sites.

Effective e-commerce sites feature customer-centric designs in which individuals can easily locate merchandise. The marketing team arranges and indexes items using terms customers typically use rather than professional or technical language. If a large number of items are sold, then the site provides a drill-down search function that features customer-friendly terms and allows individuals to find items within one or two clicks.

- Customer-centric design
- Consistent customer experience
- Drill-down search
- Channel integration
- Brand engagement

- Customer interaction
- Customization and personalization
- Online and offline marketing
- Search engine optimization (SEO)
- Shopping cart abandonment strategies

▶ **FIGURE 3**

Characteristics of Successful E-Commerce Sites

Consistent Customer Experiences Today's consumers expect a consistent positive experience every time they access a website, whether it is from a desktop computer, tablet, or mobile device. Consumers have nearly a zero tolerance for poor website performance. Poor experiences translate into dissatisfaction and lost sales, as evidenced by a number of studies:[6]

- Wal-Mart saw a sharp decline in conversion rate when its website load time increased from one second to four seconds.
- Amazon discovered that for every 100-millisecond decline in site load time, revenue increased one percent.
- Research by Torbit revealed that as load time increased, so did the bounce rate (individuals leaving the site without exploring other pages).
- Of consumers who were dissatisfied with a website's performance, 40 percent were unlikely to ever visit the site again and 25 percent were less likely to purchase the brand again.

These studies highlight the importance of a positive, consistent customer experience and the impact of load-time of pages, especially the front page, has on visitor actions.

Channel Integration Channel integration becomes essential when the business sells through additional channels beyond the web. A company that offers a printed catalog or has a retail store should match the printed catalog with its web catalog. Victoria's Secret features a "catalog quick order" system that allows customers to enter the product number from the print catalog and then go straight to checkout. The program saves considerable time in trying to find and buy a product on the web.[7] The Skyjacker website shown in this section features an extensive line of products. The site is also integrated with channel partners to ensure customers can find the right part, whether from Skyjacker's website or from their local parts store.

Sears Holdings developed the online shopping experience "Shop Your Way" that assists customers by letting them shop in the manner they feel most comfortable. The customer can access Sears.com, Kmart.com, LandsEnd.com, TheGreatIndoors.com, or the new mobile application site Sears2Go. Each gives the consumer the ability to select a product from any retail operation in the manner desired.[8]

Brand Engagement E-commerce sites create opportunities for brand engagement and customer interaction. Blogs, feedback applications, and customer reviews provide ways for e-commerce sites to encourage customers to interact with the website. Facebook and Twitter allow customers to "like" a brand and become fans. Involvement in social causes that involve customers enhances brand engagement.

Many company leaders remain hesitant about adding reviews and feedback options to websites due to the potential for negative comments;

▲ Channel integration is an important feature of Skyjacker's website.

Skyjacker Suspensions

▼ Wholly Guacamole encourages individuals to engage with the brand through Twitter, Facebook, Pinterest, YouTube, Google Plus, and Instagram.

Fresherized Foods

▲ This magazine advertisement for Community Trust Bank encourages individuals to visit the bank's website at ctbonline.com.

however, customer reviews represent an emerging trend in the Web 4.0 environment. These venues present opportunities for active interactions with customers and generate more honest relationships. They encourage customers to become brand advocates and provide a company with insights into customer thoughts and lifestyles.[9] Review and feedback pages also generate confidence for new customers visiting the site. Some e-commerce sites have also added "tell a friend" functions encouraging positive word-of-mouth recommendations.

Part of brand engagement involves personalization and customization. Personalization welcomes individuals by name as they access a site. After an individual registers, cookies deposited on the visitor's computer recall the person's name and browsing records each time the individual accesses the site. The browsing and purchase records allow the page to be customized to fit the person's history. Software can suggest additional items based on basket purchases of other customers. For instance, when someone buys a romance mystery novel, the next time she returns to the site, it suggests additional titles based on what other customers have purchased.

Most customers enjoy the convenience customization provides. Shoppers do not want to take time to sift through details. They favor the sites that remember them and the merchandise they prefer. Customization features also include the ability to:

- Locate the nearest retail store on a website or via mobile phone.
- Print coupons or other promotions from the website or use a mobile phone to access discounts at the retail store.
- Access information on the website or via a mobile phone noting that an item is in stock prior to making a purchase.[10]

Successful e-commerce sites require both online and offline marketing to build awareness and to drive traffic to the website. Most product purchases begin with someone using a search engine, which means e-commerce sites require a search engine optimization (SEO) strategy. These topics are discussed in greater detail later in this chapter.

Shopping Cart Abandonment Online retailers experience a high percentage of online shoppers abandoned shopping carts prior to checkout. The reasons vary, but the most common include hidden charges, difficulty in checking out, and sites that require customers to register in order to pay. Greg Hintz of Yahoo! Shopping offers these suggestions to keep customers from abandoning a shopping cart:

- Show any additional costs, such as shipping and handling, up front, so there are no surprises when the customer reaches checkout.
- Make checkout easy, and allow customers to make purchases without registering a user name and password.
- Make it easy for customers to enter discount codes from coupons, gift certificates, and other promotions.
- Provide a safe checkout procedure that the customer believes can be trusted.[11]

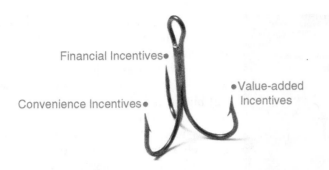

◀ **FIGURE 4**
Common Forms of Cyberbait

Fotolia/johnsroad7

E-Commerce Incentives **Cyberbait** includes any lure or attraction that brings people to a website. The most common forms of cyberbait include financial incentives, convenience incentives, and value-added incentives (see Figure 4).

Financial incentives help persuade an individual or business to make a first-time purchase via e-commerce and encourage customers to return. These incentives may take the form of a reduced price, free shipping, or an e-coupon. Financial enticements can be offered because conducting business online provides cost savings through reduced shipping and labor costs. Once the individual or company takes advantage of a financial incentive and makes the switch, continuing it may not be necessary. At that point, the convenience and added-value features help retain the customer.

Typically, the most effective financial incentives offer something free or at a discount. A BizRate Research survey suggests that free shipping remains the most popular online promotion.[12] Financial incentives require two ingredients. First, they should be meaningful to individuals visiting the site. Second, they should be changed periodically to entice new visitors to buy and to encourage repeat purchases by current visitors.

Making the shopping process easier creates a convenience incentive that can encourage customers to visit a website. Instead of traveling to a retail store, a consumer can place the order in the office, at home, or while traveling by using a smartphone or app. The order can be made at any time, day or night. The convenience and speed of purchasing merchandise online drives many consumers to e-retailers.

Value-added incentives lead consumers to change purchasing habits over the long term. They can make the difference between an ordinary and an exemplary site. The added value may be customized shopping, whereby the software system recognizes patterns in customers' purchasing behaviors and makes offers matched to past purchasing behaviors or search patterns. The Gulf Coast Seafood website shown in this section offers information about species of fish, a seasonality chart, the recipe of the week, and the top 100 seafood bloggers. It includes engagement tools such as Facebook, Twitter, and Pinterest. Visitors can download the seafood finder app and search for locations. These features add significant value to the website.

Combining incentives offers the best strategy to lure customers to a website. Cyberbait may include a discount or special price on a pair of jeans (financial-based incentive) and at the same time offer the freedom to place an order at 3:00 a.m. (convenience-based incentive). The same site may feature a game or offer a weekly fashion tip on some topic (value-added incentive). This combination entices consumers and businesses to return to the site. E-shoppers find it easy to surf the internet and search competing sites. When they do, brand names and particular websites are not as important. Consumers need reasons to regularly return to sites.

▼ The website for Gulf Coast Seafood offers a number of value-added incentives.

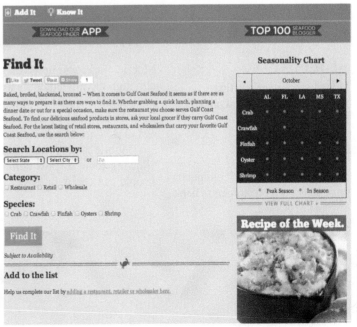

▲ An advertisement for Progressive Bank promoting "Remote Banking" convenience.

Privacy and Security Issues Consumer concerns regarding privacy and security are based on past incidents in which credit card numbers have been stolen as well as from cases of identity theft. A Javelin Strategy & Research study estimates retailers lose approximately $21 billion in online sales due to fears about identity and data theft.[13] Although still a concern, worries are declining as more consumers become accustomed to using the web. Fears about giving out credit card information are no greater now than they are for telephone orders or in-store credit card sales. Consumer confidence in e-commerce website security has risen. A recent survey revealed that three-fourths of online shoppers express faith in web security.[14]

Beyond apprehensions about identity theft and fraud are concerns that firms will sell personal information. Once this information becomes readily available, the individual loses control over who sees it and how it is used. A person might not wish to have his shopping patterns known, especially when the individual buys personal care products such as those for baldness, sexual dysfunction, weight loss, or other private matters. Further, many consumers become frustrated by being bombarded with advertising and marketing messages. Consumers also strongly express the desire to maintain control over personal information. They believe they should decide who should use it and how it should be used.

Trust remains the key to concerns about privacy and security of personal information. A KPMG survey indicates that 62 percent of consumers do not mind being tracked as long as they perceive a benefit in the form of reduced costs or free content. Consumers also want to know what a company does with the information it collects. If information is sold, then consumers want the company to request their permission first. Most consumers hate feeling spied on without permission. Tudor Aw of KPMG Europe notes, "People are happy to be tracked, but you have to be upfront and explain it."[15]

Mobile Marketing

Mobile marketing involves various forms of marketing on all mobile cell phone devices, although the movement is toward smartphones and tablets. Forty-four percent of the U.S. population owns a smartphone. Estimates suggest the figure will rise to almost 60 percent by 2016 and tablet penetration will increase to 49 percent. Individuals now spend an average of 2 hours and 21 minutes per day using some type of mobile device.[16]

Mobile phones provide a device linking individuals to social networks, thereby allowing them to post comments, pictures, and videos and read the thoughts of others. People can check in, tweet, and update their status at any time and anywhere. They can

▼ The mobile app from Community Trust Bank allows customers to bank anytime, anywhere.

- Display ads
- Search ads
- Video advertising
- Text messages

- In-app advertising
- QR codes, digital watermarks, 2D barcodes
- Geo-targeting

◁ **FIGURE 5**
Types of Mobile Marketing

download deals from companies, read reviews, check prices, and share information. Further, a mobile device offers a method for shopping. Purchases can be made with a mobile phone. Product information can be obtained. Consumers are able to check store hours, obtain directions to a business, and compare prices. These activities take place anywhere, including the retailer's store.

Effective mobile marketing involves understanding the social and shopping nature of mobile phones and incorporates it into the firm's mobile marketing strategy. Figure 5 identifies various types of mobile marketing. Forms of advertising used on the internet can be played on smartphone mobile devices such as display ads, search ads, and video ads, as will be discussed later in this chapter in the online advertising section.

Companies take advantage of mobile phones by sending text message ads to consumers. While these may be annoying, they can also be effective when created properly. A text message near lunch or dinner by a restaurant offering a special deal might entice a consumer to visit the restaurant. Two keys to text message advertising include gaining the permission of the mobile phone owner and careful timing when sending messages.

In-app advertisements offer a popular new type of mobile advertising. Globally, people download 32 billion apps to smartphones each year. Advertisers spend $2.9 billion on in-app advertising while consumers spend $26.1 billion buying apps. These apps include games, songs, and those that check weather, stocks, and current events. Advertising in this area becomes more effective when the message relates to the app's content. For instance, weather-related products should be promoted on a weather app.

QR codes, watermarks, and 2D barcodes directing consumers with a smartphone to a website now appear in magazines. Almost every magazine features some type of action code. The codes are especially popular in magazines that focus on home, family, beauty, health, travel, and fashion. The QR code placed in the Philadelphia Cream Cheese advertisement in this section offers recipes to shoppers.

Engaging customers constitutes the primary purpose of action codes in magazines. A Nellymoser study revealed that the greatest usage was for videos (35 percent). These videos may provide a behind-the-scenes look, product demonstrations, a how-to video, or entertainment. Action codes help the marketing team collect data and build opt-in lists for permission marketing. Figure 6 displays other uses for action codes.[17]

▽ This advertisement for Philadelphia Cream Cheese includes a QR code that provides consumers access to the recipe f or cheesecake.

pheel
friumphant

Philadelphia is always made with fresh milk and real cream, to help make the moment a little richer.

Scan this code with your smartphone to get the
Philadelphia Vanilla Mousse Cheesecake recipe

PHILADELPHIA

pheel the moment

www.spreadphilly.com
© 2012 Kraft Foods. QR Code is registered trademark of DENSO WAVE INCORPORATED.

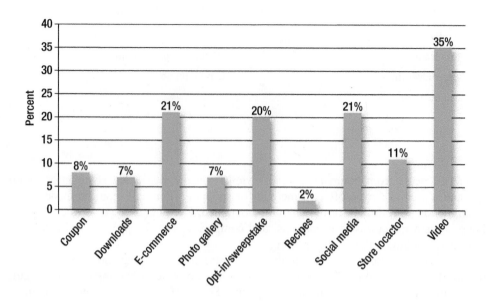

Digital Strategies

As society has shifted from desktop computers to laptops, tablets, and smartphones, marketers have adapted to these multiscreen formats. Advances in technology create new digital marketing opportunities along with the need to develop campaigns that can be viewed from any type of screen. Figure 7 identifies the primary digital marketing strategies brands feature today.

Interactive Marketing

The drive to engage consumers with a brand has led to an increase in **interactive marketing**, or the development of marketing programs that create interplay between consumers and businesses. The programs feature two-way communication and customer involvement.

The internet offers the ideal medium for interactive marketing due to the ability to track browser activities and translate the information into instant reactions. Software such as the Relationship Optimizer and Prime Response by NCR provides a powerful data analysis technique to personalize marketing messages. The NCR software analyzes customer interactions such as click-stream data traffic—any type of customer interaction with the firm—and combines it with demographic information from external or internal databases. As the data are processed, the software can launch complex interactive and personalized marketing materials in real time.

Interactive marketing emphasizes two primary activities. First, it assists marketers in targeting individuals, specifically potential and current customers, with personalized information. Second, it engages the consumer with the company and product. The consumer becomes an active participant in the marketing exchange rather than a passive recipient. Figure 8 lists online interactive tactics used by companies and the percentage of companies that utilize each method.

- Interactive marketing
- Content marketing
- Location-based advertising
- Behavioral targeting

- Video tactics
- Blogs and newsletters
- E-mail marketing

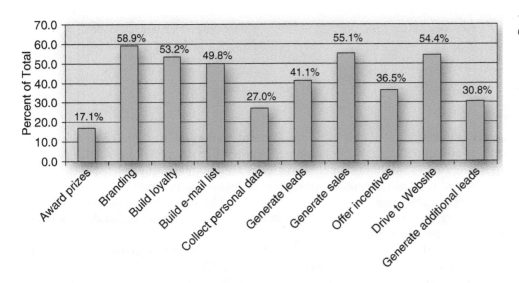

Marketing Zen's Shama Kabani describes the steps in developing an effective inter-active marketing strategy (see Figure 9).[18] It starts with cultivating an attitude of giving. Consumers should believe they will receive something in exchange for their involvement. Both sides need to receive something of value. A free gift, such as merchandise or informa-tion about some other valuable item, will be the quickest way to capture consumer attention.

The second step in gaining trust involves understanding customers, empathizing with them, and providing solutions to their problems. Consumers engage with companies and brands they trust. The company should be honest, upfront, and cannot pull surprises or use trickery to gain a sale. Otherwise, it becomes a one-time transaction.

Shama suggests that marketers should synthesize the company or brand down to one or two words that best describe what the firm offers or stands for. It might be "feminine" or "quality" or "communication" or "innovator" or "passionate." Tied closely with the one-word brand is an ultimate vision. What outcome does the company deliver? FedEx provides "overnight delivery." Gatorade delivers "energy and refreshment."

Choosing the best communication channels to present messages and to interact with customers and prospects constitutes the next step. As Figure 8 shows, several options are available. The best choice depends on the target audience and the message. Evaluation and adjusting make up the final step. These activities are especially important for digital marketing programs, because the field changes rapidly. Current channels may not exist in five years, or even by next year. Different—and perhaps better channels—may arise.

Content Marketing

Orders for in-ground fiberglass pools at River Pools and Spas declined from an aver-age of six per month to barely two. Four customers who had made deposits dur-ing the winter requested their money back because they had changed their minds. Marcus Sheridan, owner of River Pools and Spas, was spending $250,000 a year on radio, television, and pay-per-click web advertising. He reduced the budget to $25,000 and focused on providing useful information through blog posts and videos. He answered questions about costs from potential customers.[19] This approach, called

1. Cultivate an attitude of giving	**4.** Define your ultimate vision	
2. Gain trust	**5.** Choose your communication channels	
3. Identify your one-word brand	**6.** Evaluate and adjust	

▲ **FIGURE 9**

Steps in Developing an Interactive Marketing Strategy

▶ **FIGURE 10**
Content Marketing

- Information and solutions
- Authentic
- Shareable content

- Integrate content, search, and social
- Update consistently

content marketing, saved his business. **Content marketing**, or *branded content*, consists of providing useful information and product-use solutions to potential customers. Figure 10 highlights the characteristics of content marketing.

Content marketing is not self-promotion or trickery to generate sales. It focuses on providing authentic content. Marcus Sheridan shared truthful information, good and bad, about fiberglass pools. Customers appreciated his honesty and responded through interactive dialogue and purchases.

To succeed, content marketing information should be relevant and answer problems faced by customers or in some way that improves their lives. It should produce the information and solutions that site visitors will want to share with friends and relatives. Integrating content with the search and social strategies creates synergy. Using key search words in the content and providing content consumers consider to be valuable enhances the chance that a visitor seeking a solution to a problem will share the site with friends and relatives through social media.

▼ Philadelphia Cream Cheese has been successful with the branded website *realwomenofphiladelphia.com*.

phreel refreshed

PHILADELPHIA Summer Potato Salad

Prep Time: 30 min. plus refrigerating
Total Time: 1 hour 30 min. (incl. refrigerating)
Makes: 22 servings, about ½ cup each

What You Need

- 3 lb. baby red potatoes, quartered
- ½ cup water
- ¼ cup KRAFT Zesty Italian Dressing
- 1 tub (10 oz.) PHILADELPHIA Reduced Fat Italian Cheese & Herb Cooking Creme
- ¼ cup KRAFT Shredded Parmesan Cheese
- 1½ cups cherry tomatoes, halved
- 2 stalks celery, sliced

Make It

Place potatoes in 2-qt. microwaveable dish. Add water; cover. Microwave on HIGH 12 to 15 min. or until tender; drain. Place in large bowl. Toss with dressing. Refrigerate 1 hour until cooled. Add remaining ingredients; mix.

Spoon it in and make an ordinary dish, anything but.
pheel the moment

cookphilly.com

Frequency constitutes one key to obtaining search engine results. Also, the content should be updated consistently. Most experts believe two to three changes per week will be necessary. Marketers should avoid the temptation to drift into self-promotion and sales talk over time. Staying true to the mission of the branded content, providing information and solutions, is vital.

An alternative to branded content is **sponsored content**, whereby a brand sponsors the content of a blogger or related website. A YouTube video showing how to get prefect curls included references to the Remington curling iron brand embedded in the video. Spectrum Brands, which owns Remington, pays bloggers to create stories, articles, and videos for the web. An article and video entitled "Get the Right Swimsuit for Your Body" featured references to Remington embedded in the content. The goal was for the article and video to be shared through social media venues such as Twitter and YouTube.[20]

Sponsored content and content marketing share the same keys to success. The difference is that the company pays bloggers or website owners to promote content. Marketing professionals hope that potential customers will perceive the information to be valuable, share it with others, and most important, purchase the sponsored brand. The potential downside is that consumers will view it as advertising and self-promotion and not respond. Also, the company has limited control over the content and what people say. Negative comments or behaviors that do not represent the brand well might create a potentially negative or embarrassing situation that then must be addressed.

146

Location-Based Advertising

Mobile phones allow marketers to create location-based mobile advertising campaigns, often called geo-targeting. **Geo-targeting** involves reaching customers where they are located by contacting their mobile communication devices. Geo-targeting represents a unique and attractive feature of mobile marketing. By downloading an app, a fast-food restaurant can identify a person's location, show him how far he is from the nearest outlet, and then provide walking or driving directions to that unit. Many smartphone owners have check-in services at Foursquare, Gowalla, Facebook Places, and Twitter geoloca-tion. Starbuck's, McDonald's, Chipotle, and Burger King provide the largest number of restaurant check-ins. When someone checks in, software instantly sends a special promo-tion and information about the nearest locations. Marketing experts believe this location-based marketing approach will grow in use in the future. Businesses can harness the ability to drive consumers to retail outlets near where they are located, which can be an effective method to engage consumers with a brand on a one-to-one basis.

McDonald's recently ran a campaign through radio streaming on iTunes and Pandora. As the audio plays the song, copy encourages consumers to tap on the ad for the nearest McDonald's location. A map pops up and consumers can either type in a zip code or let the mobile phone's GPS find the closest locations, which are typically marked with a flag on the map. Tapping on a flag produces the restaurant's address and phone number. A click-to-call feature embedded in the ad enables the consumer to call the McDonald's with just another tap on the phone. Another version helps consumers access driving or walking directions via using the GPS feature.[21]

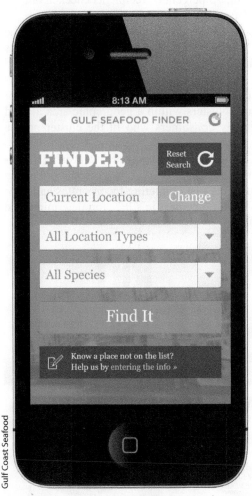

Gulf Coast Seafood

▲ This app for Gulf Seafood uses geo-information to find locations of seafood close to where an individual is located.

Gulf Coast Seafood

▲ This Gulf Seafood app utilizes location-based technology to locate nearby seafood sources with a click-to-call option as well as directions.

▶ **FIGURE 11**

Location-Based Advertising

Source: Based on Mark Walsch, "Location-Based Mobile Ads Deliver Best Engagement, Performance," *Online Media Daily*, www.mediapost.com/publications/article/192780, February 6, 2013.

- Targeting by DMAs (designated marketing areas), 30%
- Geo-fencing, 27%
- Audience-data targeting, 24%
- Geo-aware advertising, 14%
- City or zip code, 5%

Applebee's restaurant also employs location-based targeting. The brand's mobile banner ad reads "See You Tomorrow. Applebee's." When a consumer taps on the mobile ad, the content asks if it can access the person's current location through the phone's GPS. If the person responds "yes," then he is taken to a mobile landing page that provides the nearest Applebee's location, menu items, and specials. Through the app, consumers are able to purchase gift cards and receive them through Facebook, Twitter, or other social media venues.

According to Shuli Lowy, marketing director at Ping Mobile, "Mobile is no longer an option for restaurants." A study by Nielsen revealed that 95 percent of smartphone users conduct restaurant searches on their mobile device and 90 percent of those convert within a day. Sixty-four percent convert within an hour.[22]

Other brands also feature geo-targeting. Nissan, Procter & Gamble, Pepsi, Macy's, Kenneth Cole, and Timberland have conducted successful geo-targeted campaigns. Swirl is a mobile app used by retailers such as Timberland. Shoppers who agree to download the Swirl app and let it track their locations are notified of a 20 percent discount on merchandise. The app provides a consumer with a store's location and the individual has one hour to take advantage of the special. A clock within the app begins the time countdown. According to the VP of retail and digital commerce at Timberland, "Because it's opt-in ... you're receptive to it." According to Shadrin, 75 percent of recipients checked out the special offer, and 35 percent redeemed the discount.[23]

Figure 11 displays the different forms of location-based advertising and the approximate percentage quantity of each.[24] Targeting by demographic marketing areas (DMAs) is the most common approach. Everyone within the DMA that has granted permission receives the targeted message. Geo-fencing targets consumers near a specific retail location. Usually, the location is coupled with third-party demographic data or retail transactional data to determine audience clusters within a geographic area around the store. Timberland used this approach. Only consumers who fit the cluster profile receive the targeted message.

Restaurants including McDonald's and Applebee's use geo-aware advertising targeting real-time locations to deliver advertising messages based on the person's proximity to a unit's location. For other companies, audience-data targeting incorporates audience behaviors and characteristics to reach individuals. The person's location determines the exact brand and nature of the ad to be sent.

▶ Interstate Batteries launched a geo-targeted online advertising campaign to build awareness of its Battery Centers.

Interstate Batteries

Creating successful geo-targeting campaigns requires two actions. First, consumers should be in control of the engagement. They opt-in for the app. Second, the brand should provide a discount or something of value to consumers. Campaigns that follow these principles routinely yield engagement and performance measures that are higher than any other type of digital advertising.

Behavioral Targeting

Marketers for some brands can target the individuals who are most likely to purchase the item rather than merely placing ads on websites. **Behavioral targeting** utilizes web data to identify these potential customers. Behavioral targeting occurs in three different ways. It can be based on

▲ Behavioral targeting can be used to target fishing-related digital advertisements to fishermen who are most likely to make purchases.

- Pages a person visits on the internet
- Keyword searches or content read
- Past visitors to a site

The most common form of behavioral targeting involves tracking a person's movements on the internet. Cookies placed on the individual's computer track the data points as she moves from site to site. They record the types of sites visited, the information read, the searches conducted, and the products she purchased. Based on this information, ads will be placed on the websites that match her browsing history. If she has visited a number of websites about fishing, the screen will display advertisements for fishing supplies, boats, or other fishing-related products. Marketers can place a coupon or other form of cyberbait on the ad to encourage the consumer to click on it.

The second form of behavioral targeting examines an individual's search behavior. It identifies keywords typed into search engines and the content read based on keyword searches. If an individual has used a search engine to locate articles and information about new cars, then he may see an advertisement for Toyota or another car brand. If he has been reading about SUVs, then the ad may actually be for an SUV rather than a sedan or other type of vehicle. These ads typically appear on the search engine being used.

The final form is behavioral targeting based on past visitors. Amazon uses this method to suggest books and movies that may interest a person shopping on the company's website. The behavioral marketing program is triggered when an individual places a book or movie in a shopping basket or on a wish list. An ad will be generated that says "Others who purchased this book have also purchased these books." Several suggestions are made based on combinations of purchases of other customers.

Behavioral targeting takes place in seconds without a person even realizing it has occurred. Algorithms can be written to trigger these ads as the page loads. The brand being advertised may rotate or change based on the bidding process for display advertising. In the above example with keyword behavioral targeting, instead of a Toyota ad, it may be for a Ford, Nissan, or Chevrolet ad, depending on the winner of the bidding process that took place.

Video Tactics

Online video viewing has exploded over the last few years. Approximately 58 percent of the U.S. population watches digital videos, and 75 percent of internet users watch them. As shown in Figure 12, video tactics include advertising on videos, posting broadcast video ads, producing informational and cause-related videos, and product reviews.

Video ad spending has risen to $4.6 billion annually and is currently growing 20 percent to 40 percent per year, a rate much faster than any other form of advertising. Research indicates that consumers are more receptive to online video ads. The average time consumers view online video ads is 21.4 seconds, compared to 13.6 seconds for

- Advertising on videos
- Posting broadcast video ads
- Producing informational videos
- Producing cause-related videos
- Product reviews

▲ **FIGURE 12**
Video Tactics

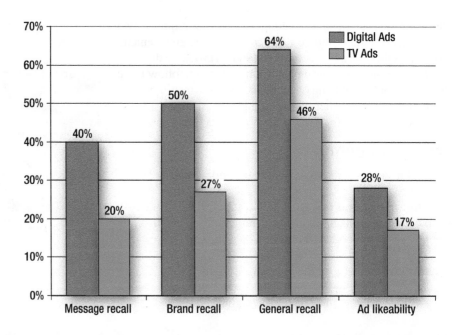

television. The completion rate for online video ads is 88 percent versus 79 percent for TV. Recall and ad likability are also higher for digital video ads (see Figure 13).[25]

Video ads can be pre-roll (before the video starts), mid-roll (in the middle of the video content), or post-roll (at the end of the content). Advertisements placed at the end of a video have a better click-through rate, because the individual has finished watching the video content. Ads at the beginning of the video have more impressions while those in the middle have the highest completion rate. Therefore, if the goal of the video ad campaign is to create impressions or enhance recall, then advertisers should front-load the ads. If the company seeks to increase brand recognition or enhance brand image, then mid-roll ads represent a better option, because viewers tend to watch the entire ad. Post-roll ads best match direct response-type of advertising with some type of call to action.

Most brands now have a YouTube channel where the company can share various types of videos. Ads prepared for television are now posted to video websites, such as YouTube. Many Super Bowl advertisers post a commercial or a snippet of it on YouTube prior to the game. Often, the digital ad will be viewed by more people than those who see the actual commercial during the Super Bowl. In addition to ads, advertisers post background scenes or videos explaining how the ad was produced. Viewers find these interesting, and this approach can increase engagement with the brand.

In addition to broadcast ads, many companies produce two other types of videos for posting online. Informational or instructional videos are the first method, using a strategy similar to the branded content approach described earlier in this chapter. Companies strive to provide useful information to consumers and answer questions they may have about the brand or product. Providing instructions on how to use a product, especially a complex item, can be useful. As with branded content, advertisers should ensure the videos will be perceived as authentic and useful—and not a sales gimmick.

▼ Television advertisements for Community Trust Bank featuring Terry Bradshaw have also been posted on YouTube.

Another approach involves posting videos with public relations or cause-related marketing messages. Duracell produced a video about firefighters and emergency personnel telling their personal stories. Advil produced a video featuring Melissa Stockwell, who lost her leg in Iraq. John Deere produced a video about a Mexican immigrant who came to the United States with nothing and now owns his own business. This type of video seeks to generate goodwill toward a brand.

Currently, numerous consumers use videos to conduct product research. Rather than visiting various websites, Amazon.com, or brand sites to obtain reviews, consumers turn to YouTube. An increase in the popularity of YouTube as a source of product information may be due to the following reasons:[26]

- Any product can be reviewed on video, and almost any product a person can think of has been reviewed on YouTube.
- Videos are more engaging because they provide both visual and spoken content.
- Videos represent the best place for early adopters to learn about a new product.

An Eyeblaster study revealed that online videos performed best when they appear next to online content or in an email, as compared to social network or gaming sites. Eyeblaster examined two metrics: dwell rate and dwell time. **Dwell rate** measures the proportion of impressions that result in users clicking an ad or mousing over it. **Dwell time** indicates the amount of time individuals spend engaged with an advertisement. Dwell rate and dwell time were both higher for video ads placed beside content or in an email rather than when they accompanied social networks and gaming sites. Ariel Geifman of Eyeblaster explains, "What we found is that people browse social networks really quickly. People spend a lot of time in social networks, but it's not on the same web page." In terms of gaming sites, Geifman said, "People are more focused on the game" and, as a result, less interested in watching a video ad.[27]

▼ Blogs and newsletters can be used effectively by fashion retailers to engage customers with the store.

Blogs and Newsletters

Blogs are online musings that cover a wide range of topics. Some permit visitors to post comments; others do not. Company-sponsored blogs can emulate word-of-mouth communication and engage customers with a brand. Fashion retailers entice customers to visit the company's blog to enjoy postings on new styles, upcoming designers, and fashion *faux pas*. In the past, customers may have relied on magazines such as *Vogue* for fashion information. Now, company blogs allow them to obtain information quicker, and, more important, interactively. This helps the marketing team engage with customers and establishes a two-way communication channel.

A company-sponsored blog provides a number of potential benefits; however, analysts stress the importance of identifying a specific reason for the blog before launching it. The goal may be to make the company more open (Dell), to humanize the organization (Microsoft), or to show a fun-and-happy company (Southwest Airlines).[28] When Coca-Cola acquired 40 percent of Honest Tea, many customers became unhappy about the move and voiced opinions on the Honest Tea blog. Honest Tea CEO Seth Goldman answered each one. While some customers still did not like the idea, "The blog at least helps people see how we think about it," Goldman said.[29]

Company leaders carefully select methods to respond to negative comments. CEO Bill Marriott of Marriott International hosts a blog for customers and employees. About 20 percent of the blog's readership consists of employees. Marriott employees monitor the comment section. No comment will be posted until it has been approved. The company does not remove comments simply because they are negative. Only those not germane to the discussion or blog are taken down. Those remaining are left up and addressed by Bill Marriott, which provides credibility to the blog through his willingness to listen to negative feedback.

For small businesses, blogs provide a relatively inexpensive way to communicate with customers. Robb Duncan began a blog for his Georgetown gelato shop, Dolcezza. When a second store was opened in Bethesda, Maryland, he announced an ice cream giveaway on opening night through the blog. More than 1,000 individuals showed up.[30]

The Thrillist (thrillist.com) and UrbanDaddy (urbandaddy.com) websites are designed to take advantage of the power that newsletters can provide. Newsletters are sent via email to approximately 1.1 million subscribers. Most subscribers are college graduates with median incomes of $88,000. The UrbanDaddy newsletter emphasizes an exclusive and luxurious approach, advising men about where to shop and how to fit in. The Thrillist newsletter features a fun and relaxed tone. Both organize free, heavily-sponsored events for subscribers of the newsletters. The newsletter becomes a means of engaging the subscribers with the websites.[31]

Both blogs and newsletters should follow the same principles as those pertaining to content marketing. The information provided should be useful and present solutions to the problems customers face. Authentic messages offering something individuals want to share receive more positive attention. They should be integrated with the brand's web content, search strategy, and social media outreach.

Effective blogs and newsletters are consistently updated. For blogs, this normally involves entries three times per week. For newsletters, publication frequency depends on the industry, content, target audience, and purpose of the newsletter. At a minimum, marketers need to add new materials once each month. A lower frequency sends the message that the company does not have anything interesting or new to provide. It also conveys the hidden message of, "We are doing this only to get your business, to increase sales."

Email Marketing

Email can become an important part of a company's digital marketing strategy. To be successful, companies integrate the email marketing program with other channels. It cannot simply be a program where addresses are purchased and mass emails are sent to individuals on the list. Most people resent spam, and response rates are extremely low, in addition to damaging the brand's reputation.

Response rates increase when an email message resembles the information presented on the company's website and in its advertisements and direct mail messages. When Data Inc. introduced new project management software, the marketing team integrated email with its webinar, direct mail, social media, and telemarketing programs. The webinar explained how the new software tool worked. Direct mail, telemarketing, and email were used to reach 600 influential decision makers. For emails that were returned undeliverable, Data, Inc. used LinkedIn to locate the contact's correct information. The email integrated approach resulted in a three percent response rate.[32]

Web analytics allow a company to develop email campaigns that offer the greatest chance of response. Emails can be based on the browsing history of an individual on a particular website. They identify those who made past purchases or items placed in the "wish" list but never purchased.

Email campaigns may be directed at consumers who abandon shopping carts without making purchases. About 40 percent of online

▼ Targeted emails can be used to contact individuals who abandon shopping carts.

Alistair Cotton/Fotolia

- Be upfront, honest with subscribers
- Build list for quality, not quantity
- Give subscribers what they want
- Be familiar to your audience

- Keep e-mails neat and clean
- Be eye-catching
- Integrate social media
- Test, test and test

◀ **FIGURE 14**
Developing Successful Email Campaigns
Source: Based on interview with Holly Betts, Marketing Zen, February 12, 2014.

shoppers abandon the shopping cart just prior to the checkout. Only about 30 percent of these shoppers return to complete the transaction. The IT department can identify individuals who abandon a shopping basket. Sending an email to them offering free shipping, a discount if they complete the order, or a simple reminder that they have items in their shopping basket can lead to greater sales. Converting these individuals to customers is much easier and more lucrative than sending mass emails. Targeted emails experience a conversion rate five to ten times higher than mass emails sent to the firm's customers. In addition, revenues from these follow-up emails are three to nine times higher than other approaches.[33]

In Figure 14 Holly Betts, an email expert with Marketing Zen, offers a number of suggestions for developing successful campaigns. It starts with individuals opting-in to the program. She emphasizes being upfront and honest with subscribers. Companies should tell recipients what they can expect, when they can expect it, and then deliver on those promises. As with branded content, emails should offer subscribers something useful that meets their needs or interests.

Marketing professionals make sure all emails come from the same source. Subscribers then instantly recognize the source and understand that it is an email they gave permission to receive. The messages should be short, neat, and eye-catching. They can include links to all of the brand's social media outlets so that recipients can increase their engagement with the brand if they wish. Email advertisers should test every campaign and keep records of what worked and what did not. This information makes it possible to build a file of best practices, based on previous results.

Web Advertising

Online advertising presents a highly effective method for reaching today's consumers, especially the younger, affluent, and internet-savvy market. Budgets for online advertising have steadily increased and are now more than $500 billion annually. Online advertising is the fastest-growing medium with annual growth rates exceeding 20 percent. Part of the growth has been fueled by multiscreen advertising, which involves media buys across the various platforms such as the web, mobile, and tablets.[34]

Figure 15 indicates the percentage of online advertising dollars allocated to each of the primary formats. Banner, media/video, and classified advertising will be presented in this section. Search spending will be described in the next section.

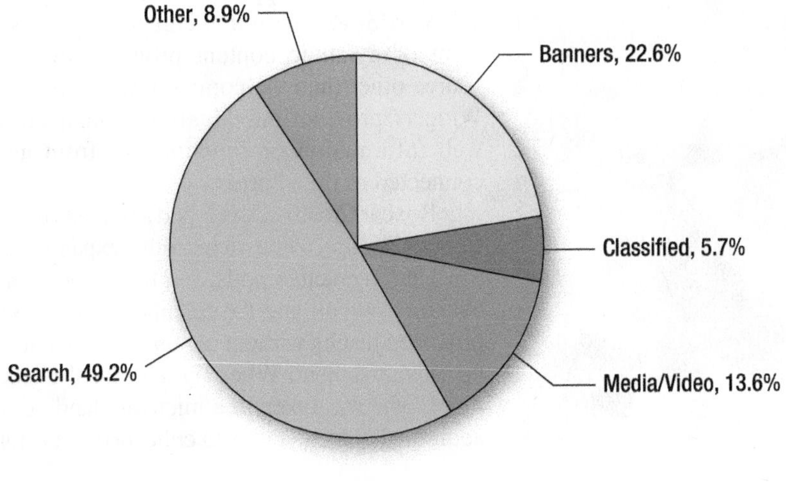

objective 6

What types of web advertising can companies use to reach consumers?

Other, 8.9%
Banners, 22.6%
Classified, 5.7%
Media/Video, 13.6%
Search, 49.2%

◀ **FIGURE 15**
U.S. Online Ad Spending by Format

153

Newcomer, Morris and Young Inc.

▲ A banner advertisement for Ouachita Independent Bank featuring images that were also used in print and outdoor ads, thereby creating continuity in the promotions program.

▼ Google's Double-Click technology can target advertisements to consumers who are browsing the web for stylish modern furniture.

Scott and Cooner, Inc.

Banner Advertising

The first form of online advertising involved the use of a display, or banner, ad. In 1994, AT&T ran one carrying the message "Have you ever clicked your right mouse here? You will." This very basic form of advertising generated billions of dollars in advertising revenues. Today, banner ads account for 22.6 percent of online advertising.[35]

Currently, banner ads can be embedded with videos, widget applications, or targeted display ads that increase the chances viewers will see and click the icon. The newest online technology, which has been taken from paid search auction systems, allows advertisers to display a banner ad only to individuals the company chooses. The system is built on a vast warehouse of user internet data and automated auction advertising exchanges such as Google's Double-Click, Yahoo!'s Right Media ad exchange, and Microsoft's AdECN. Advertisers develop messages for specific audiences. Prices can be set to entice the members of the audience who will see the banner ad.

When a consumer, such as a 20- to 25-year-old female, accesses a website featuring paid search auction technology, in a microsecond the software searches the auction exchange for advertisers that match the profile of the individual who logged onto the page. Once an advertiser has been located, a banner ad instantly flashes on the computer screen. It may be an advertisement for L'Oreal or Liz Claiborne. If a male with an interest in hunting logs on, an advertisement for hunting supplies or hunting attire may appear. The automated exchange system grants precise targeting of ads to specific consumers.[36]

Widgets Mini-applications embedded in a banner ad, or **widgets**, permit a consumer access to some form of dynamic content provided by an external source other than the company where the ad resides. Widgets provide individuals personalized access to web information or functionality from any device connected to the internet.

Boxcar Creative developed a widget application for ConocoPhillips using rich media expandable banners to create interactive polls, fun facts, and a carbon calculator. The poll and the calculator both collected and produced results without the user ever leaving the banner advertisement. When an individual clicked "learn more," she was taken to a microsite landing page with additional content and data collection opportunities.

◀ A Scott Equipment banner ad with a call-to-action "Learn More" icon.

Location-based widgets can be placed in banner ads. These ads are presented only to individuals who log on to a website in a particular region. The technology can be ideal for retailers, restaurants, and smaller businesses seeking to reach a specific region around a retail outlet.

Impact of Online Advertising

As more dollars shift to online advertising, concerns have arisen about the impact of the ads. Web users, just like television viewers, are becoming immune to advertisements. The percentage of people who respond to banner ads steadily shrinks. The click-through rate on major web destinations has declined to less than one percent. A recent measurement resulted in a response rate of 0.27 percent.[37]

To improve response rates, advertisers have created increasingly complex targeting campaigns that utilize various web metrics. MediaMind survey results indicate that the number of digital ads with two or more third-party tags increased 267 percent over the last two years. These third-party tags track items such as ad interactions, brand impact, and browsing behavior in order to optimize a campaign. Brands that utilize geo-targeting, behavioral targeting, and third-party demographic data tend have the most tags attached to the ads.[38]

According to comScore Inc., 54 percent of display ads on thousands of websites were not seen. That means almost $6 billion in display advertisements were wasted. Technical issues cause some of the problems, such as the ad appearing below the fold on a screen. The "below the fold" term describes the part a website that is not visible on a computer or smartphone screen that can only be seen by scrolling down. Unless the individual scrolls down the website, the ad will not be viewed. Another technical problem occurs when the ad loads so slowly that the web visitor either switches off the ad or goes to another site. Blocking software also prevents web ads from being visible. An increasing number of consumers has purchased software that blocks all forms of advertising. This is true especially for tech-savvy individuals.[39]

The final reason for ads not being seen is fraud. A significant number of ad impressions that brands pay for are never seen because the impressions are based on fake traffic. Malicious software makes a website record that a person is visiting the site and is viewing the ads being displayed. While both unethical and illegal, these scams generate millions of ad views and dollars for the scammers and are difficult for companies to detect.

The diminishing impact of online advertising and the high percentage of ads that are never viewed have led many advertisers to bank on new technologies designed to increase response rates and detect fraud. Advertisers are also spending more time and dollars in planning integrated campaigns that incorporate digital advertising with social media and traditional advertising.

Offline Advertising

To build a brand's reputation and brand loyalty, online advertising should be integrated with offline branding tactics that reinforce each other to speak with one voice. This

▼ Off-line advertising is an important part of building an online presence for brands such as JD Bank.

process, **brand spiraling**, involves the use of traditional media to promote and attract consumers to a website. Marketers design television, radio, newspapers, magazines, and billboards that encourage consumers to visit the firm's website in an effort to maintain a uniform brand presence and advertising message.

One recent study indicated that, after viewing a magazine advertisement, nearly half of the consumers polled said they might access a website or conduct an online search for the product. More than 40 percent were more inclined to visit a website after seeing a television or newspaper advertisement.[40] Traditional media can be the driving force behind online branding efforts.

Currently, tailor-made websites accompany many direct and email campaigns. These sites are accessed through **personalized URLs**, called **PURLs**, such as the hypothetical www.kenclow.offer.officedepot.com. A PURL contains a personalized preloaded web page that contains the customer's personal data, contact information, purchase behavior, and previous interactions with the company. A company such as Ford could display the customer's current vehicle, maintenance record, and other interactions with the company. The PURL creates a one-on-one dialogue with a customer and engages her with the company and provides messages, offers, and incentives tailored to her past data and history.[41]

Search Engine Optimization (SEO)

objective 7

What is a search engine optimization strategy?

The largest category of online expenditures is for spots on search engines. Funds devoted to search engines constitute nearly 50 percent of online advertising expenditures. About 80 percent of all web traffic begins at a search engine.[42] Therefore, making sure that a company's name or brand becomes one of the first ones listed when a person performs a search becomes a key marketing goal. **SEO**, or **search engine optimization**, is the process of increasing the probability of a particular company's website emerging from a search.

Optimization can be achieved in one of three ways. First, a *paid search insertion* comes up when certain products or information are sought. Companies can speed this process by registering with various search engines in order to have the site indexed and by paying a higher placement fee for top positions. The placement of the ad on a search page depends on the price the company pays and the algorithm a search engine used to determine the advertisement's relevance to a particular search word or phrase.

Second, a company can increase identification through the *natural* or *organic emergence* of the site. This method involves developing efficient and effective organic results that arise from a natural search process. Each search engine uses a slightly different set of algorithms to identify key phrases that match what was typed into the search box. To be listed first in an organic search requires time and effort. Normally, a new website will probably not emerge at the top of the search results. It takes time for the search engine to locate the site.

▼ The goal of search engine optimization is to increase the chances a company's brand will emerge when individuals type in particular search words.

Some studies suggest that the impact of organic listings can be impressive. For sites that come up on the first page of a search or within the top ten, web traffic increases nine fold. For second- and third-page listings, web traffic increases six fold. In terms of sales, being a top ten listing has resulted in a 42 percent increase in sales the first month and a 100 percent increase the second month.[43]

The third optimization method, *paid search ads*, includes small text boxes that pop up when a particular word is typed in or it can be paid to link boxes at the top or side of a search result. A comScore study suggests that search ads have a strong positive impact on brand awareness, perception, and

nyul/Fotolia

purchase intentions—even when consumers do not click the paid search ad.[44] The study revealed that for brands in the top search positions:

- The paid search ads generated a 160 percent increase in unaided awareness.
- Consumers were 20 percent more likely to have a positive perception of the brands.
- Consumers were 30 percent more likely to consider purchasing the brand.

Companies spend large amounts on search engine optimization. The typical click-through rate for online advertising remains around 0.2 percent; for search advertising, it is around five percent.[45] Although the early results are impressive, marketers should remember that search engine optimization represents a long-term investment. The effects do not occur quickly. Moving to the top ten listings of a search can take months or years. It requires optimizing content, programming, and finding the codes that will be picked up by search engines.

Search ads can be effective for local businesses. Barbara Oliver owns a boutique jewelry store in Williamsville, New York. She spent $50 per month in Google search ads targeted to an 80-mile radius of her store. It resulted in more customers than all of her offline advertising. With Google Places local directory, someone typing in the keywords designated by Oliver within an 80-mile radius of Williamsville was likely to see the search ad. Its effectiveness can be enhanced by smartphones and their GPS capabilities as well as Facebook and Foursquare where people sign in with their locations, which means visitors to the Williamsville area may see Oliver's search ad.[46]

International Implications

The ability to reach customers worldwide constitutes one of the major advantages that e-commerce holds over brick-and-mortar retail stores. Some online companies are still forced to turn away international orders because they do not have processes in place to fill them. This means that while the internet makes it possible to sell items in an international marketplace, some companies are not prepared to go global. Obstacles to selling across national boundaries include global shipping problems due to a lack of sufficient structure, communication barriers, and other technological barriers.[47] Also, internet companies must follow local exporting and importing laws.

objective 8

How can companies successfully conduct digital marketing programs in international markets?

Shipping Issues

One key to the effective launch of a global e-commerce site is preparing to make international shipments. Air transport may be affordable for smaller products; DHL Worldwide Express, FedEx, and UPS offer excellent shipping options. Larger merchandise normally can be shipped by a freight forwarder that finds the best mode of delivery, from ships to trucks to rail. Air transport companies and freight forwarders both offer specialized logistics software and provide the proper documentation and forms to meet importing and exporting regulations in every country served.

▼ International shipping is an important component of a global e-commerce business.

Communication Issues

Developing a website that appeals to the audience in each country will be a key task. It includes adding information that someone in another country would require, such as the country code for telephone numbers. It also requires removing or changing colors, words, or images that might offend a particular group of people in another country.

il-fede/Fotolia

New globalization software has been developed for companies expanding into other countries. One software package translates an English-language website into a large number of foreign languages. Another valuable feature that the software offers is "cultural adaptation," which adjusts a website's terminology, look, and feel to suit local norms. The software also has a feature in which the content developed in one location can easily be deployed to all sites around the world. This provides a more consistent look to the websites, without someone spending time modifying each foreign site. The software makes it easier to prepare a website in the proper native language and conform to local customs.[48]

Technology Issues

The technical side of international e-commerce remains challenging. Software compatibility continues to present unresolved technical issues. Ideally, these various technologies will eventually be merged into a single system. Currently, the bandwidth for handling internet traffic varies considerably. Information technology staff members are involved in every step of an internationalization process in order to overcome the potential technical glitches.

A coherent IMC strategy utilizes local input from the various countries involved. The brand on an internet site should stay consistent from one country to the next and present the company's primary marketing message. For IBM, this meant using local companies in each country to design individual websites and provide the information used on each site. To ensure consistency, IBM designs the main marketing messages at its central office, but then local companies translate the messages and add reseller contact and pricing information.

In the future, the growth of international e-commerce will continue to rise. Firms that get in on the ground floor are likely to enjoy a major marketing advantage.

Summary

Digital marketing combines all of the components of e-commerce, internet marketing, social media, and mobile marketing. Digital marketing includes anything with a digital footprint. An effective IMC program incorporates these new elements into the advertising and promotions plan.

The transition from Web 1.0 to Web 4.0 changed the ways in which consumers communicate and interact with companies. The key characteristics of Web 4.0 include customer engagement, cloud operations, and web participation.

An e-commerce website includes a catalog, a shopping cart, a payment collection method, and a store locator. Customers should believe the process is secure and be enticed to change buying habits. Effective e-commerce programs seek to engage customers who have abandoned shopping carts prior to making purchases. Three incentives that help people alter buying patterns are financial incentives, greater convenience, and added value. Quality programs overcome consumer concerns about privacy and security when using websites.

Digital marketing strategies begin with interactive marketing, which is the development of marketing programs that create interplay between customers and businesses. It assists the marketing department in targeting potential customers with personalized information and engages the consumer with the product and company. Content marketing can be used to provide useful information and product-use solutions to customers. Location-based advertising, or geo-targeting, involves reaching customers where they are located by contacting their mobile communication devices. Behavioral targeting utilizes web data to identify the individuals who are most likely to purchase an item. Video tactics involve placing marketing messages on various forms of video content. Further, customer engagement can take place through the distribution of blogs and newsletters. Blogs create a new form of word-of-mouth advertising. Blogs can be company-sponsored or posted by individual internet users.

Email can supplement an integrated program. Web analytics assist in directing email blasts to the most viable markets. Email newsletters help create brand awareness, drive traffic to a website, and spur sales.

Online web advertising tends to reach younger, more internet-savvy consumers. It includes banner advertising, classified and media/video advertising, search engine optimization, and paid search ads. Offline advertising can be used to build a brand's reputation and brand loyalty. Brand spiraling may be used to combine the internet program with advertising in traditional media. Tailor-made websites accompany many direct and email campaigns using personalized URLs or PURLs.

Search engine optimization (SEO) is the process of increasing the probability of a particular company's website emerging from a search. Paid search insertions, natural or organic emergence, and paid search ads can help achieve this goal.

International markets may also be served by e-commerce enterprises, especially when cultural differences, shipping problems, and internet capability problems can be solved. Information technology departments play a key role in solving the internet problems. Shipping issues and language differences also require attention in this lucrative and growing marketplace.

Key Terms

digital marketing Marketing that incorporates the components of e-commerce, internet marketing, mobile marketing, and social media

e-commerce Selling goods and services on the internet

cyberbait A type of lure or attraction that brings people to a website

interactive marketing The development of marketing programs that create interplay between consumers and businesses

content marketing (or *branded content*) Providing useful information and product use solutions to potential customers

geo-targeting Advertising designed to reach customers where they are located based on contacting their mobile communication devices

behavioral targeting Using web data to identify and target individuals most likely to purchase an item

dwell rate Measures the proportion of ad impressions that resulted in users clicking an ad or mousing over it

dwell time Measures the amount of time individuals spend engaged with an advertisement

blogs The online musings of an individual or group; the term is derived from "web logs"

widgets Mini-applications embedded in a banner ad that permit a consumer access to some form of dynamic content provided by an external source other than the company where the ad resides

brand spiraling The practice of using traditional media to promote and attract consumers to a website

personalized URLs (PURLs) A personalized web page preloaded with the customer's personal data, contact information, purchase behavior, and previous interactions with the company

search engine optimization (SEO) The process of increasing the probability of a particular company's website emerging from a search

---

MyMarketingLab

Go to **mymktlab.com** to complete the problems marked with this icon .

Review Questions

1. Define digital marketing.
2. How has Web 4.0 influenced the field of marketing?
3. What is e-commerce?
4. What is cyberbait? What are the three main forms of cyberbait?
5. What concerns do some consumers have about e-commerce?
6. What is mobile marketing?
7. What is interactive marketing?
8. Describe content marketing.
9. What is geo-targeting, or location-based, advertising?
10. What is behavioral targeting?
11. What is a blog? How can blogs be used in marketing communication programs?
12. Identify and describe the elements of an effective email campaign in marketing.
13. What primary forms of online or web advertising are used by marketing teams?
14. What is a widget?
15. What is brand spiraling?
16. What is a personalized URL or PURL?
17. What is meant by the term search engine optimization (SEO)? How can it be accomplished?
18. What challenges must be overcome to establish an international e-commerce operation?

Critical Thinking Exercises

DISCUSSION QUESTIONS

19. Examine the characteristics of Web 1.0 to Web 4.0. Discuss how the internet affects your daily life. Interview individuals in each of the following age categories about their use of the internet: 30–39, 40–59, 60+. Relate their conversations to Web 1.0, Web 2.0, Web 3.0, and Web 4.0.

20. What types of goods or services have you purchased online during the past year? Have your parents or grandparents purchased anything online? If so, compare your purchases and attitudes toward buying via the internet with theirs. If neither you, your parents, nor your grandparents have used the internet to make purchases, why not?

21. Which form of cyberbait might best help solve the problem of shopping cart abandonment? Would any form of cyberbait help alleviate consumer concerns about privacy and security? Defend your answers.

22. Look through the digital marketing strategies identified in Figure 7. Discuss each strategy as it relates to your online experience. Which strategies are the most successful at reaching you? Why? Which are the least effective? Why?

23. Have you ever experienced location-based, or geo-targeting, advertising on your smartphone? Describe your experience. If you have not experienced geo-targeting, under what circumstances would you welcome it?

24. Do you have any apps on your cell phone? If so, describe the apps you have and why you downloaded the app? Is any advertising connected with the app?

What are your thoughts about apps that utilize some type of advertising?

25. Interview five individuals of different ages about blogs. What percent have read, launched, or participated in blogging on the internet? What was each person's motivation? What is your experience with blogs? If you have never read or contributed to a blog, why not?

26. A high percentage of Internet traffic begins with someone conducting a search. Compare and contrast the concepts of paid search insertions, organic search results, and paid search ads from the perspective of a consumer wanting to locate websites that provide information and products on camping. Compare and contrast paid search insertions, organic search, and paid search ads from the viewpoint of Coleman, a company that sells camping supplies and equipment.

Integrated Learning Exercises

27. Best Buy was a late e-commerce entrant, but has developed a strong e-commerce component. The key to Best Buy's success, according to Barry Judge, vice president of marketing, is, "We do a lot of one-to-one marketing. We're not overly focused on where the consumers buy." The website carries every product that Best Buy stocks. It offers personalized services, along with convenient pick-up and fair return policies to entice consumers to shop. Consumers can purchase items on the internet and either have them shipped directly to them or pick them up at the closest store. Shoppers can use the internet to see if Best Buy stocks a particular item, to determine what the item costs, and to gather product information. What is the advantage of this strategy? Access the website at **www.bestbuy.com**. Evaluate it in terms of ease of use and product information, and then locate the Best Buy closest to you. Next, access Tiger Direct's website at **www.tigerdirect.com**. Compare it to Best Buy's site. Select a product, such as a camcorder, to compare the two websites.

28. Pick one of the following product categories and access the websites of two companies that sell the product. What types of financial incentives are offered on each company's website to encourage you to purchase? What about the other two types of incentives, greater convenience and added value? What evidence do you see for them? Compare and contrast the two companies in terms of incentives offered.

   a. Contacts or eyeglasses

   b. Water skis

   c. Clothes

   d. Cameras

   e. Camping supplies

29. The three main companies businesses use to ship small packages either overnight or 2-day delivery are FedEx, UPS, and the U.S. Postal Service. Access the websites of each shipping solution provider: **www.fedex.com**, **www.ups.com**, and **www.usps.gov**. What delivery guarantees does each offer? Which site is the most user-friendly? Which site appears to offer the best customer service?

30. Pick two of the following e-commerce sites. Discuss each of the characteristics of Web 4.0 e-commerce sites listed in Figure 2. Compare and contrast the two sites for each of the characteristics.

   a. Travelocity (**www.travelocity.com**)

   b. Wells Fargo Bank (**www.wellsfargo.com**)

   c. WeddingChannel.com (**www.weddingchannel.com**)

   d. Bluefly (**www.bluefly.com**)

   e. Diesel (**www.diesel.com**)

   f. Quiznos (**www.quiznos.com**)

31. Blogs provide opportunities for individuals and businesses to share information, thoughts, and opinions. Go to Google Blog Search at **www.google.com/blogsearch**. Type in a topic you are interested in that is related to advertising and marketing communications, such as "advertising to children." Locate three blogs on the topic you chose. Discuss who initiated the blog and the value of the information on the blog.

32. Access each of the following search engines. For each one, discuss how it handles paid search advertising when you type in a search, such as "running shoes." What ads do you see as display ads, and what ads are part of the search results? Discuss the differences among the five search engines. Which one do you like the best? Why?

    a. Google (**www.google.com**)

    b. Yahoo! (**www.yahoo.com**)

    c. AOL Search (**http://search.aol.com**)

    d. Bing (**www.bing.com**)

⭐ **33.** Use a search engine to locate three digital advertising agencies. For each agency, describe what type of digital marketing services the agency provides. If you owned a small restaurant chain, which agency would you hire for your digital marketing program? Why? (Provide the URL for each agency in your response.)

34. Access the internet and locate five banner ads. Copy and paste the banner ads in a Word document. Evaluate each banner ad in terms of design and appeal. Access each banner ad by clicking on it. Discuss the result of clicking on the banner ad. Of the five banner ads, which yielded the best results in terms of providing useful information? Why?

Blog Exercises

Access the authors' blog for this text at the URLs provided to complete these exercises. Answer the questions that are posed on the blog.

35. Advil - **http://blogclowbaack.net/2014/05/12/advil-chapter-8/**

36. Digital Marketing Strategies - **http://blogclowbaack.net/2014/05/12/digital-marketing-strategies-chapter-8/**

37. Search Engine Optimization - **http://blogclowbaack.net/2014/05/12/seo-chapter-8/**

Student Project

CREATIVE CORNER

Bluefly's marketing team wants to enhance the company's brand name and internet presence. They have asked you to be an internet advertising consultant. Access the Bluefly website at **www.bluefly.com**. Once you feel comfortable with the company, prepare a banner ad that can be used on the internet. Design a magazine ad that can be used with the banner advertisement. Then, design an email promotion that can be sent to customers who purchased from **Bluefly.com**, but it has been at least 90 days since that purchase.

CASE 1   RUNZA RESTAURANTS

Ethnic foods enjoy a unique place in the dining habits of people around the world. In the United States, one such treat goes by a variety of names and has an unusual heritage. The Runza (one of the more common names) refers to a sandwich called a Bierock or Bieroc in Kansas or a fleisckuche or Kraut Priok in other places. In essence, the sandwich consists or beef, pork, cabbage or sauerkraut, onions, and seasonings loaded into a doughy form of bread.

Various forms of runzas were first devoured in Russia according to some sources; although those are disputed, because others believe the heritage begins in Germany. In either case, family-kept recipes eventually moved to the United States and Canada. Areas in which the sandwich is most popular in the United States include North and South Dakota, Michigan, Wisconsin, Illinois, Oklahoma, and probably most notably in Kansas and Nebraska. In Kansas, the food normally will be served in a round or half-moon shaped bun; in Nebraska, the sandwich tends to be rectangular, even though other versions (square, triangular) are also used.

Perhaps the reason Nebraska may be most associated with the sandwich is that the state features the largest chain of restaurants serving the item: Runza. The chain houses the majority of its outlets in Nebraska (where the first unit was opened), Kansas, Missouri, Wyoming, Iowa, and Colorado. Currently, the Runza chain has begun opening franchise operations in numerous additional states.

A standard Runza menu includes the "Original Runza," along with a variety of new options using the same basic bun structure. Stores also sell burgers that come from fresh beef, chicken sandwiches, kid's meals, desserts, corn dog "nuggets," and homemade onion rings and crinkle-cut fries. Runza Restaurants feature a distinctive green and yellow logo. The colors appear on all cups, packages, bags, and other elements of the operation.

While Runza Restaurants would probably be considered a form of fast food, the chain differentiates itself from other sandwich and burger chains through the distinctive lead food item. This helps maintain a difference between a Runza location and McDonald's, Burger King, Wendy's, Subway, and Schlotzsky's.

In 1999, the Runza organization celebrated its 50th anniversary with a two-day block party in downtown Lincoln, Nebraska, complete with an appearance of Runza® Rex, the company's dinosaur-like mascot. Soon after, the chain signed a 10-year pact with the University of Nebraska athletic program.

Recently, new items have been added to the menu, including the Spicy Jack, which was chosen by Facebook followers in a contest containing other sandwich entrants. The organization maintains relationships with Great Books for Great Kids and seeks to maintain a positive image in every community it serves.[49]

38. Access Runza Restaurant's website at **www.runza.com**. Describe the content on the site. Examine the characteristics of successful e-commerce sites given in the chapter. Discuss each characteristic as it relates to Runza's website. What is your overall evaluation of the website?

39. What types of cyberbaits do you see on the Runza website? Give specific examples of each.

40. Explain how the Runza Restaurant could use mobile marketing. Provide details.

41. Discuss how location-based advertising could be valuable to an individual Runza Restaurant manager. Which form of geo-targeting would you use? Why?

42. Explain how behavioral targeting would be useful to an individual Runza Restaurant manager. Design a behavioral targeting program that could be used by Runza.

43. Design a banner ad for Runza Restaurants.

44. Examine Runza's website again. Make a list of ten words that could be used for a search engine optimization program. Rank the words in order from what you think would be the best search terms to the least attractive. Justify your list and ranking.

CASE 2 ▸ BLACK FRIDAY AND CYBER MONDAY

Each year, as the United States undergoes the traditional Thanksgiving to Christmas holiday season, businesses across the country hope for strong sales. The term "Black Friday" resulted from the realization that the Friday following Thanksgiving was the day many retailers moved from the "red" (loss) to the "black" (profit).

Black Friday has evolved over the years. From the traditional rush to shop, retailers began seizing the opportunity by offering special discounts on limited amounts of merchandise, opening stores in the early morning. Bargain hunters lined up in the middle of the night, and more than once physical violence broke out between patrons fighting over the last item on a sales rack. In 2011, some stores actually opened at midnight on Thanksgiving, trying to optimize sales.

In the past decade, a new phenomenon emerged. "Cyber Monday" resulted from shoppers buying online rather than in retail stores. Recently, online sales on the Monday following the Thanksgiving weekend topped $1.25 billion, an increase of 39 percent over the year before.[50] The average order

▲ Many consumers are influenced to make online purchases during Cyber Monday.

value was nearly $200. Total internet sales during the holiday shopping season reached $35 billion.

In 2013, many consumers did not wait for Cyber Monday. Internet sales on Black Friday were $816 million, also a large increase over the previous year. Shopping patterns also indicate that three additional major spending days were December 17, 23, and 26. Of note, more than ten percent of the orders placed came from mobile phone devices. Part of the reason for the rush may have been a shorter than usual Christmas shopping season, due to a late date for Thanksgiving, which cut the time by several days.

This annual rush to shop season has its detractors. Some traditionalists decry the overemphasis on materialism. Others note that the holiday shopping season has practically turned into a sporting event, complete with all its corresponding statistics. In addition, cynics note that Black Friday is not the busiest retail shopping day of the year. It actually takes place the weekend before Christmas each year.[51] Critics wonder whether those poor shoppers standing in the cold on the night after Thanksgiving are to be pitied for being exploited or laughed at for going to such extremes to save a few dollars.

In any case, marketers recognize that holiday shopping will likely continue. The methods used to reach customers continue to change. In this dynamic arena, the role of digital marketing will undoubtedly expand.

45. Describe the differences between individuals who shop in retail stores on Black Friday and individuals who participate in Cyber Monday. Are they the same individuals or different? Justify your answer.

46. Discuss your view of Black Friday and Cyber Monday. Do you participate in both or just one? Why or why not? Do you think retailers take advantage of consumers on these two special days? Why or why not?

47. How can retailers integrate shopping in the store with shopping online?

48. What types of advertising and promotions should be sent out to consumers immediately preceding the Thanksgiving weekend?

49. As some companies now begin Christmas advertising as early as mid-October, how will the roles of Black Friday and Cyber Monday be affected?

50. Design a magazine ad for some type of electronics encouraging consumers to make a purchase on Cyber Monday. Use an incentive other than a steep price discount.

MyMarketingLab

Go to **mymktlab.com** for Auto-graded writing questions as well as the following Assisted-graded writing questions:

51. A high percentage of Internet traffic begins with someone conducting a search. Compare and contrast the concepts of paid search insertions, organic search results, and paid search ads from the perspective of a consumer wanting to locate websites that provide information and products on camping. Compare and contrast paid search insertions, organic search, and paid search ads from the viewpoint of Coleman, a company that sells camping supplies and equipment.

52. Blogs provide opportunities for individuals and businesses to share information, thoughts, and opinions. Go to Google Blog Search at **www.google.com/blogsearch**. Type in a topic you are interested in that is related to advertising and marketing communications, such as "advertising to children." Locate three blogs on the topic you chose. Discuss who initiated the blog and the value of the information on the blog.

Endnotes

1. Interview with Shama Kabini, by Donald Baack and Kenneth E. Clow, January 19, 2010.

2. Brian Morrissey, "Real Time: The Web's New Prime Time," *Adweek* (**www.adweek.com/aw/content_display/news/digital/e3i15f4e2b3b4a487b3b5cd5347eb-d07cbf**), May 25, 2009.

3. Cate T. Corcoran, "Delivering the Goods: E-tailing Sales to Rise But Gains Seen Slowing," *Women's Wear Daily* 197, no. 94 (May 5, 2009), p. 94.

4. Michael Stich, Jim Leonard, and Jennifer Rooney, "Ring Up E-Commerce Gains with True Multichannel Strategy," *Advertising Age* 79, no. 10 (March 10, 2008), p. 15.

5. "Consumers Embrace Internet as Regular Shopping Tool," *Australian Giftguide* (October–December 2009), p. 10.

6. Amy Cravens, "How New Devices, Networks, and Consumer Habits Will Change the Web Experience," *Giga Omni Media White Paper*, January 22, 2013 (www.pro.gigaom.com).

7. David Sparrow, "Get 'em to Bite," *Catalog Age* 20, no. 4 (April 2003), pp. 35–36.

8. Amanda Gaines, "Leading the Charge," *Retail Merchandiser* 49, no. 6 (November–December 2009), pp. 16–19.

9. Mike Fletcher, "How to Create the Perfect E-Commerce Website," *Revolution* (March 2009), pp. 60–63.

10. Joab Jackson, "E-Consumers Get Smart," *CIO* 23, no. 7 (February 1, 2010), p. 18.

11. Gwen Moran, "Check Out Your Checkout," *Entrepreneur* 38, no. 1 (January 2010), p. 38.

12. Lisa Cervini, "Free Shipping Offers Fueling Online Sales," *This Week in Consumer Electronics* 20, no. 24 (November 21, 2005), p. 16.

13. "Data-Insecurity Fears Said to Hamper Online Shopping," *CardLine* 9, no. 13 (March 27, 2009), p. 34.

14. Suzanne Beame, "Consumer Confidence in Online Shopping Sites Is on the Rise," *New Media Age* (November 15, 2007), p. 15.

15. "Online Consumers Happy to Be Tracked," *The Wall Street Journal*, December 5, 2011, http://blogs/wsj.com/tech-europe/2011/12/05/online-consumers-happy-to-be-tracked.

16. "Multiscreen Campaign Importance Rises with Smart Device Use," *eMarketer*, November 25, 2013, www.emarketer.com/articles/print.aspx?R=1010413.

17. Roger Matus, "Mobile Action Codes in Magazine Advertising," white paper from Nellymoser, Inc. (www.nellymoser.com), p. 4.

18. Shama Hyder Kabani, "Online Marketing Plan," The Marketing Zen Group (**www.marketingzen.com**), pp. 9–13.

19. March Cohen, "A Revolutionary Marketing Strategy: Answer Customers' Questions," *The New York Times*, www.nytimes.com/2013/02/28/business/smallbusiness, February 27, 2013.

20. William Launder, "Marketers Seek Extra Edge to Go Viral," *Wall Street Journal*, http://online.wsj.com/article/SB10001424127887323980604579031391201753578, August 25, 2013.

21. Lauren Johnson, "McDonald's Puts Location at Core of iTunes Radio Launch Campaign," *Mobile Marketer*, www.mobilemarketer.com/cms/news/advertising/16531, November 5, 2013.

22. Rimma Kats, "Applebee's Drives Foot Traffic via Targeted Location-Based Mobile Campaign," www.mobilecommercedaily.com/applebees-drive-foot-traffic-via-targeted-location-based-mobile-campaign, May 15, 2013.

23. "Timberland, Kenneth Cole Track Shoppers Who Opt-In for Deals," *Advertising Age*, http://adage.com/print/243811, August 26, 2013.

24. Mark Walsch, "Location-Based Mobile Ads Deliver Best Engagement, Performance," *Online Media Daily*, www.mediapost.com/publications/article/192780, February 6, 2013.

25. Lucia Moses, "Online Video Ads Have Higher Impact Than TV Ads," *Adweek*, www.adweek.com/news/advertising-branding/online-video-ads-have-higher-impact-than-tv-ads-148982, May 1, 2013.

26. Zach James, "Forget Amazon. YouTube is Where Shoppers Do Research," *Adweek*, www.adweek.com/videowatch/forget-amazon-youtube-is-where-shoppers-do-research-152068, August 28, 2013.

27. Mike Shields, "Social Sites Not as Video Ad Friendly as Content, E-mail," *Mediaweek* (**www.mediaweek.com/mw/content_display/news/digital-downloads/metrics**), November 18, 2009.

28. Beth Snyder Bulik, "Does Your Company Need a Chief Blogger?" *Advertising Age* 79, no. 15 (April 14, 2008), p. 24.

29. Sarah Halzack, "Marketing Moves to the Blogosphere," *Washingtonpost.com* (**www.washingtonpost.com/wp-dyn/content/article/2008/08/24/AR20080824051517**), August 25, 2008.

30. Ibid.

31. Basil Katz, "Email Newsletters Aim for Inbox and Wallet," *Reuters* (**www.reuters.com/articlePrint?articleId=USTRE5894XI20090910**), September 10, 2009.

32. Karen J. Bannan, "The Mandate to Integrate," *BtoB* 94, no. 12 (September 28, 2009), p. 23.

33. "Re-Marketing Helps Boost Online Shoppers' Baskets," *Data Strategy* 3, no. 7 (May 2007), p. 9.

34. Ingrid Lunden, "Nielsen: Internet Display Advertising Grew 32% in 2013," http://techcrunch.com/2014/01/27/nielsen-internet-display-advertising-grew-32-in-2103, January 27, 2014.

35. "Online Ad Spending Consolidates Among Search, Banners, Video," *eMarkter Digital Intelligence*, February 3, 2012, www.smarketer.com/articles/print.aspx?R=1008815.

36. Brian Morrissey, "Beefing Up Banner Ads," *Adweek* (**www.adweek.com/aw/content_display/news/digital/e3if04360897e1103df4b92464543af6649**), February 15, 2010.

37. Josh Quittner, Jessi Hempel, and Lindsay Blakely, "The Battle for Your Social Circle," *Fortune* 156, no. 10 (November 26, 2007), pp. 11–13.

38. "Is Online Advertising Getting Too Complex?" *Advertising Age*, http://adage.com/print/245070, November 1, 2013.

39. Suzanne Vranica, "Web Display Ads Often Not Visible," *Wall Street Journal*, http://online.wsj.com/article/SB10001424127887324904004578537131312357490, November 10, 2013.

40. Michael Fielding, "We Can All Get Along," *Marketing News*, May 15, 2007, p. 4.

41. Paula Andruss, "Personalized URLS," *Marketing News*, September 1, 2008, p. 10.

42. "Problem Solved," *BtoB* 92, no. 15 (November 12, 2007), p. 21; "Online Ad Spending Consolidates Among Search, Banners, Video," *eMarketer Digital Intelligence*, February 3, 2012, www.smarketer.com/articles/print.aspx?R=1008815.

43. "Problem Solved," *BtoB* 92, no. 15 (November 12, 2007), p. 21.

44. Jack Neff, "Why CPG Brands Better Buy Paid Search," *Advertising Age* (http://adage.com/print?article_id=130353), August 18, 2008.

45. Josh Quittner, Jessi Hempel, and Lindsay Blakely, "The Battle for Your Social Circle," *Fortune* 156, no. 10 (November 26, 2007), pp. 11–13.

46. "Google Searches for Success in Local Ads," *Advertising Age*, March 1, 2011, http://adage.com/print/149140.

47. Lynda Radosevich, "Going Global Overnight," *InfoWorld* 21, no. 16 (April 19, 1999), pp. 1–3.

48. "The Worldly Web," *CFO* 19, no. 7 (June 2003), p. 30.

49. "Runza Restaurants," History, http://www.runza.com/about/history. Runza, http://www.food.com/recipe/runza-80204, retrieved February 21, 2014.

50. "Black Friday and Cyber Monday Sales Break Holiday Records, Magic Logix Digital Marketing Solutions, http://www.magiclogix.com/blog/ecommerce/record-holiday-sales-in-2012-for-black-friday-cyber-monday-and-ecommerce/, December 30, 2011.

51. "Lies, Damned Lies, and Black Friday Sales Statistics," Constantine Von Hoffman, CBS News, http://www.cbsnews.com/8301-505123_162-57342402/lies-damned-lies-and-black-friday-sales-statistics/, December 13, 2011.

Social Media

Social Media

Chapter Objectives

After reading this chapter, you should be able to answer the following questions:

1 What constitutes a social network?

2 What are the unique characteristics of the primary social media websites?

3 What is the nature of social media marketing?

4 Which social media marketing strategies do companies employ?

5 What social media measurement metrics are available to marketers?

6 How can marketers use social media strategies in international operations?

MyMarketingLab™

⭐ **Improve Your Grade!**

Over 10 million students improved their results using the Pearson MyLabs. Visit **mymktlab.com** for simulations, tutorials, and end-of-chapter problems.

Overview

The emergence of social media networks has altered the ways individuals interact with families, friends, businesses, and even strangers on a routine basis. The continual growth of social network websites presents opportunities and challenges to marketing departments from the smallest single family business to major corporations. Instant communication creates the potential to create buzz and excitement in a short period of time. Marketers are able to develop more sophisticated interactions with customers. At the same time, negative word of mouth and other developments may quickly damage a brand across a wide range of customers and the general public. Marketing communications experts understand the need to quickly adapt to this exciting new world. One firm that has been able to benefit from the possibilities that social media networks offer is Wholly Guacamole.

WHOLLY GUACAMOLE

The biggest problem with an avocado may be that, as soon as one is cut open, it begins to brown. Wholly Guacamole's founder, Don Bowden, sought to solve this problem. He discovered the process of High Pressure Processing, which was quickly marketed as "fresherized" guacamole. It results in a "100% all natural, fresh tasting product." Pre-made guacamole can be sold in grocery stores and in food markets. It has become a staple for many companies featuring the ingredient in sandwiches and other menu items. Wholly Guacamole's website indicates that, "We always use real Hass avocados and natural ingredients that never include preservatives (except Wholly Salsa Avocado Verde Dip), artificial flavoring or fillers."[1]

Wholly Guacamole's marketing team understands the potential impact of social media on a product's success. The company successfully leveraged it to create brand awareness, develop a strong brand, and boost sales. While social media played a significant role in recent campaigns, the messages were fully integrated with traditional advertising media channels as well as digital components in order to achieve the greatest impact.

WONG SZE FEI/Fotolia

▲ Guacamole has become a staple for many individuals to use on sandwiches.

Marketers at Wholly Guacamole increased the power of the company's limited advertising budget by creating alliances with several organizations, including *The Biggest Loser* television program, Sonic Drive-in, Disney, and the Disney movie, *Wimpy Kid*. The marketing and social media efforts designed for the co-brands led to a more powerful impact. For instance, the social media component of the alliance with *The Biggest Loser* produced 111,000 Facebook fans; 3,000 Twitter followers; comments from 200+ bloggers; more than 1,350 likes; 2,140 comments; and almost 1.6 million impressions. The connection with *Wimpy Kid* resulted in more than 46 million Facebook impressions, resulting in 3,700 new Wholly Guacamole fans. The Sonic program generated more than 1,200 tweets and 20 million impressions.

These efforts illustrate the power of social media. While the term has multiple meanings, in this context, **social media** is defined as any digital tool or venue that allows individuals to socialize on the web. A **social network** is a

Fresherized Foods

▲ A digital banner advertisement featuring the tie-in between Wholly Guacamole and the television show *The Biggest Loser*.

social structure of individuals and/or organizations that are tied together in some manner. **Social media marketing** is the utilization of social media and/or social networks to market a product, company, or brand.

This chapter first explains the basics of social networks and their relationships with marketing programs. Next, popular websites are briefly described, along with examples of how companies incorporated them into marketing and advertising programs. The third section explains the basics of social media marketing in greater detail. Social media marketing tactics are explored. A brief discussion of the additional issues associated with international social media marketing programs concludes the chapter.

Social Networks

objective 1

What constitutes a social network?

Numerous popular social networking sites currently operate (see Figure 1). **General social networking sites** are broadly based and are designed to appeal to all demographics, regardless of gender, age, race, income, or education. General sites provide venues for interpersonal communication. Individuals can stay in touch, learn what others in their networks are doing, share events in their lives, and make new friends. Facebook is the most well-known general social networking site.

A **niche social networking site** focuses on a specific interest, hobby, or demographic group. Some, such as LinkedIn, offer interactions between businesspeople. Dating sites provide an outlet to meet potential mates including target groups on sites such as OurTime, ChristianMingle, and FarmersOnly. Others cater to family or lifestyle interests such as single parents, gays, and lesbians. Special interest and hobby sites vary widely and include sites that focus on a sport such as skiing; a hobby such as photography; or special interests such as gardening. Shopping networks provide venues for individuals to share product reviews and information about brands and products. These are not e-commerce sites but rather provide a meeting place that enables individuals to share information with others about product or brand along with comments about their shopping experiences.

Social bookmarking sites allow individuals to share bookmarks of websites. While most people bookmark their favorite sites on computers, social bookmarking sites make these public. They can be organized in a wide variety of ways and accessed at any time by anyone. Individuals may also provide comments about sites they have bookmarked and encourage comments by others.

- General social networking sites
- Niche social networking sites
  - Business
  - Family and lifestyle
  - Dating
  - Special interests and hobbies
  - Shopping
- Social bookmarking sites

▲ **FIGURE 1**

Types of Social Networking Sites

Social Media Sites

objective 2

What are the unique characteristics of the primary social media websites?

The social media landscape rapidly evolves. Marketers recognize the importance of examining the major social media sites and who uses them. Some differences in the audiences of each of the major social media sites can be identified, as shown in Figure 2. Overall, females utilize social media more than men and approximately 42 percent of online consumers use multiple sites.[2] The most widely visited sites currently are Facebook, Twitter, YouTube, Instagram, and Pinterest. Facebook outpaces all other sites. Two-thirds of internet users have a Facebook page compared to between 13 percent and 16 percent for Instagram, Pinterest, and Twitter.[3]

The demographic makeup of each social media network's visitor group differs. Each site appeals to varying types of people. While the social networking sites continually change, marketers find it worthwhile to examine each one in terms of its usefulness to a brand in a social media marketing program. A brief review of the most often-visited sites follows.

Social Networking Site	Percent of Internet Users	Primary Users
Facebook	67%	Adults 18–29 Females
Twitter	16%	Adults 18–29 African-Americans Urban residents
Pinterest	15%	Adults under 50 Females Caucasians Some college
Instagram	13%	Adults 18–29 Females African-Americans, Latinos Urban residents

▶ **FIGURE 2**

Social Media Users

Source: Based on Maeve Duggan and Joanna Brenner, "The Demographics of Social Media Users – 2012," *Pew Research Center*, www.pewresearch.org, February 14, 2013.

Facebook

Facebook, the largest social media site, houses more than 1.2 billion users worldwide. It presents the largest source of display ads of all social networks, with a 17.7 share.[4] According to *AdWeek*, Facebook's popularity comes from a blend of "sheer size of fan base, record of publishing useful content, and the extent of consumer interaction that is offered."

Facebook generates almost $2 billion in annual advertising revenues. In addition to brands being advertised on its pages, Facebook recently expanded its advertising services to allow marketers to target customers on mobile devices based on an individual's activity outside of the Facebook site. This behavioral targeting tool—called "custom audiences"—allows marketers to gather information from the company's web-sites and applications, and then use that data to target individuals when they visit Facebook, whether on a mobile phone, tablet, or desktop computer.[5]

Michaeljung/Fotolia

▲ Females tend to use social media more than men; blacks trend toward using Twitter and Instagram.

Although Facebook remains the largest social media network, the number of teen users has declined by more than 25 percent in the last three years. At the same time, the number of older consumers, individuals 55 years old or older, increased 80 percent to 28 million. Part of the reason why teens leave Facebook may be the presence of their parents and grandparents. Many teens prefer the private messaging that is available on Twitter or Snapchat.

In addition to the changing demographic profile of Facebook users, only a small percentage now share details of their lives on a daily basis. Only ten percent update their status daily and only four percent update it more than once a day. Approximately 15 percent comment on photos once or more a day. Many believe Facebook has peaked in terms of number of users and frequency of use. While this may be true, the site still has more than 1.2 billion users, which makes it an attractive social network for marketers.[6] According to Brad Kim, vice president of research firm Curebit, compared to Twitter, Facebook generates ten times the number of shares, 20 times the amount of site traffic, and 20 times the number of new customers acquired. According to Kim, the reason for this vast difference in effectiveness is that Twitter tends to be a one-way message whereas Facebook features two-way communication between friends.[7]

The companies with the most successful Facebook presence, according to *Adweek*, are Starbucks, Coca-Cola, Best Buy, and Microsoft. Starbucks has 3.7 million fans, compared to 3.5 million for Coke.[8] An independent study by WetPaint and the Altimeter Group notes that these companies and others that have high levels of social media activity tend to increase revenues more than companies that lack a social media presence.[9]

Twitter

The Twitter microblogging service allows individuals and companies to send out tweets with a maximum of 140 characters per message. Twitter's users are more racially diverse than the internet as a whole or Facebook. Approximately 41 percent of the 54 million Twitter users come from a minority race. While a large number of users are Hispanics, Twitter's primary strength is among African Americans. About 18 percent of Twitter users are African American, which is almost double that of internet users. Among those in this group ages 18–29, the percentage is close to 40 percent. For companies that target minorities, especially African Americans, Twitter can be an effective social media network.[10]

Twitter offers an effective method of reaching customers. Marketers may monitor what customers

▼ An advertisement for Wholly Guacamole and Sonic appearing on Facebook.

Fresherized Foods

Michaeljung/Fotolia

▲ Starbucks utilized Twitter for a successful campaign entitled "Tweet-a-Coffee".

say about a company or brand. Software, such as Tweetscan or Summize, locates a brand or company name mentioned in tweets. Company officials are able to respond or gather the information for future use or evaluation. It provides valuable information regarding customer perceptions of the brand and what they are saying.

JetBlue, Starbucks, Comcast, H&R Block, and Southwest Airlines utilize Twitter. Starbucks launched a Twitter campaign entitled "Tweet-a-Coffee," which allowed individuals to give a $5 gift card to a friend by putting both the hashtag @tweetacoffee and the person's Twitter handle in the tweet. Within two months, the campaign generated $180,000 in purchases. In addition to the revenue generated by the program, Starbucks collected 54,000 Twitter IDs along with additional information on the Starbucks account each customer had to set up to utilize the Twitter gift card function.[11]

For small local businesses, Twitter can be an effective means of marketing. Three weeks after Curtis Kimball opened his crème pastry cart in San Francisco, he noticed a stranger who had lined up to purchase some of his desserts. When quizzed, the man said he heard about the pastry cart from Twitter. Kimball created a Twitter account and now has a fan base of 5,400 customers who wait for him to post the flavor of the day at his store.[12]

YouTube

The fastest-growing area of social media networking involves posting videos, especially on YouTube. Experts forecast that by 2017, YouTube will have more views, likes, and shares than either Facebook or Twitter. Consumers create their own videos with mobile devices; and, as a result, the number of videos produced grows dramatically every year. This proliferation of videos has led to a new venue for fans to interact with brands. They are no longer passive customers but passionate fans using videos to share their thoughts. Figure 3 highlights the ways consumers share videos online through YouTube as well as other video sharing social networks.

A large number of consumers have a YouTube channel where they post their favorite videos. They create some; others are videos they like. One type of video that has seen a sharp increase is broadcast ads produced by brands. These may be television ads or digital ads produced for the internet. Passionate fans who see an advertisement they like re-post the ad on their channels or on YouTube for their friends to see. The vast majority of ads posted by individuals are positive responses to commercials they liked. There are instances in which individuals post ads for some negative reasons. When this occurs, brand managers must be quick to react.

A second trend includes video reviews of products. Rather than write a review and post it on a blog or a website, consumers create videos in which they talk about the brand and their experiences. Most are made by positive and passionate fans praising a product, although some are negative. In one circumstance, Covergirl had 251 million total views on YouTube. 249 million of them (99 percent) were consumer-created videos talking about the brand. Similar statistics apply to other brands, such as Oreos, where 92 percent of the views are fan-created messages and Revlon, with 99 percent consumer-created videos.

- Uploading broadcast ads
- Video reviews of products
- Re-creation of ads
- Creating consumer produced how-to videos
- Capturing real-time events
- Creating branded videos

▲ **FIGURE 3**

Trends in Consumer Video Sharing

Closely tied with consumer video reviews is the re-creation of broadcast ads. Swiffer has encountered an explosion of interest in the brand on YouTube. Many of the company's ads have been posted and re-posted by fans, along with a large number of product reviews. Recently, however, 150 people have re-created one of the television ads and posted their versions on YouTube. They are shown mopping the floor with a Swiffer mop or dusting with a Swiffer product, just as in the agency-produced ad in which the actor breaks out into a dance. The total number of views for all three types of Swiffer fan-created videos exceeds 10.5 million, compared to only 225,000 views of the videos produced by Swiffer. Clearly the popularity of fan-produced material exceeds company-produced materials.[13]

In the past, when consumers wanted to know how to use a product, fix a product, or repair it, they would visit the brand's website or contact technical support. Now, many turn to YouTube. Consumers post how-to videos that show ways to use a particular product and how to fix or repair a particular item. Seeing a demonstration on video makes it easier to understand than reading a reference manual or the step-by-step instructions presented on a blog or website.

Built-in video features and still cameras in cell phones allow consumers to capture events as they occur. Many products become part of the event, either in the video or mentioned by the consumer starring in the video. Occasionally, these go viral. For instance, after Charles Ramsey rescued a captured Amanda Berry, in his interview he mentioned McDonald's. The Ramsey video resulted in more than 11 million views in less than 24 hours. McDonald's was mentioned more than 6,000 times as consumers shared the video with friends. Reacting to the buzz, McDonald's marketing team sent a tweet supporting Ramsey and gave him free hamburgers for one year. Such positive buzz can only occur when marketers actively listen to social media and quickly take advantage of real-time events.

One final marketing approach involves creating branded videos. Devin Graham is a 30-year-old filmmaker with the YouTube handle of "devinsupertramp." He creates stunt videos such as the "World's Largest Rope Swing," which had 22 million views; "Human Slingshot Slide and Slide" had 13 million views. He has almost 2 million subscribers to his YouTube channel. His popularity drew the interest of several firms. He now makes daredevil-type branded videos through sponsorships by Mountain Dew and Ford.[14]

Marketing professionals recognize that YouTube presents unique opportunities and challenges. Consumers are sharing videos, producing videos, and talking about videos. Fans create most of them, which means individual companies cannot control the content. Monitoring these videos becomes important because it allows the marketing department to support those that favor the brand and its desired image. For negative videos, company leaders must creatively respond to show they are listening. The negative reviews or posts can also be used to improve the company's products, services, and the image it seeks to project.

Community Trust Bank

▲ Popular advertisements, such as the ones with Terry Bradshaw produced for Community Trust Bank, are often posted and shared on YouTube.

Instagram

Instagram, a mobile photo and video social sharing network owned by Facebook, has enjoyed an explosion in popularity during the past few years, with more than 200 million users. Instagram users tend to be young, wealthy, and female. Almost 60 percent visit Instagram every day.

Among the brands that have established a presence on Instagram, the largest is lingerie retailer Victoria's Secret with 4 million followers. Of note, Chanel has no official presence on Instagram but has attracted 5 million photos using the hashtag #chanel. Other brands with a strong presence on Instagram include Ben & Jerry's, Bloomingdale's, Lipton, Macy's, Gucci, and Michael Kors.[15]

Amyinlondon/Fotolia

▲ Bloomingdale's developed a contest encouraging fans to submit selfies along with their favorite beauty or styling tips.

Instagram's recent emergence into social media has caused marketers for various brands to explore the best options to use on the site. Currently, the two most popular tactics are contests and crowdsourcing for photos. Bloomingdale's and Lipton held contests on Instagram. In the Bloomingdale's contest, users were asked to submit selfies with details about a favorite beauty or styling tip. To encourage participation and social sharing, Bloomingdale's posted the photos on a score board where fans could vote for their favorites. Individuals who submitted photos were encouraged to get their friends to vote for them by sharing the link through Instagram and other social media networks. In Lipton's contest, Instagram users were invited to submit "uplifting moments" via Instagram's image-sharing platform to one of four hashtags.[16]

The crowdsourcing of photos followed YouTube's pattern, except the photos were submitted through Instagram. Macy's, West Elm, and Coach recently encouraged fans to submit photos, which were placed on each brand's website, often alongside professional models.

A closely related trend in retailing involves individuals uploading personal pictures wearing a particular brand of clothing, which provides a consumer-to-consumer recommendation. Katherine Lin uploaded photos of herself with friends at the Coachella music festival on Twitter and Instagram. She was wearing a Dannijo necklace she had purchased online. Dannijo marketers saw the photo and posted it on the company's website. Lin was thrilled and instantly shared the posting with friends. Retailers realize the power of word-of-mouth communications. Some retailers post the photos on company websites; others provide a link to the photos, and another group encourages customers to upload photos directly to the company's website. Regardless of the method used, showing consumers wearing the brand's fashions is the objective. It helps consumers connect with the brand through social media and keeps them on the website longer. As a result, sales increase.[17]

▼ Pinterest is a popular social media site for food items, such as recipes by Gulf Coast Seafood.

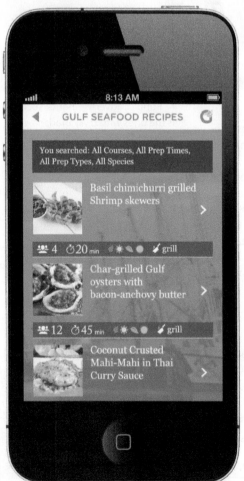

Gulfcoast Sea Food

Pinterest

Pinterest is a bulletin-board style social site that allows users to post photos and image-based articles about events, special interests, or hobbies. Currently, 70 million people use Pinterest, and 70 percent are female. Fashion and food are the two most featured topics on the site, which means retailers and food manufacturers find it to be an attractive outlet.

Land O' Lakes recently offered a promotion on Pinterest entitled "Pin a Meal, Give a Meal." Each time a meal or recipe from Land O' Lakes was pinned on Pinterest, the company donated $1 to the Feeding America foundation. Other companies active on Pinterest include Amazon, Wal-Mart, Apple, QVC, Staples, Best Buy, Netflix, and Sears. QVC and Wal-Mart currently have the most followers, but Amazon and Apple have the most pins on user pinboards.[18]

Social Media Marketing

Brand managers develop social media marketing campaigns for a variety of reasons. Figure 4 identifies some of the more common.[19] Two frequently reported rationales are to stay engaged with customers and increase brand exposure to potential customers. To do so, most brands utilize multiple social media networks.

- Engage fans
- Increase brand exposure
- Avenue for customer interaction
- Increase traffic
- Generate leads
- Enhance brand image
- Improve search rankings
- Gather customer intelligence
- Develop loyal fans
- Increase sales

◀ **FIGURE 4**

Reasons for Social Media Marketing

Source: Based on "Social Strategies for 2014," *Wildfire by Google Whitepaper, Ad Age Content Strategy Studio,* October 2013; Michael A. Stelzner, "2013 Social Media Marketing Industry Report," *Social Media Examiner,* www.socialmediaexaminer.com, 2013.

objective 3

What is the nature of social media marketing?

As an example, on its 30th anniversary, Hooters of America launched a brand overhaul aimed at winning over female customers while maintaining its predominantly male customer base. Social media provided an integral part of the brand rejuvenation. Prior to the social media launch, Hooters revamped its menu to include more "female-friendly" items, remodeled many of its restaurants, and developed a TV and radio advertising campaign. The heart of the campaign, however, was social media. Hooters fans were urged to share their experiences on Facebook, Twitter, Instagram, YouTube, and other social media platforms. Within 30 days of the launch, consumers had posted 10,000 photos. During the campaign, Hooters' Instagram account grew to more than 25,000 followers, its Facebook page produced more than 2.5 million likes, and it garnered almost 54,000 Twitter followers. The social media campaign pushed Hooters' ranking in the Nation's Restaurant News Social 200 Index from #56 to #12.[20]

When Wholly Guacamole hosted a Lion King DVD giveaway, the program generated 95,301 impressions on Facebook with more than 600 individuals making comments. It also led to an increase of 4,000 followers on Twitter.[21] Giveaways or promotions are not always needed to engage fans through social media or to gain brand exposure, but they can generate additional interest in a brand. In addition, engaging fans with a brand often creates increased customer interactions. These connections take place among fans (or customers) or between fans and the brand. Customer interactions are especially beneficial because they provide word-of-mouth endorsements for the brand. A customer relating her experience with a product carries considerably more weight with other consumers than a company touting its own merits.

Increase Traffic and Enhance Brand Image   Social media can also drive traffic, normally to the brand's website. Visitors can click on a URL embedded in a social media contact or message. Companies also take advantage of social media to drive traffic to a retail location such as a restaurant. For business-to-business programs, social media generates leads to be followed up by members of sales staff, including field salespeople, telemarketers, or the email sales force.

Social media may help enhance a brand's image. To achieve this goal, it should become more than just a sounding board for customers. It should offer a venue for solving problems, gathering useful information, and gaining insights. Research by J.D. Power and Associates revealed that, among highly satisfied customers of a brand, 87 percent said their online interactions with the brand positively impacted their perceptions of the brand and their likelihood to purchase a product. Individuals with low satisfaction scores indicated social communications negatively impacted their likelihood of purchasing the item in the future.[22]

Improve Search Rankings   Social media can boost organic search rankings with search engines. These increased rankings occur for two reasons. First, individuals more frequently mention the brand name on social media networks, because most algorithms on search engines examine numbers of mentions. Second, if content or comments made about the brand fit the search terms, then the quality of those interactions are increased and various search engines assign greater credibility to the brand.

▼ Hooters used social media in an effort to win over more female customers while retaining its male customer base.

Monkey Business/Fotolia

▲ Wholly Guacamole's marketing team used social media to engage fans with a Lion King DVD giveaway.

• React to negative feedback

• Detect problems

• Gather topics for branded content

• Predict trends

• Detect patterns or shifts in views

• Identify brand advocates

▲ **FIGURE 5**

Functions of Social Listening

Customer Intelligence **Social listening**, or listening to social chatter, often provides enlightening information to marketing professionals. Comments may be negative or positive, but in most cases visitors render honest opinions. Occasionally, social media buzz creates a situation in which the marketing team should react immediately. For instance, when General Mills launched a television advertisement for Cheerios featuring a family with parents from different races, the ad also ran on YouTube. Some of the social media response was immediate, fierce, and unfortunately racist and negative. Within days, the ad had been viewed more than 1.7 million times. Part of the language and views posted on the comment section of YouTube were not family-friendly, which led officials at General Mills to disable the comment function. Although individuals could not make comments about the ad, it could still be viewed.

Despite the negative reactions present on social media, General Mills' management team did not back down. Company leaders believed the ad reflected current American society. According to Camille Gibson, vice president of marketing for Cheerios, "There are many kinds of families, and Cheerios celebrates them all. Despite some serious, negative responses online, it's been a very positive response overall."[23] The Cheerios example illustrates one outcome of gathering customer intelligence. Seldom do marketing employees have to react as quickly as those at General Mills.

Figure 5 displays other functions related to social listening. Marketers detect potential problems with its products or some other aspect of a company before it becomes a larger issue. In listening to comments of social media, brand managers avoid reacting to a small number of individuals who may not represent the majority of brand users. Typically, those who express a view over social media are passionate about the topic. It can be a bad experience they want others to know about, or it can be a good experience they want to share. Thus, before deciding to alter a product or take action, marketers try to determine whether the view being expressed represents a small subset of its customer base or the views of a larger segment. In the case of Cheerios, General Mills decided those who expressed negative opinions on social media did not stand for the majority of the population.

Social listening provides an excellent source of ideas for branded content. Problems consumers face, along with the information they seek, can be presented on branded content pages. By listening, the company appears to be in tune with consumers and seen as striving to meet consumer needs. New software packages often have bugs that users detect. These bugs and how they can be solved can be posted on the software creator's blog or website in advance of the majority of users experiencing the problem.

Sparks and Honey is a digital agency that monitors social chatter for various brands. In addition to counting mentions for a brand, the company produces a sentiment score that indicates the level of positive or negative chatter. The agency also employs predictive analytics to estimate how quickly a trend might take effect and have an impact on its clients. The firm produces what it calls a "burst quotient." The figure tells a client how quickly or slowly they might need to respond to a trend occurring in society or whether a response will be necessary.

A trend being examined by marketing professionals involves wearable devices, such as mobile wallets and eye glasses that also serve as cameras. Listening to social interactions among consumers provides valuable information regarding what consumers think of this trend and how soon it will become part of American culture—or rather that it is a fad that will hit and then disappear.

In addition to identifying trends, marketers take advantage of social listening to detect patterns or shifts in views of consumers. In the case of the Cheerios ad featuring parents from different races, Sparks and Honey research discovered that the views expressed on YouTube were from a minority and not those of the overall society. Further, the agency detected younger consumers are more open to mixed race marriages than older consumers. Seeing this pattern and the reaction to the Cheerios ad, Sparks and Honey suggested that Gerber produce a video featuring children and young people talking about biracial couples. Rather than being reactive, the agency recommended a proactive approach.[24]

▲ Through social listening, the research firm Sparks and Honey discovered younger consumers were open to interracial marriages.

Social listening patterns assist in identifying customer advocates. According to social media marketing platform EngageSciences, 4.7 percent of a brand's fans generate nearly all of its social buzz. While other companies argue the figure should be 20 percent of a brand's fans, a small percentage of a company's customers create most of its buzz. The vast majority remains silent or seldom says anything on social media. Consequently, this small set of individuals, whether 4.7 percent or slightly more, offers great value to a brand if the members in the group can be identified. When examining social interactions, brand advocates often exhibit three characteristics:

- Behavioral commitment
- Emotional connection
- Quality communication skills

Advocates often demonstrate behavioral commitment to the brand. They make regular, frequent purchases of the brand. A company with customer purchase data in its database can track actual purchase behaviors. Individual customers can be identified, and those with emotional connections will demonstrate the ties through compliments and praise of the brand. To these consumers, the brand is the best in the world and no other brand is even worth consideration. As a result, they are willing to take extraordinary measures to purchase the item. Although advocates exhibit emotional and behavioral commitments, to be useful to marketers they also should exhibit quality communication skills.[25] They need the ability to effectively express their thoughts, feelings, and emotions. When located, brand managers are able to recruit these individuals to be advocates. Their recommendations can be extremely valuable in recruiting other brand loyalists.

For an Authorized Skyjacker® Dealer near you call 1.866.4.A.DEALER or visit us on the web at skyjacker.com

Increase Sales and Build Brand Loyalty Developing brand loyalty and increasing sales are the ultimate goals of any marketing program, including social media marketing. At the same time, if customers view a social media outreach program as merely a masquerade for selling, they might be alienated by such efforts. Instead, marketers should set the primary objective of a social media program to engage consumers with the brand. Increasing sales should be viewed as a by-product of social media marketing.

A recent study conducted by Coca-Cola suggests that online buzz, or talk on social media about the brand, did not have any measurable impact on sales. This finding stunned many outsiders because Coca-Cola has more than 61 million Facebook fans—a total more than any other brand.[26] The researchers concluded that what cannot be determined by just counting social comments or even looking at the sentiment (whether positive or negative)

▲ Placing icons for Facebook, Twitter, and YouTube on ads encourages fans of Skyjacker to interact with the brand via social media.

Foxy_A/Fotolia

▲ L'Oreal developed a successful social media marketing strategy.

is the impact on brand image and brand loyalty. Further, the researchers asked, "If Coca-Cola was not involved with social media, would the impact be negative on sales?" For megabrands such as Coca-Cola, social media marketing cannot be considered as an option. Instead, marketers use this valuable new tool to more deeply engage fans with the brand.

Although Coca-Cola did not find a positive relationship between sales and social buzz, a study by McKinsey & Co. revealed a relationship between sales and negative buzz. A telecom client of McKinsey's suffered a drop in sales of eight percent as a result of negative comments made about the brand on social media.[27]

L'Oreal   L'Oreal provides an excellent example of successful social media marketing. According to L'Oreal social media chief Rachel Weiss, "The whole point for us with our social strategy is you can touch a customer at any point within the customer's decision journey." Weiss and others at L'Oreal created a three part strategy designed to maximize the impact of the company's social media efforts.

First, the company employs differing marketing strategies and unique Facebook pages for each country in which products are sold. Georges Edouard-Dias, senior vice president of digital business for L'Oreal, argues that, "This takes us back to the roots of marketing, which is about intuition, intelligence and feeling the market, not about reading or statistics or replicating best practice." In essence, each country is unique and consequently each social media program should be tailored to suit the situation present in each region.

Second, the company seeks to create content that will lead to social conversation. As Rachel Weiss says, "Women love to talk about what lipstick they're wearing, what lipstick was Sofia Vergara wearing from the Emmys. Beauty is always part of the social conversation. Women are always interested in what other women are wearing, doing, and beauty tips." To generate conversations, the L'Oreal Facebook page asks questions, provides beauty advice, and seeks to lead customers to share stories with each other.

Third, social media works best when customers encounter it before and after a purchase. L'Oreal's strategy includes providing "how-to" instructions for consumers in the store prior to any purchase. Then, follow up and tracking takes place on social media such as YouTube, Facebook, and Twitter.[28] For instance, recently the company launched the premium hair color Casting Creme Gloss in India. To achieve the maximum impact of social media, the marketing team integrated offline sales with a Facebook app that required the user to fill in a unique code found on the pack. The app allowed the customer to upload an image with her two best friends to enter a contest to appear in an ad starring Sonam Kapoor. The combination of offline and online promotions led to a 45 percent surge in sales.[29]

Social media may not be always be linked directly to sales from clicking on a link embedded on a site or social media message, but it can still exert a positive influence on other factors, including brand exposure, fan engagement, and enhanced brand image. The quality of fans and their levels of engagement with the brand remain far more important than a company's sales figures or its overall number of Facebook fans or Twitter followers. Social media provides a unique venue for businesses to connect with loyal customers while positively influencing others.

Social Media Marketing Strategies

objective 4

Which social media marketing strategies do companies employ?

Social interaction should be the fundamental basis for social media. It involves one consumer talking to another or to many others. The primary difference is that social media facilitates these interactions rather than face-to-face engagement. Skilled marketers recognize the potential inherent in such exchanges. The newness of this type of communication means that company leaders are still developing ideas regarding the best approaches to utilize these venues. Figure 6 offers some of the current strategies.

Content Seeding

Farmers, gardeners, and homeowners plant seeds into the ground believing they will germinate and grow into a living plant that bears fruit or flowers. The same concept applies to social media marketing. **Content seeding** involves providing incentives for consumers to share content about a brand. The incentive does not have to be financial, although financial incentives tend to be the most frequently used. An incentive can be information, uniqueness, novelty, or anything that engages consumers with the brand and motivates them to share with others.

A common method of seeding is offering a coupon, rebate, contest, or other financial incentive to share content. Wholly Guacamole posted the following on Facebook about a contest in its alliance with *The Biggest Loser* television show:[30]

Wholly Guacamole
BIG APRIL CONTEST. want to go to the live finale of TBL? stay for a week at TBL resort? check out our crazy april contest eatwholly.com/thebiggestloser.com that gives away over 80 prizes.

WIN SOMETHING TODAY HERE. giving away 10 free coupon prize packs w/ wholly.jennie-o turkey products & food should taste good chips.to enter, post your guilty eating pleasure below. be honest, we won't judge (well, maybe a little).

http://eatwholly.com/thebiggestloser.com
eatwholly.com

31,950 Impressions · 0.62% Feedback

Most people like to compete, especially if they believe they can win. When Microsoft launched Windows 7, the company asked high schools to submit videos for a computer lab makeover. The "School Pride" campaign invited visitors to vote on the best video submission. To add intrigue and to encourage sharing, Microsoft used a social graph that allowed web visitors to have friends go to the site and vote for the best entry, thereby increasing a school's chances of winning. The contest generated an increase of almost 75 percent in traffic to the website.[31]

One contest that generated a great deal of social buzz was created for Esurance. Rather than spending $4 million on a Super Bowl ad, the company purchased the first ad slot after the game ended, at a cost of $2.5 million. The ad announced that one lucky viewer would win the difference, about $1.5 million, who tweeted the hashtag #EsuranceSave30 within 36 hours of the ad airing.

- Content seeding
- Real-time marketing
- Interactive blogs
- Consumer-generated reviews
- Viral marketing

▲ **FIGURE 6**
Social Media Strategies

▼ Microsoft used a content seeding contest entitled "School Pride" when it launched Windows 7.

Diego Cervo/Fotolia

The ad created a tremendous burst of Twitter shares. Leo Burnett, Esurance's agency, reported the following statistics from the campaign:[32]

- 5.4 million tweets with the #EsuranceSave30 hashtag
- More than 200,000 entries within the first minutes of the television ad
- 2.6 billion social impressions on Twitter
- 332,000 views of Esurance commercial that had been posted to YouTube
- 261,000 new followers on the official Esurance Twitter account
- A 12-fold spike in the visits to the Esurance website within the first hours of the television ad

Occasionally a mistake, or what appears to be a snafu, can create social buzz. JCPenney was the most-mentioned brand on social media that was not part of Super Bowl advertising. The retailer was mentioned 118,201 times, which is 25 times greater than its 30-day average. A typo-laden tweet from JCPenney read "Toughdown Seadawks!! Is sSeattle going toa runaway wit h this???" The tweet mystified Twitter land and was re-tweeted 40,000 times. While some thought it was a mistake or a JCPenney employee who had enjoyed too much to drink, the company revealed the jumbled message was the result of #TweetingWithMittens, a pair of Team USA mittens sold at JCPenney.[33]

A value-added incentive marketers can incorporate into a seed-sharing program is offering customers something exclusive to make them feel special. Sony artist Pitbull generated awareness for a new album prior to its launch through social media. If a person shared a message from Pitbull's website on Facebook or Twitter, it allowed that individual to listen to the CD online before the music went public. If the person got three of his friends to come back to the website, then it unlocked three bonus tracks. The idea of feeling special and offering something unique drove awareness of the album before it launched.[34]

Appealing to consumer altruism, such as a campaign to donate blood in the wake of a tragedy, offers an additional content-seeding approach. Recent storms in the United States created shortages of blood for the Red Cross. The organization used the internet to inspire individuals to share. The organization created a badge announcing the shortage and encouraged individuals to share the badge on their social networks and with their friends.

Humane societies often use social media to get word out about their work and the need for donations. Various companies may use this same tactic but must be extremely careful in how the program is announced and promoted. A brand that supports the Red Cross, a local human society, or other not-for-profit organization might encourage fans to share the information. The approach will only succeed when it appears genuine and not a gimmick to push sales by running a pseudo-advertisement.

▼ Oreo used real-time marketing to send out a tweet that it is okay to dunk Oreo cookies in the dark.

Jaimie Duplass/Fotolia

Real-Time Marketing

The idea of real-time marketing existed prior to the 2013 Super Bowl, but it was the infamous blackout during the game in the New Orleans Superdome that legitimized it as a feasible social media strategy. Oreo sent a message via Twitter that it is okay to dunk an Oreo cookie "in the dark." The message was placed on an image of an Oreo cookie, set in light, shadow, and darkness. That message became a viral hit and was re-tweeted 15,000 times within the first 14 hours.

Real-time marketing is the creation and execution of an instantaneous marketing message in response to—and in conjunction with—an occurrence during a live event. Marketers conceived and produced the Oreo tweet in just five minutes. Such a rapid reaction was possible because marketers from Oreo's parent company, Mondelez, and its agency were assembled at a "social media command center" in New York during the game. With creative and technical staff present and in place, the team was quickly able to create a response to the blackout, produce the message, and then send it.[35]

The instant success of Oreo led marketers for other brands to set up "war rooms" during major live events. These war rooms contain top marketing executives, creatives, digital technicians, and attorneys. The group seeks to strike instantly with an approved message when an opportunity occurs. During the 2014 Super Bowl, Adobe had 15 people assembled in its war room. The team employed Adobe's digital analytic tools to listen to social media chatter to determine what buzz was resonating with consumers and then congratulate whatever organization or company had initiated the buzz.

▲ Brand managers now deploy teams to "war rooms" prior to a live event to devise and launch reactions to occurrences during the event.

Adobe's message was not for consumers but rather for businesses. It was designed to acquaint other companies with Adobe's digital analytical tools.[36]

Effective real-time marketing does not occur on the fly without any thought. The approach requires upfront strategic planning before assembling a war room and prior to any live event. While seeking to display human emotions and reactions to live events, those actions must be carefully planned to ensure they resonate with consumers (or businesses) and remain consistent with the brand's overall brand image and integrated marketing communications plan. The tone featured in a real-time marketing message becomes the key. It should correlate with what is presented in other company advertisements and other social media efforts. During these preplanning sessions, company leaders discuss and sometimes even prepare messages and ads to be used for various situations that might occur during a live event. While it may seem the message was a quick reaction, it may have been talked about and designed weeks earlier.

In addition to upfront strategic planning, rules, procedures, and processes must be in place that allows the team to react quickly. Individuals with authority to approve marketing messages, advertising, and media allocation have to be present. In today's litigious society, this means that individuals from the legal team will be involved with the decision prior to initiating the message. Without prior planning, such real-time marketing does not occur.

Real-time marketing can be utilized in places other than live sporting events. During a recent snowstorm in the Northeast, Starbucks' marketing department put together a social media plan for Facebook and Twitter that focused on conversations about the anticipated blizzard. Snow-themed ads appeared on Facebook and Twitter with the focus on an image of a warm cup of java. The Twitter ads appeared when individuals clicked on #blizzard, #snowstorm, and other related hashtags.[37]

McDonald's deploys real-time marketing messages, but at a slower pace. Marketers track 2.5 million to 3 million conversations each month listening to what consumers say about McDonald's, quick-service restaurants, and other topics relevant to the company's operations. The team watches for trends that the company can feature on its social media pages. When the company launched its Cheddar Bacon Onion burger, the ads highlighted various attributes of the product; however, the chatter was about the bacon. In response, the marketing team quickly changed its promotional effort in social media to focus more on the bacon rather than other aspects of the sandwich.[38]

Interactive Blogs

The power of a blog comes from the new landscape it creates in which one consumer dissatisfied with a particular brand can now tell thousands, and in some cases millions, of people. Previously, a bad shopping experience meant that 12 to 15 people would hear

Jinga80/Fotolia

▲ Discontented consumers can now express their unhappiness through blogs and other forms of social media to thousands or even millions.

about it. Now, an individual's complaint can be sent to more than just friends and family. A discontented consumer speaks to anyone willing to listen (or read about it) via the internet. The reverse can also occur. A satisfied customer can rave about a brand and have her comments read by thousands.

Interactive blogs permit visitors to send comments or posts, making them another important component of social media. We know blogging as primarily a one-way communication device. While effective, blogs that allow and encourage active participation often become more powerful. Such interactions present a higher level of risk, because the blogging company surrenders some control over content. While employees can squelch and/or delete negative comments, doing so destroys the blog's credibility and damages its reputation. A better approach is for the company's marketing team to face any criticism honestly and humbly and react by seeking a solution to the problem or cause of the dissatisfaction.

Companies may feature three different types of interactive blogs (see Figure 7). The first occurs when a company or brand creates a blog. Blogs owned and operated by businesses find it more difficult to solicit honest interactions with consumers who may be more suspicious of their intentions. Also, company personnel operating the blog may be more sensitive to negative content and how it may be viewed by customers.

A blog sponsored by a company or brand constitutes the second form. New regulations passed by the Federal Trade Commission require an individual who is being paid by an organization with merchandise or money, or is compensated in any other way, to report that information on the blog. While these individuals have more freedom to express personal opinions, they will likely have to remain positive about the brand in order to maintain its sponsorship. Visitors to the site have more freedom to comment as well, but recognizing that a business sponsors the blog's author often tempers their views.

The third type of blog involves individuals who speak about a brand but have no financial connection to it. They truly like the brand. They take pleasure in talking about it. They enjoy interacting with others about the brand. When a brand has no affiliation with a blog, visitors feel comfortable in making comments and relating their honest opinions. These blogs can be valuable, because the marketing team learns what consumers really think about a product or service. Marketers use this type of blog to ask questions and seek opinions, if permission is granted by the blog's author.

Consumer-Generated Reviews

Word-of-mouth endorsements have changed. Many companies that vend multiple goods or services solicit consumer-generated reviews of those products. Amazon. com stands at the forefront of this approach. Each book offered online holds a space where individual customers can write reviews, with words and a one- to five-star rating. The site informs the shopper of the number of reviews, the average star rating, and notes if the reviews are written by anonymous critics or those who provide their real names. A person wishing to place his name on a review must authenticate it by presenting Amazon.com with a credit card number. Customers benefit by reading the reviews before making purchases. The system may not be perfect, because an author may use a pseudonym to write a highly favorable review and encourage friends and

- Brand blog
- Individuals sponsored by a brand
- Individual speaking about a brand

▲ **FIGURE 7**
Types of Interactive Blogs

family members to do the same. At the same time, the author cannot control posts of outside reviews.

Best Buy incorporated consumer feedback into online retailing. The company hosts a blog section for consumers to read about and discuss various topics. In each product category, such as cameras, Best Buy provides a discussion forum on a variety of related topics. In the digital camera discussion forum, consumers post photos they have taken with various cameras. Best Buy posts customer reviews of each product, both positive and negative. The reviews may influence the brands consumers consider and eventually purchase. By providing blogs, discussion forums, and consumer reviews, Best Buy offers consumers methods to search for and evaluate products and to make purchase decisions without leaving the company's website.

The growing use of online reviews by consumers has led to an increase in websites devoted to providing them, such as TripAdvisor, Zagat, Edmunds, Yelp, and Foursquare. An online panel study of 3,404 individuals revealed that 75 percent think the information presented on rating sites is generally fair and honest; however, 25 percent still believe the information is biased or unfair. The larger and more established rating sites, such as TripAdvisor, Zagat, Open Table, Edmunds, Urbanspoon, and Yelp, tend to be the most trusted.[39]

Marketers carefully study customer-generated reviews because they provide important information about how customers evaluate brands and how the brand compares to the competition. This information becomes critical when developing marketing plans,

DuPage Medical Group

▲ Blogs can be a valuable source of information for patients looking for medical care as well as to the staff of DuPage Medical Group.

Visit Baton Rouge

◀ Consumer-generated reviews are important in tourist decisions for visiting Baton Rouge.

product modifications, and service strategies. As the usage of consumer-generated reviews continues to rise, the marketing challenge will be managing this aspect of consumer word-of-mouth endorsements in ways that enhance brand equity and increase sales.

Viral Marketing

Preparing a marketing message to be passed from one consumer to another through digital means, or **viral marketing**, takes the form of an email or a video posted to a personal blog and passed to other blogs or websites such as YouTube. It can evolve into a form of advocacy or word-of-mouth endorsement. The term "viral" derives from the image of a person being "infected" with the marketing message and then spreading it to friends, like a virus. The difference is that the individual voluntarily sends the message to others.

Viral marketing messages may include advertisements, hyperlinked promotions, online newsletters, streaming videos, and games. For instance, about a dozen videos were posted on YouTube of a man claiming to be the "world's fastest nudist." He streaks through various locations in New York City wearing only tennis shoes, tube socks, and a fanny pack positioned strategically in front. The links to the videos were emailed from individual to individual. They were posted on popular blogs such as The Huffington Post and Gawker. One appeared on CNN's *Anderson Cooper 360*. The campaign turned out to be a viral video campaign for Zappos.com, an online shoe and apparel store. The viral campaign highlighted that Zappos was selling clothes because additional videos were posted that showed a van screeching up to the "fastest nudist" and several people jumping out wearing Zappos T-shirts. As the van leaves, the video shows the nudist dressed in pants and a shirt.[40]

Figure 8 provides some suggestions on how to create successful viral campaigns. The viral message should focus on the product or business. In the Zappos.com videos, the nudist receives clothes from a Zappos team. The marketing team determines why an individual would want to pass the message along or tell friends about it.

Viral campaigns do not always succeed or yield positive benefits. Most brand managers would be thrilled to have three viral videos within one year, as Kmart did. The first YouTube video that went viral was "Ship My Pants," an advertisement created by Kmart. The video was viewed 20 million times. A short time later, an advertisement posted to YouTube—"Big Gas Savings"—based on a milder naughty double entendre was viewed more than 6 million times. Then "Show Your Joe" was a holiday ad that featured men playing *Jingle Bells* with their privates, viewed more than 15 million times. Despite all three ads going viral and being viewed more than 40 million times in total, sales fell 2.1 percent for the retailer.

Research regarding the impact of viral messages suggests that 61 percent of individuals exposed to a viral message or video had favorable opinions about the brand. Purchase intentions increased around five percent but were greater if the viral message was recommended by a friend via social media rather than a company.[41]

Individuals should receive an incentive to pass the message along. A message containing entertainment value offers one type of incentive. Others may be financial, such as free merchandise or a discount for messages passed along to friends that lead to purchases, logging onto a website, or registering for an e-newsletter. The incentive should be unique. A personalized message has a greater chance of being passed along.

- Focus on the product or business
- Determine why individuals would want to pass along the message
- Offer an incentive
- Make it personal
- Track the results and analyze the data

▶ **FIGURE 8**
Keys to Successful Viral Marketing

- Keep up with activities
- Learn about products or services
- Sweepstakes or promotion
- Provide feedback
- Join community of fans
- Make purchases
- To complain

▲ **FIGURE 9**

Why Consumers Follow Brand

Source: Based on Lenna Garibian, "Digital Influence: Blogs Beat Social Networks for Driving Purchases," *MarketingProfs*, www. marketingprofs.com/charts/print/2013/10336, March 18, 2013.

- Retail sites (56%)
- Brand sites (34%)
- Blogs (31.1%)
- Facebook (30.8%)
- Groups/Forums (28%)
- YouTube (27%)
- LinkedIn (27%)
- Google+ (20%)
- Online magazines (20%)
- Pinterest (12%)
- Twitter (8%)
- Instagram (3%)

▲ **FIGURE 10**

Internet Sites Most Likely to Influence Purchases

Source: Based on Lenna Garibian, "Digital Influence: Blogs Beat Social Networks for Driving Purchases," *MarketingProfs*, www.marketingprofs.com/charts/print/2013/10336, March 18, 2013.

The many forms of digital marketing mean that viral marketing has lost some of its luster. Some consumers have lost enthusiasm and are less willing to resend messages. Still, the marketing team can take advantage of the ability to track the results of a viral campaign and analyze the results to determine whether such a program will be effective.

Following Brands on Social Media

Figure 9 highlights reasons consumers follow brands in social media. Although they vary by social media site, the two top reasons tend to be to keep up with activities of the brand and to learn about the product or service. Typically, individuals do not follow a brand with the goal of making a purchase. Typically, they have purchased a brand, like the brand, and then become a fan or follower. If they are dissatisfied with a brand, they are not likely to follow it on social media. They may use social media to lodge the complaint but will not become a fan or follower.

In summary, company leaders have become involved in social media because it does influence purchase behaviors, as shown in Figure 10. Retail sites and the brand sites have the greatest online impact on purchase behaviors. Blogs rank third in terms of influence. Of the social media sites, Facebook was viewed as having the most influence, cited by 31 percent of the respondents in the survey.[42]

Social Media Metrics

This chapter includes a discussion of social media metrics because digital platforms provide comprehensive feedback, often instantaneously, that can be used to modify social media marketing strategies. Figure 11 provides the primary social media metrics used by organizations.

A number of social media and digital research firms specialize in providing a **buzz score (or brand buzz)**, which measures the number of times a brand receives

▼ Individuals follow brands, such as Kraft, on social media because they truly like the brand and use it regularly.

Kraft Foods, Inc

objective 5

What social media measurement metrics are available to marketers?

▶ **FIGURE 11**

Social Media Metrics

- Brand buzz (total mentions)
- Reach (number of fans)
- Facebook likes
- Twitter tweets and re-tweets
- Traffic from social media
- Click-through rate to Website

JD Bank

▲ A sentiment score can be used by marketers at JD Bank to determine whether the mentions received on various social media sites were positive or negative.

▼ Scott Equipment can measure the effectiveness of this banner ad through the click-through rate.

a mention on social network within a specific time frame. While counting the number of mentions provides an indicator of the popularity of a brand in social media, examining the sentiment score will be important. "Sentiment" refers to whether the buzz was negative or positive. Marketers recognize that both are important to monitor. When positive buzz takes place, employees can join the conversation and thank fans for their support and even reward them in some way. With negative buzz, the marketing team should be prepared to react quickly to prevent the buzz from growing exponentially and going viral.

Reach measures the number of fans, friends, or followers a brand has in social media. While the quantity will be important, it does not tell the whole story. The marketing team needs to know whether those fans are active or passive. They identify whether fans merely follow the buzz or share brand stories and information with their friends. Most important however, will be, "What is the trend?" Company leaders want to know whether the number of fans is growing, stagnant, or declining. This information assists in understanding the impact of the reach of a social media marketing campaign.

While many companies try to push their customers to like them on Facebook through ads, videos, and other social media, merely liking a brand does not necessarily translate into sales, as has been noted. Many marketing professionals have started to conclude that sharing represents a better metric than likes. A passive customer may click like, but a passionate customer will share the coupon, the promotion, or brand message. Sharing grows revenue and builds loyalty.

With Twitter, tweets and especially re-tweets reflect customer passion. Seeing a brand tweet may create a mental image, but retweeting that brand message conveys a word-of-mouth recommendation from one customer to another.

Technology allows company leaders to track how individuals got to a website. To determine the effectiveness of social media, marketers determine the percentage of visits that came through social media. If contests, coupons, or other promotions are sent via social media, a company's marketing team can determine the click-through rate, which is the number of individuals who clicked on a brand message and was taken directly to the brand's website. This, in turn, reflects the value of the social media advertising or marketing program.

Scott Equipment

International Implications

Social media interactions are a worldwide phenomenon. Most Facebook users are located outside the United States. Various social networks have been involved in social movements and political revolutions. They have helped widen the worldwide marketplace for a variety of goods and service while changing the landscape of shopping and purchasing patterns in numerous companies.

Marketing professionals understand that the social network environment creates additional complexities. Among the more notable, language differences, social norms, and technological issues represent three of the greatest challenges to individual companies.

As is the case in any marketing program, language differences complicate the ways in which messages can be constructed and transmitted. In countries where internet systems allow the free flow of messages, a marketing piece designed for viewers in Spain might quickly appear in China or Greece. Consequently, the viewer cannot decipher the intent of the message. Trying to present a consistent theme across languages presents a great deal of difficulty: Language differences enhance the dilemma. One tactic used to combat the problem is an emphasis on *visual Esperanto*, a more universal, emotionally-based approach designed to tap into feelings all citizens experience.

Social norms create a significant test for marketers. Norms regarding sexuality, modes of dress, attitudes toward women and minorities, and other differences become more readily noticeable when a tweet or Facebook post is sent across national boundaries. Companies seeking to establish an international presence carefully vet all messages to make sure they do not offend the norms or sensitivities of individuals in countries where the messages or advertisements will be shown.

Technological challenges can be presented by governments or by the nature of a country's infrastructure. Many national governments try to censor various websites from appearing within their boundaries. In other settings, poor internet service creates sporadic access at best. Marketing professionals account for these issues as they design social media programs.

objective 6

How can marketers use social media strategies in international operations?

Summary

Social media includes any digital tool or venue that allows individuals to socialize on the web. A social network is a social structure of individuals and/or organizations that are tied together in some manner. Social media marketing is the utilization of social media and/or social networks to market a product, company, or brand.

General social networking sites are broadly designed to appeal to all demographics, regardless of gender, age, race, or education. The most common include Facebook, Twitter, and YouTube. Niche social networking sites focus on a specific interest, hobby, or demographic group. Marketing professionals can target both types of sites. The objective involves determining the message that best resonates with individuals who frequently visit the site. The recent explosion of video productions by individuals is changing the landscape of social networking.

Social media marketing traditionally seeks to keep customers engaged with a brand and to increase the brand's exposure. It can also drive traffic to a desired site or place, enhance a brand's image, boost organic search rankings, and collect customer intelligence through social listening systems. A quality program identifies customer advocates who exhibit behavioral commitment, emotional connections with the brand, and quality communication skills. Social media marketing can help increase sales and enhance brand loyalty.

Social media marketing strategies include content seeding, which involves providing incentives for customers to share content about a brand. Effective real-time marketing efforts involve careful planning and preparation in order to provide an instantaneous marketing message in response to a live event. Interactive blogs allow visitors to make comments or posts on the site, including those created by the company, sites sponsored by the company, and those prepared by independent fans or advocates. Customer-generated review programs, when correctly managed, provide authenticity and engagement with those who use the systems to gather information about products. Viral marketing helps a company garner interest when a message is sent along via email or a re-post by consumers. Many consumers follow brands on social media.

Social media metrics include a buzz score, reach, likes on a site, re-posts and re-tweets, and click-through rates. These measures help marketers discover whether social media programs effectively reach their audiences.

International challenges in social media include language differences, social norms, and technological complications. Effective marketing teams monitor and respond carefully to these issues.

Key Terms

social media Any digital tool or venue that allows individuals to socialize on the web

social network A social structure of individuals and/or organizations that are tied together in some manner

social media marketing The utilization of social media and/or social networks to market a product, company, or brand

general social networking sites Websites that are broadly based and designed to appeal to all demographics, regardless of gender, age, race, income, or education

niche social networking site A website that focuses on a specific interest, hobby, or demographic group

social bookmarking sites Websites that allow individuals to share bookmarks of websites

social listening A social media marketing strategy that involves listening to social chatter

content seeding A social media marketing strategy that involves providing incentives for consumers to share content about a brand

real-time marketing The creation and execution of an instantaneous marketing message in response to—and in conjunction with—an occurrence during a live event

interactive blogs A marketing strategy in which a blog allows visitors to make comments or posts

viral marketing An advertisement tied to an email or other form of online communication in which one person passes on the advertisement or email to other consumers

buzz score (or brand buzz) A measure of the number of times a brand receives a mention on a social network within a specific time frame

---

MyMarketingLab

Go to **mymktlab.com** to complete the problems marked with this icon ⭐.

Review Questions

1. Define social media, a social network, and social media marketing.

2. What are the three major forms of social media networks? Describe each.

3. What are the most commonly used social media sites?

 4. How has video posting changed the nature of social media networking?

5. What are the major objectives of social media marketing programs?

6. What is social listening?

7. What three characteristics should consumer advocates demonstrate to be effective spokespersons in social media programs?

8. What are the most commonly used social media marketing strategies?

9. Describe content seeding.

10. Describe real-time marketing.

11. What three types of interactive blogs support social media marketing programs?

12. Describe viral marketing.

13. List the reasons why consumers follow brands on social media.

14. What social media measurement metrics are available to marketing professionals?

15. What issues complicate international social media marketing programs?

Critical Thinking Exercises

DISCUSSION QUESTIONS

16. Discuss the current trends of consumer video-sharing. Examine reasons brands have become involved in social media marketing. For each of the trends you identify, elaborate on ways brands can use social media marketing to reach video-sharing consumers. Be sure to justify your choices of social media marketing.

 17. Are you on Facebook? Why or why not? If you are on Facebook, how much time do you spend online at Facebook? Do you use Twitter? Why or why not? Based on your experience with Facebook and Twitter, how can companies use them to reach you? Are you a fan of any company on Facebook or Twitter? If so, why did you become a fan? If not, why did you choose not to become a fan?

18. YouTube has gained considerable popularity in recent years. Why do you think this is so? How often do you use YouTube? What types of videos do you watch? Do your friends and relatives access YouTube? If so, how often and why? If not, why not?

19. Social listening is now being used by most brand managers. How important do you think it is for brands to listen to social media chatter? Almost all comments on social media are made by a small percentage of consumers. Do you think these comments are representative of most consumers and what they think of a brand? Why or why not? If not, why should brands even pay attention to social chatter? Lastly, should brands make marketing strategy decisions based on social chatter? Why or why not?

20. Have you made brand purchases based on comments made on social media? Why or why not? Provide specific details. Have you decided against purchasing a particular brand based on comments on social media?

Why or why not? Provide specific details.

21. Look at the social media strategies listed in Figure 6. Discuss each strategy in terms of your personal experience. Describe if the strategy impacts your purchases and views of brands. Discuss why it does have an impact or why it doesn't for each strategy. Provide details to support your thoughts.

22. Do you use consumer-generated reviews in making purchase decisions? Why or why not? How valuable do you think they are to consumers?

23. Brand managers often become excited when something the company posts on the Internet goes viral and spreads like wildfire among consumers. What factors contribute to a brand's posting going viral? Discuss how the social media strategies of content seeding, real-time marketing, interactive blogs, and consumer-generated reviews lead to a successful viral marketing attempt or unsuccessful viral marketing.

Integrated Learning Exercises

24. Pick one of the following brands. Go the company's website and locate the social media links provided. Access each of the social media brand pages and evaluate them in terms of engaging consumers with the brand. Provide specific information from each social media network that shows how consumers can be engaged. Identify the number of fans, followers, and posts on each site.
    a. Wholly Guacamole (**www.eatwholly.com**)
    b. Sonic (**www.sonic.com**)
    c. Starbucks (**www.starbucks.com**)
    d. Coca-Cola (**www.coca-cola.com**)
    e. Lucky Brand (**www.luckybrand.com**)

25. Pick a brand you really like and for which you have a high level of loyalty. Access the brand's website, Facebook page, Twitter page, YouTube Channel, and Instagram page. Discuss the information provided on each. Based on the reasons brands use social media shown in Figure 4, discuss what you think is the reason for each social media network. Evaluate how successful you think the brand is with social media.

26. Choose one of the following product categories, then select three prominent brands in that category. Access each of the brand's Facebook page, Twitter page, Instagram page, and YouTube Channel. Compare and contrast what information is provided for each brand.

Which brand has the best social media presence? Why?
    a. Sports equipment
    b. Clothing
    c. Restaurants
    d. Beverage

27. Examine the reasons brands use social media shown in Figure 4. Pick three of the reasons and identify from your personal experience a brand you believe did well with each. It could be three different brands or one brand for all three. Support your answer with specific information and links to the social media pages illustrating your discussion.

28. Figure 6 identifies strategies brands can use with social media. Find an example of each strategy in social media not described in the text. Provide the link, explain why it is an example of the strategy, and your evaluation of whether the strategy was good or bad, and why.

29. Using a blog search engine, locate an example of an interactive blog. Evaluate the blog. Is it effective? Why or why not?

30. Use a search engine to locate an example of viral marketing. Evaluate the viral marketing. Was it effective? Why or why not?

Blog Exercises

Access the authors' blog for this text at the URLs provided to complete these exercises. Answer the questions that are posed on the blog.

31. Hooters: **http://blogclowbaack.net/2014/05/12/hooters-chapter-9/**

32. Covergirl: **http://blogclowbaack.net/2014/05/12/covergirl-chapter-9/**

33. Social Media: **http://blogclowbaack.net/2014/05/12/social-media-chapter-9/**

Student Project

CREATIVE CORNER

Carlos just opened his own hot dog and pastry stand in downtown St. Louis. He believes social media could be used to build awareness of his stand and to build a customer base. Carlos believes having the unique combination of hot dogs and pastries provides him with a combination meal (hot dog, pastry, and drink) that counters what a fast-food restaurant would offer. Develop a social media marketing campaign for Carlos that includes the following elements:

- Objectives (or reasons) for the social media marketing campaign

- Social networking sites he should utilize
- Social media strategies
- Metrics he can use to measure success of the social media campaign
- Banner ad that Carlos can place on Facebook (design this for him)

In developing the campaign, be sure to provide a rationale to Carlos for your suggestions.

CASE 1   POST-IT: MAKING THE ORDINARY EXTRAORDINARY

Sooner or later, every business person comes into contact with a Post-it note. These sticky, functional tools have become part of everyday life in homes, offices, and other places. The product remains a steady, profitable staple of the 3-M portfolio. Jesse Singh, vice president for the stationery and office supplies division of 3M in Minnesota, notes "If you think about the product, it's iconic; it's been in the market over 30 years," and, until recently, the strategy to sell it was by "taking a functional view of the brand."[43]

In 2013, a new $10 million marketing campaign was launched, with a fresh intent. The new approach utilized messages in television commercials, online ads, the company's website, and through social media. The idea was to suggest Post-it notes could be so much more. The campaign emphasized "customization," or the tendency exhibited by younger consumers to want personalized messages from mass media and individualized uses for goods.

With the theme "Go ahead" driving the campaign, customers were encouraged to find new ways to use this longstanding product. Soon "Post-it" wars emerged between local offices, as employees used Post-its to create images and other designs on external windows. Further, the product's flexibility led Singh to know that "They're using it to communicate, using it to collaborate, using it to organize themselves." In a somewhat surprising turn of events, 3-M's research revealed that many customers felt a strong emotional connection to Post-its.

Post-it hosts an "Idea Headquarters" website that helps people find unique uses for the tool, including becoming more productive and reducing the tendency to procrastinate. Social media posts seek out additional methods for taking advantage of the item's distinctive characteristics.

Television commercials supported all other efforts, with messages targeting moms to show different ways they use Post-its to organize their days; millennials to be creative in posting the notes to remind themselves about events and to communicate with others (sort of a paper "tweet," according to one observer) as well as to help them remain optimistic; and to a married man who uses a Post-it note to remind himself to "keep the honeymoon going."

Post-it's marketing team faces two trends as the future unfolds. The first involves making the product itself more appealing and amenable to these novel applications. One response has been to increase the number of colors beyond the traditional yellow and more common colors. The second may become a more daunting issue over time. The "generic" problem

▲ Post-it notes have been in the market for over 30 years.

occurs when a brand becomes so well-accepted that the brand name is used to describe the item, no matter which company sells it. Examples include Band-aids, Xerox copies, and Scotch tape. Don't be surprised if you hear the product more regularly referred to as "Post-it brand" in advertisements for the product in the future. Doing so has been the most common response to the generic problem.

In the meantime, the 2013 campaign was "the first time we're including all these forms of (media) creativity under one banner," said Jeff Odiorne, executive creative director at Grey New York advertising agency. He continued, "Consumers have taken it upon themselves to figure out how to use the brand in unconventional ways. It's a brand that consumers love so much, they've made it what it is today," he adds. "The real things that real people do or have done, we want to put those on stage."[44]

34. Which social media sites are best suited to this type of promotional campaign? Why?

35. How could consumers, fans, and the company take advantage of new video-posting technologies to promote the Post-it brand?

36. What were the marketing objectives of the "Go ahead" campaign?

37. Would social listening be of value to Post-it's marketing team? If so, how? If not, why not?

38. Which social media marketing strategies should Post-it's team use? Provide justification for your response.

CASE 2 VIVE HOY

The market for carbonated soft drinks represents one of the largest and most lucrative targets in the United States and around the world. Coca-Cola and Pepsi have dominated the industry for many years. As the competition continues to evolve, each seeks out groups to attract and retain. Recently, PepsiCo reinvigorated its own efforts to capture the Hispanic share in the United States.

Advertising Age reported that in 2004 PepsiCo ranked number 6 on the magazine's list of the Top 50 Advertisers in Hispanic Media, spending $68.5 million. Then, the company had dropped to number 27, spending $41 million in 2007. The next year, the company dropped off the list and remained in that position for four years. At the same time, Coca-Cola dropped its spending dramatically to the same group, although the organization still spent $29.8 million in 2011, with a ranking of number 48 on the Top 50 list.

Javier Farfan, senior director for cultural branding at PepsiCo, noted that, "One of the key reasons I came here is to figure out how to dive deeper into the Hispanic space." Suggesting that the company had somewhat "lost its way," Farfan said, "In the carbonated category, exponentially, growth is going to come from Latinos. There's the population growth, but we're also more prone to drink soda. So it became really important and strategic for Pepsi to get into that space."

One of the outcomes was the "Vive Hoy" or "Live for Now" campaign and tagline associated with a new wave of television commercials. Farfan noted, "There's a new mainstream evolving. It's a different state of mind. Latinos don't want to be separate; they want to be included." "We want to nod and wink to them in places where they actually engage with media. Latinos watch MTV as much as Univision."[45]

To more fully attract Hispanic patrons, Pepsi launched two new products, Paradise Mango and Cherry Vanilla. Both were designed to attract Hispanic customers.

In addition to mainstream advertising and new products, *Marketing Daily* notes another fertile ground. Hispanic consumers are "Social Media Catalysts," according to the magazine. A recent study conducted for Unilever revealed that Hispanic consumers are "twice as likely to either share content or click on shared content than Americans in general." The report's data indicates that, "Hispanic consumers are also more influential on social media: content they share garners more "click-backs" (the act of clicking shared links to view the shared content) than content shared by non-Hispanic consumers."

Although Hispanic consumers read more on mobile devices than other groups, they are less inclined to share from those devices. At the same time, the youngest Hispanic consumers do not have reservations about sharing from mobile devices, which indicates the potential to reach them in ways that would lead to a larger community of advocates for Pepsi.[46]

▲ Pepsi launched the "Vive Hoy" campaign to attract Hispanic consumers.

JB325/Fotolia

The next generation of marketing efforts will likely integrate messages for Hispanic and non-Hispanic consumers as society becomes more blended. The net result will likely be an expanding marketplace for companies that are able to attract individual groups while at the same time reaching the mainstream audience.

39. The *Marketing Daily* article noted that Hispanics, "are less likely to use Pinterest or Twitter and twice as likely to use email and nearly 50 perccent more likely to use blogging channels such as Tumblr and Blogger." How should PepsiCo's marketing team respond to these statistics?

40. What social media marketing goals should PepsiCo seek to achieve with Hispanics? Why?

41. Which social media marketing tactics do you believe will be most effective for PepsiCo when seeking to reach the Hispanic audience? Which would be least likely to succeed? Defend your responses.

42. How might social listening be of value to PepsiCo with regard to the Hispanic market? Justify your answer.

43. What metrics would you use to measure the success of a social media marketing campaign directed to Hispanics? Justify your answer.

MyMarketingLab

Go to **mymktlab.com** for Auto-graded writing questions as well as the following Assisted-graded writing questions:

44. Discuss the current trends of consumer video-sharing. Examine reasons brands have become involved in social media marketing. For each of the trends you identify, elaborate on ways brands can use social media marketing to reach video-sharing consumers. Be sure to justify your choices of social media marketing.

45. Brands are excited when something the company posts on the Internet goes viral and spreads like wildfire among consumers. What factors contribute to a brand's posting going viral? Discuss how the social media strategies of content seeding, real-time marketing, interactive blogs, and consumer-generated reviews lead to a successful viral marketing attempt or unsuccessful viral marketing.

Endnotes

1. http://eatwholly.com/our-story.html.

2. Christopher Heine, "Study: Women Love Social Media More Than Men," *Adweek*, www.adweek.com/news/technology/study-women-love-social-media-more-than-men, December 30, 2103.

3. Maeve Duggan and Joanna Brenner, "The Demographics of Social Media Users–2012," *Pew Research Center*, www.pewresearch.org, February 14, 2013.

4. Daniel Frankel, "Report: Facebook, Google Overtake Yahoo in Display Ad Market Share," *PaidContent.org*, February 22, 2012, http://cnt.to/pUc.

5. Brian Womack, "Facebook Boosts Targeting Options for Advertisers," *Bloomberg*, www.bloomberg.com/news/print/2-13-10-15/facebook-boosts-targeting-options-for-advertisers, October 15, 2013.

6. Reed Albergotti, "Few Facebook Users Share Daily, Survey Says," *Wall Street Journal*, http://online.wsj.com/news/articles/SB10001424052702304485110045, February 3, 2014; Scott Martin, "Facebook's Teens Plummet as Elders Surge," *USA Today*, www.usatoday.com/story/tech/2014/01/16/facebooks-teens-plummet-as-elders-surge, January 16, 2014.

7. John Koetsier, "Twitter and Social Commerce: Facebook Generates 10X Shares, 20X Traffic, 30X Customers," http://venturebeat.com/2013/10/25/twitter-facebook-and-social-commerce-facebook-generates-10x-shares-20x-traffic-30x-customers," October 25, 2013.

8. Brian Morrissey, "Brands Seek Fans on Facebook," *Adweek.com* (http://adweek.com/aw/content_display/news/digital/e3id3d058ba458918f0fc8ec45), October 12, 2009.

9. Mark Walsh, "Study: Social Media Pays," *Media Post News, Online Media Daily*, (**www.mediapost.com/publications/?fa=Articles_aid=110120**), July 20, 2009.

10. Yoree Koh, "Twitter Users' Diversity Becomes an Ad Selling Point," *Wall Street Journal*, http://online.wsj.com/news/articles/SB10001424052702304419104S, January 20, 2014.

11. Todd Wasserman, "Starbucks 'Tweet-a-Coffee' Campaign Prompted $180,000 in Purchases," http://mashable.com/2013/12/05/starbucks-tweet-a-coffee-180000, December 5, 2013.

12. Claire Cain Miller, "Marketing Small Businesses with Twitter," *The New York Times* (**www.nytimes.com/2009/07/23/business/smallbusiness/23twitter.html**), July 23, 2009.

13. Zach James, "Fans Crush Brands When It Comes to YouTube Branded Content Pales in Comparison to User-produced Fare," *Adweek*, www.adweek.com/videowatch/fans-crush-brands-when-it-comes-youtbue-150262, June 13, 2013.

14. Tim Nudd, "Meet Devin Graham, Advertising's Daredevil," *Adweek*, www.adweek.com/news/advertising-branding/meet-devin-graham" February 11, 2014.

15. Vindu Goel, "Is Instagram Another Path to Riches for Facebook?" http://bits.blogs.nytimes.com/2014/02/18/is-instagram-another-path-to-riches-for-facebook, February 18, 2014.

16. Joe McCarthy," Bloomingdale's Balances Selfies with Beauty Tips in Instagram," www.luxurydaily.com/bloomingdales-balances-selfies-with-beauty-tips-in-instagram, October 31, 2013; Steve Smith, "Lipton Rides Instagram's Positive Mood," www.mediapost.com/publications/article/192807, February 6, 2013.

17. Christina Binley, "More Brands Want You to Model Their Clothes," *The Wall Street Journal*, http://online.wsj.com/article/SB100014241278873242160045784830, May 15, 2013.

18. Chris Heine, "Amazon is Among Pinterest's Best Retailers for the Holidays," *Adweek*, www.adweek.com/news/technology/amazon-is-among-pinterests-best-retailers-for-the-holidays, December 12, 2103; Karlene Lukovitz, "Land 'O Lakes Pinterest Promo Helps Fight Hunger," *Marketing Daily*, www.mediapost.com/publications/article/195218, March 7, 2013.

19. "Social Strategies for 2014," *Wildfire by Google Whitepaper, Ad Age Content Strategy Studio*, October 2013; Michael A. Stelzner, "2013 Social Media Marketing Industry Report," *Social Media Examiner*, www.socialmediaexaminer.com, 2013.

20. Karlene Lukovitz, "Hooters Dives into Social Media," *Marketing Daily*, www.mediapost.com/publications/article/206785/hooters-dives-into-social-media, August 14, 2013.

21. Galen Callen, *Wholly Guacamole & Disney Report*, October 2011.

22. Aaron Baar, "Social Interactions Affect Brand Perceptions," *Marketing Daily*, www.mediapost.com/publications/article/193609, February 19, 2013.

23. Bruce Horovitz, "Hate Talk Won't Derail Mixed-Race Cheerios Ad," *USA Today*, www.usatoday.com/story/money/business/2013/06/02/cheerios-general-mills-commerical-mixed-race-ad/2384587, June 3, 2013.

24. "How Social Data Influenced Hyatt to Pull Part of Campaign Days Before Launch," *Advertising Age*, http://adage.com/print/243539, August 8, 2013.

25. Doug Pruden and Terry Vavra, "How to Find and Activate Your Best Potential Advocates," http://smartblogs.com/social-media/2014/01/27//how-to-fin-and-activate-your-best-potential-advocaates, January 27, 2014.

26. Jack Neff, "Buzzkill: Coca-Cola Finds No Sales Lift from Online Chatter," *Advertising Age*, www.adage.com/article/cmo-strategy/240409, March 18, 2013.

27. "McKinsey Finds Social Buzz Can Affect Sales–Negatively Anyway," *Advertising Age*, http//adage.com/print/242039, June 11, 2013.

28. Lara Vogel, "L'Oreal on Social Media: 3 Ideas Worth Stealing." *Hoosh Meaningful Numbers*, September 3, 2013, http://blog.hoosh.com/loreal-on-social-media-3-ideas-worth-stealing/, retrieved March 10, 2014.

29. Amit Bapna and Ravi Balakrishnan, "Brand Using Social Media to Learn About Consumer Preferences, *The Economic Times*, December 4, 2013, http://articles.economictimes.indiatimes.com/2013-12-04/news/44757376_1_facebook-app-facebook-india-social-media, retrieved March 10, 2014.

30. *Wholly Biggest Loser Final Report*, June 2011.

31. "5 Ways to Encourage Customers to Share Your Content," *Marketo White Paper*, www.marketo.com, 2013.

32. "Esurance Hands Out That $1.5 Million, Releases Mind-Boggling Stats," *Adweek*, www.adweek.com/adfreak/esurance-hands-out-that-15-million," accessed February 10, 2104.

33. Adam McKibbin, "These Brands Scored Big on Sunday Without Expensive TV Spots," *Adweek*, www.adweek.com/brandshare/these-brands-scored-big-on-sunday-without-expensive-tv-spots-155290, February 3, 2014.

34. "5 Ways to Encourage Customers to Share Your Content," *Marketo White Paper*, www.marketo.com, 2013.

35. Paul Farhi, "Oreo's Tweeted Ad Was Super Bowl Blackout's Big Winner," *Style*, http://articles.washingtonpost.com/2013/-02-4/lifestyles/36741262, February 4, 2013.

36. "Adobe Readies Its Super Bowl Real-Time War Room," *Advertising Age*, http://adage.com/print/291400, January 30, 2014.

37. Christopher Heine, "Starbucks Pushes Snow Day on Facebook, Twitter," *Adweek*, www.adweek.com/news/technology/starbucks-pushes-snow-day-on-facebook-twitter," February 8, 2013.

38. Rick Wion, "McDonald's Finds Quick Social Response Requires Nimble Planning," *eMarketer*, www.emarketer.com/articles/print/1009716, March 8, 2013.

39. David Ensing, "Consumers Take Online Reviews with a Grain of Salt," www.quirks.com/articles/2013/20131026, October 2013.

40. Andrew Adam Newman, "A Campaign for Clothes by a Guy Not Wearing Any," *The New York Times* (**www.nytimes.com/2009/10/29/business/media/29zappos.html**), October 29, 2009.

41. Todd Wasserman, "So Your Ad Went Viral–Big Deal," http://mashable.com/2013/12/12/so-your-ad-went-viral-big-deal, December 12, 2013.

42. Lenna Garibian, "Digital Influence: Blogs Beat Social Networks for Driving Purchases," *MarketingProfs*, www.marketingprofs.com/charts/print/2013/10336, March 18, 2013.

43. Stuart Elliot, "3-M says, 'Go Ahead, Make Something of It," The New York Times, January 28, 2013, http://www.nytimes.com/2013/01/28/business/mutfund/3m-says-go-ahead-make-something-of-it.html?pagewanted=all&_r=1&, retrieved March 5, 2014.

44. Ibid.

45. Natalie Zmuda, "Pepsi Refocuses on Hispanics," *Advertising Age,* July 24, 2013, http://adage.com/article/hispanic-marketing/pepsi-refocuses-hispanics-flavors-tagline/236269/, retrieved March 6, 2014.

46. Karl Greenberg, "Hispanic Consumers Are Social Media Catalysts," *Marketing Daily,* February 20, 2014, http://www.mediapost.com/publications/article/219954/hispanic-consumers-are-social-media-catalysts.html, retrieved March 6, 2014.

Alternative
Marketing

From Chapter 10 of *Integrated Advertising, Promotion, and Marketing Communications,* Seventh Edition. Kenneth E. Clow, Donald Baack.

Alternative Marketing

Chapter Objectives

After reading this chapter, you should be able to answer the following questions:

1. How can buzz marketing, guerrilla marketing, lifestyle marketing, and experiential marketing enhance a marketing communications program?

2. What methods can be used to effectively employ product placements and branded entertainment?

3. Why has the use of alternative media venues, especially video game advertising, grown in marketing communications programs?

4. How have in-store marketing and point-of-purchase displays evolved into effective communication and sales tools?

5. How can brand communities enhance brand loyalty and devotion?

6. What methods are used to adapt alternative marketing programs to international marketing efforts?

Overview

Traditional mass media advertising faces many challenges. Although advertisers are not ready to abandon radio, television, magazines, newspapers, and out-of-home programs, they know that many new and valuable media outlets have emerged. As a result, alternative marketing programs and alternative media are on the rise. Marketers spend increasing numbers of dollars finding ways to reach potential customers in new and innovative formats. Successful advertising and promotional programs often take advantage of these new alternative approaches, including those targeted to individual segments domestically and consumers in other countries for international firms.

Gourmet Hot Dogs

Hebrew National makes gourmet Kosher hot dogs. Kosher literally means "fit to eat." According to the company's website, "For more than 100 years, Hebrew National® has followed strict dietary law, using only specific cuts of beef that meet the highest standards for quality, cleanliness, and safety—so artificial flavors, colors, fillers, and by-products simply don't make the cut." The company began as a mom-and-pop operation located on the Lower East Side of New York City that has grown into the largest, most recognized Kosher brand in America.[1]

The Bratskeir Company, a full-service advertising and marketing communications agency, described the problem faced by Hebrew National this way: the brand's "higher price was a barrier to trial and purchase of its better-tasting, higher-quality franks." The insight drawn by the company was, "Moms who try Hebrew National hot dogs love the taste and quality and understand why they cost more. They are influenced by, and readily influence, other moms. They like to do good for others as do well for their families."[2]

The company's agency searched 12 cities for 250 PTA presidents, Hispanic community leaders, and Jewish mothers to serve on "mom squads." The moms' sport-utility vehicles were emblazoned with the Hebrew National logo. The "mom squads"

Tyler Olson/Fotolia

▲ "Mom squads" were recruited to host backyard hot-dog barbecues and pass out coupons for Hebrew National Kosher hot dogs.

hosted backyard hot dog barbecues and distributed discount coupons at community events. Bratskeir noted that, "They took their show on the road, holding sampling events at Little League games, soccer tournaments, and other neighborhood events, all summer long" and "Moms distributed coupons everywhere they went. For every coupon redeemed, we donated a package of hot dogs to ConAgra's Kid's Cafés, which feeds thousands of children from poor families."

Mark Kleinman, vice president of sales and marketing, used to think only outrageous products were worthy of alternative marketing strategies. He stated, "But even a loved American food like the hot dog can generate a lot of discussion." The net result was an impressive growth in sales and visibility for this company and its products.[3]

This chapter presents four topics. First, it identifies major alternative marketing programs: buzz marketing, guerrilla marketing, product placements and branded entertainment, and lifestyle marketing. Next, it describes a series of marketing tactics associated with alternative media. Third, in-store marketing will be examined. Finally, brand communities are discussed. The international implications of these new forms of alternative media are also presented.

Alternative Marketing Programs

Developing alternative marketing programs requires creativity and imagination. Marketers identify new places where a consumer's path intersects with a brand's presence or creates a new intersection point. They then prepare attention-getting marketing messages for those points of contact, which provides the opportunity to supplement or replace mass media advertising with more targeted methods.

In essence, the goal remains the same as for traditional media. Marketing professionals continue to look for innovative ways to reach a target audience. Alternative marketing programs and alternative media venues provide widely accepted options.

objective 1

How can buzz marketing, guerrilla marketing, lifestyle marketing, and experiential marketing enhance a marketing communications program?

Shown: Flying Flames LED candle chandelier.

BRASS FLICKERING FLAME
CHANDELIERS
BELONG TO THOSE
WHO LOVE THEM.

Dallas 1617 Hi Line Dr. Ste. 100 214.748.9838 Austin 512.480.0436 Visit scottcooner.com

Scott Cooner, Inc

▲ Traditional media advertising is an important component of any alternative marketing program.

Figure 1 lists common alternative marketing choices. These programs seldom operate independently. A guerrilla marketing campaign might also include buzz and lifestyle marketing components. The same campaign may contain digital components and traditional media.

Alternative marketing relies on buzz, word-of-mouth, and lifestyle messages at times when consumers are relaxing and enjoying hobbies and events. Integrating these venues into a coherent integrated marketing program that speaks with a clear voice and message should be the goal.

Buzz Marketing

Buzz marketing has become one of the fastest-growing areas in alternative marketing. Estimated expenditures for these programs total more than $1 billion annually. **Buzz marketing**, or *word-of-mouth marketing*, emphasizes consumers passing along information about a product. A recommendation by a friend, family member, or acquaintance carries higher levels of credibility than an advertisement. Buzz can be more powerful than the words of a paid spokesperson or endorser. As shown in Figure 2, word-of-mouth endorsements can be supplied by consumers who like a brand and tell others, consumers who like a brand and are sponsored by a company to speak to others, or by company or agency employees who talk about the brand.

Consumers Who Like a Brand

A consumer who truly likes a brand and tells others about it creates the ideal marketing situation. Enthusiasts deliver these messages in person or via the internet in various ways. Many musical groups have achieved fame through this type of word-of-mouth support by those who have seen the bands in bars or as part of a small concert or tour. The ad for Five Star Fitness Center on the next page features Rheagan, who is passionate about exercise and a fan of Five Star Fitness. She shares this enthusiasm with anyone who will listen.

Sponsored Consumers

Many companies sponsor individuals as agents or advocates to introduce new products. It works best when these individuals, or ambassadors, also like the brand. A program can involve individuals talking one-on-one to others, or they can host house or block parties to present the product to a group of friends and family.

- Buzz marketing
- Guerrilla marketing
- Lifestyle marketing

- Experiential marketing
- Product placement and branded entertainment

- Individuals who truly like a brand
- Individuals who are sponsored by a brand
- Company or agency employees

▲ **FIGURE 1**

Forms of Alternative Marketing

▲ **FIGURE 2**

Types of Buzz Marketing Approaches

Brand Ambassadors Customer evangelists, or brand ambassadors, are typically individuals who already like the brand that they sponsor. The company offers incentives and rewards in exchange for advocacy. Marketers select an ambassador based on his devotion to the brand and the size of his social circle. Once recruited, an ambassador delivers messages to her family, friends, reference groups, and work associates. Some are asked to develop grassroots, no- or low-cost marketing events and to promote the brand on the internet through blogs or on social networks such as Facebook. Brand advocates are advised to be upfront and honest about their connections with the brand.

On move-in day at the University of North Carolina, students wearing American Eagle Outfitter shirts volunteered to help new students move into their dorms. They cheerfully unloaded cars and lugged belongings to dorm rooms. They passed out American Eagle coupons, water canisters, and Eagle pens as they helped the students. The helpers were student brand ambassadors. An estimated 10,000 college students work as ambassadors for a variety of companies, including American Eagle, Red Bull, NASCAR, Microsoft, and Hewlett-Packard. In exchange for promoting a particular brand, they receive discounts and/or merchandise.[4]

Procter & Gamble took advantage of a similar approach for a series of products through the efforts of Justin Breton, a student at Boston University. He spent about 15 hours per week talking about PUR, a water filtration system from Procter & Gamble. Justin was one of 100 college ambassadors hired by P&G to pitch items ranging from PUR to Herbal Essences hair products. The students prepared their own marketing plans and earned up to $2,500 per semester. They were required to submit regular reports and were monitored by P&G and RepNation.[5] The approach helped Procter & Gamble place products in the hands of consumers and provided students with opportunities to create unique marketing ideas.

House or Block Parties Many brand ambassadors host house or block parties. Nestlé Purina spent $50,000 on 1,000 house parties to market a new line of dog food, Chef Michael's Canine Creations. Purina identified childless individuals with household incomes greater than $60,000 who love to pamper their pets. House Party, a firm that matches brands with party hosts, located the homes for Purina. Dianna Burroughs hosted a party in her Manhattan West Village condo. Fourteen guests and their dogs arrived to sample the filet-mignon-and-potato-flavored kibbles from Chef Michael's Canine Creations. House Party's other clients include Avon, Procter & Gamble, Kraft, Mattel, Hershey's, and Ford.[6]

▲ Rheagan generates buzz for Five Star Fitness Center because she is passionate about exercise and the facility.

▼ Many companies employ college students to pitch products ranging from air filtration systems to cell phones to computer software.

Vgstudio/Fotolia

▲ BzzAgent recruits individuals who are influencers among their friends and associates to serve as brand ambassadors.

BzzAgent offers parties and the ambassador approach for its clients. Suzanne Ermel, a 30-year-old unemployed lawyer, serves as a BzzAgent ambassador for a boxed wine, Black Box. At the grocery store, when she sees a shopper put a box of wine in her shopping cart, Suzanne stops the shopper, declaring "Don't do it! This [Black Box wine] is just a couple of dollars more and you're going to like it a lot more." She adds, "I've pointed Black Box out to random people shopping for wine." She invites friends to her house for a blind tasting party and serves Black Box wine without mentioning the brand name. She then solicits comments from her guests and reveals the name of the wine. The Black Box buzz marketing campaign sought to "increase trial, advocacy, and impact sales."[7] The key to these events was that the host was an influencer among his or her friends and associates.

Company Employees

A final group of advocates includes company or agency employees. The company or agency decides whether they should pose as customers or identify themselves as being affiliated with the company. The Word of Mouth Marketing Association (WOMMA) argues that individuals should be upfront and clearly identify themselves as being with the company.

A few years ago, Wal-Mart featured a blog about two ordinary people, Laura and Jim, trekking across the Unites States in an RV and staying in Wal-Mart parking lots. The blog appeared to be written by a couple who were avid customers of Wal-Mart. The blog received considerable attention after *BusinessWeek* exposed Jim as a professional photojournalist employed by Edelman, Wal-Mart's public relations firm. Both Wal-Mart and Edelman received considerable criticism regarding the program because of the lack of transparency.[8]

The Word of Mouth Marketing Association provides guidelines for companies seeking to generate word-of-mouth communications through employees, agency employees, or even sponsors or agents. It encourages:

- Honesty of relationship—be honest about the relationship between consumers, advocates, and marketers.
- Honesty of opinion—be honest in presenting opinions about the brand, both good and bad.
- Honesty of identity—identify honestly who you are.[9]

Buzz Marketing Stages

As shown in Figure 3, some compare buzz marketing to how a virus replicates. The process consists of three stages: inoculation, incubation, and infection.[10] The inoculation stage corresponds to the product being introduced. During incubation, a few innovators or trendsetters try the product. In the infection stage, widespread use of the product occurs.

- Inoculation—the product is introduced
- Incubation—the product is used by a few innovators or trendsetters
- Infection—widespread use of the product occurs

▶ **FIGURE 3**
The Stages of Buzz Marketing

▲ Wholly Guacamole's marketers used social media to create buzz about its alliance with the TV show *The Biggest Loser*.

Only a few companies have been successful deploying buzz marketing during the inoculation stage, or product introduction. In most cases, buzz marketing does not work well at this stage unless the company employs brand agents or brand ambassadors. Otherwise, generating word-of-mouth communication can be virtually impossible. Previous research suggests that true customer-generated buzz occurs only after awareness of the product has emerged. That awareness typically requires advertising through traditional channels.[11] Now, however, social media can provide an alternative method for developing awareness of a new product or brand. Through blogs and social networking, brand managers can generate awareness and buzz, especially if they can locate some early adopters who are passionate about the brand and are willing to share that enthusiasm within their spheres of influence.

Buzz Marketing Preconditions

Advertising and buzz communication programs from actual customers typically cannot create a successful buzz by themselves unless the preconditions listed in Figure 4 are met. The brand must be unique, new, or perform better than current brands. It should stand out and have distinct advantages over competitors. Although not essential, memorable advertising helps to produce buzz. Intriguing, different, and unique advertising captures attention and can inspire talk among people. Getting consumers involved can enhance word-of-mouth communications.

Stride Sugarless Gum developed a website to complement the company's traditional advertising. The campaign featured the tagline, "Stride gum lasts a ridiculously long time." The company invited consumers to share what they would like to do for a ridiculously long time and post photographs of these activities on the Stride microsite developed for Sugarless Gum.[12]

Buzz marketing works for two primary reasons. First, as noted, people trust someone else's opinion more than paid advertising. Second, consumers like to render their opinions and share their thoughts. Many exhibit an innate desire for social interaction and are concerned about the welfare of others. Sharing an opinion can build a person's ego and sense of self-worth, especially when the opinion leads to happiness or satisfaction with a particular product.

Stealth Marketing

A special form of buzz marketing, **stealth marketing**, applies surreptitious practices to introduce a product to individuals while not disclosing or revealing the presenter's true relationship with the brand. Someone posing as a tourist might ask people to take a photo with a new camera and then talk to them about the camera. An attractive model ordering a beer or soft drink can tell everyone about how great it tastes. In both instances, the company pays someone to extol the product's benefits.

One stealth marketing ploy that received national attention was a 6-minute video entitled "Bride Has Massive Hair Wig Out" featuring a young bride-to-be who was unhappy with her haircut. In the video, she starts hacking off her hair just prior to the wedding ceremony. Her friends try in vain to stop her. It turns out she was acting. It was a cleverly produced video ad for Unilever's Sunsilk Haircare brand produced

- Product must be unique, new, or superior
- Brand must stand out
- Advertising should be
  - Memorable
  - Intriguing
  - Different
  - Unique
- Consumer involvement with the brand

▲ **FIGURE 4**

Preconditions of Buzz Marketing

203

▲ After asking someone to take her picture, this individual can then talk about the camera.

by its advertising agency. Thinking it was a real bride and real situation, the "Wig Out" video attracted millions of online viewers, was tweeted to thousands, appeared on blogs, received a feature story on CNN, and became the subject of talk shows before Unilever revealed the truth about the stealth marketing campaign.[13]

Stealth marketing thrives in the online world, most notably on social media, due to the ease of creating videos and offering brand endorsements. Most people are not likely to pass along traditional advertisements and clips. The result has been a rise in stealth approaches as an alternative.

Some argue that stealth marketing represents a shrewd way to reach consumers and generate buzz. At the same time, the Word of Mouth Marketing Association emphasizes the importance of honesty of relationship and honesty of identity. The Federal Trade Commission (FTC) has issued an opinion letter supporting the Word of Mouth Marketing Association regarding the full disclosure of any paid individuals in ads. The enticement to create stealth marketing campaigns that generate buzz remains, and the debate over its ethical implications will likely continue.

Guerrilla Marketing

Guerrilla marketing programs obtain instant results using limited resources. The concept was developed by Jay Conrad Levinson. Historically, guerrilla marketing offers one of the most successful alternative media marketing programs. Its tactics rely on creativity, quality relationships, and the willingness to try unusual approaches. These programs were originally aimed at small businesses; however, now a wide array of firms takes advantage of guerrilla marketing tactics. Guerrilla marketing emphasizes a combination of media, advertising, public relations, and surprises to reach consumers.

Guerrilla marketing utilizes alternative tactics and venues to focus on finding unique ways of doing things. To be successful, the marketing department must change its thinking process in the marketing department. Discovering "touchpoints" with customers constitutes the first step. Touchpoints include the places where the customers eat, drink, shop, hang out, and sleep. Next, the marketing team identifies unique and memorable ways to reach consumers at one or more of those touchpoints. To do so requires imagination and unorthodox thinking.

Social media and guerrilla marketing tactics were part of the re-launch of Twinkies after Hostess went bankrupt and the brand disappeared from store shelves. Brand loyalists passed along the tagline "sweetest comeback in the history of ever" throughout social media. Guerrilla teams, Twinkie the Kid mascot, and food trucks were sent to major markets. The campaign cost $3 million and generated so much demand that the company could barely keep up. Customers purchased 85 million Twinkie cupcakes, with another 100 million ordered by retailers.[14]

Figure 5 compares guerrilla marketing to traditional marketing. Guerrilla marketing tends to focus on specific regions or areas. Rather than a national or international campaign, the approach concentrates on personal communication. The objective should be to create excitement that spreads to others by word-of-mouth. Guerrilla marketing involves interacting with consumers, not just sending out a message. Building relationships with customers should be the outcome. By enticing individuals to react or to do something, the program enhances the chance that a message will hit home. Advertisements reach consumers where they live, play, and work in ways that are noticed. The eventual

AntonioDiaz/Fotolia

◀ **FIGURE 5**

Traditional vs. Guerrilla Marketing

Traditional Marketing

- Requires money
- Geared to large businesses with big budgets
- Results measured by sales
- Based on experience and guesswork
- Increases production and diversity
- Grows by adding customers
- Obliterates the competition
- Aims messages at large groups
- Uses marketing to generate sales
- "Me Marketing" that looks at "My" company

Guerrilla Marketing

- Requires energy and imagination
- Geared to small businesses and big dreams
- Results measured by profits
- Based on psychology and human behavior
- Grows through existing customers and referrals
- Cooperates with other businesses
- Aims messages at individuals and small groups
- Uses marketing to gain customer consent
- "You Marketing" that looks at how can we help "You"

relationships that evolve help create brand loyalty and positive recommendations to other consumers. Consequently, guerrilla marketing requires an aggressive, grassroots approach to marketing. It should produce buzz. When carried out properly, guerrilla marketing becomes a powerful marketing weapon. Figure 6 identifies six reasons why companies should use guerrilla marketing tactics.

Pink Jacket Creative generated buzz about Engobi, a caffeine-enhanced snack chip, during the inoculation stage of the buzz process, which can be extremely difficult. As shown in the photo in this section, "Engobi Girls" were employed to distribute free samples of the chips and to generate interest in prospective customers as part of an ingenious guerrilla marketing campaign.

◀ **FIGURE 6**

Reasons for Using Guerrilla Marketing

- To find a new way to communicate with consumers
- To interact with consumers
- To make advertising accessible to consumers
- To impact a spot market
- To create buzz
- To build relationships with consumers

Pink Jacket Creative

◀ "Engobi Girls" were a central component of the guerrilla marketing campaign created by Pink Jacket Creative for a new type of snack chips.

Karns foods

▲ Karns Foods can use lifestyle marketing to acquaint consumers with its quality meat department.

Lifestyle Marketing

Another program that assists companies making contacts with consumers in more offbeat and relaxed settings, **lifestyle marketing**, involves identifying marketing methods associated with the hobbies and entertainment venues of the target audience. Lifestyle marketing includes contacting consumers at places such as farmer's markets, bluegrass festivals, citywide garage sales, flea markets, craft shows, stock car races, and other places where large concentrations of potential customers convene. A local grocer such as Karns Foods can use these types of venues to acquaint consumers with its quality meat department.

A wide range of consumer lifestyles creates potential target groups, from relatively standard habits to more edgy and extreme behaviors. The energy drink Red Bull and the producers of the energy snack PowerBar gave free samples to people attending sports events, including football and baseball games. The concept was that people who watch sports would be more inclined to try the product. Covergirl offered cosmetics to women attending a fashion show with the idea that females in attendance would be more concerned about personal appearance. Finding a venue where consumers go for relaxation, excitement, socialization, or enjoyment and then matching it with the brand's target market constitutes the key to lifestyle marketing.

Experiential Marketing

Another alternative marketing form, **experiential marketing**, combines direct marketing, personal selling, and sales promotions into a single consumer experience. It typically involves direct marketing through interactive means such as special events and free samples. Experiential marketing seeks to engage consumers with the brand, rather than merely providing free samples. Bruce Burnett, chief executive of i2i Marketing suggests that experiential marketing, "gives consumers the opportunity to question as well as gain hands-on experience with a brand, allowing them to be more intimate with it, leading to a higher conversion rate."[15]

▼ Tracy is passing out samples of a new drink as part of an experiential marketing program.

Cadillac developed a three-part experiential program aimed toward current and perspective buyers. All three events were by invitation only. The first element featured a series of 14 golf clinics that paired golf instruction by the David Leadbetter Gold Academy with test drives of the Cadillac. The second element included a culinary tour in 13 different markets paired with the Cadillac SRX model. The third element, a five-track based event, displayed a souped-up V-Series Cadillac sedan in a half-day of high-performance driving and education session led by the Skip Barber Racing School. Invitees participated in three modules: slalom breaking, lane change, and lap driving. GM's head of North American marketing Chris Perry stated that the experiential programs fit the Cadillac brand well because "the Cadillac customer is one who is more entrepreneurial spirited, perhaps more interested in the latest technology, always looking for the new ideas and thinking, more outer directed."[16]

Jack Morton Worldwide created an experiential marketing campaign for Cotton, Inc. aimed at 18- to 34-year-old women. The traveling mall exhibit presented the songs "The Fabric of Our Lives" and "Dixie" sung by contemporary artists Zooey Deschanel (indie rock), Miranda Lambert (country), and Jazmine Sullivan (R&B). Mall shoppers were able to look into the singers' closets, which were filled with cotton clothes. Shoppers could also record a personal version of "The Fabric of Our Lives." The campaign's budget was $500,000 to $1 million. The exhibit provided mall shoppers with hands-on contact with cotton fabrics.[17]

To increase the probability that a positive experience will occur from an experiential marketing event, companies should follow these steps:

Step 1   Choose a clear, concise market segment to target.
Step 2   Identify the right time and place to involve consumers with the brand. Choose opportunities that fit with consumers' lives and when they can engage with the brand emotionally and logically.
Step 3   Make sure the experience reveals clearly the brand's promise and represents the brand well to consumers.

Allowing consumers to enjoy the benefit of a good or service before actually making a purchase gives the program the greatest chance for success.[18]

Product Placements and Branded Entertainment

Most marketers believe getting a product noticed has become increasingly difficult. In response, many firms increased product placement and branded entertainment expenditures. Each couples the popularity of an entertainment venue with a product or company.

Product Placements

The planned insertion of a brand or product into a movie, television show, or program, a **product placement** serves the purpose of influencing viewers. Product placements have been a part of motion pictures since the beginning of the industry in the 1890s. Lever Brothers placed the company's soap brand in some of the early films. In the 1930s, Buick created a ten picture deal with Warner Brothers for placements. Several tobacco companies paid actors to endorse and use the brands. Early television programs, such as the *Colgate Comedy Hour*, were sponsored by brands.

The biggest surge in product placement occurred in 1982 after Reese's Pieces were used to lure E.T. out of hiding as part of the plot of the movie. The placement of the Reese's Pieces spurred a 65 percent increase in sales following the movie's release.[19] With that surge, product placements continued to grow for both brands and TV shows. During a recent month, *American Idol* led all television shows with 208 paid product placements. The top brand in terms of product placement was Coca-Cola.[20] Figure 7 displays the top six brands and top six television shows for product placements.

objective 2

What methods can be used to effectively employ product placements and branded entertainment?

Top Brands (Total occurrences/month)		Top Shows (Total occurrences/month)	
Coca-Cola	99	American Idol	208
AT&T	76	Celebrity Apprentice	127
Chevrolet	45	America's Next Top Model	88
Ford	39	Biggest Loser	88
Apple	32	Amazing Race	69
Everlast	32	Shedding the Wedding	40
Nike	32	Dancing with the Stars	38

◀ **FIGURE 7**
Top Television Production Placements

Advertisers believe product placements lead to increased awareness and more positive attitudes toward the brand. In a few isolated cases, sales of a brand have increased. In most instances, however, no immediate impact on sales occurs. Research by Nielsen reveals the following about product placements:

- Brands placed within "emotionally engaging" television programs were recognized by 43 percent more viewers.
- Brand recognition increased 29 percent for brands placed in highly enjoyed programs.
- Positive brand feelings increased by 85 percent for brands placed in popular programs.[21]

Brand placement presents the advantage of a low cost per viewer, especially for movies. After a movie has finished at the cinema, it will usually be converted to a DVD format for movie rentals. From there, the movie may be adapted for television viewing on syndicated outlets or one of the premium movie channels. It might also be made available on TV through video-on-demand. This expands a movie's reach beyond the cinema screen to other venues where it may be seen multiple times by individuals.

Harley-Davidson hired Davie Brown Entertainment to locate appropriate product placement opportunities in movies, television, music, and video games. For the first time in Harley-Davidson's history, the company relied on product placements as its core marketing strategy. According to Dino Bernacchi, director of advertising and promotions for Harley-Davidson, "We want to use [product placement] to socialize Harley-Davidson motorcycling.... Entertainment can sensationalize the excitement and thrill of riding to the point of moving people to check it out." Only three percent of American consumers own a motorcycle, but another 15 to 20 million have the desire to buy one. Harley-Davidson's marketing team believed strategic product placements would encourage those on the edge to go ahead and make purchases.[22]

▲ Harley Davidson emphasized product placement in television shows, movies, music, and video games in a recent marketing campaign.

M.Camerin/Fotolia

Recently, MillerCoors signed an exclusive product placement deal with Turner Broadcasting. Only MillerCoors products would be shown on TNT- and TBS-created shows. Product placement included cans of beer, barware, taphandlers, and trucks. While MillerCoors did not have control of the scripts for the various television shows, the brewery's marketing team provided input on each of its brands and how they could be used. For instance, Blue Moon appeals to women and was therefore featured in *Rizzoli & Isles*. Miller Lite was featured in *Dallas* because the city of Dallas contains a large group of Miller Lite customers.[23]

Branded Entertainment

The integration of entertainment and advertising by embedding brands into the storyline of a movie, television show, or other entertainment medium is **branded entertainment**.[24] In an episode of the CTV drama, *The Eleventh Hour*, for example, Nicorette was integrated into a story about a character trying to quit smoking. The movie *Up in the Air* starring George Clooney prominently displayed American Airlines and Hilton Hotels. The movie's plot involves Clooney's character logging ten million miles on American so he can have his name emblazoned on the plane and ride along with American Airlines' chief pilot. Actual American Airlines planes were used in the film. Many of the hotel scenes were filmed at

Hilton locations. Integrating the brands into the story made them much more noticeable to the viewing audience.[25]

The use of branded entertainment has increased with the rise of reality television shows that simulate "real-world" situations. The success of branded entertainment in reality shows has led to its use in scripted television shows. Branded entertainment may also be found in novels, plays, songs, and movies.

Achieving Success

Figure 8 identifies the major factors that influence the success of brand placements and branded entertainment. The specific medium or media involved has an impact on effectiveness. Placement clutter has caused some television programs to lose clout. For instance, 4,349 product placements were used during Fox's *American Idol* show from January to May in one season.[26] Only the prominent brands were noticeable, such as the red plastic cups of Coca-Cola in front of the judges. Most were lost in the mass of brands appearing on the show.

Product placements and branded entertainment work because no "call to action" appears. Instead, increasing brand awareness and generating positive feelings toward the brand are the goals. When a consumer's favorite actor enjoys a particular brand or her favorite show contains a particular brand, it becomes more likely that the individual will transfer those positive feelings to the brand. People between the ages of 15 and 34 are more likely to notice brands placed in a movie or show. Also, individuals in North America and the Asia-Pacific area are more receptive than viewers in Europe. When a consumer sees a brand placement of a product that he has purchased, it may reinforce the idea that a wise decision was made, further validating the original purchase decision.[27]

Company Tactics   The manner in which marketers place the brand into a movie or show will be important. Brand insertions work best when they seem logical. In other words, the most effective placements are those woven into the program in ways that appear to be natural parts of the story. Brands shown in the background that seem to be artificially inserted will be less effective.

For some companies, product placements in movies deliver the advantage of bypassing legislation and guidance intended to control advertising to children and young adults. A study of the top 25 box office movies revealed that 32 percent were rated for viewing by adolescents and contained prominent brand placements for tobacco products. If these companies would have tried to advertise directly to teens, they would have encountered numerous regulations and possibly severe penalties.[28]

Budgets for product placements and branded entertainment have been increasing for several reasons. First, a brand's appeal may be stronger when it appears in a non-advertising context. Second, the perception of what others think of a brand is important to consumers. For many, it can be more important than how the consumer views the brand. Seeing the brand used in a television show, a movie, or a book makes the brand appear to be acceptable and even desirable. Third, seeing others use the brand provides reassurance for individuals who have already purchased the item.

Fourth, for individuals who place little value in brand names and branded products, having a brand placed in a program provides evidence of the brand's advantages. The evidence may be strong enough for them to consider purchasing the item. In these cases, the brand does not have to directly persuade the consumer of its merits. It does so through the acceptance and use of the product by the actor or the story in the program.

The Media's Perspective   For moviemakers and television producers, money represents the primary motivation behind product placements and branded entertainment. In the past, brand mentions were incidental or used by movie producers to create realism in a film. They now generate additional income. Martha Stewart charges $10,000 for a 30-second placement on her

- Media
- Supporting promotional activities
- Consumer attitudes toward placements
- Placement characteristics
- Regulations

▲ **FIGURE 8**
Key Factors Influencing the Effectiveness of Product Placement and Branded Entertainment

▼ Seeing brands used in television shows and movies can make the brand look more acceptable and desirable.

show. For a one-time mention in the show with a product close-up, the price goes up to $100,000. For a 2-minute branded entertainment segment with two or three talking points, the price rises to more than $250,000.[29]

In summary, brand placements present an excellent method to increase share of mind and build brand awareness. Although some believe that certain programs have become saturated with product placements, they continue to be utilized. If clutter becomes too severe, usage will likely decline, but only if the impact on consumer responses and attitudes also declines.

Alternative Media Venues

objective 3

Why has the use of alternative media venues, especially video game advertising, grown in marketing communications programs?

In upper New York, before crossing one of the five bridges operated by the New York State Bridge Authority, a driver must pay a toll or present an EZ-pass. Advertisements now appear on the mechanical arms that come down at the toll booth for a popular tourist attraction called Headless Horseman Hayrides and Haunted Houses. Owner Nancy Jubie reported, "This is so in-your-face advertising, we couldn't pass it up." The cost to put the name of her business on a toll booth arm for 3 months was $18,000.[30] Many companies look for unusual and unlikely places to attract attention. Figure 9 identifies some of the alternative forms of media.

Video Game Advertising

Product placements in video games have become common. Products can be part of a stand-alone game purchased at a retail store and played on the computer, or they can be placed in an internet video game. In-game brand placement enjoys all of the advantages of brand placements and branded entertainment. Video game advertising reaches young people who have become more difficult to contact through traditional media. In addition, it has the added feature of interactivity. Advertisers spend approximately $7 billion per year on in-game advertising because it presents an attractive market for the following reasons:

- 75 percent of all U.S. internet users spend at least one hour a month playing online games.
- 27 percent average 30 hours a month playing games.
- The primary game-playing market segment is 16- to 34-year-old males.
- The fastest-growing video game market segment is females.[31]

Video game advertising takes several forms (see Figure 10). The original and most widespread form of video game advertising involves locating a brand placement in the game. It can take the form of a billboard in a racing game, a Coke vending machine, or a McDonald's restaurant that is permanently integrated into the game. With the cost of producing a game now in the $20 to $30 million range and $1 to $5 million more to launch a game, game producers welcome product placement advertising as a source of revenue.

The number of game-related websites has exploded in recent years. Rather than placing ads in the game itself, advertisers place ads on these gaming sites. Although the exact number of gaming websites has not been identified, estimates suggest that more than 6,000 exist. Some receive as many as seven million visits per year.[32]

Numerous companies offer video games to be played on branded websites. These branded video games are called **advergames**. Axe, Maxwell House, Holiday Inn, Arby's, Baskin-Robbins, and Suave are companies offering advergames. Instead of creating a special microsite for these games, the advergames are usually placed on free gaming portals such as Kewlbox (www.kewlbox.com). Ninety percent of the games on the site are advergames and are offered for free. They are played 500,000 to 700,000 times per day.[33] Blockdot.com research indicates that consumers have

- Video games
- Cinema
- Subways
- Street and mall kiosks
- Stairs
- Escalators
- Parking lots
- Airlines
- Shopping bags
- Clothes

▲ **FIGURE 9**

Examples of Alternative Media

- In-game advertisements
- Rotating in-game advertising
- Interactive ads
- Game-related Websites
- Advergames
- Sponsored downloads
- Mobile game apps

▲ **FIGURE 10**

Video Game Advertising

positive feelings about brands that sponsor advergames. More specifically, 83 percent of consumers think positively about companies that underwrite advergames, and 70 percent are more likely to buy products from companies that sponsor the games.[34]

In addition to game-related websites, advertisers are attracted to the social gaming market. According to Nielsen, gaming has passed email as the second most popular online activity just behind social networking. Of the 800 million individuals on Facebook, 53 percent have played games on the site, and 20 percent play them regularly.[35]

Another popular new approach involves mobile gaming that drives traffic into retail outlets. Buffalo Wild Wings, for instance, features a fantasy football game app that requires consumers to play it in the store to be eligible for prizes. Cosi, a newly established sandwich restaurant, requires gamers to visit a store to determine if they are winners. In both instances, the mobile game apps drive customer traffic to retail outlets where they are more likely to purchase food items.[36]

Benefits IGA Worldwide research revealed that the majority of gamers hold positive attitudes about seeing ads in video games, if the ads are well done and fit the scene. The study noted that 82 percent of gamers find the games to be just as enjoyable when ads were present. A 44 percent increase in recall of brands resulted from ads presented in games when compared to awareness prior to exposure in the video game. Positive brand attribute associations also increased.[37]

Online video games present advertisers with the luxury of generating quality web metrics. Advertisers can track the length of ad exposure in an online game. In most cases, the marketers are able to tie in demographic information to find out who views the in-game ad, how long they play, and how often. These metrics then make it possible to target ads specifically to the consumer, demographic group, location profile, or type of player.[38]

New Video Game Technology Product placements within a game face the disadvantage of soon becoming static. Consequently, the player no longer notices it. To combat this problem, Massive, a new media company, has pioneered a technology that rotates or changes ads in online video games in real time. Advertisers insert new ads and products into the online game each time the person plays it. By changing the ads, the marketing team delivers time-sensitive promotions, and the advertising remains current. Massive can make the advertisement interactive, allowing the player to click on it for additional information. Additional technology can measure how much of a billboard or product placement a player sees during the game depending on their in-game actions. Technology can then fine tune the player's surroundings so that the missed ad will reappear later in the game.[39]

Females and Video Games In the past, most marketers believed that mostly teens and young adult males enjoyed video games. Today, IDC Research estimates that females constitute 40 percent of all gamers. One recent estimate suggests that more than 130 million females play video games.

The introduction of new games, such as *Littlest Pet Shop* and *Charm Girls* for girls plus *Your Shape, Just Dance, Wii Fit Plus*, and *Sports Active* for women, has built demand. Ubisoft's *Imagine* video game series, which sold 14 million copies in 3 years, features games

▲ The primary game-playing market segment is 16- to 34-year-old males.

▼ Approximately 40% of gamers are now female, many starting to play games at a young age.

AlexandreNunes/Fotolia

Eleonore H/Fotolia

▲ More women are needed to design and produce games for the female market.

in which girls can play the role of a ballerina or explore female-dominated professions. WomenGamers.com connects with women who enjoy video games. The site offers reviews of games and posts various types of commentary articles.

Many believe more can be done to entice women into the market. Courtney Simmons, public relations director for Sony Online Entertainment (SOE), recently spoke to an invitation-only crowd at the Game Developers Conference in San Francisco. Simmons enjoys playing video games with her three children. She argues that women are being "gamed down to," because "there is a lack of understanding about how women play." Simmons wants "more women making games," she says, "making more games that women want to play."

EA conducted extensive market research about what female users want in a game. The company's marketing team discovered that girls like it better when the pets make eye contact with the player. Studies and sales data indicate that women are more likely to play handheld casual games, such as the Nintendo DS, along with more socially-oriented games.

From a marketing communications perspective, gaming offers considerable potential. As more females purchase gaming devices and play games tailored to them, sales will increase. Further, the ability to reach girls, young women, and mature women with products placed in the games or advertising messages embedded in them presents a potentially powerful new method to develop brand awareness and brand loyalty in an alternative medium.[40]

▼ A street kiosk advertisement for Unleashed Dog Parks created by the Pink Jacket Creative advertising agency.

Cinema Advertising

Prior to a movie showing, most theaters present advertisements during pre-feature programming. Some products may have direct relationships with the movie; others are totally unrelated. Although clutter exists in the sense that the commercials often run consecutively and will be mingled with new movie previews, they are delivered to what is essentially a "captive" audience waiting for the feature to start.

Cinema advertising rarely appears at the center of an integrated ad campaign, but that was the case with HP's launch of the Photosmart Premium printer with TouchSmart Web. According to Tariq Hassan, HP's vice president of marketing, "We had to create more awareness; we had to touch the consumer. The theater was a natural fit." The cinema campaign included a 30-second spot in the pre-feature programming at 17,300 theaters and 2,600 plasma screens in theater lobbies. It also executed an interactive "lobby domination" strategy in 15 theaters in New York, Chicago, San Francisco, San Diego, Miami, and Houston. Theater lobbies were turned into branded events with banners, signage, holographic 3-D kiosks, and large manned booths where the printer was demonstrated. The campaign delivered 50,000 product demonstrations averaging 6 minutes in length and a total of 700,000 lobby impressions.[41]

Other Alternative Media

A number of additional media alternatives are available. Ads now appear on subways and other public facilities as local and state governments struggle to balance budgets. Parking lots, stairs, and escalators all feature advertising displays. Airlines increase revenues by presenting advertisements on flight-ticket jackets and using in-plane signage. Shopping bags, clothes, and restaurant menus provide additional advertising venues.

Alternative media provided an important component of the advertising campaign for Unleashed Dog Parks created by the Pink Jacket

◀ A bus wrap advertisement for Unleashed Dog Parks created by the Pink Jacket Creative advertising agency.

Creative advertising agency. As shown in the two photos in this section, Pink Jacket added a street kiosk ad and a bus wrap ad to reinforce the billboards that were running. The objective was to reach people during routine moments in their daily lives.

The out-of-home component of a recent Kraft Lunchables with Fruit campaign was unique in its use of alternative venues. The company descended on the three largest U.S. markets—Chicago, New York, and Los Angeles—with news about fruit offered on numerous street corners. In partnership with Feeding America, interactive storefronts were developed. Consumers could engage with the storefront materials to contribute to Feeding America. In addition to the interactive storefronts, Lunchables took over bus shelters with dynamic lenticular printing, dominated billboards, sides of buildings, and Times Square.

A new innovative form of alternative media utilizes facial recognition technology. A digital display in a shopping mall with this technology can recognize a female in her 20s standing in front of it. Ads touting makeup, shoes, fashions, and ice cream then pop up. If a man in his 50s moves in front of the display, a different set of ads appears.

The popularity of using nontraditional formats to deliver advertising messages continues to increase. Each time an innovative marketing professional identifies a new venue, a segment of the advertising community jumps on board. These methods make it possible to send messages that either cut through or go around clutter to reach people in moments when they may be more receptive to an advertisement's content.

In-Store Marketing

Consumers make approximately 60 percent of all purchase decisions while in a retail store.[42] Except for point-of-purchase (POP) displays, many marketing departments do not pay much attention to in-store marketing. Funds devoted to it represent a small percentage of advertising and marketing budgets. This may mean that some companies are missing opportunities.

To understand the potential of in-store advertising, consider what affects consumers as they purchase clothing. In a survey of about 600 consumers, 52 percent said that in-store signage, displays, or point-of-purchase displays influenced their decisions, far outdistancing print advertising and word-of-mouth communications.[43] Figure 11 displays a complete list of these influences.

objective 4

How have in-store marketing and point-of-purchase displays evolved into effective communication and sales tools?

pressmaster/Fotolia

▶ **FIGURE 11**

Types of Advertising that Most Influenced Clothing Purchases

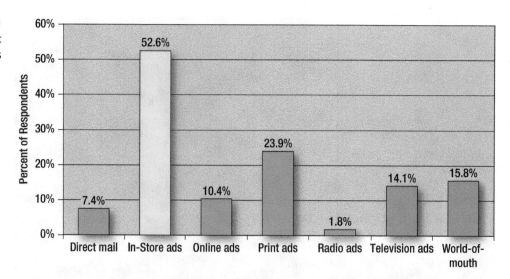

▲ Approximately 60 percent of all purchase decisions are made in the retail store.

In-Store Marketing Tactics

The in-store shopping experience has a major impact on purchase decisions. In a survey of shoppers, 69 percent called the in-store time the "make or break" experience. "Understanding high potential shopper strike zones has become increasingly critical, given the intensified battle for consumer loyalty and share of mind in-store," commented D'Anna Hawthorne, strategic director at Miller Zell, a retail consulting firm. Companies now try to engage consumers, not just merchandise items on a shelf. According to consumers, end-aisle displays and merchandise displays are the most engaging. Ceiling banners and overhead mobiles are the least engaging.[44]

The use of color, light, and sound has long been a part of in-store marketing. Retailers may also add *motion*. Placing and using video screens and television monitors to present messages represents the newest and most expensive in-store marketing tactic. Many static signs have been replaced with high-technology mediums. Also, shopping carts with static signs that are broken or unreadable are being replaced with video screens. Digital media within the store offers retailers the opportunity to customize messages to fit the store and the aisle where the display is located.[45]

Airplay America produces The Salon Channel, a retail television channel and digital signage network for beauty salons. Programming consists of human interest and lifestyle stories. Beauty shop patrons spend an average of 30 to 45 minutes per salon visit. The Salon Channel provides entertainment, including features about nationally recognized stylists and the latest hairstyles, along with advertisements for products and services, many of which are related to beauty and fashion.[46]

Wal-Mart follows the same path. In the past, Wal-Mart's ads appeared on all in-store televisions at the same time. With new technologies, the marketing department distributes ads geared to each department within a store and for specific aisles. Rather than hanging television monitors from the ceiling, flat-screen panel monitors are placed at eye level in the aisles, which leads to greater ad recall. Marketers placed digital monitors at end-caps and near other displays. These television monitors contain advertising pertinent to the end-cap or the merchandise being displayed. To fully appreciate the potential impact of this form of in-store advertising, consider each week 68 million viewers watch the combined national television newscasts on ABC, CBS, and NBC. The number of shoppers at Wal-Mart each week tops 127 million. The potential audience for a commercial on the

Wal-Mart television system will be nearly twice as large as an advertisement on the three national newscasts.[47] In addition, the Wal-Mart ad reaches consumers as they shop and while they consider purchasing options.

Social Media and In-Store Tactics

The rise of social media usage has led to attempts to use it to drive store traffic. Social media can be integrated with other in-store tactics. Marketers place QR codes on the product's package or label and on store shelves that offer instant coupons. Mobile coupons may be accessed via social media that can then be redeemed at the retail store.

Banana Republic recently offered a unique alliance with Match.com. The clothing store sponsored an in-store Valentine's Day meet-and-greet mixer in key markets of Chicago, San Francisco, Los Angeles, and New York. Individuals from Match.com met each other after hours at the selected store to become acquainted. Fashion and lifestyle blogger Joy D. Cho was enlisted to share her personal love story on her blog *Oh Joy*. Cho and her husband re-created their first date in a Banana Republic outlet. Photos of the date were posted on Facebook, Twitter, Instagram, and Pinterest. Individuals were also encouraged to share their favorite photos taken inside the store on social media for a chance to be included in the Valentine's Day album posted by Banana Republic on Facebook.[48]

Point-of-Purchase Marketing

Traditionally, one of the most important components of in-store marketing has been **point-of-purchase (POP) displays**, which include any form of special exhibit that advertises merchandise. Retailers locate point-of-purchase displays near cash registers, at the end of an aisle, in a store's entryway, or anywhere they might be noticed. Point-of-purchase advertising includes displays, signs, and devices used to identify, advertise, or merchandise an outlet, service, or product. POP displays can serve as an important aid to retail selling.

Point-of-purchase displays remain highly effective tools for increasing sales. Coca-Cola reports that only 50 percent of soft drink sales are made from the regular store shelf. The other 50 percent results from product displays in other parts of the store. American Express discovered that 30 percent of purchases charged on the American Express card came from impulse decisions by customers seeing the "American Express Cards Welcome" sign.

Research indicates that an average increase in sales of about nine percent occurs when one POP display is used. Only about half of POP displays actually impact sales; however, those that increase purchases do so by an average of nearly 20 percent. Consequently, point-of-purchase advertising remains attractive to manufacturers.[49]

Currently, manufacturers spend more than $17 billion each year on point-of-purchase advertising materials. Manufacturers place the greatest percentage of POP materials in

Boyer's

SHOP FAST
Park closer and get in the store faster!

Boyer's

SHOP FASTER
Get everything you want faster without traveling down long aisles

Boyer's LESS THAN 3 GUARANTEE
If there are more than 3 people in line we will open another register

Boyers Foods

▲ In-store signage at Boyer's offering a faster, better shopping experience.

▼ Point-of-Purchase displays are often located near cash registers to encourage impulse buys.

Tyler Olson/Fotolia

restaurants, food services, apparel stores, and footwear retailers. The fastest-growing categories include fresh, frozen, or refrigerated foods and professional services.[50]

Manufacturers view point-of-purchase displays as an attractive way to display a brand more prominently in front of customers. Many retailers hold a different perspective, believing that POP materials should either boost sales for the store or draw customers into the store. Retailers are not interested in the sales of one particular brand, but instead want to improve overall sales and store profits. Retailers prefer displays that educate consumers and provide information. As a result, retailers are more inclined to set up displays to match the retailer's marketing objectives.

Designing Effective Point-of-Purchase Displays

Effective POP displays clearly communicate the product's attributes. A quality display incorporates the price and other promotional information. It encourages the customer to stop and look, pick up the product, and examine it. A customer who stops to examine a product on display becomes more likely to buy the item.

A successful display makes a succinct offer that the customer immediately understands. In most cases, a display has a limited time to capture the customer's attention. If it fails, the customer simply moves on to other merchandise. Colors, designs, merchandise arrangements, and tie-ins with other marketing messages are critical elements of effective POP displays.

The best point-of-purchase displays are integrated with other marketing messages. Logos and message themes used in advertisements appear on the display. A study by the Saatchi & Saatchi advertising agency revealed that consumers make purchase decisions in just four seconds. On average, a consumer only looks at a display or signage for three to seven seconds.[51] Tying a POP display into current advertising and marketing messages increases the chances it will be noticed. Effective displays present any form of special sales promotion that a company offers. Customers quickly recognize tie-ins with current advertising and promotional themes as they view displays. Figure 12 lists some additional pointers for point-of-purchase advertising.

Measuring Point-of-Purchase Effectiveness

Manufacturers and retailers both seek to measure the effectiveness of POP displays. Linking the POP display into a point-of-sale (POS) cash register

◀ Using POP displays that are integrated with Kraft's advertisements for Kraft Parmesan Cheese increases the chances of being noticed by shoppers.

Kraft Foods, Inc.

▶ **FIGURE 12**
Effective Point-of-Purchase (POP) Displays

- Integrate the brand's image into the display.
- Integrate the display with current advertising and promotions.
- Make the display dramatic to get attention.
- Keep the color of the display down so the product and signage stand out.

- Make the display versatile so it can be easily adapted by retailers.
- Make the display reusable and easy to assemble.
- Make the display easy to stock.
- Customize the display to fit the retailer's store.

makes it easier to gather results. Items on the display are coded so that the POS system picks them up. Then, individual stores measure sales before and during a point-of-purchase display program by using cash register data. The data also helps the retailer's management team decide when it is time to withdraw or change a display as sales begin to decline. The technology enables retailers to identify the displays that generate the largest impact on sales. A retailer might deploy this method to test different types of POP displays in various stores. The most effective displays can then be expanded to a larger number of stores.

From the manufacturer's viewpoint, point-of-sale data helps to improve POP displays. The data may also be used to strengthen partnerships with retailers. These bonds help the manufacturer weather poor POP showings. Retailers are more willing to stay with a manufacturer that tries to develop displays that benefit both parties.

Brand Communities

The ultimate demonstration of brand loyalty and brand devotion takes the form of **brand communities**. In most cases, a symbolic meaning behind the brand links individuals to the brand community and other owners of the brand. Interactions between the customers and the product lead to a sense of identity and inclusion. A set of shared values and experiences that integrate with feelings about the brand becomes the result.

Brand communities do not form for every product or company. They cannot be created by the product itself; however, a marketing department can facilitate and enhance a community experience. A company with a strong brand community maintains a positive image, has a rich and long tradition, occupies a unique position in the marketplace, and enjoys a group of loyal, dedicated followers.[52] Figure 13 highlights some of the reasons that brand communities exist. Most brand communities require some type of face-to-face interactions, although the internet does provide a venue for members to contact each other and to blog about the product.

Jeep, Harley-Davidson, and Apple all enjoy loyal brand communities. In each case, the brand owners come from diverse populations. The highly successful Jeep Jamboree and Camp Jeep events give owners opportunities to share driving experiences, tell stories, and share ideas. Most of the interactions among customers occur during the company-sponsored barbecue. They also take place during roundtable discussions hosted by a Jeep engineer or other Jeep employee.

Many, if not most, of the attendees at a Camp Jeep event have no experience driving a Jeep off-road. Among those who have, some use a "tread lightly" ethos, whereas others have mud-covered vehicles from heavy off-road adventures. First-timers at the camp

objective 5

How can brand communities enhance brand loyalty and devotion?

- Affirmation of the buying decision
- Social identity and bonding
- Swap stories
- Swap advice and provide help to others
- Feedback and new ideas

▲ **FIGURE 13**

Reasons Brand Communities Form

◀ The popularity of the reality TV show *Duck Dynasty* has increased enthusiasm for the brand community around the Skyjacker brand.

Skyjaker Suspension

▶ **FIGURE 14**
Ways to Enhance Brand
Community Spirit

- Create member benefits to encourage new customers to join a group.
- Provide materials to the group that are not available anywhere else.
- Involve firm representatives in the groups.

- Sponsor special events and regular meetings.
- Promote communications among members of the group.
- Build a strong brand reputation.

are often timid and afraid they might not fit in, but soon find they do as repeaters fully welcome anyone and everyone to the Jeep community. The vehicle provides the common bond that brings individuals together, regardless of demographic and psychographic differences.

Harley-Davidson features a highly successful brand community program. Several years ago, the company's leadership team helped create a unique brand community spirit. An organization called HOG formed around the Harley brand. In return, Harley-Davidson offered benefits, such as information about community gatherings along with special marketing offers for accessories, to HOG members. The benefits are only available to the HOG group, which encourages new Harley-Davidson owners to join the HOG brand community.

Marketers seek to facilitate and enhance the community in which owners can interact. Figure 14 provides information on ways a marketing team can assist in creating a brand community.

Building a brand community begins with sponsoring events that bring product owners together. As noted, Jeep sponsors the jamborees and a camp. Harley-Davidson sponsors rides, rallies, and local events. These events help create a brand community spirit that leads to bonding between owners. Eventually, this produces a sense of social identity.

Company representatives should become involved in club events. Jeep engineers attend events and mingle with customers. They provide advice and encouragement to any new owner about to take his or her vehicle off-road for the first time. Harley managers, including the CEO, ride Harleys to rallies to talk with owners.

In addition to company-sponsored events, other venues for interaction can be encouraged. The internet offers another place for owners to talk. They can visit through blogs, chat rooms, or social network microsites. A company can become involved in these exchange venues. Employees should openly identify themselves. Brand communities enjoy company involvement and want an honest exchange of comments.

While providing venues and means for enhancing a brand community spirit, the company continues other advertising and marketing programs. Brand communities normally emerge for brands with strong images. Such images must be maintained. Marketers feature the pride of owning the brand in advertisements, making its uniqueness and position in the marketplace clear.

International Implications

objective 6

What methods are used to adapt alternative marketing programs to international marketing efforts?

Alternative marketing can be used to reach minority groups within the United States. An example of buzz marketing occurred when the Clamato company sought to increase brand awareness among U.S. Latinos. The firm gave 2,000 agents a 32-ounce bottle of Clamato and 10 coupons. The agents reached 34,000 potential customers, and positive opinions of the drink rose from 32 to 78 percent.[53]

Alternative marketing methods are also being tried in other countries. Starbucks and Pepsi combined efforts to produce a movie series called *A Sunny Day*. The film follows a girl from the Chinese countryside to the big city, where she discovers love, blogging, Starbucks, and Pepsi. The series was tailored for Shanghai's subway and the 2.2 million who ride it each day. The story was made into a soap opera-style script featuring short daily segments. A website featured story snippets each day for those who missed seeing it on the subway and wanted to know what happened. The Shanghai subway has a network of 4,000 flat-screen monitors that provide train information, clips of soccer highlights, entertainment news, and advertising. Marketers pay to run ads, just like they would on television. *A Sunny Day* was the system's first venture into a short miniseries, with episodes each day for 40 weeks.[54]

Brand communities have emerged in other countries. Jeep employed the brand community concept to build a brand presence in China. The first Jeep was introduced in China in 1983 by American Motors through a joint venture in Beijing; however, recent sales of Jeep have slowed. In response, the first three-day Camp Jeep in China was created. It attracted 700 Jeep owners and 3,000 participants. The event included off-road courses, bungee jumping, a hiking course, wall climbing, a soccer field, and an off-road ATV course. Musical entertainment and time slots for karaoke enthusiasts were provided.[55] The event's purpose was to renew Jeep's strong brand name and to create a strong sense of community among current Jeep owners in China. Through these individuals, Jeep's marketing team hoped to generate word-of-mouth, or buzz, for the Jeep brand, driving new customers to the Jeep brand.

The clutter problems that plague U.S. advertisers are present around the world. The tactics used to overcome it domestically may be adapted to international operations. Firms from other nations can adapt alternative media tactics. International conglomerates will likely respond with new and creative alternative marketing programs.

INTEGRATED campaigns in action

Interstate Batteries

Interstate Batteries employed its internal marketing department to launch a geo-targeted online media plan for all company battery centers located in cities throughout the United States. The objectives of the campaign were to:

- Increase awareness of all Interstate Battery Centers
- Drive traffic to all Interstate Battery Centers
- Create awareness of key brand messages

Interstate Batteries featured an online display advertising to create awareness and provide information about the location of its stores. The campaign was geo-targeted by each store's market ZIP codes. Consumers who clicked on the ads were taken to a geo-specific landing page that provided information about the closest All Battery Center. The campaign targeted the 25 to 54 age group with the selected ZIP codes surrounding each of the battery stores.

Online metrics to measure the success of the campaign were determined prior to the launch. Metrics included click-through rates, coupon redemptions, changes in sales, and the number of transactions at the retail stores. Additional online metrics included the number of individuals who enlarged the map, submitted information by email, and printed the coupon.

The Interstate Battery Center digital campaign is located at the Pearson Instructor's Resource Center (www.pearsonhighered.com). The campaign includes a PowerPoint presentation outlining the details of the campaigns and examples of the collaterals. Video by the Interstate Batteries marketing team explaining the campaign is available.

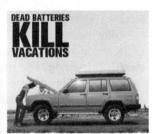

Interstate Batteries

Summary

Alternative media enjoys many success stories. Well-known brands, such as Ben & Jerry's and Starbucks, have emerged using very little traditional advertising. Each found new methods to establish a brand presence, including alternative media and alternative marketing methods. Starbucks built a community of coffee lovers through local involvement and word-of-mouth.

The four forms of alternative marketing programs are buzz marketing, stealth marketing, guerrilla marketing, and product placement. Buzz marketing, or word-of-mouth marketing, places the emphasis on consumers passing along information about a brand. The consumers can be those who like a brand, sponsored consumers, or company insiders. Some consider using company insiders to be unethical, which means care should be given before starting such programs.

Stealth marketing uses surreptitious practices to introduce a product to individuals or fails to disclose or reveal the true relationship with the brand. It has also drawn ethical criticism.

Guerrilla marketing programs are designed to obtain instant results with limited resources through creativity, high-quality relationships, and a willingness to try unusual approaches. Lifestyle marketing involves the use of marketing methods associated with the hobbies and entertainment venues of the target audience. Experiential marketing combines direct marketing, field marketing, and sales promotions into a single consumer experience.

Product placements are planned insertions of a brand or product into a movie, television program, or some other media program. Branded entertainment facilitates the integration of entertainment and advertising by embedding brands into the storyline of a movie, television show, or other entertainment medium.

Numerous alternative media venues exist. They include mobile phone advertising, video game advertising and advergames, cinema advertising, airline in-flight advertising, and others. Use of these media has been on the increase.

In-store marketing programs take two forms. New tactics include the use of high-tech video screens and television monitors in new and more visible places. This includes tailoring messages to individual parts of the store. Traditional point-of-purchase advertising continues to be widely utilized. Recently, POP advertising incorporated newer technologies to increase its effectiveness.

Brand communities evolve when consumers feel a great deal of brand loyalty and devotion. They form around events, programs, and exchanges of information. A company with a strong brand and a devoted marketing team can assist in the formation and continuance of brand communities.

Alternative media choices are utilized to reach minority groups in the United States in unique new ways. They are also expanding into international markets. As advertising clutter increases, the use of these media is likely to grow and will likely become cluttered as well.

Key Terms

alternative marketing The use of buzz, word-of-mouth, and lifestyle messages at times when consumers are relaxing and enjoying hobbies and events

buzz marketing An emphasis on consumers passing along information about a product to others; also known as *word-of-mouth marketing*

stealth marketing The use of surreptitious practices to introduce a product to individuals without disclosing or revealing the true relationship with the brand

guerrilla marketing Programs designed to obtain instant results through the use of limited resources by relying on creativity, high-quality relationships, and the willingness to try new approaches

lifestyle marketing Marketing methods associated with the hobbies and entertainment venues of the target audience

experiential marketing A program that combines direct marketing, field marketing, and sales promotions into a single consumer experience

product placement The planned insertion of a brand or product into a movie, television show, or some other media program

branded entertainment The integration of entertainment and advertising by embedding brands into the storyline of a movie, television show, or other entertainment medium

advergames Branded video games

point-of-purchase (POP) displays Any form of special display that advertises merchandise

brand communities A link that forms due to an association between the brand, a consumer, and others who own or purchase the brand

MyMarketingLab
Go to **mymktlab.com** to complete the problems marked with this icon

Review Questions

1. What are the main alternative media programs described in this chapter?

2. What is buzz marketing?

3. What three types of consumers can pass along buzz marketing messages?

4. Why is buzz marketing effective? What preconditions should be met to ensure its effectiveness?

5. What is stealth marketing?

6. What is guerrilla marketing? How does it differ from traditional marketing?

7. What is lifestyle marketing? What types of locations are suited to lifestyle marketing?

8. What is experiential marketing?

9. What are product placements and branded entertainment? What do they have in common?

10. Identify the alternative media venues described in this chapter.

11. Describe the forms of video game advertising, including advergames.

12. What is in-store marketing? Why is it important?

13. What new in-store marketing tactics are being utilized?

14. What is point-of-purchase advertising? Why is it important?

15. How have new technologies changed some forms of point-of-purchase advertising?

16. What is a brand community?

17. What should a company's marketing team do to assist in the development and growth of brand communities?

18. Is the use of alternative media growing or declining in international markets? Explain why.

Critical Thinking Exercises

DISCUSSION QUESTIONS

19. Think about a product category where you have a high knowledge of the various brands. Pick one of the major brands. Discuss the characteristics the brand would want for a brand advocate, ambassador, or evangelist. What type of offers would it take from the company to create a strong brand ambassador? Discuss each of the stages of buzz marketing as it relates to the brand you identified. Which stage is the brand in now? Justify your answer. Discuss each of the preconditions of buzz marketing as it relates to your chosen brand.

20. Consider a recent purchase you made at the recommendation of someone else. Why did you trust that person's recommendation? How important is a recommendation by someone else in your purchase decisions?

21. Can you think of a lifestyle marketing program or an experiential marketing campaign that you encountered? What was your reaction? Was the approach effective? Why or why not? What about with other consumers? If you have not experienced lifestyle or experiential marketing, think of a situation and brand where you think it would be effective. Explain why.

22. Imagine being approached by the owner of a small clothing boutique. She has heard about guerrilla marketing and wants to try it. Why should she use guerrilla marketing? What are the pros and cons? What guerrilla marketing techniques would you suggest?

23. Find a movie or television show that you have already watched and enjoyed. Watch it again, but this time, make a list of all of the product placements in the file. Identify if each was a prominent placement, if the actor used the brand, or if it was just in the background. When you finish, discuss the product placements that were the most effective and those that were the least effective. What made the placement effective? What made it ineffective?

24. Do you play video games? If so, approximately how many hours a month do you play games (including online games)? What advertising have you noticed in the games? How effective was the advertising?

25. Go to a nearby retail store. Examine the point-of-purchase displays in the store. Which ones were the most impressive? Why? Which ones did not succeed at getting your attention? Why not? Go back to the store a week later. How many of the displays have changed? What is your overall evaluation of the point-of-purchase displays used by the retailer?

26. Go to a nearby retail store and talk to the manager or one of the employees. Ask them about the store signage, including point-of-purchase displays. Ask the employee to discuss what signage is effective and why. As a customer, did you agree with the manager's or employee's viewpoint? Why or why not?

Integrated Learning Exercises

27. Access **http://women.igda.org**. What is your overall opinion of this website? How can it be beneficial to a marketing manager? How can it be beneficial to females who want to pursue video game design? Go to the parent website **www.igda.org**. What types of information are available at this site?

28. Access the Word of Mouth Marketing Association website at **www.womma.org**. What features did you find on the site? What resources are available? What benefits does the site provide to a business? Is there any value for a consumer?

29. Type "buzz marketing" into an online search engine. Find two advertising agencies or marketing agencies that offer buzz marketing expertise. What types of buzz marketing services does each provide? Which company do you think offers the best buzz marketing program? Why?

30. Type "guerrilla marketing" into an online search engine. Find two agencies that offer guerrilla marketing services. Describe what type of services each offers. Go to an article database and type in "guerrilla marketing." Find two articles about guerrilla marketing that interest you. Summarize the articles.

31. Soap is a digital creative agency that brings brands and consumers together through gaming. Access the agency's website at **www.soapcreative.com**. What information is available on the website? Who are some of the agency's clients? Describe some of the games created by Soap and why they have been successful.

32. Point-of-purchase displays should be an important component of a firm's IMC program. Research indicates that effective displays have a positive impact on sales. Access the following firms that produce point-of-purchase displays. Which firm's site is the most attractive? Which firm would be the best from the standpoint of developing displays for a manufacturer? Explain.

   a. Displays2Go (**http://www.displays2go.com**)
   b. Vulcan Industries (**www.vulcanind.com**)
   c. Display Design & Sales (**www.displays4pop.com**)

Blog Exercises

Access the authors' blog for this text at the URLs provided to complete these exercises. Answer the questions that are posed on the blog.

33. Coca-Cola: **http://blogclowbaack.net/2014/05/12/coca-cola-chapter-10/**

34. Harley Davidson: **http://blogclowbaack.net/2014/05/12/harley-davidson-chapter-10/**

35. Buzz marketing: **http://blogclowbaack.net/2014/05/12/buzz-marketing-chapter-10/**

Student Project

CREATIVE CORNER

Ugg is the brand name for an Australian company that sells big, bulky sheepskin boots. The company's marketing team wondered if it would be possible to get fashion-conscious consumers to even consider the boots. Instead of advertising to the fashion-conscious consumer, Ugg's marketing team targeted high-profile fashion influencers. They successfully contacted and convinced Kate Hudson and Sarah Jessica Parker to wear the items. Then Oprah Winfrey praised Uggs on one of her shows. At that point, the boots became fashionable, and retailers couldn't keep them in stock.[56]

Ugg became successful using unique alternative marketing methods. Access Ugg's website at **www.uggaustralia.com** to learn about the company's products and the company itself. Suppose Ugg wanted to initiate a buzz marketing campaign at your university and that the company leaders contacted you for marketing advice. First, they would like to recruit some brand ambassadors as advocates for their brand. Your first task, therefore, is to design a flyer to post around campus announcing that Ugg wants to hire brand ambassadors. Before you can design the flyer, you must decide on the relationship the ambassador will have with Ugg and the type of reward or payment she will receive. After you design the flyer, your second task is to design a buzz marketing program that you believe Ugg and the new brand ambassador should use on your campus.

CASE 1 — AFTER THE RUSH: WHAT'S NEXT FOR RED BULL?

In today's active world, people need help. At least, that would be the position presented by any of the companies that sell energy drinks. Red Bull and other products are designed to jolt a consumer into action.

Red Bull's ingredient list begins with taurine, which occurs naturally in the human body. Red Bull helps to replace the taurine lost during conditions of high stress or physical exertion, which, in turn, helps the person recover more quickly. The carbohydrate glucuronolactone, which also is found naturally in the human body, is added to help with the detoxification processes as well as support the body in eliminating waste substances. The amount of caffeine in a serving of Red Bull is nearly double the amount present in Mountain Dew, a product perceived by many as the highest-energy soft drink. Red Bull also contains acesulfame K, sucrose, glucose, B vitamins, and aspartame, which is well-known as the key ingredient in NutraSweet. The company's marketing materials emphasize that the formula took 3 years to develop. The 8.3-ounce can drink was first launched in Australia in 1984. Red Bull tastes sweet and lemony, and, as one fan put it, "like a melted lollypop." The price of a single can is typically higher than a 16-ounce bottle of soda.[57]

When Red Bull was introduced into the United States, the product clearly struck a chord in some markets. Those pulling all-nighters for school, work, or partying, as well as those engaged in extreme sports, quickly gravitated to Red Bull. By 2010, the drink continued to hold a 60 to 70 percent share of the U.S. market for similar drinks and annual sales.

Many marketers view Red Bull's entry into the United States as one of the first and classic uses of alternative and buzz marketing. Red Bull's brand management team began by identifying a target audience—those who would most likely want the buzz created by an energy drink. One key constituent group would be college-age consumers. Consequently, the company provided free samples of the drink to college and university students, who were encouraged to throw big parties where cases of Red Bull would be served.

Red Bull's marketing team created a group of "consumer educators" who traveled to various locations giving out free samples. The brand managers organized and sponsored extreme sporting events, such as skateboarding and cliff diving, for consumer educators to attend. The concept was that the participants and fans of these types of sports had buzz-seeking desires and an interest in products that were positioned as "sleek, sweet, and full-throttle."[58] From the parties and the extreme sports, word-of-mouth communications about the brand spread. The buzz-seeking target audience became Red Bull's first customer base.

The traditional soft-drink companies were slow to react. Eventually, Pepsi created a competing product called Adrenaline Rush; Coca-Cola entered the market with KMX; and Anheuser Busch developed 180, which is supposed to turn a person's energy level around by 180 degrees. Pepsi may be less

▲ Red Bull used alternative marketing to establish a presence in the United States.

Jeffrey Blackler/Alamy

concerned with Red Bull due to its ownership of Gatorade. Still, both Coke and Pepsi have concentrated efforts on garnering shelf space in convenience stores and superstores.

More recently, Red Bull's marketing efforts have been expanded to include traditional advertising. At the same time, endorsers tend to be edgier figures, such as famed kayaker Tao Berman, and the commercials themselves remain offbeat. Red Bull creator Dietrich Mateschitz summarized it best, "If we don't create a market, it doesn't exist." And $1.6 billion later, he clearly has a point.

Two challenges have begun to emerge. First, Red Bull has been banned in some countries, including France and Canada. Other nations have examined the product and express fears about its impact on health. The second is keeping Red Bull on the cutting edge. A series of new energy formulas are available, including the heavily advertised 5-Hour Energy drinks. Can Red Bull maintain its edgy marketing presence over a sustained period of time?

36. What alternative marketing methods does Red Bull use?

37. Visit Red Bull's website (**www.redbull.com**) and identify the alternative media venues used by Red Bull's marketing team.

38. What role should traditional media play in Red Bull's future, especially when compared to alternative media?

39. Are there ways to build brand communities around Red Bull? What role might Twitter, Digg, or Facebook play in supporting such communities?

40. Red Bull's marketing team believes that staying with alternative approaches best fits its image. As you think about all of the alternative marketing methods and alternative media, what suggestions would you make to Red Bull for the future? Describe a campaign for Red Bull using one or more alternative methods.

CASE 2 — TANNING AND VOLLEYBALL: REVITALIZING A LIFESTYLE

Jessica Jones faced a difficult challenge as she took control of the Sun Products, Inc., account. As a relatively new account executive, Jessica knew it was important to establish measurable results when conducting various marketing communication campaigns. Sun Products sells items oriented toward beach-related activities, the most successful of which is the company's line of sunscreen products.

The tanning industry faces a unique set of challenges as a new generation of consumers emerges. First, consumers are now more aware of the dangerous long-term effects of tanning than ever before. These include more wrinkles and vastly increased chances of developing skin cancer in later life. In Australia, where the ozone layer is the most depleted, exposure to the sun is even more hazardous. More important, however, is a potential shift in cultural values regarding appearance.

As the new millennium commences, a certain set of consumers might believe that tanning equals "foolishness"—or at least that a suntan is not as "sexy" as it had been for many years. Beach bums and bunnies continue to run counter to this trend. The question remains, however, whether being bronze is a good idea.

Suntan lotion companies can counter these problems by developing new products designed to screen out the sun rather than enhance the sun's tanning properties. Creams with higher SPF (sun protection factor) values generally sell at higher prices. Higher-quality sunscreens do not wash off in a pool or while swimming. Further, items containing herbal ingredients and new aromas are designed to entice new interest. Products with aloe vera and vitamin E may help reduce the pain of and heal sunburns more quickly. Products that "tan" without exposure to the sun are being developed for those who want the beach look without doing time in the sand.

At the same time, to promote more "traditional" products to college students on spring break and others who still enjoy a deep, dark tan requires careful promotion. Advertisements often stress the "fun" aspects of being outdoors.

Hawaiian Tropics, one of the chief competitors in the tanning industry, has taken a unique approach to the promotion of its products. The company holds an annual contest in which the Tropics team of beach girls is chosen to represent the firm. Contestants are female, beautiful, and have good tans. Those who win the contest tour the country promoting Hawaiian Tropics products and appear on television programs. At individual events held at beaches across the United States and in other locations, free samples of Hawaiian Tropics are given out, along with coupons and other purchase incentives. Giveaways of beach towels and other beach equipment are used to heighten interest in the product at various stores.

Beach Volleyball Magazine notes that it features not a sport, but a lifestyle. The activity has the benefit of being included as part of the Summer Olympics. Some women, such as Misty May-Treanor and Kerri Walsh-Jennings, have recognizable

Beach volleyball is a natural tie-in with sun tanning products.

Alvaro GermanVilelia/Fotolia

names on the national stage and enjoy immense popularity within the women's volleyball fan base. In addition, there are professional beach volleyball tournaments across the United States each year.

Promotion of women's beach volleyball tends to focus on tans, bikinis, and the sexy, athletic competitors. Many of the marketing materials available online, on posters, and in other places feature photos of beach volleyball players in skimpy swimsuits. Fans also tend to attend events wearing outfits designed to show off a fit body and a great tan.

Jessica suspects there is a natural tie-in available with beach volleyball, especially on the women's side. Instead of tanning for its own sake, getting a tan while doing something healthy seems like a great appeal. The primary issue is whether the appeal can move beyond volleyball fans to the larger public. The secret would be to find a theme for a tie-in that would appeal to a larger audience.

An entire range of promotional items can be utilized. Items include coupons, premiums and giveaways, contests, samples, bonus packs (with various ranges of SPF values in the same pack), and refunds for higher-priced lotions.

Jessica knows the key is to maintain a consistent message and theme for her company. It must stand out in the crowd of Coppertone, Bain de Soleil, and Hawaiian Tropics. She realizes that to succeed, she needs Sun Products' point-of-purchase displays placed prominently in as many places as possible, from drugstores to swimming specialty stores.

41. Is a buzz marketing program possible for Sun Products? Why or why not?

42. Design a complete lifestyle marketing program for Sun Products based on a tie-in with women's beach volleyball. Include both traditional and nontraditional advertising venues.

43. Name any opportunities you can identify for product placements or brand entertainment for Sun Products.

44. How could Sun Products use guerrilla marketing? Describe a possible guerrilla marketing campaign.

45. Is there a potential overlap between the brand community that loves beach volleyball and a brand community for Sun Products? Describe the ways that Sun Products' marketing department could build and enhance a connection between the two.

MyMarketingLab

Go to **mymktlab.com** for Auto-graded writing questions as well as the following Assisted-graded writing questions:

46. Think about a product category where you have a high knowledge of the various brands. Pick one of the major brands. Discuss the characteristics the brand would want for a brand advocate, ambassador, or evangelist. What type of offers would it take from the company to create a strong brand ambassador? Discuss each of the stages of buzz marketing as it relates to the brand you identified. Which stage is the brand in now? Justify your answer. Discuss each of the preconditions of buzz marketing as it relates to your chosen brand.

47. Access Ugg's website at **www.uggaustralia.com**. Evaluate the website in terms of its effectiveness, freshness, and the use of alternative marketing methods. What traditional marketing methods did you see? Do you think Ugg has effectively merged traditional and nontraditional advertising methods? Why or why not?

Endnotes

1. Hebrew National, http://www.hebrewnational.com/kosher-products, retrieved March 16, 2014.

2. Bratskeir Company, "Woman Bites Dog: Trumping Price with Taste, http://www.bratskeir.com/hebrewnatl.html, retrieved March 16, 2014.

3. Bloomberg Business Week Magazine, July 29,2001, "Buzz Marketing," http://www.businessweek.com/stories/2001-07-29/buzz-marketing, retrieved March 16, 2014.

4. Natasha Singer, "On Campus, It's One Big Commerical," *The New York Times*, September 11, 2011, www.nytimes.com/2001/09/11/business-at-colleges-the-marketers-are-everywhere.

5. Laurie Burkitt, "Procter & Gamble Taps Co-Eds to Sell Products," *Forbes.com* (**www.forbes.com/2009/09/09/procter-gamble-repnation-cmo-network-readyu_print.html**), September 9, 2009.

6. Laurie Burkitt, "Marketers Break Into Homes By Sponsoring Parties," *Forbes.com* (**www.forbes.com/2009/08/19/purina-house-party-cmo-network-houseparty_print.html**), August 19, 2009.

7. Andrew Adam Newman, "Putting Boxed Wine to the Taste Test," *The New York Times*, October 11, 2011, www.nytimes.com/2011/10/12/business/media-boxed-wine-firms-claim-theyll-pass-the-taste-test.

8. Angelo Fernando, "Transparency Under Attack," *Communication World* 24, no. 2 (March–April 2007), pp. 9–11.

9. Ibid.

10. Jim Matorin, "Infectious 'Buzz Marketing' Is a Smart Way to Build Customer Loyalty at Your Operation," *Nation's Restaurant News* 41, no. 18 (April 30, 2007), pp. 18–20.

11. Kate Niederhoffer, Rob Mooth, David Wiesenfeld, and Jonathon Gordon, "The Origin and Impact of CPG New-Product Buzz: Emerging Trends and Implications," *Journal of Advertising Research* 47, no. 4 (December 2007), pp. 420–26.

12. Ibid.

13. Chris Powell, "The Perils of Posing," *Profit* 26, no. 2 (May 2007), pp. 95–96.

14. T. L. Stanley, "Twinkies Relaunch as Dude Food," *Adweek*, www.adweek.com/news/advertsing-brand/hostess-twinkie-relaunch-brands-treat-dude-food-151734, August 7, 2013.

15. Becky Wilkerson, "Bringing Brands to Life," *Marketing* (**www.marketingmagzine.co.uk**), February 18, 2009, pp. 35–38.

16. "Karl Greenberg, "Cadillac in the Performance Swim Lane With V-Centric Events," *MediaPost News, Marketing Daily*, April 20, 2011, www.mediapost.com/publications/?fa=articles.printfriendly&art_aid=149076.

17. Stuart Elliott, "King Cotton Goes on Tour," *The New York Times* (**www.nytimes.com/2009/08/24/business/media/24adnewsletter1.html**), August 24, 2009.

18. Derek Drake, "Prove the Promise of Your Brand," *Adweek* 50, no. 35 (October 5, 2009), pp. S11–S12.

19. Simon Hudson and David Hudson, "Branded Entertainment: A New Advertising Technique or Product Placement in Disguise?" *Journal of Marketing Management* 22, no. 5/6 (July 2006), pp. 489–504.

20. "Product Placement Hits High Gear on American Idol, Broadcast's Top Series for Brand Mentions," *Advertising Age*, April 18, 2011, http://adage.com/pring/227041.

21. Linda Moss, "Nielsen: Product Placements Succeed in 'Emotionally Engaging' Shows," *Multichannel News* (**www.multichannel.com/index.asp**), December 10, 2007.

22. Stacy Straczynski, "Harley-Davidson Revs Product Placement," *Adweek* (**www.advweek.com/aw/content_display/news/agency/e3i84436228620cd549875945**), November 12, 2009.

23. "The Only Beer in TNT and TBS Shows Now Comes from MillerCoors," *Advertising Age*, http://adage.com/print/240451, March 20, 2013.

24. Simon Hudson and David Hudson, "Branded Entertainment: A New Advertising Technique or Product Placement in Disguise?" *Journal of Marketing Management* 22, no. 5/6 (July 2006), pp. 489–504.

25. Andrew Hampp, "How American Airlines Got a Free Ride in 'Up in the Air,'" *Advertising Age* (http://adage.com/print?article_id=141059), December 14, 2009.

26. Cecily Hall, "Subliminal Messages," *Women's Wear Daily* 195, no. 2 (January 3, 2008), p.12.

27. Marc Graser, "More Ads Set for Videogames," *Variety*, September 13, 2011, www.variety.com/article/VR1118042795; Simon Hudson and David Hudson, "Branded Entertainment: A New Advertising Technique or Product Placement in Disguise?" *Journal of Marketing Management* 22, no. 5/6 (July 2006), pp. 489–504.

28. Raj Persaud, "The Art of Product Placement," *Brand Strategy*, no. 216 (October 2007), pp. 30–31.

29. Burt Helm, "Marketing: Queen of the Product Pitch," *BusinessWeek* (April 30, 2007), pp. 40–41.

30. "Hey, Advertisers: New York Has a Bridge to Sell You," *Advertising Age*, October 26, 2011, http://adage.com/print/230643.

31. Jessica E. Lessin, "Expenses Mount for App Launches," *The Wall Street Journal*, http://online.wsj.com/article/SB10001424127887324345804578425, April 17,2013; Theresa Howard, "As More People Play, Advertisers Devise Game Plans," *USA Today* (July 11, 2006), p. Money, 3b.

32. Ibid.

33. Ibid.

34. Rita Chang, "Advergames: A Smart Move, If Done Well," *Advertising Age* (http://adage.com/print?article_id=131786), October 16, 2008.

35. Heather Chaplin, "Players Lend a Helping Hand or Thumb," *Adweek*, April 20, 2012, www.adweek.com/print/139461; "Brands Friending Social Gaming Amid New Web Craze," *The Wall Street Journal*, August 8, 2010, http://online.wsj.com/article/SB10001424052748704657504575411804125832426.html.

36. Rebecca Borison, "Fall Into Cosi Sweepstakes," www.mobilecommercedaily.com/cosi-drives-in-store-traff-with-game, accessed October 10, 2013.

37. Mike Shields, "IGA: Most Gamers Cool with In-Game Ads," *Mediaweek.com* (http://mediaweek.com/mw/content_display/news/digital-downloads/gaming/e3i8d91a7147083886bfb91a8ee5978c1a7), June 17, 2008.

38. Susan Catto, "Are You Game?" *Marketing Magazine* (November 26, 2007, Supplement), pp. 18–19.

39. Ibid.

40. WomenGamers.com (**www.womengamers.com/news/2010/03/11/breaking-down-female-demographic**), May 3, 2010; Yukari Iwatani Kane, "Videogame Firms Make a Play for Women," *The Wall Street Journal* (http://online.wsj.com/article/SB100014240527487048824045744463652777885432.html), October 13, 2009; CNN.com (www.cnn.com/2008/TECH/ptech/02/28/women.gamers/index.html), May 3, 2010.

41. Katy Bachman, "HP Employs Cinema Experience to Push Printer," *Mediaweek* (**www.mediaweek.com/mw/content_display/news/out-there/place-based/e3i4cb8ab6**), November 29, 2009.

42. Kenneth Hein, "Study: In-Store Marketing Beats Traditional Ads," *Sales & Marketing Management* 161, no. 6 (November 2009), p. 57.

43. Amy Johannes, "Snap Decisions," *Promo* 18, no. 11 (October 2005), p. 16.

44. Kenneth Hein, "Study: In-Store Marketing Beats Traditional Ads," *Sales & Marketing Management* 161, no. 6 (November 2009), p. 57.

45. Tim Dreyer, "In-Store Technology Trends," *Display & Design Ideas* 19, no. 9 (September 2007), p. 92.

46. Ibid.

47. Michael Bellas, "Shopper Marketing's Instant Impact," *Beverage World* 126, no. 11 (November 15, 2007), p. 18.

48. Sarah Mahoney, "Banana Republic, Match.com Spread V-Day Love," *Marketing Daily*, www.mediapost.com/publications/article/192845, February 6, 2013.

49. "POP Sharpness in Focus," *Brandweek* 44, no. 24 (June 6, 2003), pp. 31–36; David Tossman, "The Final Push—POP Boom," *New Zealand Marketing Magazine* 18, no. 8 (September 1999), pp. 45–51.

50. Betsy Spethmann, "Retail Details," *Promo SourceBook 2005* 17 (2005), pp. 27–28.

51. RoxAnna Sway, "Four Critical Seconds," *Display & Design Ideas* 17, no. 11 (November 2005), p. 3.

52. Catja Prykop and Mark Heitmann, "Designing Mobile Brand Communities: Concept and Empirical Illustration," *Journal of Organizational Computing & Electronic Commerce* 16, no. 3/4 (2006), pp. 301–23.

53. Sinclair Stewart, "More Marketers Using Word of Mouth to Whip Up Sales," *Seattle PI* **www.seattlepi.com/business/344656_wordofmouth24.html**, December 23, 2007.

54. James T. Areddy, "Starbucks, PepsiCo Bring 'Subopera' to Shanghai," *The Wall Street Journal Online* (http://online.wsj.com/public/article_print/SB119387410336878365.html), November 1, 2007, p. B1.

55. Thomas Clouse, "Camp Jeep Comes to China," *Automotive News* 82, no. 6281 (November 12, 2007), p. 48.

56. Jeff Weiss, "Building Brands Without Ads," *Marketing Magazine* 109, no. 32 (October 4–11, 2004), p. 22.

57. "Red Bull's Good Buzz," *Newsweek* (May 14, 2001), p. 83.

58. Jeff Weiss, "Building Brands Without Ads," *Marketing Magazine* 109, no. 32 (October 4–11, 2004), p. 22.

Database and
Direct Response
Marketing and
Personal Selling

From Chapter 11 of *Integrated Advertising, Promotion, and Marketing Communications,* Seventh Edition. Kenneth E. Clow, Donald Baack.

Database and Direct Response Marketing and Personal Selling

Chapter Objectives

After reading this chapter, you should be able to answer the following questions:

1. What role does database marketing, including the data warehouse, data coding and analysis, and data mining, play in creating and enhancing relationships with customers?

2. How can database-driven marketing communication programs help personalize interactions with customers?

3. How do database-driven marketing programs create sales and build bonds with customers?

4. When should direct response marketing programs be used to supplement other methods of delivering messages and products to consumers?

5. What are the tasks involved in developing successful personal selling programs for consumers and businesses?

6. How should database marketing and personal selling programs be adapted to international settings?

Overview

This chapter examines database programs, direct response marketing, and personal selling. Database marketing provides a new communication link with customers. This, in turn, helps to produce higher levels of customer acquisition, customer retention, and customer loyalty. Database marketing has become increasingly crucial. New technologies associated with the internet and computer software make it easier to build and develop strong database programs.

Successful businesses continually acquire new customers and work to retain them. Repeat customers purchase more frequently and spend more money. Maintaining repeat business is far less expensive than constantly replacing those who turn to other companies. Personal selling, such as that carried out by Paula Ramirez, plays a key role in many organizational marketing outcomes.

SELLING PHARMACEUTICALS

Paula Ramirez

Courtesy of Paula Ramirez

O f the many forms of selling that take place, one of the more complex tasks involves convincing physicians about the merits of new drugs. Doctors are extremely busy and do not have time to listen to a sales pitch or read lengthy articles or literature about drugs. For a salesperson to see a physician requires patience, because getting past secretaries, receptionists, and nurses (gatekeepers) can be challenging.

Paula Ramirez is a sales representative for Strativa Pharmaceuticals. She has been successful because she understands the classic steps of selling to business clients, whether she calls on a CEO of a large corporation or a physician at a local medical clinic. Her approach includes collecting information, making sales calls, leaving samples, developing relationships, closing, and following up.

When collecting information about physicians, Paula stated, "Right now we're using an online system that allows me to take the physician's name and upload his or her information from a database. Further details regarding the physician's practice then becomes available. I try to learn about the staff, including their names, like and dislikes of each person—as much information as I can." Paula maintains personal information about each employee, such as "Kids in Little League" or "from Wyoming" in the client's file in order to make a personal connection. She says, "The more I know about each individual, the easier it is to interact with them and develop a personal

relationship. I have found that friendship is an important key to personal selling."

Through her selling experience now and in the past with other companies, Paula has learned the importance of handling objections and closing sales. She recognizes that objections mean the person is interested. "Your task at that point is to answer the objection in terms of your product," she says. Once objections have been answered sufficiently, it is time to close, to ask for the sale. "You have to ask. You can't be afraid of a no answer because a "no" does not always mean "no," it means not right now. Don't give up. Go back, because there is another objection that you have not sufficiently answered."

The first part of this chapter examines database marketing, including data warehouses, data coding, and data mining as well as data-driven communications and marketing programs. Three data-driven marketing programs are permission marketing, frequency programs, and customer relationship management systems. Databases are used for direct response marketing techniques, including direct mail, email, television programs, telemarketing, and traditional and alternative media. Databases are a key component of personal selling. Finally, international differences in these programs are considered.

Database Marketing

Database marketing involves collecting and utilizing customer data for the purposes of enhancing interactions with customers and developing customer loyalty. Successful database marketing emphasizes identifying customers and building relationships with them.

objective 1

What role does database marketing, including the data warehouse, data coding and analysis, and data mining, play in creating and enhancing relationships with customers?

▶ **FIGURE 1**
Overview of Integrated
Marketing Communications

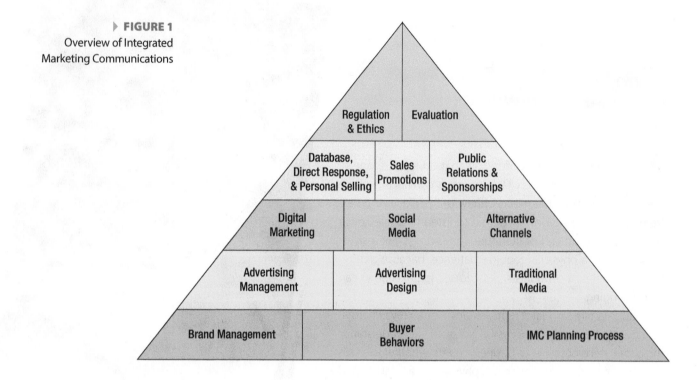

The primary focus of database marketing is customer retention and developing positive relationships.

This includes understanding the lifetime values of various customers and the development of customer retention efforts. Enhancing customer loyalty constitutes the primary benefit of database marketing. Although database marketing can be used for selling products, retention and relationships remain the primary focus.

A number of retail boutiques have captured the power of database marketing. When shoppers visit the store, the sales staff can access data regarding their preferences, sizes, previous purchases, and other information. Purchases are followed up with thank-you notes. Customers receive notices when new shipments of clothes arrive and are sent invitations to special events. Loyalty to these boutiques remains high. Some customers who have moved away return to buy merchandise. One vital ingredient stands out: Data are used to make customers feel special and develop relationships with them. Although selling occurred, it does not drive the database program. Figure 2 displays the tasks associated with database marketing. Of these, building the data warehouse and data coding are the two key activities described next.

- Building a data warehouse
- Database coding and analysis
- Data mining
- Data-driven marketing communications
- Data-driven marketing programs

▶ **FIGURE 2**
Tasks in Database Marketing

Building a Data Warehouse

Successful database marketing requires a quality **data warehouse**, which holds all customer data. The IT department and marketing team distinguish between an operational database and the marketing database when building a data warehouse. An *operational database* holds the individual's transactions with the firm and follows accounting principles. The marketing department manages the *marketing database*, which contains information about current customers, former customers, and prospects. Examples of data and analyses found in a standard marketing data warehouse include:

- Customer names and addresses
- Email addresses and digital records of visits to the company's website
- History of every purchase transaction
- History of customer interactions such as inquiries, complaints, and returns
- Results of any customer surveys
- Preferences and profiles supplied by the customer
- Marketing promotions and response history from marketing campaigns
- Appended demographic and psychographic data from sources such as Knowledge Base Marketing or Claritas
- Database coding such as lifetime value and customer segment clusters

Collecting customer names and addresses is the easiest part of developing the database. Gathering the other information that turns the data warehouse into a powerful marketing and communication tool can be more challenging.

The marketing team typically employs a system for updating addresses, because approximately 20 percent of Americans move each year. When individuals fill out a change of address form with the U.S. Postal Service, the information is sent to all of the service bureaus authorized to sell the information to businesses. A company that sends database names to one of these bureaus receives address updates for only a few cents per hit, or per individual that moves. Updating mailing addresses occurs at least once each year, depending on how often the company uses the database and the frequencies of contacts.

Email and Internet Data

Email addresses continue to be essential elements of a quality database. The internet and email provide cost-effective channels of communication to be used in building relationships with customers. Most database programs take advantage of digital tracking to register and store website visits and browsing patterns. This information allows for personalization of the firm's website for each customer. When someone logs on to the site, a greeting such as "Welcome back, Stacy," can appear on the screen. The tracking technology makes it possible for the system to recognize that Stacy, or at least someone using her computer, is accessing the website. If Stacy has purchased products or browsed the catalog, then the content of the pages can be tailored to contain the products she has an interest in buying.

Purchase and Communication Histories

Effective database programs maintain detailed customer purchase histories. The database records every interaction between the company and customer. When a customer sends an email to

▼ Contact information is an important component of building a data warehouse for a business-to-business company such as Scott Powerline & Utility Equipment.

Bobbie Williams/Scott Equipment

tech support, the information will be placed in the database. Any person who returns a product or calls customer service to complain has the information documented. Purchases and interaction histories determine future communications with customers and assist the marketing team in evaluating each customer's lifetime value and other customer value metrics.

Personal Preference Profiles

Purchase and visit histories do not provide complete information. Quality database marketing programs include profiles with specific information about each customer's personal preferences. These profiles and personal preference files may be constructed in various ways, including customer surveys and through information provided on an application for a loyalty card.

Every time the company initiates a contact with a customer, the information should be placed in the database, along with the customer's response. This information provides a rich history of what works and what does not. It further allows for customization of communication methods for each customer, which leads to the highest probability of success.

Customer Information Companies

Oftentimes, demographic and psychographical information are not available through internal company records. In these cases, the information can be obtained by working with a marketing research firm that specializes in collecting customer data. Knowledge Base Marketing, Donnelly, Dialog, and Claritas are four companies that market this type of information.

Data from website visits can be combined with offline information provided by firms such as Acxiom and Datran Media. Once merged, companies can store the information in cookies to allow for future customization and personalization of websites and communications with customers. For instance, based on income level and past purchasing habits, two women in adjoining offices can access the same cosmetics website; one might see a $300 bottle of Missoni perfume and the other might see the $25 house brand.[1]

▼ Geocoding allows a boutique, such as Chic Shaque, to target customers in specific geographic areas around its retail stores.

Geocoding

The process of adding geographic codes to each customer's record so that customer addresses can be plotted on a map, or **geocoding**, helps decision makers finalize placements of retail outlets and directs marketing materials to specific geographic areas. Geocoding combines demographic information with lifestyle data. This assists the marketing team in selecting the best media for advertisements.

One version of geocoding software, CACI Coder/Plus, identifies a cluster in which an address belongs. A group such as Enterprising Young Singles in the CACI system contains certain characteristics such as enjoying dining, spending money on DVDs and personal computers, and reading certain magazines. A retailer might then target this group with mailings and special offers.[2]

Database Coding and Analysis

Database coding and analysis provide information for the development of personalized communications. They assist in creating marketing promotional campaigns. Common forms of database coding include lifetime value analysis, customer clusters, and location-data tracking.

Joplin Globe

Lifetime Value Analysis

The **lifetime value** figure for a customer or market segment estimates the present value of future profits the individual or segment will generate over a lifetime relationship with a brand or firm.[3] Many marketing experts believe a market segment value provides more accurate information, because it sums costs across a market segment. Individual lifetime value calculations normally only contain costs for single customers.

The figures needed to calculate the lifetime value of a consumer or set of consumers are revenues, costs, and retention rates. Revenue and costs are normally easy to obtain, because many companies record these numbers for accounting purposes. Retention rates require an accurate marketing database system.

The cost of acquiring a new customer constitutes a key figure. It can be calculated by dividing the total marketing and advertising expenditures in dollars by the number of new customers obtained. As an example, when a company spends $200,000 dollars and acquires 1,000 new customers as a result, the acquisition cost becomes $200 per customer ($200,000 divided by 1,000).

The cost of maintaining the relationship represents another important amount. It measures all costs associated with marketing, communicating, and maintaining the database records. Obtaining these records may be more problematic, because such costs are usually for a campaign, which makes allocating costs to a single customer difficult. Computer and database technology can average or allocate a portion of these costs to individual customer records or to a lifetime value segment.

The lifetime value figure will be the end product for either individual customers or a customer segment. A lifetime value figure for a customer segment of $1,375 represents the amount of revenue, on average, that each customer will generate over his or her lifetime. By communicating with and marketing to the customer segment, the company may be able to increase the lifetime value. A lifetime value analysis informs the company's customer contact and service personnel regarding a customer's potential worth to the company.

Customer Clusters

Marketers use coding systems to group customers into clusters based on a wide variety of criteria. A bank may group customers based on the number of accounts, types of accounts, and other relationships a customer may have with the organization. For example, customers with home mortgages above $100,000 with balances of 30 to 60 percent remaining may be targeted for a home equity loan. A clothing retailer might group customers by the type of clothing each group purchases and then develop marketing programs for the various groups. Teenagers who purchase Western wear would be in a different cluster than teenagers who prefer hip, trendy fashions.

Unified Western Grocers, a wholesale cooperative association serving more than 3,000 grocery stores, used a customer cluster analysis to reduce 19 different advertising campaigns and programs for the various stores it served down to four, based on customer commonalities. The four clusters that emerged from the analysis were affluent urban and suburban households; mid-downscale rural seniors; large, low-income urban households; and non-acculturated

▼ Progressive Bank can take advantage of customer clustering to identify the best prospects for its trust and wealth management services.

French Creative

Hispanics. The marketing team designed advertisements and created shelf allocations of brands for each of the four customer clusters. The approach reduced advertising design costs and led to more effective advertising.[4]

Location-Data Tracking

The newest form of data analytics is based on information provided by mobile GPS technology. Cell phone companies such as Verizon can track customer locations and combine it with profile information. This type of information may be valuable to sports properties as well as restaurants and retailers. For instance, the Phoenix Suns basketball team's marketers took advantage of the technology to better understand fans who attended games. This information helped target specific businesses as potential sponsors.

A company such as Verizon can obtain location data to track the movement of individuals inside a sports arena as well as their activities outside the facility. These data are aggregated and then *hashed*—the process of anonymizing the data so that specific individuals cannot be identified. The data provides information regarding the restaurants or businesses patrons visited prior to attending a game as well as after a game. The marketing team then adds profile data from companies such as Experian in order to segment consumers by demographics. The ability to target specific market segments based on their actual patronage behavior at the game and the businesses around the facility becomes the result.[5]

▼ Data mining can be used by Weaver to build profiles of its customers that would be good targets for the company's various services.

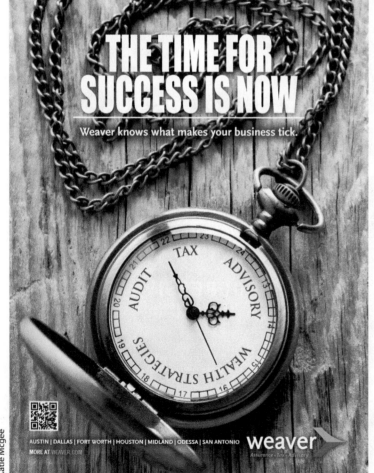

Data Mining

Data mining involves using computer data analysis software to study data to find meaningful information and help build relationships. Data mining includes two activities: building profiles of customer segments and/or preparing models that predict future purchase behaviors based on past purchases.

Data mining assists the marketing team in building profiles of the firm's best customers. These profiles, in turn, help identify prospective new customers. They can be used to examine "good" customers to see if they are candidates for sales calls that would move them from "good" to a higher value. Companies offering different types of goods and services develop multiple profiles. The profiles assist in targeting sales calls and help identify cross-selling possibilities.

The marketing team at First Horizon National Bank employed data mining tactics to expand the company's wealth management business by studying consumer groups. Data regarding existing customers from the mortgage side of the firm's business made it possible to locate the best prospects for investment services. Linking the data mining program with cross-selling resulted in an increase in company revenues from $26.3 million to $33.8 million in just one year.[6]

Marketers for the retailer American Eagle developed a data mining method to analyze consumer responses to price markdowns. The information helped the team determine when to cut prices and by how much in order to optimize sales. Markdown programs were geared to individual stores, because consumers responded differently in each outlet.[7]

The second data mining method involves developing models that predict future sales based on past purchasing activities. Marketing professionals at

Staples, Inc. prepared a modeling program to examine the buying habits of the company's catalog customers. The program identified the names of frequent buyers who were then sent customized mailings.

The specific type of information needed determines the dating mining method. Once the information contained in the data has been analyzed, the team can design targeted marketing programs. Profiles and models assist in creating effective marketing campaigns. A direct-mail program to current customers differs from one designed to attract new customers. The data provide clues regarding the best approach for each customer segment.

Data coding and data mining serve three purposes (see Figure 3). First, they assist in developing marketing communications. Marketing employees utilize the information to choose types of promotions, advertising media, and the message to be presented to each group of customers. Second, they help in developing marketing programs. Third, companies that employ salespeople can use the information to qualify prospects and make personal sales calls on those individuals or businesses that offer the greatest potential. Specific sales activities are described in the following sections.

- Develop marketing communications
- Develop marketing programs
- For personal sales
  - Qualify prospects
  - Information for sales calls

▲ **FIGURE 3**

Purposes of Data Coding and Data Mining

Database-Driven Marketing Communications

Building a database, coding the information, and performing data mining make it possible to utilize the output for the purpose of establishing one-on-one communications with customers. Personalized communications build relationships and lead to repeat business and customer loyalty. They may help move the company and its products from brand parity to brand equity. A database marketing program contains tools to personalize messages and keep records of the types of effective and ineffective communications. The internet offers the key technology for database-driven communications. Figure 4 highlights the importance of the internet in customer interactions.

objective 2

How can database-driven marketing communication programs help personalize interactions with customers?

Identification Codes

A database-driven marketing program starts with assigning individual customers IDs and passwords that allow them to access components of the website that are not available to those who simply visit the site without logging on. IT professionals tie IDs and passwords to cookies on each customer's computer in order to customize pages and individual offers. When the system works properly, the customer does not have to log in each time. Instead, the cookie automatically does it for the person. For example, each time a user accesses Barnes & Noble, he receives a personalized greeting, such as "Welcome, Jim." Next, when Jim places an order, he does not have to type in his address or credit card information. The database contains this information and it comes up automatically, which saves Jim time and effort and increases the probability he will buy something.

Companies send specialized communications after the sale. A series of messages follows the purchase. First, the buyer receives an email confirming the order and thanking her. The email contains a tracking code that she can access to locate her order at any time. The message includes an estimated shipping date. Some companies include

- It is the cheapest form of communication.
- It is available 24/7.
- Metric analysis reveals that the customer read the message, the time it was read, and how much time was spent reading it.
- Customers are able to access additional information whenever they want.
- It can build a bond with customers.

◄ **FIGURE 4**

The Importance of the Internet in Customer Communications

Sending birthday wishes to customers can enhance brand attitude, brand patronage, and brand loyalty.

an email in the interim stating that the order has reached the warehouse. Then, another email can be sent when the order is pulled and shipped.

Personalized Communications

An effective database-driven communication program relies on customer profiles and any other information about customer preferences to help individualize messages. Clothing retailers often send emails about new fashions that have arrived. These emails do not go to every person in the database. Only to those who have indicated a desire to have access to the information or who have indicated they have an interest in fashion news receive the messages. These customers often believe they are receiving special "inside" information.

Marketing employees build lists of loyal patrons who will be sent birthday greetings based on customer profile data. Recently, a steak and seafood restaurant sent a card and offered a $10 birthday discount to 215,600 persons who provided their birthdates. The cost of mailing the birthday card and discount was $90,000. Patrons redeemed approximately 40 percent of the cards. Each birthday customer brought an average of two other people, and those individuals paid full price for their meals. The result was $2.9 million in revenues derived from the program.[8]

A survey by Fulcrum revealed that 74 percent of individuals who received a birthday message from a business thought more positively about the company, and 88 percent of the positive reactions translated into increased brand loyalty. Greetings from brands in the food and beverage industry generated the most positive responses. Birthday wishes with discounts were more effective than birthday greetings sent without incentives. Clearly personalized communications offer an effective means of increasing brand loyalty.[9]

Customized Content

In addition to personalized communications, data can be analyzed in order to customize content. Netflix tracks what movie buffs watch, search for, and rate. The company tracks the time of day, date, the device used (smartphone, tablet, or PC), where individuals browsed, and where they scrolled on a page. The information aids the company in suggesting movies to the person and helps stream the suggestions to the individual's most-often checked device at the best time. For instance, if the browsing history indicates that an individual searches for and watches romantic comedies on Friday nights, then a suggestion would be sent to the person's mobile phone or tablet that morning or the day prior. Netflix estimates that 75 percent of viewer selections result from these data-driven recommendations.[10]

In-Bound Telemarketing

Contacts made by telephone work the same way as internet contacts. The service-call operator immediately sees the identity of the person calling. Customer data appears on the screen in front of the in-bound telemarketer. The operator treats the caller in a personalized manner. When the company calculates a lifetime value code, the operator knows the customer's value and status. The operator asks about a recent purchase or talks about information provided on the customer's list of preferences or a customer profile. The operator greets and treats each customer as an individual, not as a random person making an in-bound call.

WavebreakMediaMicro/Fotolia

Reward.   Reward Plus!

Treat Yourself to High Interest Checking PLUS Savings!

MEMBER FDIC

NOW MOBILE!

Newcomer, Morris and Young Inc.

◀ A bank such as Ouachita Independent Bank can incorporate trawling to identify individuals who have just moved into the community and may be looking for a banking institution.

Trawling

Database marketing includes a procedure called **trawling**, or the process of searching the database for a specific piece of information for marketing purposes. Home Depot's trawling program locates individuals who have recently moved. The company's marketing team knows that when people buy new homes, they often need home improvement merchandise. Most of the time, these items include merchandise sold at Home Depot.

Other marketers trawl a database to find anniversary dates of a special purchase, such as a new car. Car dealerships send a correspondence on each year's anniversary of a car purchase to inquire about customer satisfaction and interest in trading for a newer vehicle. A retailer can trawl for individuals who have not made a purchase within the last three months or who purchased a lawnmower last year. Trawling presents a wide variety of ways to communicate with specific individuals who meet a particular criterion.

Database-Driven Marketing Programs

Database-driven marketing programs take many forms. They may be undertaken in conjunction with other marketing activities. Some of the more common programs include permission marketing, frequency programs, and customer relationship management efforts.

objective 3

How do database-driven marketing programs create sales and build bonds with customers?

Permission Marketing

A strong backlash by consumers against spam and junk mail continues to grow. Consequently, many marketing departments have turned to **permission marketing**, a program in which companies send promotional information to only those consumers who give the authorization to do so. Permission marketing programs can be offered on the internet, by telephone, or through direct mail. Response rates are often higher in permission programs, because customers only receive requested marketing materials or those for which consent was given. Results are enhanced when permission marketing programs utilize database technology to segment customers, although not every person who signs up for permission marketing becomes a valuable customer.

Figure 5 lists the steps of a permission marketing program. Permission can be obtained by providing incentives for volunteering, such as information, entertainment, a gift, cash, or entries in a sweepstakes. Any information provided should be primarily educational and focus on the company's product or service features.

Reinforcing the relationship requires an additional new incentive beyond the original gift. Relationships can be enhanced when marketers acquire more in-depth information

▶ **FIGURE 5**

Steps in Building a Permission Marketing Program

1. Obtain permission from the customer.
2. Offer the consumer an ongoing curriculum that is meaningful.
3. Reinforce the incentive to continue the relationship.
4. Increase the level of permission.
5. Leverage the permission to benefit both parties.

about a consumer such as hobbies, interests, attitudes, and opinions. The information may be tailored to entice additional purchases by offering special deals.

Keys to Success in Permission Marketing For a permission marketing program to succeed, the marketing team ensures that the recipients have agreed to participate. Unfortunately, some consumers have been tricked into joining permission marketing programs. One common tactic involves automatically enrolling customers in permission marketing programs as they complete online surveys or purchase items online. Opting out of the program requires the individual to un-check a box on the site. Although this approach increases the number of individuals enrolled, the technique often creates bad feelings.

The marketing materials should be relevant to the consumers receiving them. Far too many people who have joined permission marketing programs encounter situations in which they provide no input and are bombarded with extraneous marketing messages. This does not create loyalty and runs counter to the purpose of a permission program.

One recent survey revealed that 80 percent of consumers stopped reading permission emails from companies because they were shoddy or irrelevant. Another 68 percent said the emails came too frequently, and 51 percent reported they lost interest in the goods, services, or topics of the emails. On the whole, consumers delete an average of 43 percent of permission emails without ever reading them.[11]

To overcome these challenges, the marketing team monitors responses and customizes the permission program to meet individual customer needs. Database technology allows for customization by tracking responses and browsing behavior. When a customer regularly accesses a website through a link in an email sent by the company to read the latest fashion news, the behavior can trigger email offers and incentives on fashions related to the news stories and links the customer followed. An individual who does not access the website and does not appear to be interested in fashion news receives a different type of email offer. By capitalizing on the power of database technology, a firm can enhance the permission marketing program and make it beneficial to the company and the customer.

Permission Marketing Enticements Figure 6 notes the top reasons for opting into email programs. Winning a sweepstakes tops the list. Also, individuals who are already customers of the company may be more inclined to examine the company's products.[12] Enticing them into the permission marketing program will be easier than trying to attract new patrons.

Figure 7 provides a list of motives that help retain customers in a permission marketing relationship. As shown, consumers remain with such programs for many reasons.[13]

Permission marketing programs have the potential to build strong, ongoing relationships with customers when they offer something of

▼ Permission marketing can target individuals interested in fashion news.

.Shock/Fotolia

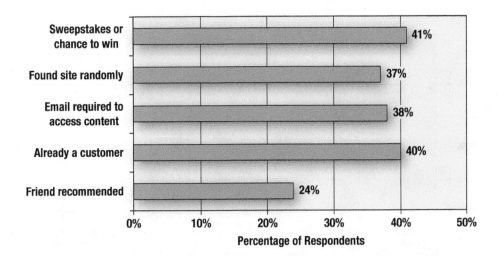

◀ **FIGURE 6**
Reasons Consumers Opt into Email Permission Programs

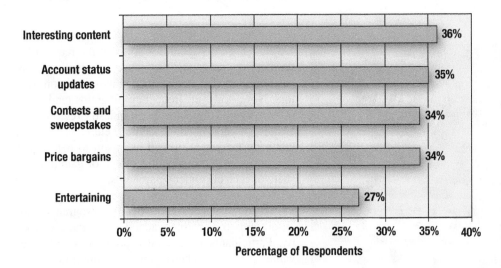

◀ **FIGURE 7**
Reasons Consumers Remain in a Permission Marketing Program

value. To optimize permission marketing, firms feature empowerment and reciprocity. **Empowerment** means consumers believe they have power throughout the relationship and not just at the beginning when they agreed to join the program. They can make decisions and have choices about what to receive.

To maintain positive attitudes, consumers should be given rewards along the way, not just at the beginning. This creates feelings of **reciprocity**, or a sense of obligation toward the company. Only rewarding customers for joining the program will be a mistake. Empowerment and reciprocity lead the customer to believe the company values the relationship, which increases the chances the consumer will continue to be an active participant.

Frequency Programs

A company offers free or discounted merchandise or services for a series of purchases in a **frequency program** or **loyalty program**. These enticements encourage customers to make repeat purchases. In the airline industry, frequent-flyer programs offer free flights after a traveler accumulates a certain number of miles. Grocery stores grant special discounts when purchase totals reach a certain amount within a specified time period.

Chief Marketing Officer (CMO) Council research indicates that two-thirds of consumers belong to loyalty programs. On average, households are enrolled in 14 programs, but only actively participate in about six. Figure 8 provides a list of benefits of such programs mentioned by customers and the percentage that cites each benefit.[14]

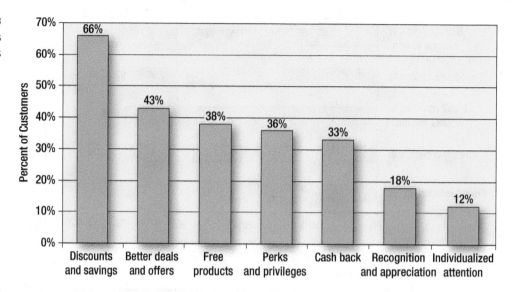

▶ **FIGURE 8**
Benefits of Loyalty Programs Cited by Consumers

▲ An advertisement for Karns Quality Foods encouraging consumers to sign up for the store's loyalty program.

Goals Figure 9 identifies some of the reasons for developing frequency programs. Originally, many were developed to differentiate brands from competitors. Now, however, frequency programs tend to be offered by all companies in an industry (credit card, airline, grocery, hotel, restaurant, etc.). As a result, company marketers instead use them to help retain customers, match competitor offers, or gain a larger share of each customer's purchases.

Principles Successful loyalty programs are based on two principles: added value and reciprocity. Participants in a loyalty program should feel value accrues from belonging to the program. When the customer in turn rewards the perceived value by making additional purchases, it creates a sense of reciprocity. When the customer and the company both benefit from the relationship, it continues.

Recent research suggests that the more effort a customer expends to participate in a frequency program, the greater the value of the reward becomes. Many consumers are willing to put forth greater effort to obtain luxury rewards as opposed to necessity rewards. Shoppers at a grocery store are more likely to give higher levels of effort in order to receive a free overnight stay at a nearby local resort or a free meal at a nice restaurant than they would for a $20 gift certificate for food.

Data-Driven Customization Collecting data assists the marketing team in customizing loyalty programs to meet each individual's needs. Mass offers may not be as effective, because customers feel they are being "sold" rather than "rewarded." CVS Pharmacy's marketer understood this principle when they launched the ExtraCare loyalty program. Individuals who belonged to ExtraCare received a tailored version of the weekly print circulars. The data collected from the member's purchases leads to suggestions of sale items along with individualized discounts and coupons. These promotional offers were not for competing brands or products that do not interest card members. Instead, they were for brands and products card members regularly purchased. In the

- Maintain or increase sales, margins, or profits
- Increase loyalty of existing customers
- Preempt or match a competitor's offer
- Encourage cross-selling
- Differentiate the brand
- Discourage entry of a new brand

◀ **FIGURE 9**
Goals of Frequency or
Loyalty Programs

words of one customer who likes to drink Coke products rather than Pepsi, "For me to be able to get a coupon to buy more Coke is a lot more relevant. I value more getting coupons for products I like, not for products I don't care for, which is wasting my time."

Maximize Motivation Effective loyalty programs maximize a customer's motivation to make another purchase. Many times, marketers target moderate users with frequency programs. Light users seldom make purchases and cost more to maintain in the program than they spend. High users already make frequent purchases and are unlikely to increase their purchasing levels. Consequently, moderate users represent the most valuable target group.

Research indicates that a *variable ratio reward schedule* is superior to regularly scheduled rewards in motivating additional purchases. A variable ratio means that customers receive intermittent reinforcements. They do not know exactly when a reward will be given or the size of the incentive. The random reward schedule should be frequent enough to encourage them to make ongoing purchases.[15]

Although many consumers have frequency cards, they may not always use them. The marketing manager of a locally-owned restaurant noticed he had a large number of customers who had not recently used their Frequent Diner Club cards. Trawling identified 4,000 Frequent Diner Club members who had not earned any points during the previous three months. To motivate these past customers, the restaurant sent a letter to each of the 4,000 offering a $5 discount on dinner. The offer was good for 35 days. The cost of the mailing was $1,800. Results were:

▲ Restaurants often use loyalty cards to encourage customers to return more often.

- The average number of member visits per day increased from 25 to 42 during the promotion and to 29 per day after the promotion ended.
- Average visits by individual members holding cards increased both during and after the promotion.
- Incremental sales increased by $17,100 during the promotion and by $4,700 after the 35-day promotion.

By spending $1,800, the promotion led to reactivations by about 600 people who had not dined at the restaurant in 3 months. Of the nearly 600 who were motivated to come back during the promotion, 147 dined at the restaurant after the promotion was over.[16]

Customer Relationship Management

Customer relationship management (CRM) programs provide a method to employ databases that customize products and communications with customers, with the goals of higher sales and profits. Successful CRM programs build long-term loyalty and bonds with customers through a personal touch, facilitated by technology. Effective customer relationship management programs go beyond the development of a database and traditional selling tactics to the mass customization of both communications and products.

Two primary CRM metrics are the lifetime value of the customer and share of customer. The lifetime value concept measures the potential level of purchases to be made by an individual or market segment.

The second metric, share of customer, is based on the concept that some customers are more valuable than others and that, over time, the amount of money a customer spends

▲ Centric Federal Credit Union can use a CRM program to enhance relationships with its current customers.

with a firm can be increased. **Share of customer** refers to the percentage of expenditures a customer makes with one particular firm compared to total expenditures in that product's category. Share of customer measures a customer's potential value. The question becomes, "If more is invested by the company in developing a relationship, what will the yield be over time?" When a customer makes only one-fourth of his purchases of a particular product category with a specific brand, increasing the share of the customer would mean increasing that percentage from 25 percent to a higher level, thus generating additional sales revenues. The ultimate goal would be leading the customer to make 100 percent of his purchases with one brand.[17]

Kellogg's CRM database holds information from 18 million consumers. Among these, 3.5 million individuals have become part of Kellogg's Family Rewards Program. Each Kellogg product package provides a unique, 16-digit code. Members submit these codes online in exchange for points that can be redeemed for discounts or free prizes, such as toys or sports equipment. The code tells Kellogg the type of product, the package size, and the store where the product was purchased. The information creates a history of every Kellogg purchase the individual made, when it was made, and where it was made. These data allow the company's marketing group to prepare specific offers designed to match the person's past purchasing behaviors. In addition, the data assist in developing marketing communications that are better aligned with consumer preferences and that facilitate the cross-selling of Kellogg products.[18]

In general, CRM marketing programs should enhance customer loyalty. When a hotel's check-in person knows in advance that a business traveler prefers a nonsmoking room, a queen-size bed, and reads *USA Today*, these items can be made available as the guest arrives. Training hotel clerks and other employees to rely on the database helps them to provide better service, thereby increasing loyalty from regular customers. Any organization's marketing department can adapt these techniques to fit the needs of its customers and clients.

In addition to permission marketing, frequency programs, and CRM systems, other marketing programs can result from database analysis. Internet programs, trade promotions, consumer promotions, and other marketing tactics may be facilitated by using the database.

objective 4

When should direct response marketing programs be used to supplement other methods of delivering messages and products to consumers?

Direct Response Marketing

One program closely tied to database marketing, **direct response marketing** (or **direct marketing**), involves targeting products to customers without the use of other channel members. Figure 10 identifies the most typical forms of direct response marketing

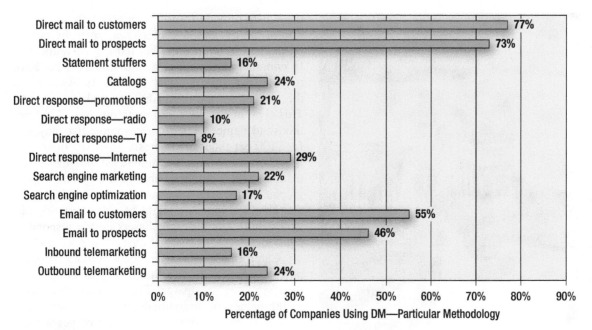

▲ **FIGURE 10**

Methods of Direct Response Marketing

and the percentages of companies using them. Notice that direct marketing can be aimed at customers as well as prospects. According to the Direct Marketing Association, about 60 percent of a typical direct marketing budget targets prospecting for new customers; the other 40 percent is spent retaining current customers.[19]

Many pharmaceutical companies employ direct response advertising, especially on television and in magazines. A recent study revealed that this direct response approach works. Ads for prescription medications by pharmaceuticals prompted almost one-third of Americans to ask their doctors about a particular brand of medicine and 82 percent of those who asked doctors received some type of prescription. The prescription was for the advertised brand 44 percent of the time; for another drug, 56 percent of the time. Sometimes, doctors prescribed the advertised brand as well as another brand.[20]

Individuals and companies respond to direct response marketing in a number of ways, such as by telephone, email, visiting a retail location, or using a PURL (personalized URL). PURLs offer the advantage of preloading all of the individual's personal data to a website, which can then customize the information and any offer. They also assist in tracking the individual's onsite activities and in making real-time changes to offers.[21]

Direct Mail

As shown in Figure 10, direct mail remains the most common form of direct response marketing. Direct mail targets both consumers and business-to-business customers. The quality of the mailing list normally determines the success of a direct mail program. Companies utilize two sources when compiling a mailing list: the firm's internal database and/or a commercial list.

The company's marketing department parses an internal list and separates active members from inactive members. Prospective new customers receive different direct mail pieces with messages designed to entice repeat purchases. Mailing direct offers to individuals (or businesses) who have not purchased recently but who have purchased in the past often yields a better response rate than cold-call mailing lists from brokers.

Types of Commercial Lists A company can purchase a commercial list as either a response list or a compiled list. A **response list** consists of customers who have made purchases or who have responded to direct mail offers in the past. Brokers selling

▲ Progressive Bank can take advantage of direct mail to target specific financial service customers.

these lists provide information about the composition of the list and how much was spent by buyers on the list. In addition, a *hot list* can be requested. It contains the names of individuals who have responded within the past 30 days. Individuals on the hot list are the most likely to make purchases. This type of list costs more: as much as $250 per thousand names. A regular response list may sell for $100 per thousand names.

The second form, a **compiled list**, provides information about consumers who meet a specific demographic profile. The disadvantage of a compiled list is that although someone might fit a demographic category, most American purchasers do not respond to mail offers.

Caterpillar's marketing team wanted to reach potential buyers in the Southwest as part of the "Eat My Dust" campaign. The company purchased 1,700 names of individuals who had purchased industrial loaders during the past five years from Equipment Data Associates, a Charlotte, North Carolina, firm that compiles detailed purchasing histories of more than 870,000 U.S. contractors. Rea & Kaiser's Nichols agency designed a sweepstakes to win a new Cat 414E. An eye-catching direct mail piece urged contractors to sign up either online, by mail, or at a local Caterpillar dealer. Standard response rates are less than one percent; the response rate for the "Eat My Dust" direct mailer was 18 percent.[22] The highly targeted list made the difference.

Catalogs

Many consumers enjoy catalogs and view them at their leisure. Catalogs have a longer-term impact because they are kept and shared. Catalogs feature a low-pressure direct response marketing tactic that gives consumers time to consider goods and prices. Many marketers believe that online shopping has replaced catalogs; however, some research suggests that this is not the case. More than half of online shoppers browse a catalog prior to making the online purchase and more than 30 percent have a catalog in hand when placing the online order. More than 85 percent of survey respondents said they had purchased an item online after seeing it in a catalog first.[23]

Successful cataloging requires an enhanced database. Many catalog companies, such as L.L.Bean and JCPenney, create specialty catalogs geared to specific market segments. The specialty catalogs have a lower cost and a higher yield, because they reach individual market segments.

Catalogs are essential selling tools for many business-to-business marketing programs. They provide more complete product information to members of the buying center as well as prices for the purchasing agent. When

▲ Catalogs are an important component of Skyjacker's Integrated Marketing Communications Program.

combined with an internet presence, a catalog program can facilitate a strong connection with individual customers.

Mass Media

Television, radio, magazines, and newspapers provide additional tools for direct response advertising. Direct response TV commercials are slightly longer (60 seconds), which allows a potential buyer time to find a pen to write down a toll-free number, an address, or a website. Catchy, easy-to-remember contact information is often used, such as "1-800-Go-Green" or "www.gogreen.com." Repeating the response format helps customers remember how to respond. Often a "call-now" prompt concludes the commercial.

Television also features infomercials for various types of products, such as exercise equipment and cooking tools. Cable and satellite systems have led to the creation of numerous direct response channels. The Home Shopping Network remains one of the most successful. Essentially, the channel runs 24-hour infomercial programs. Other channels feature jewelry, food, and shoes.

Direct response techniques are also presented on radio stations and in magazines and newspapers. Radio does not have the reach of television, but it can be designed to match the type of station format. Radio ads repeat the response number or website frequently so that consumers can make contacts.

Print media can be sent to various market segments. Newspaper advertisements may feature website information and other quick-response formats. The same holds true for magazines. Both contain website information and toll-free numbers.[24] The more ways provided to respond to an ad, the higher the response rate.

Internet and Email

The internet offers a valuable form of direct marketing. Consumers can respond directly to ads placed on a website, and direct response advertisements can be placed on search engines and used in emails.

As shown in Figure 10, email continues to be a frequently used form of direct response marketing. Email provides a cost-effective method of reaching prospects. It helps build relationships with current customers through personalization of communications and by presenting marketing offers tailored to each consumer's needs, wants, and desires. For business-to-business marketers, email works better than postal mail and other direct marketing forms when the recipient is familiar with the company.[25]

By placing ads on search engines and using search engine optimization, firms make direct response offers directly to individuals and businesses in the market for particular products. A direct response ad for fruit trees that appears when a person types in "apple trees" will be more effective than one that appears when a person searches on "iPad" or "office furniture."

Direct Sales

In the consumer sector, companies such as Amway, Mary Kay, and Avon rely on direct sales. The salesperson contacts friends, relatives, coworkers, and others and provides them with small catalogs or marketing brochures. Alternatively, individuals host parties and invite friends and relatives to see products.

Mark is the Avon flanker brand designed for teenagers and women under 30. In launching a new line of cosmetics, Mark's marketing group brought direct selling into the digital and social media age by hiring 40,000 "Mark Girls" to work in the United States. Mark Girls are primarily women between

▼ More than 40,000 "Mark Girls" work in the United States for Avon.

© SerrNovik/Fotolia

the ages of 18 and 24 who use grassroots methods to sell Mark cosmetics and fashion accessories in dorms, through sororities, and via Facebook. The brand offers personalized e-boutiques, iPhone apps, and a Facebook e-shop. Kristiauna Mangum is a marketing major at Ohio State University. She is also a sales manager for Mark and manages 155 other Mark girls, earning commissions that range from 20 to 50 percent of the product's price.[26]

Telemarketing

Telemarketing takes place in two ways: inbound or outbound. *Inbound telemarketing* occurs when an individual initiates a call to a company. When a customer places an order, cross-selling can occur by offering other products or services. At times, customers make inbound calls to register complaints or talk about problems. Direct response marketing can provide information about how to solve the problem. For example, when a customer calls a mortgage company because of a late fee, the person can be encouraged to sign up for a direct pay program, which means the customer does not have to worry about possible mail delays.

The least popular method for direct marketing is *outbound telemarketing*. New legislation now requires prior consent before outbound sales calling or texting to a cell phone. This law has greatly reduced the attractiveness of outbound telemarketing. Successful outbound programs are tied into databases that identify the customers or prospects who have had prior relationships with the company. Only those individuals are contacted. An outbound telemarketing program that contacts customers who have not purchased in a year can help bring those customers back. A company that purchased a copy machine can be called to inquire about interest in paper and toner.

Personal Selling

Personal selling offers a face-to-face opportunity to build relationships with consumers. It takes place in both consumer and business-to-business transactions. Personal selling may result in the acquisition of new customers in addition to influencing current customers to increase levels of purchases. It can also be used to service and maintain existing relationships. The goal of personal selling should not be limited to making sales. Developing longer-term relationships with customers represents a second key objective. **Relationship selling** seeks to create a customer for life, not for a single transaction.

Figure 11 identifies the standard steps in the selling process. A quality data warehouse accompanied by effective database technologies provides key tools that assist in personal selling.

Generating Leads

Producing quality leads constitutes the first personal selling task, especially for business-to-business programs. Figure 12 identifies some of the most common methods. Personal sales calls are costly, which makes generating quality leads crucial.

Referrals generate the most ideal leads, because most recommendations are made by satisfied individuals. Referrals give the salesperson a head start. Making contact with purchasing agents or buyers in business organizations can be difficult. Dropping the name of the person who gave the referral helps the salesperson get past a gatekeeper.

objective 5

What are the tasks involved in developing successful personal selling programs for consumers and businesses?

- Generating leads
- Qualifying prospect
- Knowledge acquisition
- Sales presentation
- Handling objections
- Sales closing
- Follow-up

▶ **FIGURE 11**
Steps in the Selling Process

Also, if someone has given a referral, then the potential lead becomes more receptive to the sales call and has a more positive attitude toward the salesperson. The best referrals come from current customers. Those made by other channel members, vendors, and acquaintances can also be useful because they allow the salesperson to get a foot in the door with a potential prospect.

For generating leads, databases provide quality information, especially internal databases. Most of these leads originate from some type of advertising or inquiry. Direct response ads in various media can generate leads. Online ads on various websites or search engines also produce leads. Individuals may send an email inquiry or request additional information through the company's website. Databases provide quality leads through trawling and analytical techniques, such as data mining. These methods identify leads with higher sales potential.

Other less desirable means of generating sales leads are networking, directories, and cold calls. Although these approaches may produce some leads, they are time consuming and less productive. Networking in civic and professional organizations allows salespeople to make personal contacts. Directories may be obtained from the federal government, professional organizations, or research firms that provide the names of companies that purchase specific products or those in a given industry. The challenge becomes locating quality leads from the list. Cold calls are the worst method of generating leads. The salesperson has no idea whether the company or individual has any interest in the product.

- Refferals
- Database-generated leads
- Networking
- Directories
- Cold calls

▲ **FIGURE 12**
Methods of Generating Sales Leads

Qualifying Prospects

Every name or prospect may not be viable. Also, all prospects do not offer equal value. With this in mind, qualifying prospects means evaluating leads on two dimensions: (1) the potential income the lead can generate and (2) the probability of acquiring the prospect as a customer. Based on the outcomes of these evaluations, determinations can be made regarding the best methods of contact and what happens with the lead. The high cost of making personal sales calls means that only the best leads warrant personal visits. Some prospects receive telephone calls or emails from an inside salesperson. Others may be mailed or emailed marketing materials but are not contacted directly by a salesperson.

Once the leads are analyzed using the two categories—sales potential and probability of acquisition—they are then placed into categories, or buckets, with the leads high on both dimensions as the best, or "A" leads. These leads normally receive a call from the sales staff. The second best group, or "B" leads, often will be contacted by a telemarketer or through email. "C" leads receive marketing materials and are encouraged to make inquiries if interested. Leads that score low on both dimensions may be kept in a database and monitored for future action in case the lead's situation changes.

Knowledge Acquisition

During the knowledge acquisition phase, the company's salespeople or other members of the sales department gather materials about the prospect. Figure 13 identifies typical information. The more a salesperson knows about a prospect before making the sales call, the higher the probability of making a sale or gaining permission to demonstrate the company's prospect.

▼ Leads can be generated through business personnel clicking on this digital banner ad for LUBA Workers' Comp.

WORKERS' COMP IS THE LAST THING
ON MY MIND

LUBA Workers' Comp
Because, it's the biggest thing on ours.
888.884.5822 • LUBAwc.com   Rated A- Excellent by A.M. Best.

LUBA Workers' Comp

▶ **FIGURE 13**
Knowledge Acquisition Information

- Understand the prospect's business.
- Know and understand the prospect's customers.
- Identify the prospect's needs.
- Evaluate the risk factors and costs in switching vendors.
- Identify the decision makers and influencers.

The Sales Presentation

The initial sales call can be designed to gather information, discuss bid specifications, answer questions, or to close the deal with a final pitch or offer.[27] The exact nature of the first sales call depends on the information gathered prior to the call. Also, the stage of the buying process affects the presentation. The types of sales presentations used typically fall into one of these categories: stimulus-response, need-satisfaction, problem-solution, and mission-sharing.[28]

A **stimulus-response** sales approach, or a "canned" sales pitch, involves specific statements (stimuli) designed to elicit specific responses from customers. The salesperson normally memorizes the stimulus statement (the pitch). Telemarketers, retail sales clerks, and new field sales reps often rely on this method.

The **need-satisfaction** sales approach strives to discover a customer's needs during the first part of the sales presentation and then to provide solutions. The salesperson should skillfully ask the right questions. She should understand the customer's business and customers. Once a need has been identified, the rep then shows how the company's products meet that need.

The **problem-solution** sales approach requires employees from the selling organization to analyze the buyer's business. It usually involves a team of individuals such as engineers, salespeople, and other experts. The team investigates a potential customer's operations and problems, and then offers feasible solutions.

In the last approach, **mission-sharing**, two organizations develop a common mission. They then share resources to accomplish that mission. This partnership resembles a joint venture as much as a selling relationship.

.shock/Fotolia

▲ Understanding customer needs provides the basis for the need-satisfaction sales approach.

Handling Objections

Companies and individuals seldom make purchases after a sales presentation without raising some objections or concerns. Salespeople anticipate objections and carefully answer them. Figure 14 lists the most common methods of handling objections.

With the *head-on approach*, the salesperson answers the objection directly. Doing so, however, suggests that the customer or prospect is wrong. Consequently, the salesperson should use tact. No one likes being told he is in error. The salesperson takes care to not offend the customer.

To avoid a confrontation, some salespeople employ an *indirect approach*. This method allows the salesperson to never really tell the customer he is wrong. Instead, the salesperson sympathizes with the customer's viewpoint and then provides the correct information.

When the customer's objection is partially true, the salesperson may utilize the *compensation method*. With this approach, the salesperson replies "yes, but…" and then explains the product's benefits or features that answer the customer's objection.

Some customers do not have specific objections but are anxious or worried about the consequences of switching to a new vendor. For this situation, a sales rep can apply the *feel, felt, found* method. The salesperson permits the customer to talk about her fears or worries. In response, the salesperson can relate personal experiences or experiences of other customers who had the same fears and worries and how the product resulted in a positive experience.

- Head-on approach
- Indirect approach
- Compensation method
- "Feel, felt, found"

▲ **FIGURE 14**
Methods of Handling Objections

Closing the Sale

Often, the most important element of the sales call is the closing; however, it may also be the most difficult part. Salespeople often experience feelings of rejection or failure when prospects or customers say "no." Successful salespeople are masters at making the close. Figure 15 identifies some of the most common sales-closing methods. The one to be used depends on the personality of the salesperson, the personality of the prospect, and the situation surrounding the sales call.

With the *direct close*, the salesperson asks for the order outright. The approach may be used when objections have been answered and the salesperson believes the prospect is ready to buy.

When the salesperson cannot be sure if the prospect is ready, he can try the *trial*. With this approach, the salesperson solicits feedback that provides information regarding the customer's reaction, without asking directly for the sale. A positive reaction leads the salesperson to ask for the order. If not, then he returns to the sales presentation. The salesperson may also *summarize* the product's benefits and how it meets the customer's needs prior to asking for the order.

Sometimes a salesperson asks a serious of questions along the way, ensuring the customer will *continuously* respond "yes." By answering "yes" to smaller questions about the benefits of a product, when it comes time to ask for the order the customer may be more likely to respond with a "yes."

A salesperson can also *assume* the customer will say "yes." She might ask, "How many cases do you want?" or "How would you like this to be shipped?"

- Direct close
- Trial close
- Summarization close
- Continuous "yes" close
- Assumptive close

▲ **FIGURE 15**
Methods of Closing Sales

▼ With the summarization close, the salesperson shows how the product meets the customer's needs.

Creativa/Fotolia

Follow Up

Keeping customers happy after a purchase can result in repeat business, customer loyalty, and positive referrals. Quality follow-up programs are cost-effective ways to retain customers, which is much cheaper than continually finding new ones. Unfortunately, following up may be neglected by the sales staff, especially if the salesperson receives commission on new sales but not on follow-up activities. In this situation, the company must designate other employees to follow up to ensure that customers are satisfied with their purchases.

International Implications

objective 6

How should database marketing and personal selling programs be adapted to international settings?

Database marketing faces the same challenges as other aspects of an IMC program when a firm moves into the international arena. These include differences in technology, which make data collection and analysis more difficult due to issues such as language and internet availability. Further, local laws may limit the methods by which information can be collected as well as the types of information a company seeks and/or shares with other companies.

In many parts of the world, customers may only live a few miles apart yet reside in different countries. For example, the European Union consists of many nations in close proximity. Therefore, decisions must be made as to whether data will be country specific.

Programs such as permission marketing, frequency, and customer relationship management are subject to legal restrictions as well as cultural differences. In some instances, they may be highly accepted. Such is the case for permission marketing in Japan. In many Asian cultures, the giving of gifts takes on added meaning. This may indicate that stronger bonds between customers and companies are important in personal selling.

Direct marketing programs should be adapted to local conditions. Mail delivery systems may be easier to access in some countries than others. The same holds true for telephone systems, internet access, and other technologies. Infomercials may not be possible in countries with state-run television systems. A company's marketing team considers all local legal, social, cultural, technological, and competitive conditions before embarking on an international database-driven marketing program or direct marketing program.

Some international companies have moved to the forefront of data-based marketing programs. For example, Land, a Russian high-end supermarket chain, has implemented interactive kiosks that create recommendation-styled grocery lists for customers who use the brand's loyalty cards.[29]

Marketers also adapt personal selling tactics to specific countries. Local culture and customs must be carefully observed prior to making a sales call. A cultural assimilator will often be assigned help the sales team understand the nuances of a specific region or nation such as methods of greeting people, the manner in which gender differences are treated, dining customs, time awareness, personal space in communication, and other factors that affect interpersonal interactions.

Summary

Database marketing has become a vital element of a complete IMC program. The two key activities involved at the most general level—identifying customers and building relationships with them—have an impact on numerous other IMC tasks. It is more cost-effective to retain customers than to seek out new ones. Further, the actual message may change when communicating with long-time, loyal customers.

Building a data warehouse begins with collecting data to be used by the marketing department. Beyond basic information, such as a customer's name, address, and email address, other key data include the customer's purchase history and preferences. Geocoding involves adding geographic codes to customer records, which assists in selecting media and creating messages targeted to specific groups.

Database coding and analysis leads to either lifetime value analysis of customers or the clustering of customer groups based on customer spending patterns. Data mining programs involve building profiles of customer segments and/or preparing models that predict future purchase behaviors based on past purchases. The information gathered from data coding and data mining leads to the development of data-driven marketing communications and marketing programs.

Database-driven marketing communication programs are facilitated by effective identification codes that allow for personalization of messages and interactions. An effective database-driven communication program relies on customer profiles combined with other information available regarding specific customers. In-bound telemarketing programs, trawling, advertising, and lifetime value segment programs can be fine-tuned for individual customers.

Database-driven marketing programs include permission marketing, frequency programs, and customer relationship management systems. Permission marketing is a selling approach in which the customer agrees to receive promotional materials in exchange for various incentives. Frequency programs are incentives customers receive for repeat business. Both are designed to create customer loyalty over time. CRM is designed to build long-term loyalty and bonds with customers through the use of a personal touch facilitated by technology.

Direct response or direct marketing efforts may be made by mail, catalog, phone, mass media, the internet, or email. Direct mail programs remain popular as outbound telemarketing programs continue to diminish.

The goal of many personal selling programs—relationship selling—should be to create a customer for life rather than for a single transaction. The steps involved in personal selling include generating leads, qualifying prospects, knowledge acquisition, designing effective sales presentations, handling objections, closing the sale, and following up. Each of these activities can be made more effective through the use of quality database management programs.

Key Terms

data warehouse The place where customer data are held

geocoding Adding geographic codes to customer records to make it possible to plot customer addresses on a map

lifetime value The present value of future profits a customer generates over his or her life in a relationship with a brand or firm.

data mining The process of using computer data analysis software to mine data for meaningful information and relationships

trawling The process of searching the database for a specific piece of information for marketing purposes

permission marketing A form of database marketing in which the company sends promotional materials to customers who give the company permission to do so

empowerment Consumers believe they have power throughout the seller–consumer relationship, not just at the beginning when they agreed to join a frequency program

reciprocity A sense of obligation toward a company that results from receiving special deals or incentives such as gifts

frequency (or loyalty) program A marketing program designed to promote loyalty or frequent purchases of the same brand (or company)

customer relationship management (CRM) Programs designed to build long-term loyalty and bonds with customers through the use of a personal touch facilitated by technology

share of customer The percentage of expenditures a customer makes with one particular firm compared to total expenditures in that product's category

direct response (or direct) marketing Vending products to customers without the use of other channel members

response list A list of customers who have made purchases or who have responded to direct mail offers in the past

compiled list A list consisting of information about consumers who meet a specific demographic profile

relationship selling Developing long-term relationships with customers rather than focusing on a single transaction

stimulus-response A sales approach, often called a "canned" sales pitch, that uses specific statements (stimuli) to elicit specific responses from customers

need-satisfaction A sales approach in which the salesperson strives to discover a customer's needs during the first part of the sales presentation and then provides solutions to those needs

problem-solution A sales approach that requires employees from the selling organization to analyze the buyer's operations and offer ways to solve their problems

mission-sharing A sales approach in which two organizations develop a common mission and then share resources to accomplish that mission

Review Questions

1. What two activities are part of a successful database marketing program?

2. What is a data warehouse? What is the difference between an operational database and a marketing database?

3. List the tasks associated with database marketing.

4. Describe geocoding, customer clusters, and location-data tracking.

5. Define lifetime value. How is it determined?

6. What are the two primary functions of data mining?

7. Explain how identification codes are used in database-driven marketing communications.

8. Explain how consumer profile information is used when sending communications to customers.

9. What is trawling?

10. Describe a permission marketing program. What are the key benefits of this approach?

11. What are the keys to an effective permission marketing program?

12. Describe a frequency program.

13. What is customer relationship management?

14. What is meant by the term share of customer?

15. What is direct response marketing?

16. Explain how response lists and compiled lists are used in direct mail programs.

17. Explain the two ways infomercials are presented as parts of a direct response program.

18. What is relationship marketing?

19. What steps are involved in the personal selling process?

20. Identify the four types of sales presentations typically used by sales reps.

21. What types of closing methods are available to salespeople?

Critical Thinking Exercises

DISCUSSION QUESTIONS

22. Assume you are the account executive at a database marketing agency. A local music retailer with four stores has asked you to develop a database for the company. How would you build a data warehouse? What information should be in the databases? Where and how would you obtain the data?

23. Hickory Outdoor is a retail store that sells fishing, hunting, camping, and other outdoor equipment and supplies, including various items for a number of outdoor sports. The company has built a database of its customers over the last five years. The marketing team can use data mining to improve their marketing efforts. Suggest ways data mining can be used. What type of marketing programs would you suggest based on data mining? What other types of marketing programs can be developed from the database?

24. Karen's Formal Dress is a retailer specializing in formal and wedding wear. She has a database with more than 3,000 names of individuals who have purchased or rented formal wear. She would like to develop a permission marketing program. How can the marketing team encourage individuals to give permission to receive marketing materials? Once the company has the customer's permission, how can the relationship be continued to make it beneficial to both the consumer and to Karen's Formal Dress? Describe the methodology Karen should use in her permission marketing program, including the types of materials, methods of distribution, and incentives.

25. A primary reason for developing a frequency program is to encourage customers to be loyal to a business or brand. For each of the following products, discuss the merits of a frequency program. What types of incentives would individuals need to join the frequency club and then to continue participation in the program?

    a. Local restaurant

    b. Auto repair service

    c. Printing service

    d. Clothing retailer

26. Examine the forms of direct response marketing shown in the graph in Figure 10. Which ones have you responded to in the past? Which ones are most likely to influence your purchase decisions? Which ones are the least likely? Explain for each method your personal responses over the last year.

27. The marketing team for Hickory Outdoor (see question 23) is seeking to use direct response advertising to accomplish two goals: (1) to sell specific merchandise and (2) to encourage individuals to visit the store or its website. Which types of direct response advertising would be the most effective? Why? What type of direct response offers should Hickory Outdoor make?

28. Examine the direct marketing methods highlighted in Figure 10. Evaluate each method for the following types of businesses. Which ones would be the best? Which ones would not work as well? Justify your answers.

   a. Shoe store

   b. Sporting goods retailer

   c. Internet calendar and game retailer (sells only via the internet)

   d. Manufacturer of tin cans for food-processing companies

29. Interview five individuals. Ask each person to list the catalogs they have received during the past six months. Have each person discuss why he or she receives certain catalogs. Ask how often each person orders something out of a catalog and how the order is usually placed. Is anyone accessing the internet for information offered in a catalog or ordering from a catalog after accessing a website? Discuss how important the catalog market is today and what you see as the future of catalog marketing.

30. Think about a recent personal purchase experience that involved a salesperson. Describe how the salesperson handled you during the sales call. Which sales presentation approach did the salesperson use? Which methods of handling objections were used? Evaluate how well the objection was handled. Which closing did the salesperson use? How well did the salesperson handle the closing?

Integrated Learning Exercises

31. Pick a company that sells clothing. Go to the company's website. What evidence do you see of database marketing and of personalization of the website? Describe a database marketing program the company could use to reach consumers such as yourself.

32. Go to website for Scotts Miracle Gro at **www.scotts.com**. What evidence do you see of database marketing and of personalization? Review the concepts presented in the section "Database-Driven Marketing Communications." What steps could Scotts take to develop data-driven communications with visitors to the website as well as individuals who make purchases?

33. A number of companies specialize in database marketing. You are the manager of a small chain of eight Chinese food restaurants. Review the websites of each of the following companies. Outline what each company offers. Which one would be the best for your company? Why?

   a. Database Marketing Group (**www.dbmgroup.com**)

   b. Advanced Marketing Consultants (**www.marketingprinciples.com**)

   c. Dovetail (**www.dovetaildatabase.com**)

34. *DMNews* is a trade journal for database marketing and CRM programs. Access the website at **www.dmnews.com**. What types of information are available on the site? How could this help companies with database marketing and CRM programs? Access and read one of the articles from the journal. Write a paragraph about what you learned.

35. CentricData is a database marketing firm that specializes in mid-size to large retailers. Access the website at **www.centricdata.com**. What types of services does CentricData offer? How could this company help a retail store develop a database marketing program?

36. The Direct Marketing Association (DMA) is a global trade association of business and nonprofit organizations that use direct marketing tools and techniques. Access the trade organization's website at **www.the-dma.org**. What services does the DMA provide its members? What value would this be to a business in developing a direct marketing program?

37. A primary key in successful direct marketing is the quality of the list used. One company that specializes in compiling lists is U.S. Data Corporation. Access the company's website at **www.usdatacorporation.com**. What types of lists does the company offer? Access one of the lists and discuss how a company could use U.S. Data Corporation for a direct response marketing campaign. What services does U.S. Data Corporation offer?

38. Suppose you are the marketing manager for a chain of 15 beauty salons and have decided to use a direct response marketing campaign. Access the website of US Data Corporation (**www.usdatacorporation.com**). Select five different lists you could purchase from the company and explain why they were chosen. Identify two different services offered by US Data Corporation that would be of interest to you. Explain how that service could be used in your direct response marketing campaign.

39. Use the internet to find three websites of companies and organizations that offer advice to salespeople. Write a report about the methods the sites suggest and how those tactics compare to the materials presented in this chapter.

Student Project

CREATIVE CORNER

Lilly Fashions sells fashionable, trendy clothes. The company's primary target customer is 20- to 30-year-old females with an average income of $40,000 and some college. Lilly's marketing team wants to capitalize on the concepts of database marketing and direct response marketing. Design a newspaper advertisement that encourages females in the company's target market to visit the retail store and join Lilly's loyalty program. In addition, design a direct mail piece that would go to individuals who are currently in the database but who have not made a purchase within the last three months. Prepare another email that can be sent to members in the database on the person's birthday offering them a free meal at a local restaurant, if they come to the store to pick up the meal voucher. This promotion is a joint promotion with the restaurant, which shares in the cost, which means the restaurant must also be part of the email.

Blog Exercises

Access the authors' blog for this text at the URLs provided to complete these exercises. Answer the questions that are posed on the blog.

40. Database marketing: **http://blogclowbaack.net/2014/05/12/database-marketing-chapter-11/**

41. Direct response marketing: **http://blogclowbaack.net/2014/05/12/direct-response-marketing-chapter-11/**

42. Personal selling: **http://blogclowbaack.net/2014/05/12/selling-chapter-11/0**

CASE 1 — SALON SENSATIONAL

The world of beauty enhancement continually changes. Jennifer Swann, owner and manager of Salon Sensational, recognizes that she must constantly adapt to new trends in order to keep her company on top. Jennifer owns four salons, located in Medford and Portland, Oregon. The salons serve both male and female clients. Her current operation offers hair care of all types, manicures, pedicures, and includes space rentals to two popular local massage therapists. The company also sells a line of top quality hair care products including shampoo, conditioner, and coloring rinses.

Salon Sensational has been involved in local community events. Most notably, each year the salon provides low-cost pink hair accents to sponsor Breast Cancer Awareness efforts. Also, twice each year stylists provide free services to low income members of the community as part of a city-wide program for the disadvantaged, held at the local city auditorium.

Jennifer has created a program designed to keep her stylists on the cutting edge. Each receives financial incentives in order to attend training sessions for creating the newest hair styles. She also maintains an incentive system designed to encourage stylists to sell and cross-sell the hair care products that the salon offers.

Five years ago, Jennifer purchased a sophisticated computer software system that allows her to track all customer interactions with the salon, including records of past appointments, purchases of products, methods of payment (cash versus charge), along with notes about past complaints as well as past compliments. The system maintains appointment schedules and also identifies customers who have routinely canceled or not kept their appointments.

Repeat business represents the staple of the salon industry. When customers routinely return, stylists stay busy and the total company benefits. Customer referrals also help to build volume in terms of appointments.

Currently, Jennifer is looking for ways to increase purchase frequencies and facility utilization. She recognizes that care must be given to avoid alienating clientele members by appearing to "hard sell" them hair care products or additional visits. At the same time, she knows that part of the frequency displayed by customers is the result of building strong bonds and relationships between individuals and their stylists as well as Jennifer herself.

One approach to building revenues would be to add new services, such as cosmetology. In that way, a person getting ready for a major event, such as a prom or wedding would be able to have her hair styled, nails polished, and make-up set up, all in the same location. The question is whether sufficient

▲ Jennifer styling the hair of one of her customers.

JackF/Fotolia

demand for such a new service exists. She would have to invest in a minor amount of remodeling in order to be able to provide the service.

At the same time, Salon Sensation enjoys a positive reputation in both cities. Many customers report high levels of loyalty. The goal is to build on those aspects in order to continue to succeed.

43. Identify the types of data Jennifer should collect from her customers and how she could obtain it.

44. Suppose Jennifer wants to start a loyalty card program to build her database. Design a flyer that could be handed to customers of the salons encouraging them to join the loyalty program. What benefits would customers receive? In exchange, what information would Jennifer request from each customer?

45. Once the database is built, what database-driven marketing communications should Salon Sensational send out to individuals in its database?

46. Which direct response marketing programs would be helpful to Jennifer? How would they be of value? Explain how Jennifer could use each to increase purchase frequencies and visits to her salons.

47. What types of personal selling tactics should stylists use? Which should not be used? Why?

48. What methods for overcoming objections would best serve Salon Sensational when selling hair care products?

CASE 2 — THE TRAVEL AGENCY DILEMMA

Leisure time travel remains a common pursuit across a variety of markets. Numerous forces influence consumers as they seek out restful, adventuresome, romantic, and family-oriented vacations. Factors such as gasoline and airline ticket prices, economic conditions, political unrest, and the changing world of technology factor into personal and family decisions regarding places to go, things to do, people to see, and events to enjoy.

Travel agencies experience the influence of these forces as directly as any other group. When gas prices rise, consumers take shorter trips. When airline tickets are at a premium, travelers look for bargains or seek other alternatives. Unemployment, political turmoil in places such as Mexico and Europe, and other considerations cause people to either stay at home or change travel plans.

The most direct influence on the travel agency business has been the internet and its popular travel sites. Travelocity, Priceline.com, and other airline booking sites allow consumers to shop online for the best air fares and travel times. Hotels.com plus numerous hotel chain-run booking sites, which also offer frequency programs, make it possible to find the most ideal hotel arrangement without the use of a travel agency. Many internet-savvy consumers no longer feel the need to call or drive to a local travel agency. These individuals have become convinced that they are able to match any price or travel arrangement that an agency can find.

To compete in this intense environment, agency managers seek ways to deliver value-added services that entice consumers to continue to utilize their companies. Among the potential methods to maintain customer loyalty are offers of convenience, skill at finding better prices than consumers can obtain online, and the ability to package travel into one-price programs. Many travel agencies create agreements with hotels, cruise lines, and airlines to offer better prices than consumers will receive from other vendors.

Travel agencies can also offer suggestions regarding combinations of activities such as fine dining with an elaborate hotel. Many agency employees visit numerous destinations, seeking to obtain better quality information about local attractions that would go unnoticed by travelers to a specific area.

In the future, the question remains as to whether travel agencies will be able to continue to compete. Only with carefully constructed service programs and quality marketing efforts

▲ With access to the internet, many tourists see little value in the services provided by travel agencies.

1000words/Fotolia

will it be possible to maintain a set of clientele as the world of internet shopping continues to increase.

49. How might database marketing, including the data warehouse, data coding and analysis, and data mining, help a travel agency create and enhance relationships with customers and potential customers?

50. How could data-driven marketing programs, including permission marketing, frequency programs, and customer relationship management systems, be useful to travel agencies?

51. Discuss each of the direct response marketing techniques in relation to marketing travel agencies.

52. What personal selling tactics are most important to travel agency employees as they work with customers and potential customers?

53. Discuss the pros and cons of each of the methods of handling objections in personal selling in relation to a couple who are hesitant to purchase a vacation to one of the Caribbean islands.

54. Discuss the pros and cons of each of the closing methods in personal selling in relation to a couple who are hesitant to purchase a vacation to one of the Caribbean islands.

MyMarketingLab

Go to **mymktlab.com** for Auto-graded writing questions as well as the following Assisted-graded writing questions:

55. Karen's Formal Dress is a retailer specializing in formal and wedding wear. She has a database with more than 3,000 names of individuals who have purchased or rented formal wear. She would like to develop a permission marketing program. How can the marketing team encourage individuals to give permission to receive marketing materials? Once the company has the customer's permission, how can the relationship be continued to make it beneficial to both the consumer and to Karen's Formal Dress? Describe the methodology Karen should use in her permission marketing program, including the types of materials, methods of distribution, and incentives.

56. Pick a company that sells clothing and go to its website. What evidence do you see of database marketing and personalization of the website? Describe a database marketing program the company could use.

Endnotes

1. Stephanie Clifford, "Ads Follow Web Users, and Get More Personal," *The New York Times* (**www.nytimes.com/2009/07/31/business/media/31privacy.html**), July 31, 2009.

2. Leo Rabinovitch, "America's 'First' Department Stores Mines Customer Data," *Direct Marketing* 62, no. 8 (December 1999), pp. 42–45.

3. Jason Q. Zhang, Ashutosh Dixit, and Roberto Friedman, "Customer Loyalty and Lifetime Value: An Empirical Investigation of Consumer Packaged Goods," *Journal of Marketing Theory & Practice* 18, no. 2 (February 2010), pp. 127–139.

4. Elliot Zwiebach, "Wholesalers Segment Shoppers Using Lifestyle Clusters," *Supermarket News* 55, no. 7 (February 12, 2007), p. 23.

5. "Verizon Uses Phone Data to Connect Consumer Dots for NBA Teams," *Advertising Age*, http://adage.com/print/245178, November 8, 2013.

6. Howard J. Stock, "Connecting the Dots," *Bank Investment Consultant* 13, no. 3 (March 2005), pp. 28–31.

7. Jordan K. Speer, "Digging Deep: Extreme Data Mining," *Apparel Magazine* 45, no. 12 (August 2004), p. 1.

8. Arthur M. Hughes, "The Importance of Customer Communications," *Database Marketing Institute* (**www.dbmarketing.com/articles/ART233.html**), August 23, 2007.

9. "Consumers Appreciate Birthday Wishes from Brands," *Quirk's* http://quirksblog.com/blog/2013/12/04/consumers-appreciate-birthday-wish-from-brands, December 4, 2013.

10. "Data Mining Boosts Netflix Subscriber Base," *Advertising Age*, http://adage.com/print/243759, September 2, 2013.

11. Joseph Gatti, "Poor E-Mail Practices Provoking Considerable Customer Defection," *Direct Marketing* (December 2003), pp. 1–2.

12. Joseph Gatti, "Most Consumers Have Reached Permission E-Mail Threshold," *Direct Marketing* (December 2003), pp. 1–2.

13. Ibid.

14. Mark Dolliver, "Gauging Customer Loyalty," *Adweek* (**www.adweek.com/aw/content_display/news/agency/e3i4a73f5d7451749a37c7fca20**), February 16, 2010.

15. Mark A. Santillo, "Active Engagement," *Greater Games Industry Catalog* 12 (Spring 2010), p. 14.

16. Arthur M. Hughes, "The Importance of Customer Communications," *Database Marketing Institute* (**www.dbmarketing.com/articles/ART233.html**), August 23, 2007.

17. "CRM Metrics," *Harvard Management Update* 5, no. 3 (March 2000), pp. 3–4.

18. "Kellogg Cracks the Code on Loyalty," *Advertising Age*, http://adage.com/print/243342, July 29, 2013.

19. Richard H. Levey, "Prospects Look Good," *Direct* 16, no. 6 (December 1, 2004), pp. 1–5.

20. Julie Appleby, "As Drug Ads Surge, More Rx's Filled," *USA Today* (**www.usatoday.com/news/health/2008–02–29-drugs-main_N.html**), February 29, 2008.

21. Paula Andruss, "Personalized URLs," *Marketing News*, September 1, 2008, p. 10.

22. Jeff Borden, "Eat My Dust," *Marketing News* 42, no. 2, February 1, 2008, pp. 20–22.

23. Kyle Stock, "Why the Analog Catalog Still Drives Digital Sales," *Bloomberg Businessweek*, www.businessweek.com/printer/articles/165812, November 7, 2013.

24. Based on Jay Kiltsch, "Making Your Message Hit Home: Some Basics to Consider When…," *Direct Marketing* 61, no. 2 (June 1998), pp. 32–34.

25. Daniel B. Honigman, "Sweet Science," *Marketing News* 41, no. 16 (October 2, 2007), pp. 16–17.

26. Camille Sweeney, "Avon's Little Sister Is Calling," *The New York Times* (**www.nytimes.com/2010/01/14/fashion/ 14SKIN.html**), January 14, 2010.

27. Ken Le Meunier-FitsHugh and Nigel F. Piercy, "Does Collaboration Between Sales and Marketing Affect Business Performance," *Journal of Personal Selling & Sales Management* 27, no. 3 (Summer 2007), pp. 207–220.

28. Patricia R. Lysak, "Changing Times Demand Front-End Model," *Marketing News* 28, no. 9 (April 25, 1994), p. 9.

29. Christopher Heine, "Grocery Chain will Pitch Store Patrons with Amazon-Like Recommendations," *Adweek*, December 9, 2013, http://www.adweek. com/news/technology/grocery-chain-will-pitch-store-patrons-amazon-recommendations-154379, retrieved March 21, 2014.

Index